❧ RINGLING ❧

Florida A&M University, Tallahassee
Florida Atlantic University, Boca Raton
Florida Gulf Coast University, Ft. Myers
Florida International University, Miami
Florida State University, Tallahassee
New College of Florida, Sarasota
University of Central Florida, Orlando
University of Florida, Gainesville
University of North Florida, Jacksonville
University of South Florida, Tampa
University of West Florida, Pensacola

University Press of Florida

Gainesville

Tallahassee

Tampa

Boca Raton

Pensacola

Orlando

Miami

Jacksonville

Ft. Myers

Sarasota

RINGLING

The Florida Years, 1911–1936 & **David C. Weeks**

First cloth printing, 1993
First paperback printing, 1993

17 16 15 14 P 13 12 11 10 9

Library of Congress Cataloging-in-
Publication Data
Weeks, David Chapin.
Ringling: the Florida years, 1911–1936/
by David C. Weeks.
p. cm.
Includes bibliographical references
(p.) and index.
ISBN 978-0-8130-1242-1 (alk. paper). —
ISBN 978-0-8130-1243-8 (pbk.: alk. paper)
1. Ringling, John, 1866–1936.
2. Circus owners—United States—
Biography 3. Sarasota (Fla.)—History.
1. Title.
GV1811.R52W44 1993
338.7′617913′092—dc20
[B]   93-11189

Frontispiece: John Ringling at his estate in
Alpine, New Jersey, c. 1926. Courtesy of
Henry Ringling North.

The University Press of Florida is the
scholarly publishing agency for the State
University System of Florida, comprising
Florida A&M University, Florida Atlantic
University, Florida Gulf Coast University,
Florida International University, Florida
State University, New College of Florida,
University of Central Florida, University
of Florida, University of North Florida,
University of South Florida, and Univer-
sity of West Florida.

University Press of Florida
15 Northwest 15th Street
Gainesville, FL 32611
www.upf.com

❧ CONTENTS ❧

❦ FOREWORD ❦

Raymond Arsenault

OVER THE CENTURIES Florida has attracted more than its share of larger-than-life characters. From Pensacola to the Florida Keys, the peninsula has been a repository for all manner of personal and imperial ambitions, as dreamers and builders, schemers and scoundrels, have sought to leave their mark upon the land. The result is a modern landscape punctuated with sprawling subdivisions, gaudy theme parks, oversized Mediterranean Revival hotels and mansions, man-made islands, drainage ditches masquerading as canals, and acre after acre of manicured flora. Exotic and eclectic, Florida is a jumble of contradictions, of natural beauty and unnatural creation, of artful genius and misplaced pietism.

No single individual is wholly representative of this complexity. But those seeking an understanding of modern Florida's unique regional culture could hardly find a better starting point than the life of John Nicholas Ringling. Known to millions of Americans simply as "the circus man," Ringling was actually a man of many talents and varied interests, a middle-brow polymath who used his time and fortune to recast his physical and cultural surroundings. As a circus promoter, an inveterate patron of the arts, a self-styled art critic and connoisseur, and a real estate developer, he sought to bridge the often disparate worlds of popular and high culture. Self-taught but sophisticated, Ringling mediated between the marketplace and the gallery, between the dictates of American pragmatism and the values of European aestheticism. The tangible results of this cultural fusion—most notably the choreography of the Ringling Bros. and Barnum & Bailey Circus, his extensive collections of Baroque paintings, European decorative objects, and Italian statuary, and his ostentatious Sarasota mansion Ca' d'Zan—seldom satisfied purist conventions or expectations. But Ringling's achievements were never dull or mundane, and even his harshest critics acknowledged his enterprising and adventurous spirit. Here was a man who was not afraid to think or live on a grand scale, who knew what he wanted from life and from art.

During the past sixty years, several million visitors have marveled at the artistic treasures in the John and Mable Ringling Museum of Art, and countless others have toured the Venetian splendor of Ca' d'Zan or wandered the grounds of the Ringling estate. Many of these visitors must have come away with a touch of puzzlement. What manner of man created this empire of whimsy and pretension? How did he do it? Why did he do it? The most persistent questioners could test the knowledge and patience of docents or even track down a curator; but authoritative answers were scarce. Nearly everyone in Sarasota could tell a John Ringling story or two, but no one had made an extended effort to separate fact from folklore, or to examine carefully the textual and contextual nuances of Ringling's life and times. Despite a wealth of information on the artistic legacy and material culture of John Ringling's world, the man himself remained a shadowy enigma, until now.

Fortunately, David Weeks has rescued John Ringling from the shadows. Based on a decade of research and writing, the present volume offers a carefully crafted analysis of the public and private lives of one of American history's most colorful and influential culture brokers. Weeks chronicles Ringling's early life and the remarkable ascent of the Ringling circus family, which transformed a small harness-making business in the upper Midwest into an international entertainment empire. But the book's primary focus is on the final quarter-century of Ringling's life, from his arrival in Sarasota in 1911, at the age of forty-five, to his death in 1936. Ringling's Sarasota years stretched from the pre–

World War I era, when most of central and southern Florida remained raw and unpopulated, to the fabled Florida boom of the 1920s, to the subsequent hard times of the 1930s. Like Florida's other leading dream merchants—Carl Fisher of Miami Beach, George Merrick of Coral Gables, Perry Snell of St. Petersburg, and the Mizner brothers of Boca Raton and Palm Beach—Ringling helped to create an age of excess that was followed by an age of want and desperation. Though his life in Sarasota was a bittersweet saga—he lost much of his fortune during the Great Depression and outlived his beloved wife Mable and all six of his brothers—he left an artistic and philanthropic legacy of incalculable value. David Weeks recaptures the triumphs and the tragedies, the genius and the decadence, the generosity and the self-indulgence, in this even-handed and compelling biography.

❦ Raymond Arsenault is professor of history at the University of South Florida, St. Petersburg. He has written extensively on the history of Florida and the American South.

THE IMPETUS that led to the writing of this book stemmed from an awareness that the custodians and interpreters of John Ringling's bequest to the people of Florida wanted a reliable account of the man and his uniquely mixed career. Accordingly, the reader will find that the book follows the circus man, the corporate entrepreneur, and the art connoisseur and collector who applied a degree of showmanship to each of those diverse interests.

For more than a century, the name Ringling has meant *circus* to millions in Europe and America, relegating his other interests to local antiquarians and art specialists. Yet an exploration of the intimate relationships among John Ringling's multiple roles discloses that his ideas and sentiments were only superficially understood by the public and the pragmatic men of affairs with whom he shared the business life of Sarasota. This last phase of his many-sided career gave Ringling an enduring place in a short, colorful epoch—the charmed fantasy of Florida in the mid-1920s. It was a time when Florida spelled romance to celebrities, the newly rich, families with inherited wealth, and thousands of more ordinary Americans. Ringling was a vivid example of life in that fanciful and often bizarre period between World War I and the Great Depression. He typifies the Florida venturer of the 1920s, who is too late to emulate the early moguls such as Henry Flagler and Henry Plant, and too early to join the corporate builders of the post–World War II era.

The theme that follows his career is the pursuit of two contrasting threads that run through Ringling's life. A picture emerges of two men: one prideful but outgoing, a man of humor and good company; the other aloof and secretive, confiding in no one. This latter trait lent dignity and reserve to a man so much in public view, a man who from childhood was driven by a passion to become important and to move in the society of important people. He came from the Midwest into the new pleasure-seeking life of New York City at a time when financiers and millionaires were beginning to enjoy the sporting pleasures that a center of commerce and wealth can afford. As a major shareholder in Madison Square Garden, Ringling entered such company because of his money and convivial spirits. Yet his genuine but superficial image as a showman with Bohemian tastes, a partner in the great Ringling Bros. and Barnum & Bailey shows, was in continual conflict with his excessive diffidence, which was almost a compulsion to retain a personal privacy. While his newly won wealth purchased for him a public image of a rich and important figure, his parallel wish for a seclusion that left the public image at his doorstep led to a rejection of intimacy by this man who could name a thousand acquaintances but no close friend.

Ringling's character and his life in Sarasota, as far as they merited public interest, assured him a special place in the social history of Florida as well as the nation itself. His varied roles in the Sarasota community disclose a unity of purpose and action that his contemporaries did not always understand or appreciate. Florida's heroes were not soldiers, magistrates, artists, or writers. They were developers of railroads and hotels. Because Ringling was a leading player in Sarasota's most important industry of development, his every action was described and analyzed in hundreds of news reports that appeared in the local press. In their eagerness to present a full account of his actions, some reporters wrote prematurely about Ringling's plans and transactions, although many of those business dealings never took place.

Upon his death, his executors and several government probers, including examiners from the Bureau of Internal Revenue, found that he kept few personal records of many transactions and of his thirty-five corporate roles. Like others of his time, Ringling was not averse to using a certain amount of financial legerdemain, transferring assets into and out of accounts depending on his momentary need to increase or cache his apparent wealth. His overt ideas and plans for Sarasota are found in his few public expressions, which tend to be understated and lacking in animation. Often his announcements were made by proxy, that is, voiced by an associate at his direction. There was another, warmer side to Ringling's personality, shown rarely in a brief reference or an allusion to the color and light of the bay and the shore of Sarasota. His letters (except those to his sister Ida) are uniformly impersonal and are sometimes excessively brusque, because that was his chosen public posture.

This account of Ringling's life in Sarasota starts with his 1911 arrival and closes with the discharge of the executors of his estate once they fulfilled the terms of his will and transferred his unencumbered bequests to the people of Florida. An epilogue traces the way his art collection and Ca' d'Zan were revived and protected from the threat of decay, and how in the process the name and the repute of the donor were restored.

I wish to acknowledge the assistance and encouragement given to me by the Ringling Museum staff members whom the director, Lawrence J. Ruggiero, named to act as liaison between me and the many individuals and sources within and beyond the museum where access was essential. They include Nancy Glaser, then head of education, Myriam Springuel, Kathleen Chilson, and Elisa Hansen. Kathleen Chilson has given innumerable after-business hours, applying her expertise as museum editor to transform the initial manuscript to a product for publication. Museum volunteer Barbara Arnay donated both editorial and computer skills.

For expert guidance on the Ringling collection I am greatly indebted to Rosilyn Alter, curator of Italian painting, and to Michelle Scalera, head of conservation. Their suggestions greatly improved the quality of the sections that deal with paintings in the collection; remaining shortcomings are wholly my own. I owe much to the research assistance given by Lynelle Moor, head of the museum's art library, and by her assistants, Wilma Kestler and Corinne Beggy.

I am especially grateful to Henry Ringling North for interviews and to Lillian Burns for permitting me to use her father's correspondence with John Ringling, and for her help with the details of Sarasota history. I was provided access to important primary sources by John McCarthy, then archivist of Sarasota County records; the director and staff of the library at Florida Southern College; and the records staffs of the Sarasota County Court and the Florida State Archives. I thank Harriet Burket Taussig, Dorothy Kahle McDaniel, Maxine Baylor, Alice Myers, and William Perry for their interviews. Credit is due the owners of many unpublished photographs, including Henry North, Lillian Burns, and Maxine Baylor. Pauline Scott labored over the chapter notes and compiled an index to the *Sarasota Times* and *Sarasota Herald* for items relating to the Ringling family for the years 1911–37. Armando Rufini of the museum security staff was most helpful in assembling Ringling papers from obscure corners in Ca' d'Zan. Debbie Walk, recently named to the post of archivist, has never failed to provide whatever elusive facts were needed. Among my many friends and colleagues at the museum who also love this splendid bequest, I thank the docents who generously shared their knowledge and suggestions for searching out details of life at Ca' d'Zan. For eight years of patience and understanding in the midst of a sea of paper, I thank my wife, Frances.

❧ CHRONOLOGY ❧

1847 August Rüngeling (1826–98) migrated to Canada, then to United States.

1852 Marriage of August (now Ringling) to Marie Salomé Juliar (1833–1907) in Chicago. Albrecht (Albert) born in Chicago, Illinois; d. 1916.

1854 Augustus born in Milwaukee, Wisconsin; d. 1907.

1857 Otto born in Baraboo, Wisconsin; d. 1911.

1863 Alfred Theodore (Alf T.) born in McGregor, Iowa; d. 1919.

1864 Charles born in McGregor, Iowa; d. 1926.

1866 John Nicholas born 31 May in McGregor, Iowa; d. 2 December 1936.

1868 Henry born in McGregor, Iowa; d. 1918.

1874 Ida (later Mrs. Henry North) born in Prairie du Chien, Wisconsin; d. 1950.

1882 Ringling family moves to Baraboo, Wisconsin. The four brothers organize winter-season hall shows (performed at town halls).

1884 Circus formed with Yankee Robinson ("Yankee Robinson and Ringling Bros. Double Show").

1885 Ringling Bros. organized as sole proprietors.

1890 Circus travel converts from wagon to railroad.

1905 Marriage of John Ringling and Mable Burton in Hoboken, New Jersey.

1906 Ringling Bros. buy half-interest in Forepaugh-Sells Circus from James A. Bailey heirs.

1907 Ringling Bros. purchase Barnum & Bailey Circus from Bailey heirs.

1911 John and Mable purchase twenty acres at Shell Beach, Sarasota, Florida from Ralph Caples (includes Charles N. Thompson home).

1916 John Ringling purchases defunct Sarasota Yacht and Automobile Club property, including Cedar Point (Golden Gate Point).

1918 John Ringling purchases summer home at Alpine, New Jersey, on Hudson River.

1924 Construction begun on Ca' d'Zan, new winter home for John and Mable.

1925 Old Madison Square Garden demolished. (New Garden opens in 1926. John Ringling no longer the major shareholder but continues as a director.) Ringling's major projects begun at Sarasota: causeway across the bay, Ritz Carlton Hotel, Ringling Isles.

1927 John and Mable Ringling Museum of Art chartered and established. Circus winter quarters moved from Bridgeport, Connecticut, to Sarasota.

1929 Death of Mable Ringling, age 54, on 8 June 1929, in New York. John Ringling purchases the five circuses of American Circus Corporation.

1930 Marriage of John Ringling and Emily Haag Buck in Jersey City, New Jersey.

1932 Museum opened permanently to the public, 17 January 1932. Ringling's first attack of thrombosis; he convalesces in New York City, July–December. Circus partnership dissolved; corporation formed by Ringling's creditors; Ringling continues as president with no duties.

1933 First suit for divorce filed by John Ringling; dismissed.

1934 Second suit filed by Ringling; divorce granted, July 1936.

1936 Death of John Ringling, 2 December 1936 in New York. John

Ringling North and Ida Ringling North appointed executors of his estate.

1946 John and Mable Ringling Museum of Art and Ca' d'Zan transferred to the State of Florida.

1947 Final settlement between the executors of Ringling's estate and the State of Florida.

John Ringling at age eighteen in 1885, the first year of the Ringling brothers' sole proprietorship of the circus. Courtesy of Henry Ringling North.

A Prologue: Ringling, the Showman

OHN NICHOLAS RINGLING was one of those rare, powerful personalities who are found in every generation of American businesspeople. They become phenomenally successful in their day; their names become nationally known. Ringling achieved that status as the unquestioned circus king; in Sarasota he became a prominent millionaire-entrepreneur and the only art patron of his time. His prodigal spending in large development projects and an insatiable acquisitiveness lasted until the Great Depression and a long illness led to financial ruin. Excluded by his creditors from his accustomed position of command and stripped of his authority in the circus, he found himself deprived of strength when he needed it most. Meanwhile, his financial toboggan careened out of control. Even then, adversity could neither subdue him nor prevent him from looking ahead, however vainly, to when he might recapture the initiative.

Ringling was favored with a commanding appearance. About six-feet-one in height, he was not quite as massive as his younger brother Henry but was taller than all the other brothers. Like many men of formidable size, he spoke with a soft, quiet voice. He was remembered by his longtime friend and circus associate Fred Bradna as a powerful, swarthy man with heavy, drooping eyelids and a deep, low voice.[1]

As a young man, he appears to have been somewhat overweight. In the 1890s and the early 1900s, excess weight was still accepted as a mark of the good life that accompanies wealth. Later, skilled tailors were able to conceal a heavy figure that had ceased to be fashionable. Moreover, he chose to wear a curious, rounded haircut that defied the taste and style of his time but became a distinctive mark of his appearance.

The name Ringling became a symbol for the great tent shows and their unique place in America's popular culture in the late nineteenth and early twentieth centuries. As part of the Ringling Bros. Circus, John achieved international recognition. Yet a fund of restless energy and a driving ambition to move among important people sent him plunging into a second career. He became an investor-operator in ventures that varied widely, ranging from bicycle racing in New York City to locomotive repair in Oklahoma. He spread his interests from New York to Florida to Texas and Montana. With a good share of the fortune that these interests provided him, Ringling created a legacy to the state and people of Florida. That legacy included a major art museum and a Venetian palace residence in Sarasota, Florida, the city that he helped to build and where he spent part of every year from 1911 to 1936. Yet he would always be remembered as the circus man, the greatest showman since P. T. Barnum. In fact, Ringling himself, at the very end of his life, turned his thoughts to the circus and his plans to regain his lost control of the show. Shortly before his death on 2 December 1936, Ringling outlined his ideas for a circus spectacular to his friend, Melvin Hildreth, an old-time circus man like himself. The two met for dinner and an evening of reminiscing. Ringling described his spectacular as a pageant, which he planned to call "Golden Are the Days in Memory."[2] Whatever golden days John Ringling could then recall must have reached well back in time to earlier, happier days.

That dinner and its sweep of memories came at a time when Ringling had recovered some of the mobility that his four years of illness had impaired. He even looked forward to a measure of better financial health, although that may have been an illusion. Then, an unexpected attack of pneumonia in late November 1936 proved fatal. He had lived seventy years, outliving his six brothers. Four of them—Albert, Alfred,

Charles, and Otto—had been his original partners in the circus. After the summer of 1932, while he was ill with the effects of thrombosis and his affairs were in an increasingly critical state, one asset after another was pledged or mortgaged to satisfy the interest of his debts. A conspiracy evicted him abruptly from his position as operator of the circus. Through these hard times he contrived to keep Ca' d'Zan, his Sarasota home, out of the reach of creditors.

Of the many calamities that befell Ringling in later years, the final blow was the threatened loss of his Sarasota home. The Federal Court in Tampa had ordered Ca' d'Zan to be auctioned on 7 December 1936 to satisfy an old debt. Built under his wife Mable's direction and greatly loved by her, Ca' d'Zan was the scene of the Ringlings' happiest moments before Mable's death in 1929. John and his nephew, John Ringling North, tried many times to stave off a final disaster by pulling together funds raised from one sacrifice after another. Had he been stronger, Ringling might have survived this last threat. But he was weakened by stroke, thrombosis, and semiparalysis. He needed help to cross a room or to sign a paper. This was the man whose very appearance had once suggested great reserves of power. The approaching auction of his home left him with no will to fight.

Fifty years later, John Ringling's image remains elusive. He has seemed to be many different things to people. First among them is John Ringling, the circus king—his most enduring persona. His other interests and achievements are always overshadowed by the image of parades, calliope music, daring performers, and exotic animals. Even after Ringling had been a local winter resident for more than ten years, his name in the *Sarasota Times* was usually qualified with a phrase such as "the well-known showman." The title does, indeed, name his lifelong vocation. Yet among his neighbors he would not be known, first and foremost, as a showman. To them he was the urbane owner of Palms Elysian, his first Sarasota home, and later of its successor, Ca' d'Zan. Having acquired all the outward finery of the millionaire-entrepreneur, he lived in grand style, often coming and going on his private railway car to New York and to other centers of finance and corporate action.

Among his partner-brothers, he alone was not satisfied to immerse himself altogether in the circus and its unconventional life. He was driven to share the status and deference accorded to men whose fortunes came from banking, railroads, and other solid, publicly esteemed enterprises. His role in the circus required him to travel far ahead of the circus train. Contracts, logistics, rail schedules, all sent him among the people whose status he coveted.

To art dealers and auctioneers in New York and London, he became the Sarasota art collector, buyer of major and minor works of varying quality. Some in that world saw him as a knowledgeable and astute buyer; others claimed that he measured art in square yards of canvas.

During his twenty-five years in Sarasota, he became the owner of several short-line railroads, large land holdings in Montana, and oil properties in Oklahoma. In all, he held positions in thirty-five companies, although not at the same time. And he became the principal land developer in Sarasota during the 1920s.

John Ringling was forty-five and Mable was thirty-six when they established their first winter home in Sarasota. Except for occasional visits to their Montana ranch, they had been city dwellers since their marriage in 1905; life in a small town by the Gulf of Mexico would be different from life in Chicago, New York, and European cities. They had never owned a home or lived in a house. Mostly they lived in hotels and apartments in Chicago until 1910, when they took an apartment at 636 Fifth Avenue in New York City. For several Sarasota winters, they brought their social life with them. Their guests were usually business acquaintances, New York and New Jersey political figures, and entertainers. John's acquaintances were numbered in the hundreds. With his remarkably accurate memory, he never forgot the name of anyone in that throng who could be useful to him.

At the time of his move to Sarasota, Ringling had already spent nearly thirty years as a showman. He had traveled immense distances with the circus and its affairs in this country, in Canada, and in Europe, where he continually searched for new talent. His name was known internationally for his part in building one of the great circuses in the world.

❧ The beginnings of the Ringling family in America were not unlike those of many families who migrated from northern Europe to become nonfarming settlers in the cities and towns of the upper Midwest. The family traced its name to the French Richelin, which became Rüngeling when the Huguenot family fled from France in the exodus that began before the revocation of the Edict of Nantes in 1685. August (1826–98), father of the five brothers who would later give their name its wide recognition, changed it again to Ringling after migrating to America in 1847. After his marriage to Marie Salomé Juliar at Milwaukee in 1852, the couple began a series of moves. First they went to Chicago, where their first son, Albrecht (Albert), was born in 1852. From there they went to Wisconsin, to Iowa, and back to Wisconsin, seeking a suitable home for their increasing family, always hoping to find a promising location for August's harness-making and saddlery shop.[3]

Although the Ringling name can be found in Germany, the bearers of the name are not related to this family. John searched for ancestors in parish and local records. But as his brother Charles observed, the Ringlings "were descendents of no kings, princes, barons or dukes." Records indicated that one (on the father's side of the family) had been with Napoleon's staff; one (on the mother's side) had been taken as a prisoner of war and incarcerated in England during the Napoleonic wars. "That," noted Charles, "is the very best that I can do."[4] Some of the Huguenot Rüngelings had migrated to the Dutch provinces of the Netherlands; others moved from Germany into Denmark. But a search after John Ringling's death in 1936 failed to locate any surviving Danish heirs.[5]

August Rüngeling migrated alone to America, to be joined later by his father, mother, and sister. His journey brought him first to Canada, then up the St. Lawrence River and across into the United States. Marie Salomé Juliar came in 1845 with her parents, three sisters, and one brother from the Alsace region of France to a farm near Milwaukee. Marie Salomé's sister, Marie Magdalene, later Mrs. Gottlieb Gollmar, also became the mother of a circus family. Four of her sons, partners like their Ringling cousins, organized a wagon show in 1891, in time to buy the Ringling circus wagons no longer needed after the changeover to rail. One Gollmar brother, newly qualified as a physician, became chief surgeon for the Ringling show in 1892.[6] The Gollmar Bros. Circus outlasted many small rivals, but upon its demise, Silas

Gollmar moved to Sarasota to become an official at the Ringling Bank and Trust Company, which was opened and headed by Charles Ringling.

August and Salomé Ringling moved often. Of their seven sons who lived, four were born in McGregor, Iowa: Alfred T., Charles, John, and Henry. The market for custom-made harnesses was declining because of competition from factory products, a process hastened by the 1861–65 wartime demands on industry. The Ringlings became steadily poorer as the town grew. In the boom that followed the Civil War's end in 1865, the more fortunate families became rich, with conspicuous and costly furniture, paintings, and diamonds. Men gained status with their fine, blooded horses, which were paraded through town each Saturday evening. The contrast between such luxury and the Ringling family circumstances was extreme.[7] Even at age four, John was old enough to notice the deference paid to McGregor's wealthy families. Here, no doubt, began his compulsion to become rich and to be admired.

There were many in McGregor who did not share in the new prosperity. This was a noisy river town where Iowa's eastbound freight was barged across the Mississippi to the rail terminal at Prairie du Chien on the Wisconsin side. The Ringlings eventually moved to Prairie du Chien and finally settled in Baraboo, Wisconsin. They typified the class of small artisans, mechanics, and tradespeople who avoided the roistering riverfront but lacked the money that would admit them to the town's more affluent society.

In later life the Ringlings were reluctant to describe the privations in their home when they were growing up. Neither of the family histories, Alfred's 1900 romance entitled *Life Story of the Ringling Brothers* and Henry Ringling North's *Circus Kings* (1960), offers a candid image of growing up in the family home, but the parental influence must have been enduring. August and Marie Salomé, both grave in manner and anxious for their children's good, lived out their thoroughly puritan precepts of unfailing honesty, self-discipline, and fidelity. They provided a homely example of the Teutonic work ethic. August doggedly refused to give up the harness maker's craft even as he watched the market's continual decline, and Marie Salomé kept their home and family standards with a rigor equal to her husband's.

The Ringling family, c. 1890. Back row: Albert, Alfred T., Augustus, Otto, Charles. Front row: John, Marie Salomé, August, Ida, Henry. Courtesy of Henry Ringling North.

The same industrial revolution that was ending the demand for the father's craft was creating opportunities for the sons to make their fortunes. Expansion of industry, westward farm migration, and a new flow of European immigration to the prairies followed the war in 1865. Federal and private resources were freed from wartime demands. By the time the Ringling brothers were ready to organize and to take to the road, their audiences in midwestern towns were eager for some colorful, exciting entertainment. The novelty of a circus, coming to town with its strange animals and skilled performers, could fill the need.

Several accounts purport to explain how the Ringlings got started in the business of outdoor tent shows. One legend tells of an incident caused by "Popcorn George" Hall, owner of a small show of the 1870s. His unpaid bill for repairs at August Ringling's harness shop brought two husky Ringling brothers to his circus entrance, sent by their father to remain there until the bill was paid. Their experience that day stirred

The Ringling family home in McGregor, Iowa. John Ringling was born here 31 May 1866. Courtesy of the John and Mable Ringling Museum of Art.

their determination to become owners of a circus. Another account, by Alfred Ringling in his *Life Story of the Ringling Brothers*, relates that Dan Rice's riverboat show stopped at McGregor, Iowa, in 1870. In return for some harness work, August, Sr., received several passes along with payment.[8] Although these stories generated useful publicity, they can hardly be accepted as single events that set in motion the building of the Ringling Bros. show. In 1870, the time of Alfred's story, John was four years old and Charles was six. Whatever circus games the younger boys may have engaged in, the elder ones began their circus careers by traveling with small tent shows. Albert had no less than ten years' experience with such shows as the Parsons' Circus, and Alfred worked with the Gregory Brothers for several seasons before the Ringlings organized at Baraboo, Wisconsin, in 1884.[9] The Parsons and Gregory shows were typical of the more than seventy small circuses that rolled out of Wisconsin in the latter half of the nineteenth century.

Six of the brothers (Albert, Otto, Alfred, Charles, John, and Henry) started their own enterprise with a town hall concert and comedy show in 1882, when John was sixteen. For several winters they performed, paraded as a band, and managed and transported the show by train; they soon learned to drop unstable characters from their troupe. In 1884, teaming with an experienced showman, they organized a circus: "Yankee Robinson and Ringling Bros. Double Show . . . Ringling Brothers and Yankee Robinson, Proprietors and Managers."[10] Robinson, who was elderly and frail, did not survive the rigors of the first joint season on the road. With his death, Albert, Otto, Alfred, Charles, and John became sole owners. No other name ever again preceded their own in circus billing.

The five brothers (Henry had dropped out) divided the management tasks; each one assumed a role that he found suited to his personal choice. Soon these roles followed an established pattern. Al (Albert), the eldest, was the only true performer. He started as equestrian director, or ringmaster, and held the post for life. His reputation among circus people was that of a man who was "modest, unassuming, affable, and courteous."[11] His wife, Louise, was a skilled equestrian, the only performer among the Ringling wives; she also helped out as a snake charmer in the side show, made costumes, and filled a dozen needs on the lot. One of Al's strategies to make the show seem larger was to have performers change costume and reappear in another ring, creating the illusion of a much larger troupe.

Otto started as treasurer, a post well suited to his frugal, almost penurious nature. He too held the job for life. He never married and, unlike his brothers, never built or owned a home either modest or splendid, never traveled in a limousine or permitted himself to own any of the ornaments of wealth that his brothers came so quickly to enjoy. Otto was almost a recluse, nearly bereft of social graces. But he was also a man of limitless ambition, the taskmaster of the partners, and a rigid guardian of circus assets.

Alfred Theodore, who was always called Alf T. to distinguish him from his older brother Al, led the band. Later in his career, as director of press relations and publicity, he used his skill at hyperbole and his ability to excite a feeling of wonder. When he made his home in New Jersey, Alf T. owned a lavish estate where circus animals from their smaller circus were kept in winter quarters. Like his younger brothers,

Herald from the Ringling Bros. first season, 1884, when they joined with Yankee Robinson. This "mammoth show" consisted of twenty-two performers; there were no performing animals and no ring. Courtesy of the John and Mable Ringling Museum of Art.

he also became a millionaire through his astute management of real estate and other assets.[12]

Charles began as the circus's orchestra leader and violinist. Like his brothers, he had a flair for self-taught skills—playing a variety of band instruments in the winter hall shows. Through the big show years, even when the circus had a full professional band, he continued to play at least once each season from a seat among the musicians. His lifelong management role (until his death in 1926) was to be the administrator of the whole crew—performers and work force alike. For this he was well suited; he could manage the tumult of circus life, yet he was always "Mr. Charlie" to the whole organization, a name suggesting their respect and affection.

John was not long in giving up his initial character part as a comedian. His act as a Dutch clown in the hall shows disappeared when he took on the tasks of scheduling, contracting, and arranging circus bookings at selected towns and small cities. An important part of his work depended on his ability to assess local conditions so that the circus could bypass towns where money was short. Any local conditions that would tighten the purse were to be avoided in favor of others where freer spending could be expected.

Nothing less than total commitment could have made bearable the bare-knuckle, harshly demanding life of the early wagon show seasons. Circus life was hard and often dangerous. A strict social barrier separated a circus from its audience in the towns and smaller cities of the nation. Fights were not unusual between the circus crew and townsmen.[13]

Whatever small surplus of capital accumulated went into equipment, horses, and tents until the show began to succeed. After one of the more successful seasons, Grandmother Juliar spoke to John of her concern. She was unhappy with the unorthodox life the circus imposed on the brothers. She was quickly mollified when John pointed out that their profit that year was $15,000.[14]

The changeover from wagon to rail in 1890 led to the Ringlings' sustained successful growth, allowing their show to travel greater distances and reach larger audiences almost daily in the season. By 1891 the big top had grown from one ring to three, and the first of the

John Ringling at about age twenty-five. This style of dress was favored by the five brothers to promote their circus image as "The Sunday School Show." Courtesy of Henry Ringling North.

glittering "spectaculars" was produced. Titled *The Crusades*, it was composed by Alfred and one of their hired assistants.[15] That feature was one of the circus's great attractions. The show became larger each year, with more acts, more animals, more apparatus, and more rail cars to move it.

In 1906, when the Ringlings had gained stability in the Midwest, they bought half of the Adam Forepaugh-Sells Circus from the heirs of James A. Bailey (of Barnum & Bailey). The brothers were moving toward a monopoly with the profits from their success. Augustus and Henry—the two brothers who had remained outside the Ringling partnership—were made joint managers for the next two seasons. This purchase was the Ringlings' first move to halt a price and advertising war that was cutting into the profits for all the major shows. The next logical step was the formation of a trust by the Ringlings and their two principal rivals, the Wallace circus and the Bailey heirs.[16] These three were expected to divide the territories and to agree on prices, precisely the kind of move that the antitrust laws were, even then, being designed to prevent. However, the trust idea folded when the Wallace shows rejected the territory assigned to them. The Ringlings tried another tactic. After much family debate, they bought the entire Barnum & Bailey Circus, its assets, and its famous name.[17] Having demolished their principal rival, they went on to reap enormous profits, recouping their entire investment of $410,000 in one season.

Devotion alone could not make such a fragile enterprise grow and prosper. The Ringlings brought to it no experience, credit, capital, or family influence. Instead, they invested their genius, their personalities, and their judgment of public taste to put together an exciting, fast-moving program of entertainment. They added a principle of clean enjoyment, free from the vulgarity they regarded as unnecessary in a circus, particularly since they were aiming for a family audience. People in their territory wanted a show that adhered to the prevailing Protestant code of acceptable language and action. George Ade (1866–1944), an American journalist and dramatist, believed that this explained their success. After a close look at their operation, he wrote, "They found the business in the hands of vagabonds and put it into the hands of gentlemen. . . . [They] became circus kings of the world by adopting and observing the simple rule that it is better to be straight than crooked."[18] Ade was perhaps somewhat harsh in his sweeping judgment of circus owners of his day, for there were others who also tried to run clean and honest shows.

The Ringling circus, like others, suffered its share of accidents and misfortunes, some of them serious. Weather hazards, wrecks, blowdowns, and animal diseases were unrelenting. Yet as long as each of them lived, the brothers never ceased to fight for and hold onto first place. As a result, their show attracted top talent. Ringling performers were commonly hired for less than they asked, but no one in the organization was ever cheated out of his promised wage.

Although they faced the same hazards as their competitors, the Ringlings introduced systematic management to an industry that was haphazard in the extreme. Every performance was personally supervised. For more than forty years and more than 19,000 performances, one or more of the brothers was in charge.[19]

With their division of tasks, John recalled, each brother was able to specialize: "Each assumed complete control of his own department, and the others never questioned or criticized unless asked for an opinion, each man concentrated on his own work and kept off the others. . . . in what we refer to as the 'opposition' days, a circus life was full of thrills. It was real warfare against powerful enemies, a fight for existence on our part."[20]

John Ringling's reminiscence about conflicts suggests that, on some occasions, he enjoyed them. He learned useful stratagems for both open and subtle conflict. As a self-taught businessman, he learned to hold in his own hands complete control of whatever he perceived to be his responsibility. He felt no need to share authority or to be questioned. He made decisions known when he was sure of the desired impact. While he found this habit useful, it effectively distanced him from the circus people, and later from his business associates.

The death of the dour, thrifty Otto Ringling in 1911 may have lessened a certain restraint on the other brothers' spending habits. They all added Florida vacations to their winter schedules. While his brothers continued their intense, almost passionate interest in their two circuses, John began to move into more conventional business arenas. He was often miles away, dealing with rail executives, Interstate Commerce Commission officials, and others to whom the circus was an alien world.

The circus was different. Its social niche was unclear; as an enterprise, its only assets were movable property. Its record of failures was surely unequaled. But by the standards of the day, John Ringling was a capitalist, and not merely because he was rich. He was one of many who acquired fortunes in the expansive years between 1880 and 1929. He and his brothers were like other aggressive owners of proprietary businesses who swept ahead in their field, striving for a monopoly unrestrained by government regulation. They held the essentials of economic power: they owned and controlled the enterprise and they controlled the labor that made it run. Profits in those days mounted at unprecedented rates, and, like their industrial counterparts, the Ringlings put much of theirs back into the business. It was their good fortune to be part of a capitalist-proprietor era that lasted until the Great Depression.

Not surprisingly, when John Ringling began his separate career

John Ringling with the circus train, c. 1929, being interviewed by a reporter. Courtesy of Henry Ringling North.

he retained his established habits. He of course preferred the un-challenged control that he and his partners enjoyed in the circus. However prominent he became, both nationally and locally in Sarasota, Ringling remained an intensely private person, and he displayed an arrogance that family members have attributed to the uncritical adulation lavished upon him by his mother and grandmother.[21] He rejected intimacy and withheld warmth in both social and business relationships. His sister Ida perhaps knew him best. As the elder brother in their home (after the older boys had left), John shared Ida's childhood, and it kept them close through life, as a recollection of shared early hardships often does.

Reactions in the press to John Ringling's personality were uniformly superficial. O. O. MacIntyre, columnist of *New York Day by Day,* saw him as a man of wry and subtle humor.[22] Most writers stressed Ringling's aloof, diffident manner and did not seem able to get past that barrier. A profile in *Fortune* magazine from 1930, however, presents an animated composite of Ringling the millionaire. It was clearly gathered from several informants as well as from observing the subject himself.

> He is an enormous, thick powerful man with sad, heavy eyes and an arm like a wrestler's. He talks rapidly in a low voice. He smokes a great number of cigars, removing the butt between quick puffs of smoke and throwing half the length away. He dresses superbly. He has a vast fortune, one of the largest in America and he spends it magnificently on a Fifth Avenue home, a Venetian palazzo in Sarasota, Florida, with a steam yacht and private car.
>
> There is no legend under the big top of his battles or his rage. He is known as a cold and phlegmatic man. . . . where the fictional circus captain would have been feared and loved by his employees and called by some odd title, Ringling is feared, not loved and called merely Mister John. . . . Ringling is noted for his domesticity. His parties are "at homes." His lavishness ends there also.[23]

Shortly after he made a big splash by purchasing his principal competitor, the American Circus Corporation, the *Literary Digest* offered a somewhat critical view: "At the top of this pyramid is the powerfully built, huge and silent man, about 62, with thousands and thousands of acquaintances, but no intimates, a lover of art, a man with a punch that could fell a steer, an excellent picker of sub-ordinates . . . ."[24]

In 1931 the NEA services, a features syndicate, found him to be "a huge production in at least three rings and four stages." A staff writer for the *Brooklyn Eagle* saw a different Ringling. He stressed the quality that others had termed diffidence, even shyness.[25]

> John Ringling in no way resembles the traditional showman. He has none of the gay garrulity, the extravagances and eccentricities of a man like, say, P. T. Barnum.
>
> There is a reticence, almost a sardonic reticence about him, a great sense of physical power and energy, and with all that charm

Mable Burton Ringling at Atlantic City, New Jersey, at about the time of her marriage, 1905. Courtesy of Henry Ringling North.

which all men must have whose success depends on domineering people and making them like it. John Ringling is not your chatty type of man. He answers questions as economically as possible, shuts his lips and gazes at the interviewer in a way that makes the silences between answers and questions nervously formidable—for the interviewer. It is the least known element in his minutely publicized business.[26]

When Ringling was ill and had been driven from his place with the circus, many former performers remembered him. He kept some of their letters, which expressed real affection and concern. Their messages tend to contradict the *Fortune* writer's idea of his being "only feared" among the circus people. However, these letters came primarily from memories of an earlier time when John, like his brothers, was often present on the circus lot and more closely identified with the show. For example, in June 1933 the DeKos family, some in America and some in Europe, wrote, "(Greetings from) friends who think the

Studio portrait of Mable
Ringling, photographed in
Chicago shortly after her
marriage in 1905.
Courtesy of Henry
Ringling North.

world and all of you and no one will take your place in our hearts."[27]
Another former employee recalled an event from forty years earlier:
"You have probably forgotten me and the good turn you did for me in
giving me a job as a biller with your show in 1897. That's 41 years ago
and a lot of water has run under the bridge since then; nevertheless, I
am ever mindful of that favor, for it was the stepping stone to whatever
success I have attained . . . ."[28]

George Ade first encountered the Ringlings at Baraboo, Wisconsin,
in the early days. At the suggestion of his friend, the prominent editor
and novelist William Dean Howells, Ade spent a month on the road
with the Ringling Bros. Circus to experience circus life. Later, in 1924,
Ade described Ringling as "still diffident and smiling and quite as
genuine as he was back in the days at Baraboo, Wisconsin, when money
was not so plentiful and prosperity hid around the corners." Whereas

John and Mable Ringling traveling with the circus, c. 1919. Courtesy of
Henry Ringling North.

the stereotype of the circus man was a "loud, cursing vulgarian," he had found the Ringlings to be quiet, reserved, courteous, and kindly.[29]

Fred Bradna, a top-level manager with the Barnum & Bailey Circus and then with the Ringling Bros., was less concerned with the brothers' personal attributes than with management practice. Bradna found John a demanding employer, always exacting a high standard of performance and appearance. Bradna found annoying his "inability to consolidate a decision." He saw John Ringling's management style as an indifference to small matters. Ringling often agreed to a request from an assistant without even listening or knowing what he had approved. However, although he was known to give cursory attention to small matters and to minor functionaries, he chose his assistants carefully and trusted their judgment within the areas of their duties. Furthermore, the same John Ringling whom Bradna found indifferent to small matters would stand at the entrance during a performance and rebuke a performer whose shoes were not properly shined. These contradictory subtleties were characteristic of him.

Bradna (the only circus man invited to stay the night at Ringling's Sarasota home) also remembered vividly that Ringling "conducted his affairs like a Moorish potentate; ornately, glitteringly, incredibly. No scene concocted by Cecil B. DeMille of Hollywood rivaled the manner in which he lived from day to day."[30]

May Wirth, who had come from Australia with her adoptive parents to perform for the Ringlings, was one of the great equestriennes of her generation. In a journal she kept of her career in America, she wrote that she sensed a continual rivalry or competition between Charles and John. Each, she believed, sought to discover and present the finest acts to dazzle their partners and audiences. She found Charles invariably considerate, accepting without question any omissions she considered too dangerous in poor riding conditions. John, she recalls, was just the opposite. "He would want to know why I was cutting them out. I'd explain that it was a bad ring, and he'd say 'OK,' still chewing on his famous cigar and spitting over my head. But he was a good boss and proud of having me first in America."[31]

Ringling became known for the panache and the somewhat florid style that marked his rich social life in Chicago, Los Angeles, and New

Hudson River Palisades at the Ringlings' summer home. The 100-acre estate is now within the palisades park developed by the Rockefeller interests. Courtesy of Henry Ringling North.

Mable Ringling at the Ringling summer home with one of her four miniature Dobermans, 1926. Courtesy of Henry Ringling North.

York. In 1905, after twenty years on the road as a bachelor, he settled into marriage at age thirty-nine, taking on some, if not all, of its responsibilities. By then his habits and life-style were firmly established. Armilda Burton, who had changed her name to Mable, was at thirty a woman of uncommon wisdom. She never attempted to change him or to demand a domesticity that he could not have endured, and in return received his lifelong love.

Mable (4 March 1875–8 June 1929) came from a small farm community near Washington Courthouse, Ohio. Her parents, George and Mary Burton, with their five daughters and one son, lived in the town of

Mable Ringling in the garden at their Alpine, New Jersey, estate. The New Jersey state police maintained an office at the far end of the garden.
Courtesy of Henry Ringling North.

Moons. Mable's early life on the farm is obscured by her reticence, which she retained throughout her life. While living and working in New Jersey, she apparently met Ringling at Atlantic City, although neither family nor friends ever knew much about the first encounter.

John and Mable Ringling at their summer home, Alpine, New Jersey, 1926.
Courtesy of Henry Ringling North.

They were married in Hoboken, New Jersey, on 29 December 1905, at
the city clerk's office. Mable brought to the marriage several valuable
assets that promised well for future marital harmony. She was beautiful,
poised, and blessed with a warm personality that nicely balanced her
husband's habitual reserve. However, she never consented to be photographed for the press, and only once did she agree to be interviewed. In
that conversation, with a writer for the *Seattle Post Intelligencer,* she spoke
little about her life except her travels with the circus and the art and
museum that were vital to her life in Sarasota.[32]

At the time of their marriage, John was gaining affluence, but he
derived most of his income from the circus rather than the multiple

interests that later helped to make him rich. For several years Mable took advantage of the quiet interval between seasons to be tutored in the arts and English. Their twenty-five years of marriage were characterized by an enduring affection and compatibility, a notable achievement in view of John's years of bachelor freedom. While his restless nature and varied interests kept him moving about the country, Mable became content to stay more often at Sarasota or at their summer home in Alpine, New Jersey. She limited her circus role to that of an affectionate spouse traveling with her husband on their private rail car attached to the circus train.

Sarasota's Golden Promise

ONG BEFORE developers transformed Sarasota into a metropolitan resort, a community began to form and to assume a character that distinguished this village from others on the Gulf coast. From the arrival of its first permanent residents, Sarasota's scenic assets attracted settlers. Few coastal cities can boast such a favored location. Sarasota faces a well-protected bay about fifty miles long; passes enter the Gulf of Mexico between barrier keys that protect the mainland from storms. In the 1920s, the city was advertised by the Ringling Bros. Circus as one of the fairest regions of the earth. But for early settlers, the demands of daily life left little if any leisure for enjoyment of nature's gifts. Many years would pass before the idea of Sarasota as a resort for winter visitors became a viable notion.

The area that was to include Sarasota gained identity in the 1840s when the first white settlers came to Hillsborough County, later subdivided to create Manatee and then Sarasota counties. Previously, only Spanish conquistadors, Cuban fishermen, and Indians had visited the area. When the Second Seminole War ended in 1842, the huge Indian territories of South Florida were open to settlement. During the Indian war years, the threat to isolated settlers kept even the hardiest people away. The peace of 1842 removed—for a time—the threat of Indian attack. Some rough roads were cleared and steamers came to some of the rivers. In a rush to spur settlement, Congress enacted the Armed Occupation Act. One hundred and sixty acres of homestead land were available to eligible settlers who would occupy, farm, and defend five acres for five years. Yet in this large county, fewer than fifty settlers received homestead grants.[1] Apart from the William Whitaker family, the Sarasota area had no permanent white residents until after 1865.

The peace of 1842 was brief. The Third Seminole War erupted in 1855, and for three years the countryside was overrun with conflict. Peace was restored in 1858, and settlers returned to their neglected land. After another short interval, secession and the Civil War brought new turmoil. Through the Civil War years, Florida was a major supplier of meat, salt, and leather to the Confederacy. Union gunboats blockaded the Gulf coast, lurking among the Keys to capture or destroy any vessel that risked attempting a run to Havana or one of the British islands. Still, some wily boatmen evaded capture in the hidden island waterways. On the Gulf coast, Union raiding parties destroyed whatever they encountered—crops, livestock, citrus trees—anything that belonged to the hapless residents near the shore. These raids, along with intermittent guerrilla activities among pro-Confederates, brought waves of destruction to the sparsely settled areas of Florida's Gulf coast. Although Florida witnessed few battles between the armies, many of its homes lost their men, dead or maimed in distant scenes of the conflict.

After the war, settlers began to arrive. Some came looking for cheap, fertile land; others wanted to make a fresh start. A few wished merely to find a freer life away from the restraints of close neighbors. Such hopes brought single men and families from northern and central Florida, from the Carolinas, Georgia, Virginia, and even from New England. An old military road near the coast and a few trails offered what little communication there was, apart from access by sea.

During and after the chaotic period of Reconstruction (1865–77), there was a concerted attempt to rebuild the state's economy. Enterprising settlers, some new residents and some of longer standing, put their energies and their fortunes to work. Soon after (in the early 1880s) came the wave of new railroad building, significant in part because most of the older lines, such as David Yulee's east-west line from Fernandina to Cedar Keys, had been destroyed. Unlike the many pre–Civil War lines, most of the new railroads were built on a wider gauge, making transport feasible throughout the state, as well as into Georgia and beyond.[2] By the turn of the century, nearly all the short lines were merged into four major networks, but not before millions of acres of land had been granted to both genuine and fictitious rail companies.

Sarasota was too far south to be served by the first system of new rails or to share in the growth of Florida resorts that followed the coastal railroads. Henry Plant brought his Savannah, Florida and Western line from Sanford to Tampa and its port, thus joining ocean shipping to rail. In 1891 he built the huge and opulent Tampa Bay Hotel, described in the *New York Times* as one of the two or three greatest hotels in the world.[3] Meanwhile, Henry Flagler's Florida East Coast Railroad opened three Atlantic coastal centers to affluent winter visitors. His line went first to St. Augustine in 1885, with its two hotels luring prosperous northerners away from shooting and hunting at their Georgia plantations. Three days each week, "Florida Specials"—consisting entirely of "vestibule parlor cars and sleeping cars"—rushed their passengers south. At Palm Beach, after extending his line to Lake Worth in 1890, Flagler offered the richest travelers two hotels of surpassing splendor. Then in 1896 he continued his line to Miami. Now he could offer the whole east coast to visitors eager to try the novelty and luxury of a Florida winter.

Plant and Flagler demonstrated what outside capital could do for Florida. Both men were prime examples of the multimillionaire-entrepreneur, investing their own millions in high-risk ventures. While Plant sought to increase his wealth, Flagler apparently financed great projects for the personal satisfaction of seeing new railroads and cities grow from his initiatives.[4] Their resorts brought large sums into the local economies, sustaining a host of residents who built, served, and supplied the splendid hotels. The guests expected to find the amenities that they enjoyed at home; thus, Palm Beach and Miami grew into communities of trades and services catering to tourists. Palm Beach quickly gained its special character as the center of status and wealth, while other resorts such as St. Augustine and Miami attracted a more middle-class clientele.

The implication of Flagler's experience was clear to would-be developers: hotel and rail in combination with warm Florida winters meant economic success. Rail travel from northern urban centers took scarcely more than a night and a day. But visitors wanted more than sun and sand. Some were celebrities seeking publicity; others were rich old families in search of isolation. And then there were the newly rich who wanted to share Florida's glamour. The shrewd developers gave their clients hotels catering to specific classes of travelers. At the best hotels, houseboats, golf courses, and elegant shops charmed the guests, bringing more people and more money into Florida each season. Those who would become developers on Florida's Gulf coast eventually applied the same formula, but circumstances made the smaller Gulf resorts less ostentatious than their east coast predecessors.

Sarasota had to wait for its age of fine hotels and flocks of tourists. Its potential as a tourist mecca came nearer with each rail transaction. One trail of related events began in 1881. In that year, the Internal Improvement Fund, a state agency that controlled public lands, sold four million acres to Hamilton Disston of Philadelphia for a million dollars. The thirty-three-year-old heir to a saw and tool company became the largest landholder in the country. The agency had grown nearly moribund during Reconstruction; there was some activity, but holders of railroad bonds took court action, forcing the agency to earmark its meager income to pay off state obligation on these prewar bonds. With Disston's million, the Fund revived and went on to grant several million acres to prospective railroad companies.[5] Florida's rail lines grew from 528 miles in 1881 to 3,250 in the next twenty years.[6]

Disston sold much of his land to syndicates. One such syndicate based in England resold 50,000 acres in and around Sarasota to the Florida Mortgage and Investment Company.[7] A company director, Sir John Gillespie of Edinburgh, sent to Australia for his son to assist the site manager handling company affairs in Sarasota. Nearly one hundred Scottish colonists (known as the Armiston Colony) were already preparing for homes in the Sarasota region, and the younger Gillespie traveled halfway around the world ahead of them, making the final leg of his journey from Manatee to Sarasota by horse and buggy.

The Scots had an agreement with the promoter, Selwyn Tait. Each colonist was to have forty acres within five miles of Sarasota and a rental house in the town; the house had to be purchased by the end of a six-month period. They were also led to expect a community with a hotel, a boardinghouse, and a store. Late in December 1885, when the weary travelers arrived, they found almost nothing of what they expected. The Scottish syndicate, though acting in good faith, had been misled by its principals in London and land agents in Florida.[8]

Although given temporary shelter by the people of the countryside, the newcomers were bitterly disappointed and convinced that they had been cheated. Soon after arrival, nearly all left for other parts of Florida or northern states, though one family and a few individuals stayed for several years. A few returned to Scotland—sadly disillusioned about the wonders of the New World and chilled by the freezing weather of an unusually cold winter.

Fortunately for Sarasota, J. Hamilton Gillespie stayed, first to assist the company manager, later to replace him. The young Gillespie gave pioneer Sarasota a measure of urbane civility and affluence. He became the first mayor of the town in 1902 and headed the movement to make Sarasota a community that could attract new residents and develop a viable economy. Of course, his employer, the Florida Mortgage and Investment Company, still owned most of in-town Sarasota and 50,000 acres nearby. Gillespie, acting for the company, started at once to build a hotel and a boardinghouse, then a dock and a store. All were completed within a year, but that ended the company's building program.

Nearly a decade after that modest start, Sarasota was able to accommodate a small number of visitors and provide some amenities, including the opportunity to participate in the increasingly popular pastime of sport fishing. During the late nineteenth century, a number of rich Americans and Europeans discovered the thrill of tarpon fishing. One of the more distinguished proponents of the sport was the fourth duke of Sutherland, who came each year in the early 1890s to fish for tarpon, to visit his friend Thomas Edison at Fort Myers, and to inspect his huge land holdings near Clearwater on the Pinella peninsula. The duke's yacht, *Sans Peur*, was much too large to enter Sarasota Bay, but his steam launch brought him to the village dock. When he dined as Gillespie's guest at the DeSoto Hotel, his piper marched up and down and played his bagpipes outside the windows of the hotel while his grace was entertained within.[9]

Sarasota had some of the ambience of southern culture, but not in the mold of the antebellum South. Rural-based sectionalism did not dominate Sarasota history—it was at most a minor theme in the early, pioneer stage. Nevertheless, the town had its share of locals who resented outsiders and believed that almost any northerner was a threat to the established order. Vigilantes and Ku Klux Klan members were capable of acting on such resentment.

Sarasota was divided by passions fanned by the vigilantes, some Ku Klux Klan activities, and at least one murder. In late 1884 C. E. Abbe, Sarasota's Republican postmaster, was ambushed and murdered on 27 December by vigilantes as he walked toward his home with a Chicago visitor. Abbe was from Illinois; he had migrated to Sarasota in 1877. There he became the object of frequent harassment, primarily because he was believed to have reported squatter occupation of land, ostensibly to pave the way for colonization by northern land-grabbers. Chicago and New York newspapers attributed the shooting to Abbe's supposed efforts to bring numbers of northerners to Sarasota: "He was a Republican and as such almost alone in the town. . . . his appointment intensified the feelings of the ignorant 'crackers.'"[10]

After the Abbe murder, vigilante action rarely disrupted Sarasota life. A brief period of turmoil startled the few residents in 1886, when Gillespie brought transient laborers to Sarasota to build the DeSoto Hotel and other company-sponsored projects. But with the exception of those workers, the community had little trouble assimilating newcomers into the existing social order. Unlike some older southern towns in the late nineteenth century, Sarasota was a relatively open community. Partly because of its late settlement, there was no antebellum tradition. The local leadership was drawn from a broad middle class rather than from a single, hierarchical faction. In the first slow stage of growth in the 1880s and 1890s, status and influence were shared among small merchants, prosperous landowners, and a few professionals. They were led by Gillespie, whose status stemmed from his connection with the landowning syndicate in Scotland. In time, Sarasota was to develop a local aristocracy based on money.

During Sarasota's early years the economy was based largely on nature's bounty—fishing and farming. The hasty exodus of the Scottish settlers had withdrawn a potential population of educated, skilled mechanics and small proprietors whose presence, had they stayed, would have helped materially to develop a varied economy. During those years, the black population was small by Florida standards; the overall state average had been close to 50 percent before emancipation—a figure distorted by uneven distribution that ranged from 74 percent in Leon County, with its great cotton plantations, to 2 percent in mostly vacant Dade County in the far south. In 1860 Manatee County (including later Sarasota County) had a population of 681 white residents and 254 slaves, most of whom lived on the former Gamble plantation on the Manatee River.[11] Sarasota's free black settlers were few until 1903. In that year, jobs created by the building of the railroad brought several hundred black laborers to the area. Many of the blacks moved on to other construction projects, but some settled to make Sarasota their home.

Black residents, from then on, formed a significant laboring class for the growing village that became a city in 1914. They worked in fisheries (some as independent boat operators), on farms, in small businesses such as livery stables, and as day laborers. Despite a chronic housing problem, a developing black community took shape steadily between 1903 and 1920. Black families first occupied the old prefabricated houses built by the Florida Mortgage and Investment Company. Their crowded quarters, known as "Overtown," were eventually displaced by a subdivision of 240 lots on forty acres outside the city limits. The settlement was named "Newtown" by its originator, Charles N. Thompson of Shell Beach, who was one of the Ringling circus managers. Thompson sold small plots of land to black residents and donated land for two churches and a schoolhouse.[12] By 1916 there were 280 blacks in a total population of 1,700, double the number of all residents only five years earlier.[13] Although a majority of Sarasota's black community continued to work as day or domestic laborers, their community included several black-owned businesses and even supported a small black middle class.

Despite the growing black presence in the area, local white officials were slow to accept responsibility for educating black children. At first there were only private schools—Josie Washington's kindergarten in her home was among the first when she started it in 1912.[14] Through the 1910–20 decade, black teachers were hired by the county, but only rental space was provided. Finally, in the 1924–25 school year, the Sarasota Grammar School became the first public school for black children.

Principal occupations for Sarasota's white working class gradually expanded to include new jobs in retail and building trades as the town grew. Steamers and finally the railroad replaced the former yawl and sloop transports that had moved local products to Tampa. Small boats still took farm products, cattle, and dried and smoked fish (at about three cents a pound) to Key West and Havana. A ranching economy developed rapidly in the region along the Myakka River. Thanks to the ranchers' lucrative trade with the cattle market in Havana, they were soon an economic and political force in the county.

Despite continuing economic ties with Havana, Sarasota remained a relatively dormant community with a lagging economy well into the twentieth century, bypassed by Henry Plant's railroad network that served Tampa on the north and Punta Gorda via Arcadia on the south. Rail and steamer brought increasingly rapid but sporadic growth to scattered communities along Florida's Atlantic and Gulf coasts, most of it financed by northern investors. Some of the eastern cities, like St. Augustine, had old colonial ties. But more peculiar to Florida was the distinct character found in each new town. In 1890 a writer for the *New York Times* noted, after a tour of the state, that "Florida places within a few miles of each other are so widely different that they do not seem to belong to the same section."[15]

Plant's rail lines were making notable changes at points along the Gulf. In 1892 the *New York Times* advised its readers that the west coast of Florida was now opened to the settler, the tourist, and the sportsman: "indeed, almost every point north of the Everglades worthy of mention—may be reached by rail."[16] The West India Fast Mail from New York to Tampa ran daily, connecting to steamers for Charlotte Harbor and Havana. Readers found exciting accounts of tarpon fishing, hunting, and shooting, enticing those with money to visit the Gulf coast. Towns from Tampa to Naples were described, but Sarasota was not among them.[17] For Sarasota, the age of steamship and rail would not begin until 1895; even then, reliable rail service was yet to come. Before the mid-1890s, there were few obvious reasons for extending either rail or steamship networks to Sarasota. The land was less fertile than what was found north of the Manatee River, much of it soft sand; some proved to be hardpan below the surface. Apart from the village and nearby farms, most of the county was covered with pine woods, palmetto thickets, and cedar forests abounding with game. Moreover, the Scottish syndicate still owned large tracts of the Sarasota region, and its shareholders wanted too much for the land.

In 1892 Gillespie made a valiant but eventually futile effort to bring rail service to Sarasota, not only to benefit the village economy, but also to generate some dividends for the floundering syndicate that he still represented. Gillespie and four northern associates formed the Manatee and Sarasota Railway and Drainage Company. Their venture was badly underfinanced and had to be bailed out by the Arcadia, Gulf Coast & Lakeland Railroad of Florida, a firm with just enough capital to complete the nine miles of track from Bradentown (later Bradenton) to Sarasota and to purchase one wood-burning engine and two primitive passenger cars—one with a canvas top and another open to the weather. Unlike most rail lines, this one did not connect with another line at either end. It was intended to connect at Bradentown with steamers to Tampa, where travelers could go by rail to northern cities. Service opened in May 1892 and ended in 1895. The line, which was dubbed the "Slow and Wobbly," never achieved a schedule or viable service. But it did generate new energy in Sarasota: a few tourists risked travel over its unstable track, some merchandise moved in, and citrus was shipped out. In all, this was one of Gillespie's less successful efforts. His initiative failed to produce the hoped-for dividends demanded by the angry syndicate shareholders in Scotland. They had agreed to a land grant for the railroad with an expectation of future profits from development along the line.[18]

Gillespie's railroad failed, not merely because it was poorly constructed and without serviceable equipment, but because there was no market for rail service. Sarasota might well have reverted to its comfortable isolation had other changes not intervened. In 1895, the same year in which the "Slow and Wobbly" became defunct, a steamer began regular service to Bradentown and Tampa. Sarasota fishermen finally had a way to send their catch to northern markets, packing the fish in ice from a new municipal plant. In 1899 gasoline for marine engines was brought to Sarasota. First used for recreation and charter boats, the gasoline engine (replacing earlier naphtha-fueled engines) offered a material improvement over sail for commercial fisheries.

The impact of these changes was slow and, by itself, only moderately conducive to greater change. In 1898 came the Spanish-American War, which had an immediate and lasting impact on Florida's west coast. Tampa became the Gulf coast headquarters for transshipment from rail to ship for men, materiel, and supplies. Money flowed into Tampa on soldiers' paydays, and Henry Plant's huge Tampa Bay Hotel overflowed with people whose business led them to converge on wartime Tampa. Some of them—both civilian and military—enjoyed boating along the coast. For the first time, numbers of northerners had the opportunity to see for themselves the natural beauty of the Gulf coast.

War changes everything it touches, and the Gulf coast of Florida was no exception. The pace of life quickened, and even Sarasota felt the change. Residents realized they could no longer expect their town to grow without ties to more distant centers of commerce and wealth. The alternative was to remain like Boca Grande, a quiet village stirred briefly each year by the rich sports enthusiasts who came for the tarpon season. Among the first to perceive the commercial and tourist potential for Sarasota if rail service could be brought from Tampa was Ralph C. Caples. Caples came in 1899 on a delayed honeymoon with his wife, Ellen.[19] On one of his later visits, he bought a Shell Beach estate from C. N. Thompson.

A rail executive himself, Caples (then with the New York Central) saw the urgent need for bringing a line into Sarasota, and he formed the Florida West Coast Railroad Company. But he lacked the necessary financing to convert his scheme into reality. In 1903 his plan was preempted by another source with plenty of money to invest. The United States and West Indies Railroad and Steamship Company was well financed and able to bring to Sarasota the needed freight and passenger service.[20] The impact was immediate; the economy grew stronger and the population increased. The pioneer era was all but over. Permanent reliable service was assured by a tie to the Seaboard Airline Railroad that absorbed the line to Sarasota, thus bringing the resources of a major trunk line to the area. Modern facilities were slowly introduced— an electric power plant and its companion, an ice plant, helped to move Sarasota into the new century.

In a welcome to the long-awaited rail line, a writer for the weekly *Sarasota Times* grasped for metaphors in his praise: "The coming of the Seaboard Railroad was like sunshine to the rosebud, when the sunshine of civilization awoke this quiet little village into new life, and like the rosebud it opened and by the gentle sea breeze, its fragrant perfume was wafted on the wings of butterflies in all directions and like magic took hold of the enthused people so anxiously seeking the sunniest spot in all sunny Florida as the haven of rest."[21]

The new railroad had, in fact, been built to meet a less romantic purpose. The Seaboard's initial object was to transport fish and citrus products to northern markets. To that end, the tracks were extended on a pier in the bay with fish houses where fishing boats could tie up alongside, so that the fish could be iced and loaded directly onto the trains. However mundane the directors' motive, the railroad enabled visitors to reach Sarasota in Pullman comfort.

Energized by the presence of a trunk line, Sarasota's residents began to demand amenities such as paved streets, sidewalks, and telephone service—the very minimum of contemporary town life. Sarasota had never lacked vocal boosters who saw in its ideal climate and healthful waters all manner of benefits. The *Sarasota Times* loyally supported every effort to improve the town. Promoters such as landowners J. H. Lord and Harry Higel joined J. H. Gillespie and others in campaigns for improvements. Street paving for the town and surrounding areas was perhaps the most widely discussed topic and the most active issue in the town council for the entire decade following.

The village that had been barely functioning in 1899 achieved mea- surable signs of success, proudly listed in the *Sarasota Times* in 1911: one hundred and sixty-five telephones, four miles of paved roads, two miles of good sidewalks, three daily trains, a waterworks and sewer system soon to be installed. By the end of the year, another mile of paved road and six miles of sidewalk had been added. There were eight hotels, a nine-hole golf course,[22] and twelve real estate agencies. While Florida's population increased 42 percent from 1900 to 1910, Sarasota's grew 280 percent, to 840—a figure that would double in the next five years.

The keys were still largely unpopulated, their development impeded by lack of access. Longboat Key, which became significant in the future of Sarasota in John Ringling's plans, offered nearly twelve miles of beautiful, unspoiled Gulf beaches. In 1911 Longboat was settled by about twenty families, most of whom had come to homestead on the fertile land where they engaged in tomato farming. At the very time when Ringling bought his first Sarasota property, some Longboat residents were eager to start subdividing their land. A firm of developers, Godding and Manning, laid out a town, put down an artesian well, and promised to establish a regular ferry service to the mainland.[23] That autumn, the U.S. Army Corps of Engineers resumed dredging a deep-channel inland waterway from Sarasota to Venice. In 1909 on Sarasota Key there was more activity. Harry Higel and his associates laid out on its northern tip a development they named "Siesta."[24] The Bay Island Hotel prospered despite the lack of a bridge to the mainland. The social life on these islands was restrained by their separation from the mainland, helping to establish Sarasota's image as a quiet retreat. Those who demanded greater splendor and more glamour would have to look elsewhere.

By 1911 events in other parts of the country were creating an effect in Florida. The panic of 1907 had almost halted the expansion of American industry, delaying investment that would open new areas. Then the resurgence of energy and investment that followed recovery from the panic brought a new stimulus to business and migration into Florida. From its 1910 data, the Bureau of the Census found that the South was growing faster than other parts of the nation and Florida was gaining population faster than most other southern states.[25] The forthcoming completion of the Panama Canal encouraged high but unfounded expectations of a wave of prosperous trade moving through the ports of Florida. The dream of a deepwater port was alive in Sarasota as early as the 1880s. A truly splendid future seemed assured for Sarasota, a terminus for ship and rail. To the *Sarasota Times,* such a destiny seemed imminent: "The star of empire has halted in its westward course, and it now hangs, poised over the northern shore of the Gulf of Mexico, with its brightest rays illuminating the resources and beauties of the flowered state."[26] To a less biased observer, the Sarasota waterfront, with its array of fish houses and tidal flats, presented anything but a prideful strand lighted by a star of empire. Transition to a bright future was slow at best. However, many of the drab frame buildings had vanished from Sarasota's Main Street, or at least were disguised with false fronts. In 1913 there were still more than thirty wood frame buildings, but several brick and concrete business buildings were helping to establish a new look for Main Street.

The climate, the beaches, sport fishing, and golf brought two types of visitors. The first group were winter visitors who came because they liked the location and the pleasant life of the season. These families bought property on the bay and later on the keys. Their presence contributed to the local economy. The number of private railway cars, the status symbol of the rich, might be taken as an indicator of the wealth represented. Sometimes four or five cars, including those of the Caples and the Ringlings, awaited their owners' pleasure. Like Palm Beach and Miami, Sarasota had gained a character that was to endure through the boom years ahead.

Among the first areas to be readied with platted lots for the real estate market were Indian Beach in 1891 and its northern neighbor, Shell Beach, in 1895. Both came too early to arouse much interest among potential buyers.[27] The first fine home to be built on one of the keys was New Edzel Castle in 1911 on Bird Key, a small island in Sarasota Bay. When it was opened, the public was invited to inspect this splendid home lighted by its own electric system with a backup bottled gas facility.

A second small group of newcomers, who liked what they saw in Sarasota, chose to play a role in the town through investment and enterprise. Bringing wealth into Sarasota from their previous careers, they made their homes and businesses in the town itself. This was the first substantial advance and it lasted until 1914 and World War I. After the war, this stage resumed its energy and lasted through the early 1920s, until the Florida boom ended.

Several figures dominate that stage of Sarasota's history. The two most significant ones for the town's future were Berthe Palmer and Owen Burns, who was to become Ringling's associate in nearly all of his development projects in Sarasota. (John Ringling, who came at about the same time, took no part in its business or social life until later.)

In February of 1910 Berthe Palmer of Chicago, widow of hotel magnate Potter Palmer, visited Sarasota and immediately became the town's most publicized new landowner. Several accounts speculate on the reasons behind her interest in Sarasota. In January 1910, J. H. Lord, who maintained businesses in Chicago and Sarasota, advertised land from his own large holdings in the *Chicago Tribune*. Palmer's inquiries were promptly followed by an inspection tour.[28] On this occasion, her private railway car brought her with her father, H. C. Honoré, her brother Adrian C. Honoré, her business manager, and an array of servants and retainers.[29]

Sarasota had no available accommodations for a party of that size. The Belle Haven was in disrepair, but rooms at the more modest Halton were readied for the visit. A series of land purchases began. Ultimately, Palmer holdings would amount to some 100,000 acres, including 400 on the southern tip of Longboat Key. She chose for her home the former Webb property, facing the bay at Osprey, south of Sarasota, the same spot chosen by Osprey's first white settler.

Almost overnight Palmer became Sarasota's most widely publicized winter resident, conspicuous in her French-built Cadillac limousine and, at first, an object of intense curiosity. She contributed generously to all appeals and charities but remained a patron without participating in Sarasota social life. Photographs show her with Osprey neighbors; she seems to have been gracious without condescending. There was, however, no mistaking her business acumen in promoting family interests. Her one overriding concern was to increase the Palmer fortune.

That fortune and the eminent family name conveyed prestige. Palmer's social leadership in Chicago and abroad inevitably brought nationwide publicity to Sarasota as her chosen winter home. In effect,

Sarasota had suddenly become fashionable. After her death in 1918, her brother and her sons, Honoré and Potter, Jr., became the focus of Palmer transactions. During her lifetime, Palmer enjoyed a prestige and dignity that was, in fact, a tribute to her strong personality and commanding presence rather than to the size of her fortune, which was not large for that time.

It is unlikely that Berthe Palmer and John Ringling ever found themselves at the same social event. Her life in Sarasota ended before John and Mable played any active role there. They were perhaps kindred spirits. Worlds apart in social background, each was accustomed to taking command. Each was surrounded by family members and retainers. The social ties of both households were in Chicago or New York, whence most of their guests and friends came during the winter months. Despite the social distance that separated them, their experiences were not without a certain parallel. Her climb to the top of the social ladder of a great city at the turn of the century was accomplished by overcoming some very determined rivals.

The Palmers initiated land and stock improvement programs that propelled the farming and ranch industries toward a better economic level. Similarly, other newcomers to Sarasota joined with residents of longer standing to provide initiative and capital. They were energetic, relatively young people who had enough money to invest in local businesses. The growth was indirectly stimulated by the resurgence of national investment that followed recovery from the 1907 panic. Men like Caples, Lord, and Higel were needed to engage the confidence of investors and builders from outside Sarasota. It was this initial growth spurt that Ringling saw when he viewed Sarasota as a somewhat transient winter resident.

Owen Burns (1869–1937) moved to Sarasota later in 1910. Reportedly he came for a weekend of sport fishing (his lifelong hobby). But he never returned to his prior interests in Chicago or New York, except for short business visits and one trip to New York for his marriage. He came to Sarasota at the height of the tarpon season, and in a few days was caught up in the sport. Burns was the ideal entrepreneur for the time and place. By chance, Dr. Joseph Halton, physician, landowner, and owner of the Halton Hotel, was ready for a larger hotel and had secured the lease of the floundering Belle Haven (once Gillespie's DeSoto). Burns bought the Halton and established a series of other enterprises, among them varied real estate, banking, construction, cast stone, paving, and dredging.[30] One of his first ventures was the Burns Realty Company, formed when he purchased all the town property then held by Hamilton Gillespie. Those in-town lots—many of them intended for the Scots of 1886—comprised about 75 percent of the town. The agreed-upon price was $30,000.[31] In 1918 Burns acquired a large piece of Cedar Point adjoining John Ringling's 1917 purchase of the Sarasota Yacht and Automobile Club property. Their two Cedar Point subdivisions became the largest dredge-and-fill operations in Florida at the time. In the process, the two owners created some of the most attractive property on the bay, with an extended seawall fronting its entire length.

The scope and variety of Burns's ventures attest to his role as Sarasota's principal developer in the years immediately after 1910. His paving and sidewalk construction contracts alone made a major improvement in the town's appearance. His personality was totally unlike that of John Ringling, for he was reluctant to attract publicity with his business affairs or his personal life-style. Yet those same qualities and his business facilities in Sarasota made him an ideal choice to become Ringling's associate. He was to be the working colleague, appointed to carry out the plans for Sarasota's golden future.

Bird Key was among the many parcels of land that Burns bought as a speculation. He held it only briefly, then sold it to John Ringling in 1922.[32] When Ida Ringling North returned to Sarasota after some years in the Ringlings' hometown of Baraboo, Wisconsin, she made the house on Bird Key her home, living there until her death in 1950.

The local business and professional people had their forum in the Board of Trade, which also served as a lobby for county and state concerns. The board held its first meeting on 1 January 1910, in a room offered by their leader, J. H. Gillespie. At this initial meeting members voted to purchase a table, a lamp, an oil can, and one gallon of oil—the total to cost not more than five dollars.[33] Second only to the constant appeal for better roads was the board's demand for a bay channel five or six feet deep from Tampa to Sarasota and on to Venice. That year Congress authorized $30,000 for the project, though its completion would be interrupted by World War I. In 1910 the *Sarasota Times* joined the board in a promotion campaign to attract new business enterprises. It soon became evident that such publicity was beginning to succeed and that the town was going to develop in two directions: as a resort for winter visitors and as a locale for land investment and speculation.

Several new residents who became active investors in Sarasota were to be associated later in some way with Ringling. Ralph Caples, the railroad executive, was foremost among them, the leader in backing Ringling's plans. He too saw that Sarasota had great potential, but only if its Gulf coast location could become accessible to northerners.

Caples continued his railroad career for several years. Later, as owner of a Chicago advertising agency, he represented a number of rail lines and food companies. In Sarasota he speculated in land, including a joint purchase with Ringling of 130 acres at Shell Beach, where he built his own home.[34] His principal role in Sarasota was that of a civic leader, an unpaid publicist for the city, and a promoter of local participation in ventures initiated by developers like Ringling. His appearance was forbidding; he had a somewhat dour expression combined with a forceful personality. Yet he liked to display a visible presence in local charity efforts during the Depression, when hardship was common in the homes of many local families. Ellen Caples, like her husband, was a central figure in the society that brought together the local elites and the wealthy new families from the North.

As an ardent supporter of Sarasota, Caples encouraged people of substance and ability to make their homes there. He was influential in bringing John Ringling as a winter resident. Among the friends whom he persuaded to relocate was John F. Burket, a young attorney from Ohio who was named town attorney and then city attorney when Sarasota became a city on 1 January 1914. Burket often acted as Ringling's local attorney. Still later, he was the principal Sarasota attorney in the liquidation of Ringling's estate.

Another prominent figure in Sarasota's early years of change was Ohio native A. E. Cummer. An inventor and businessman, he became one of Ringling's colleagues in purchasing control of the Bank of Sarasota. Clarence E. Hitching, an experienced banker, came from Bradentown to help organize the Bank of Sarasota. He stayed until the bank closed in 1932, a victim of the Depression.[35]

These men, like their counterparts in many other American cities, shared a spirit of enterprise, a fund of energy, and a strong desire to see Sarasota develop into a modern city. It was this spirit that gave them a common ground, made the same names appear and reappear in nearly every step that moved Sarasota into the twentieth century. For a generation, they helped to shape the decisions of public officials. The Board of Trade drew a vivid picture of Sarasota's charms in its 1915 invitation to new business:

> Sarasota beautiful . . . lies in calm and supreme dignity on the shores of Sarasota Bay, adjacent to the Gulf of Mexico. This harbor is almost perfectly land-locked and the most scenic water body in America. From early morning's radiant sunrise, throughout the day's brisk bustle of a modern business center, Sarasota stands in bold relief, exemplary for its progress, foremost in its improvements and ultra-famous for its diversified environments in social and business life, blessed by its golden sunsets, its cooling breezes and ever invigorating climate.[36]

A more convincing and less poetic description might have noted the willingness of many older residents to admit newcomers to their community, and the general acceptance of southern ways by the newly arriving families. The disposition to merge with so little friction was apparent. Although the new businessowners were all northerners, they did not challenge the established patterns of southern social life. This was an issue on which white southerners were particularly sensitive, for many could still recall the excesses of the Reconstruction era. Indicative of the change in Sarasota's leadership was the decline and eventual displacement of the earlier paternalism of J. H. Gillespie.

This was the character of Sarasota when the Ringlings came for their first winter season in 1911–12. The community was a small one, having in the Palmer family one great, seigneurial house at the southern tip. However, the Palmers limited their participation to the pursuit of family wealth and to generous aid to local charities. Similarly, at the north end of town, the Ringlings—John and Mable, Charles and Edith—showed little disposition to enter either the business or the social community of Sarasota, preferring to confine their social life to their own family members and their business interests to the circus. This was one feature that was common in towns where a seasonal population existed side by side with residents. Sarasota families did not seek out social contact with winter residents unless they in turn showed an interest in the town and its concerns.

A Decade of Quiet Affluence

JOHN RINGLING and his brothers owned three successful shows by 1910: the Ringling Bros., the smaller Adam Forepaugh-Sells, and the large Barnum & Bailey. No rival could approach the size and prestige of their giant enterprise. All their self-taught management techniques were needed to operate these unwieldy organizations, but there were compensating pleasures in the greatly increased profits. The years of steady reinvestment and self-discipline had paid off. At last, the partners were rich. Except for Otto, who never indulged in creature comforts, the others were ready to discover new ways to spend their money. All turned to Florida as an alternative to the wintry blasts of Chicago and Wisconsin. Florida's potential as a market for the largest circus shows in the country was coupled with the improved national economy, which had recovered from the losses suffered in the panic of 1907. Several new stands, such as Tampa, were added to the itinerary as the Ringling Forepaugh-Sells show moved through the southern states in the latter part of the season.

The months when the circuses were in winter quarters allowed the owners to enjoy the dual luxury of leisure time and freedom from the demands of almost daily travel. However, the unconventional life of the circus tended to separate even the proprietors from society in general. Florida offered a welcome change from the rapacious demands of circus life on the road. For one or two seasons, John and Mable tested the life-style of winter residents at Tarpon Springs, then a sport fishing resort north of Tampa. The rich sportsmen wintering there formed a small, closed community. This exclusive company was cool to "new money" and disinclined to accept circus people.[1]

From Tarpon Springs, Sarasota was within cruising range for the small yacht *Louise II*, registered in Mable's name with its home port at Tampa.[2] On trips to Sarasota, John and Mable were entertained by their friends (the Ralph Capleses and the Charles Thompsons) at Shell Beach. Their adjoining properties had been part of the original estate that Thompson bought and platted as Shell Beach in 1895.[3] Caples and Thompson urged the Ringlings to leave Tarpon Springs for Sarasota. Thompson, himself a circus manager, assured John and Mable that they would not find there the same unfriendly bias and social barriers encountered in Tarpon Springs.

Another winter came; the Ringlings were again at Tarpon Springs, but no more content than before. After one of their visits to Sarasota in February 1911, Ringling bought about twenty acres from Charles Thompson, but he still delayed a decision about building a winter home. Some months later, the Thompsons sold their large frame house and built a new home on the estate. This time the buyer was a stranger who at once converted the old house into guest accommodations. He soon was advertising it as "a private hotel with running water in every room, and an excellent table."[4] This was perhaps too close a commercial neighbor for Caples' taste. Within a month or two after the boardinghouse opened, he bought the property and promptly hired a New York specialist in renovations to modernize the 1895 house. Although the Shell Beach houses had been wired for electricity in anticipation of service from Sarasota, the lines had not been extended from the center of town.[5]

Caples seemed to be preparing the Thompson house for a residence, but he decided instead to keep and enlarge his present home, a log bungalow he had purchased from W. H. English. It had a unique charm, somewhat dimmed by a preserved thirty-foot python that had come with the house from its former circus-man owner. The Capleses stayed in their unusual home (the only modern log house in Sarasota) for another fifteen years. By 1925 Caples was ready to replace the bungalow with a small Italianate villa that was more in keeping with his posture and wealth.[6]

The time had come too for John and Mable to own a home, something more personal than the temporary arrangements in hotels and apartments of their first seven years of marriage. Now, with an apartment in New York, the idea of a Florida home was both appealing and practical. They bought the renovated Thompson house from Caples in October 1911—a move that Caples probably planned but allowed his friend Ringling to believe was his own. John and Mable were not an especially domestic couple. The idea of owning a house had never before captured their interest, and they were often on the move in their private car, the *Wisconsin*. If they had any "home" in those first years, it was in Chicago, where the Ringling Bros. Circus operated its central office. In time, both came to think of Sarasota as home. Servants and a cook were soon engaged to staff their new ménage. Sophie Collins, who came from Alsace like Grandmother Juliar, presided over their kitchen for twenty-five years. (Sophie, John Ringling, and Jacob, his gray African parrot from Germany, could carry on conversations in German.)

The vacant area north and south of Shell Beach was only starting to develop. Both Caples and Ringling were willing to speculate on the property with a joint purchase of 130 acres of Shell Beach land near their homes and a part of neighboring Indian Beach, where only a few waterfront lots had found buyers. Soon featured in a somewhat exaggerated 1915 developers' sales promotion were "the magnificent homes of rich winter residents from all over the U.S.A. and from abroad . . . the Ringling brothers, Charles Thompson, Mrs. Jack Phillips, widow of Admiral Phillips, commander of the battleship *Texas* of Spanish War fame."[7] In 1911–12, bayfront property was the most costly real estate in the area. Lots with streets, curbs, and paved entrances were offered at $2,500, twice the amount the Thompsons had paid fifteen years earlier for their entire 100 acres. Land on Longboat Key, accessible only by boat, was going for around $150 per acre.

Charles and Edith Ringling next joined the Shell Beach colony. They were the first to buy part of the joint Caples-Ringling purchase. Only

Entrance to the Ringlings' first Sarasota home, Palms Elysian, formerly the 1895 home of Charles N. Thompson, a circus manager. Ringling bought part of the estate in 1911. Courtesy of Sarasota County Department of Historical Resources.

the new Thompson house separated the estates of John and Charles.[8] These two were closer in age than their other brothers. Their nearly adjoining Florida homes suggest not only that they were compatible companions, but also that they were accustomed to and preferred a close family circle as the center of their domestic and social life. Charles built a frame house large enough for his family of four and a few occasional visitors. From the outset, the difference in the personalities of the two brothers was visible in the plans for their new homes. John Ringling began at once to improve the landscaping; he removed utility buildings from view and generally made certain that "Palms Elysian," as the house was known, would become a showplace. In contrast, Charles planted a small grove of citrus trees, and added a token harness shop (as a reminder of his apprentice days) and a barn for his cows.[9]

The two Ringling purchases in Sarasota were, in effect, a signal to the other Ringling family members to join them. Otto had died in 1911,

Palms Elysian as it appeared in 1911. The Ringlings occupied the house for
part of every year until 1924. Courtesy of Manatee County Historical
Society, Eaton Florida History Room.

the first such loss in the close family. At various times until his death in
1916, Al, the oldest, and his wife, Louise, rented a winter home in
Sarasota. However, Al and Louise were so immersed in the circus that
they were never content to be far from its sights and sounds. They

Tamiami Trail near the present Sarasota–Manatee County line. This was one of the last unimproved sections of the Tamiami Trail, which was completed in 1925–26. Courtesy of John McCarthy.

hastened to Baraboo early each spring before going on the road with one of the shows. Alf T. and Elizabeth bought a large estate that once had been the home of former Confederate General George Riggins.[10] Henry and his wife, Ida, preferred inland Florida. They settled at Eustis, but left their launch *Salomé* at the John Ringling dock for Mable's pleasure. (The wooden dock extended more than 1,800 feet across the shallow bay before it reached enough water to float a launch.)[11]

Florida's Gulf coast offered a total contrast to the grinding routines of a circus and its ever-moving one- or two-day stands. The three circuses, each in its own self-contained world, were inactive in winter; hence, the winter quarters could be left to trusted managers. Unlike the work force, which was mostly composed of transients, many of the same performers were hired every season. Most of the stars and some of the lesser performers continued their acts elsewhere—some in Europe, others in South America during the winter. Many signed contracts for vaudeville appearances in theaters across the country. New acts came and went each season, in a continuing search for novelty and new feats of skill and daring. A Ringling Bros. or a Barnum & Bailey contract was the aim of many solo acts and family troupes. Each year several hundred applied for places in one of the Ringling programs.

John and Mable usually came to Sarasota in late November or early December. The house was closed again in time for the two big circuses to open in Chicago and New York in mid-March. John continued to carry on his other business affairs in both cities. His attorneys and associates in the world of entertainment and rail travel were there. He corresponded primarily by telegraph, a favorite substitute for letters among show people and many types of businesses. Long-distance lines had not yet reached Sarasota for calls to New York, and it was essential for Ringling to travel in and out of New York throughout the year. While there, he worked at the small office in his apartment at 636 Fifth Avenue or at one of his clubs, the Lotus or the Lambs; both were meeting places for figures in the entertainment business. Later he opened a business office at 331 Madison Avenue, where he and his confidential aide, Richard Fuchs, carried out the many convoluted deals that composed Ringling's affairs.

Given his occasional appearances in Sarasota, it is not surprising that a decade passed before Ringling was described as other than a "circus man" in the social columns of the *Sarasota Times*. Gradually his image changed as he became an established and active winter resident. At length, he progressed to "circus owner," "capitalist," and finally "financier," the pinnacle of status. He was named a "capitalist" when he started to buy real estate and City of Sarasota bonds on a large scale (he rescued an entire issue that was almost wholly unsold) and a "financier" when he began his island development.

Unlike Berthe Palmer, Ringling did not come to Sarasota with a mission. He brought with him no plan to introduce improvements or to increase his own fortune. If his initial visits on board *Louise II* led him to form any ideas of future land development, he kept them to himself for a decade. (He would later find that Sarasota was not ready for the scope of the projects that he and Owen Burns introduced.) Moreover, this was still the era when investors used their personal capital for exploiting opportunities. Ringling simply did not then have the money to fund large-scale developments such as those on Florida's Atlantic coast.

He had moved his personal center of business operations from Chi-

cago to his Fifth Avenue apartment in New York.[12] With his friend Tex
Rickard, whom he brought in as manager, he was increasingly active in
efforts to rescue New York's floundering Madison Square Garden.
Stanford White's monumental structure was never able to show a profit,
and several of the more prominent financiers such as J. P. Morgan and
William Vanderbilt withdrew from its board of directors. Some stayed
on, Ringling among them. He also held a seat on the board of New
York's Chatham & Phoenix National Bank, a move that later brought
him into contact with Manufacturers Trust. Ringling was one of an elite
group of men who were close to the center of the nation's financial
structure.

Each of his new interests brought Ringling closer to his goal of being
accepted in the conventional business world. Prudently, he kept his
ambition within reasonable bounds. He did not aspire to become a great
mogul among financial bankers, nor did he choose to seek a career in
the control of trunk line railroads. He looked to short line rails; his
capital went to buy or to build such lines in Missouri, Ohio, Oklahoma,
Texas, and Montana. For some twenty-five years Ringling the circus
man had coveted the status accorded to bankers and rail executives.
Now he was becoming one of this favored class, not by abandoning his
circus career but by combining one with the other.

With the increasing diversity of his interests, Ringling's home in
Sarasota was at most an intermittent retreat for him in the winter
months. For Mable, however, Palms Elysian presented an opportunity
to develop a niche for herself, a chance to be more than the beautiful
wife who accompanied her connoisseur husband in his private car. Both
she and John enjoyed New York life and evenings at the theater, especially Florenz Ziegfeld and George White productions. Mable also
found pleasure in attending the opera, a taste that John did not fully
share. While he was traveling and conducting circus affairs, Mable soon
began to spend more time in Sarasota. She was happy with the Florida
climate, her home and gardens, and the pleasure of being close to the
Gulf, where she enjoyed cruising. For both, the new home meant an
opportunity to entertain guests. Some were personal friends; others
were invited from among John's extensive business acquaintances. Almost immediately after the purchase of the estate, Mable's parents, the

George M. Burtons, arrived and occupied the guest cottage that had come with the property.[13]

The Ringlings began to refurbish the main house, a somewhat old-fashioned frame structure of twelve rooms. Mable was eager to start remodeling, continuing Ralph Caples's earlier plan for modernization. Porches were enclosed, bathrooms were added, and other improvements helped to make the house suitable for fashionable guests and for entertaining. Like many homes of its time, the interior was dark and the furniture was ponderous and lacked grace. Except for the grounds, the estate had no special character to suggest that this was the winter home of a rich and discriminating owner. Yet visitors enjoyed its informality and its air of comfort and ease; sometimes they experienced the thrill of hearing an alligator roar from a safe distance beyond the estate.

Progress and change in the house were followed with considerable local interest, or more correctly, curiosity about this Mr. Ringling, "manager of the famous Ringling Brothers Circus," as he was often identified in the *Sarasota Times*. It was important to Ringling for the estate to display all the outward refinements of a gentleman's residence. The barn and outbuildings that stood near the house were moved so they would no longer offend the eye.[14] Over the next twenty-five years, he spent about a quarter of a million dollars on landscaping, fountains, statues, and walks.[15] The improvements were not solely intended to impress visitors with Ringling's wealth. John and Mable's eagerness to proceed suggests that they desired a home that reflected their own self-image.

The steam yacht *Wethea*, Ringling's next boat-owning venture, was the largest pleasure craft docked at Sarasota's city pier.[16] Over the years, each steam yacht that he bought was larger and more luxurious than its predecessor. Owning a fine yacht and membership in prestigious clubs such as the New York, the Columbia, and the Larchmont yacht clubs were status symbols that he enjoyed. Throughout her Florida winters, Mable shared her enjoyment of gulf cruises with her guests. The Ringling yacht would move slowly along, touching at various ports along Florida's west coast.

John and Charles Ringling were among the first winter residents to bring luxury to the city pier. Charles and Edith enjoyed fishing, often

John Ringling's first steam yacht, *Wethea*, at the city pier in Sarasota, 1914. The Belle Haven Hotel is in the background. Courtesy of Sarasota County Department of Historical Resources.

using their yachts for fishing trips in the Gulf and rivers, but it is doubtful that John Ringling derived more than a sense of prestige from possessing such elegant playthings. In later years, when he became the developer of the Sarasota islands, his yachts became an adjunct to sales promotion. Prospective investors and buyers were invited to inspect desirable properties from the deck of a millionaire's yacht, which suggested the prestige that might accompany ownership of the land.

A succession of losses plagued John Ringling in Sarasota waters. No harm befell the *Wethea*, but its successor, the larger and more powerful *Vidoffner II*, and Henry Ringling's launch *Salomé* were both destroyed by fire while docked in Tampa. Two crewmen were killed and a third was severely burned in the *Vidoffner*. The *Salomé* caught fire, burned, and sank during a thunderstorm in the bay. Guests were burned by the flames and Mable's arms were permanently scarred, but no lives were lost.[17]

❧ In the years of peace and war between 1910 and 1918, each spring the Ringling brothers put aside their yachts and their plans for winter

John Ringling's yacht *Vidoffner II*, with Captain Arthur Rowe and crew of eight. The yacht was destroyed by an explosion in Tampa. Courtesy of Sarasota County Department of Historical Resources, Arthur Rowe, Jr., Collection.

homes and turned their attention to the three circuses. The brothers were not only circus owners, they were circus managers—national leaders in an industry that was like no other. Ringling shows were big, lavish, and extravagant, assembled with what appeared to be a mechanically perfect organization.[18] The Ringling presence meant constant, vigilant attention to every detail. Every moment of each season was critically supervised. The Ringlings' entire pattern of life was determined by the routines of their circuses. During a season, life was filled with constant travel and endless crises that arose from breakdowns, accidents, and natural hazards. As owners, they had to calm quixotic tempers and resolve unpredictable conflicts among performers. The seven-month annual route meant absence from home and isolation from friends and all associates except those who traveled with the circus. Only John seemed to demand something more.

The brothers had lived in this unconventional pattern for their entire adult lives. In consequence, social life centered around their collective family. During the lifetime of the elder Ringlings, annual Christmas gatherings brought the brothers to Baraboo for holidays at the parental home of August and Marie Salomé. John, however, rarely attended these family reunions after his mother's death in 1907.[19] Some family members continued to meet there during the holidays. The move to Sarasota was, in effect, a further withdrawal from Baraboo and from what John perceived to be its small-town life-style.

John Ringling was separating himself from his early life, from his start as a clown in the winter shows, and from his seasons as a circus wagon driver. He changed his appearance to suit his new role as a finely tailored businessman whose homes were on New York's Fifth Avenue and in Sarasota. Thus, more than mere distance separated him from his less sophisticated life in a small Wisconsin town.

Although Sarasota was also a relatively small city, its residents and winter visitors included families who were as wealthy as the Ringlings. Several participated in the business life of the nation's northern cities. Some spent the entire winter season in Sarasota, while others came only for a short stay, usually for the sport fishing in the Gulf. Life seemed to move slowly in the years before World War I. The *Sarasota Times* presented a relaxed view of world affairs while giving full coverage to local events.

Editorial policy and limited funds had decreed many years earlier that Sarasotans would find little of world events in the local *Times* and none on the front page. The first nomination of Woodrow Wilson as president appeared as a paragraph within the general news on page two.[20] Little news of the war ever made the front page from 1914 to 1917. In 1914 the war in Europe seemed infinitely remote, a matter of concern only to Europeans. Prospects of a brisk winter season took precedence: "An army of tourists and settlers will invade Florida, while in Europe the war scare creates fear of invaders. . . . invaders in Europe will march with gun and sabre, in Florida with stuffed pocketbooks."[21] Not long after that, the war first touched Sarasota. Former mayor J. H. Gillespie left for England, hoping to serve in the British forces with his former regiment.

Sarasota entered the war years without having gained recognition as a resort that could compete with those on the Atlantic coast. Something was lacking. Boosters and an enthusiastic press could accomplish little. Despite its new facades of brick and concrete, Main Street scarcely seemed another *Promenade des Anglais*. The Seaboard Airline Railroad transported its passengers in coaches furnished with cast-off equipment, without lights, and in need of much repair. The *Times* urged visitors to note the eight miles of sidewalks and the nearly five miles of paved streets.[22] A growing awareness of the need to improve the city's image renewed the latent conflict between an urban and a traditional country life-style. Early in 1914, an ordinance put an end to the nuisance of wandering hens and chickens by requiring owners to keep them penned.[23] Two years earlier a similar ordinance, bitterly fought to a referendum by cattlemen, had forced the confinement of livestock. For the first time residents could enjoy their lawns and plantings undisturbed by their neighbors' domestic animals and fowl.

Little about the war stirred the community until the spring of 1917, when young men went into active service with the Navy or the American Expeditionary Force. All attention suddenly focused on the war, for which the nation was almost wholly unprepared. The young men of Sarasota's Naval Militia had been actively training for more than a year, using the defunct Yacht and Automobile Club for their drills. The militia was immediately called to duty. Sixty-three men marched to the railroad station on a rainy Sunday and left amid the farewells and tears of the city.

Patriotic fervor at once replaced indifference. Charles Ringling's yacht *Zumbrota* sailed away to the Atlantic coast to be prepared for service with the Navy as a submarine chaser.[24] (No enemy action marked her wartime service.) John Ringling's *Vidoffner II* followed, commanded by Captain Rowe, whose crew was to be assisted by three gun crews for Atlantic patrol. Sarasota joined the nation's other towns and cities with bond drives and a new Red Cross chapter. Comfort packages were assembled and sent off to the troops. Names of bond buyers were published; first Charles and then John Ringling joined the lists.

This same fervor in turn led briefly to shooting pelicans to prevent them from eating fish that were needed for human consumption. One store owner experienced the misdirected intensity of such aroused emotion. He gave some children a flag no longer suitable for display, and his remarks about its being no good were misquoted. That evening a committee of citizens visited him, charged him with disrespect to the flag, and offered him until morning to leave town safely.

The pace of growth in Florida had slowed during the years before the United States entered the war, in part because of a shrinking flow of investments. By 1917, money from outside the state had largely dried up. Reduced investment in industry was in general accompanied by increased unemployment in the industrial North that was more severe in 1914 than at any time since the panic of 1907. The war in Europe reduced unemployment in America and thus intensified pressure for social change. Growing demands upon industry and the absence of imported goods from Europe also resulted in some minor gains for labor because the number of men in the work force was depleted by enlistment and the draft. Employers were unable to resist some labor demands for better working conditions and higher wages. At the richer end of the social scale, those who customarily sailed their yachts into the Mediterranean were now forced to stay nearer home. They were left to choose among the fashionable Florida resorts of St. Augustine, Palm Beach, and Miami. In the first years of the war, a number of smaller yachts transported their owners to Key West, and then along the Gulf coast.

As more visitors headed for east coast resorts, some sought the quieter retreats or the superior sport fishing along the Gulf. When the war ended, the Seaboard Airline Railroad began to promote Sarasota in its northern advertising. Ralph Caples and John Ringling were surely instrumental in convincing S. Davies Warfield, the line's president, that the Seaboard and Sarasota had common aims and interests. Northern directors of the rail line were more concerned with extending their line to Miami for shipping freight, but Sarasota could share in any increase in the resulting southward flow of visitors and tourists.

The war either initiated or hastened several fundamental changes in the area's social and economic framework. Without those changes, Florida would have remained an underdeveloped region even longer. Before 1914, wage earners enjoyed little if any surplus that they could regard as freely disposable income. Paid vacations were uncommon, especially among the minor functionaries of business. Travel abroad was a luxury reserved for the rich. Within the country the mode of tourist travel was essentially limited to the railways. That too was an indulgence dependent on leisure time and funds that were available to only a small fraction of the populace. Automobile travel was an adventure. Any journey farther than local driving was attempted by only the few who were brave and sporting enough to risk impassable roads in unreliable vehicles.

Victory in the Great War brought further changes that soon were felt in Florida. Most welcome was an immense increase in wealth. Profits from wartime industry and private savings were distributed over a greater number of owners, shareholders, and proprietors. Some invested this money as capital, while others simply spent and enjoyed it. For some, an increase in income meant a chance to enjoy the winter months as tourists or homeowners in Florida. Before long speculators appeared, ready to create the excesses of Florida's land boom.

Another related development was the result of wartime production. The improvements that were demanded for military vehicles reappeared in the civilian market in the form of the family automobile. Makers quickly overcame some of the worst defects in the quality and production methods of America's prewar motor industry. As the numbers of vehicles multiplied, new sources of revenue enabled the states to improve and expand the network of roads for intercity travel.

These pervasive changes, which brought a new mobility to middle-class Americans, were bringing opportunities to Florida land developers, hotel builders, and resort promoters. The state was to benefit profoundly from the new class of American traveler—middle-class families with a trustworthy automobile and sufficient money to finance a trip, and perhaps even own a vacation home there.

So long as the finest sport fishing was enjoyed by small colonies of rich visitors, the west coast could remain an uncluttered preserve, inaccessible to larger numbers of tourists.[25] But the potential for wider popularity of Gulf fishing was clear. Publicity and more frequent rail service could make the difference, but only if some modern resort hotels, apartments, and houses were available.

Both Ringlings were by now firmly entrenched capitalists, as the term was then understood. In the circus they held a near monopoly, and they still wielded firm control over the labor that was needed to operate the shows. In Sarasota they assumed a more modern capitalist role as investor-developers without seeking to form a trust or monopoly. Both recognized the opportunity offered by a combination of improved rail service, persuasive advertising, and holdings in land, hotels, and homes.

John Ringling and others like him influenced friends who were rail executives to provide better service to the Gulf resorts. Several among them weighed the advantages of investing in the kind of development that made the east coast resorts successful. Like that of many other entrepreneurs, John Ringling's wealth grew rapidly from 1915 to 1920. His oil revenues rose steadily; railroads carried maximum loads in the war years. The circus continued to bring in handsome returns. He freely spent money on improving his Sarasota home. New servants' quarters were built, which left more space for guests in the house. An elaborately designed rose garden was improved by adding freight-car loads of red Georgia clay; more clay was brought in for the tennis courts. Charles also built new servants' space, but otherwise he did not attempt to imitate his brother's style; he invested in new barns.

John and Charles took little part in local affairs, and even after several seasons in Sarasota an undefined distance remained. The Ringlings were still strangers who needed to be reintroduced more than once. Charles was identified in the *Sarasota Times* as "one of the brothers who own quite a number of circuses, the best known of which is the Ringling Bros."[26] Among the many "strangers" in the area, the social news reported, were Ida Ringling North and her family, the Norths of Baraboo. At that time Ida spent few winters in Sarasota. After her husband's death, she remained in Baraboo, where her brothers arranged for her to live in the former Albert Ringling home.

Sarasotans were not entirely sure how to handle the Ringling colony, whose members, except for Alf T. and his son Richard, did not show much inclination to join in the city's life.[27] The Ringlings did not come to Sarasota as socially prominent people, yet they were rich and nationally known. The senior couples were seen mostly as they arrived or departed by train or moved about in their new Pierce Arrow and Packard motor cars, the grandest vehicles to glide through town, equaled only by Berthe Palmer's limousine. The *Times* reported little about the Ringlings other than the movements of John and Mable in their private railway car, now named *Sarasota.*

Mable and Edith were accustomed to living almost wholly in the shadow of their husbands. Circus and family surrounded them. Hence, they took little interest in local women's activities such as card parties (where they usually played "500") and woman's club meetings. Contract bridge had not yet become a national pastime. When it did, the bridge table proved to be a popular meeting place, and Mable and Edith became active players.

John was absent during the circus season, while Mable often stayed in Sarasota. Curiosity about his local interests was satisfied only by a reporter's conjecture. Intermittently between 1915 and his death in 1936, he was reported to have plans of all sorts, from building homes to purchasing and selling land and constructing hotels and resorts. Few of these rumors were verified by events that followed. The more conspicuous he became in the city, the more his name excited speculation. He denied only some of the more outrageous rumors, such as one about his becoming a Republican candidate for Congress.[28] Since he had no office or enterprise in Sarasota where he could be seen and interviewed, he remained an outsider for nearly a full decade until he formed a working relationship with Owen Burns.

From about 1912 to 1922, Ringling was busy elsewhere. He was expanding his interest in oil operations and in short line railroads. His interest in the national trunk lines was limited to buying bonds, but he moved directly into owning several short connecting lines. In his role as contracting manager for the circus, he gained not only a detailed knowledge of the nation's rails, but also much useful information about several hundred towns and small cities the rail lines served, and where the directions of growth seemed to lead. Jake Hamon, a promoter of rail expansion in the Southwest, convinced Ringling in 1912 that the Ardmore region of Oklahoma was ideal for investment in a line that would serve the cattle country. Thus, in northwest Oklahoma, Ringling became known first as a railroad and town builder and oil investor, and only second as a national figure in the circus. Drawing on the tradition of circus hyperbole, Ringling named his line the Oklahoma, New Mexico, and Pacific.[29] Perhaps in his vision of the future, he saw it reaching the ocean a thousand miles to the west. Hamon became a vice-president of the line.

Rails had scarcely been laid from Ardmore to its terminal when oil was found in wells drilled not far from Ringling's right of way. Circus attorney John Kelley rushed to the scene, where he and Hamon secured oil leases for 8,000 acres and title to a similar amount of acreage. Ringling's Chicago attorney, Eugene L. Garey, helped him to form the Cardinal Oil Company, which was intended to hold the land titles and to operate the Oklahoma oil properties. Before long, Ringling changed his mind and formed two companies—Rockland Oil and Sarasota Oil—which he wholly owned.[30] The oil discovery was celebrated by a town named Ringling, which Ringling laid out himself.[31]

The oil rights were never sold, and the oil never ceased to flow. It continued to provide income to Ringling until his death and to his estate afterward. The complex arrangements that were to deny him the use of that income and the ultimate settlement of ownership had to wait until his estate was untangled. In his lifetime, the flow of money reached several million dollars. His later rail losses were more than compensated by oil revenues. The Bureau of Internal Revenue showed no sympathy for his claim of a million-dollar loss on the Oklahoma rail line.

His next venture was even more ambitious. He bought the St. Louis and Hannibal Railroad, a nearly defunct line 105 miles long in junk condition. To revive the failing line, he added about forty miles of spur line and improved the whole with new bridges. He bought or reconditioned sound rolling stock and rebuilt the shops where locomotives and passenger cars were refurbished and put back into service. He had at one time thirty-two locomotives in shops for repair or ready for sale or lease. He learned that there was an immense supply of sand and gravel in the nearby Salt River, and that the state of Missouri needed a constant supply of both for road building. Taking advantage of the opportunity, he promptly formed the Northeast Missouri Land and Gravel Company. His dragline was set up to load forty freight cars a day from the river bed, and his rail line moved the gravel, which he sold to the state.[32]

Not satisfied with two railroads, Ringling went on to buy three more. In Texas, following the route of oil exploration, he acquired the Eastland, Wichita Falls and Gulf Railroad. In Ohio he added to his collection the Dayton, Toledo and Chicago line. One more line completed his portfolio: the White Sulphur Springs and Yellowstone Park Railroad in Montana. His 49 percent ownership remained in his possession and passed into his estate intact. The terminus was named Ringling, and he bought large blocks of ranch land in the area between 1916 and 1919, in checkerboard fashion with the Union Pacific Railroad.[33]

John Ringling paid an exceedingly high price for the gratification of naming himself president of several railroads. He could not manage those lines personally despite his unusually extensive technical knowledge. The circus was becoming more and more demanding as the number of partner-brothers dropped to three and then to two. Nor did he appear to have current knowledge of the economics of the farm and ranch states. Somehow he failed to perceive that the growth era of the railroads was ending. The great fortunes had been made by the builders of the trunk lines or by those who controlled the rate structures. Labor troubles, strikes, monopolies, and preferential rate structures were the chief characteristics of rail systems in the 1920s. Ringling's failure was colored by his own experience. Seen from the circus train, America looked different than it did from the centers of finance. John Ringling's railway ventures, all acquired in a short period, brought only fleeting profits, and the profitable years ended with the peace of 1918.

For almost a decade, Ringling's multiple interests made him an absentee owner in his western rail lines. Had he moved early enough to salvage his railroad investment by selling to the trunk lines, he probably could have reduced his losses. But defensive actions were rare in the history of his career. Ever completely confident in his own abilities and judgment, he always expected to find a solution to any setback—if only by doing nothing.

Ringling's interest in rail ownership was marred by what now seems to have been certain flaws in his judgment. The motivation that led him to make those investments—besides the desire to make money—seems to stem from relentless ambition. He wanted status in the fraternity of rail executives. His mistake was not in his initial investments, but in his failure to get out. He held to a perception of the prairie states that was formed before World War I. Cotton and wheat were then feeding an expanding market, bringing new prosperity that was dependent on the railroads to move the products. After the war, conditions changed. Overcultivation and sharp market decline were forerunners of the natural and manmade disasters that came later. Although Ringling was at least a generation too late to reap large benefits from the nation's railroads, he did make several friends who were later useful in his plans to make Sarasota a metro-resort served by two major lines.

His steady accumulation of Montana ranch and farm lands was most likely speculative and was not mixed with the pursuit of status or other ulterior motives. Much of the land was acquired early in his career, when the future of that remote area was still highly uncertain. By 1916 he had accumulated some 80,000 acres, much of it intended for resale. For several years during World War I, he owned and operated the Smith River Farm Company, which encompassed one large farm and four ranches. The company also ran a sales agency that dealt in sheep, cattle, and horses for local ranchers. His manager, R. M. Calkins, Jr., handled the marketing of livestock, hay, grain, and farm products. In addition to this typical western sales operation, Calkins managed a small number of reconditioned railroad cars such as *Minerva*, an old Pullman that had been restored and leased for tourist use on the run to Yellowstone Park. Some details of this otherwise obscure episode in Ringling's career are contained in the reminiscences of Taylor Gordon, a young man who recorded his experience as one of Ringling's servants in his autobiography, *Born To Be.*[34]

Ringling's Montana livestock was a source of substantial profit. In 1916 he was already thinking of the heavy demand for cattle, especially dairy breeds, that would erupt once peace returned to Europe. He was certain that when the war ended, Germany, France, and Belgium would be in great need of cattle and horses, and European farmers would be forced to borrow funds to pay for restocking their devastated farms. Accordingly, the price for farm animals was certain to rise sharply as soon as the rebuilding of Europe's economy began.[35] Ringling and Calkins agreed that their best plan was to run a herd of Holsteins or some other milk strain to be ready for the forthcoming European market.

Had he given careful attention to such matters in postwar reconstruction, Ringling might well have become an international trading figure in the livestock industries, but he let the opportunity go by. By the time the war ended, he had other, more compelling concerns with the circus. The unexpected deaths of Al in 1916 and Alf T. in 1919 left only John and Charles to manage their behemoth of a circus. The Montana venture and its potential for a European market never recaptured his attention. His failure to exploit such a clear, brief opportunity for making a fortune suggests that Ringling was sometimes prone to superficial and transitory interests. His rail and ranch investments were never made into productive assets, largely because of his own lack of perseverance; he could readily have engaged others to oversee a marketing program had he chosen to do so.

Ringling held most of his Montana land after selling part of it to his nephew Richard. Barely twenty at the time, Richard decided to abandon the circus as a career and to settle as a rancher. He bought up many thousands of acres as well as a home. After his marriage, he raised his family in Yellow Springs, Montana.

Ringling began to report losses on his western railroads and lands in 1919. He was not alone among people of wealth who failed to prepare for their new adversary, the income tax; many considered the tax to be nothing less than confiscation. Unlike those who refused to file, Ringling regularly met the deadline, but his haphazard personal accounting led him into serious, lasting trouble. Even in the free-wheeling days of the Harding administration, the bureaucracy was more than a match for those who tried to evade the tax. Whatever his reasons, and they may have been as mundane as indifference, Ringling failed to establish a cost basis for many of his investments.[36] Disclosure was anathema to him. Throughout his life, he could not bring himself to share details about his private affairs, and he was ill prepared to face the consequences. His tax returns were challenged year after year, leaving him and later his estate with disallowed deductions of several million dollars.[37]

In 1921, pleased with his rapid success in acquiring oil leases in Oklahoma, Ringling was prepared to challenge the nation's most sophisticated oilmen. Ringling, his nephew Richard, and J. M. Kelley (the circus lawyer) joined with several more experienced operators to negotiate with the Business Council of the Crow Indian tribe for an oil lease on 500 acres of tribal land in Montana.[38] The Ringlings soon found that while the Business Council was dominated by younger, less traditional, men, the tribal elders opposed the scheme. The elders supported a powerful opposing group operating as an arm to Standard Oil interests.[39] Unless the Ringlings could obtain a court order banning the competing group as trespassers, there was little chance that John and Richard would gain the required approval from the secretary of the interior. To activate their tribal leases, the two Ringlings joined with a Wyoming firm calling itself the New York Oil Company, whose employees had the technical resources and the kind of understanding needed for maneuvering to gain possession of oil lands. Even with their allies, however, John and Richard Ringling were no match for big oil, despite their acquaintance with Harry Sinclair and their access to President Harding (through Interior Secretary Fall in Washington and Ralph Caples in Sarasota). Their attorney, Kelley, urged that the leases were untenable. Court battles, he said, would be costly, and there was little chance of winning, pitted against more powerful interests supported by tribal elders.[40]

The Crow Indian venture ended with little more than an exciting insight into the arcane dealings of speculators who worked with Indian tribes and the legal maneuvers that surrounded the politics of oil leases in the Northwest. The Oklahoma property, by contrast, was acquired purely by chance before major interests appeared, ready to demand an ascendant position. Hence, that first success lacked the drama of the Montana scheme, but it proved to be an enduring, profitable investment. After their oil failure, John and Richard confined their Montana interests to ranch lands that were available at prices not unlike those of the Florida backcountry. John Ringling was never one to be put off by uncertain titles to land he wished to buy. His Montana purchases produced a mass of poorly recorded titles that were complicated further by his own manipulation of his deeds to support other operations. The consequences did not arise until his executors tried to sell these ranch lands.

❧ From the close of 1918 until the middle of the next decade, national and local conditions combined to present the right opportunities for Ringling in Florida. At the war's end he decided that Sarasota would be the focus of his future capitalist role. To turn this decision into a reality, he was prepared to withdraw much of his accumulated capital and to invest in Sarasota land and development. No new venture could displace the circus from the center of his life, but he had shown that he was quite capable of dividing his time and attention. His decision also marked a turning away from the West and from the faltering railroads and his Montana lands. He showed no disposition to sell off those assets, but he made no effort to increase their productivity or value.

In the freewheeling environment of the 1920s, Florida developers and speculators engendered their own destruction, ultimately ruining their bank creditors and their clients as well. Because land was Florida's principal commodity, the resulting losses brought widespread damage to the state's economy. The physical environment—the islands, shores, and submerged land—was equally free from controls that might inhibit exploitation. In Sarasota, only the management of coastal waterways came under federal control. U.S. Army Corps of Engineers and War Department permits were needed for bridges, for major structures in the bay, and for the passes between the islands and the Gulf. Development of the keys and the bay shore was expensive and dependent on dredge-and-fill operations. Dredging deepened the channels, while the addition of sand extended and raised the ground level of the islands or made new land, all of which had to be held in place by seawalls. In these circumstances, development projects in the 1920s belonged to a few well-financed individuals, such as John Ringling and Owen Burns. Burns's construction company had the equipment and the knowhow for the job. Ringling could put up the money, although he did that somewhat reluctantly when the bills were presented. Together, Ringling and Burns were prepared to rebuild the natural configuration of Sarasota into several hundred salable house lots.

In his emerging role as a Florida developer, Ringling seemed to adopt an entirely new life-style. He was beginning to spend freely for elegant possessions, and he also developed a more sober appearance, wholly unlike the stereotypical showman of the past. His entrepreneurial decade in Sarasota was enhanced by steadily acquiring objects of art and furnishings for his homes and by surrounding himself and Mable with the physical evidences of wealth. From careful examination of hundreds of auction catalogs, he continually increased his knowledge of how to furnish a home in a splendid manner. At first he bought things because he liked them, but before long he was buying to create a grand stage setting for his role in Sarasota.

Rejecting the fashions of his own day, Ringling favored those of the owners of the 1880–90 era, such as his late friend Stanford White, the architect whose love of sumptuous materials had been reflected in the bills he presented to his clients. Mable shared and indeed encouraged this taste for the palatial decor of this period when European court styles had been so popular. Gilt wood furniture and fine tapestries came to decorate the Ringlings' home and apartment.

In 1919 Ringling bought a summer home at Alpine, New Jersey, overlooking the Hudson River. The hundred-acre property was about one mile north of the Alpine ferry, on the great Palisades. The large house was of no particular style, but it had the dignity of stone and frame construction and a certain quiet charm. It was surrounded by extensive, well-landscaped grounds, a feature that John found necessary in a home. Mable was happy with the gardens, especially the long rose garden. The estate was close to New York City for John's many business affairs, yet it was removed from the urban heat and dust of summer.

Among the Ringlings' purchases in Europe during the summer of 1920 was their first Rolls Royce, the ultimate symbol of wealth and prestige. The elegant but ungainly limousine had been built in 1914 for the empress of Russia, but had been halted at Berlin on its eastern journey when the war erupted.[41] In 1920 it was already somewhat antique but still altogether regal. Soon, one Rolls was not enough. The Ringlings acquired several more: one to be kept in New York, a new one in 1924, and another in 1925 for Sarasota, as well as two Pierce Arrows, a sedan for public appearances, and a phaeton (touring car) for Mable.

To perceive of him at this stage as a new John Ringling would be a misconception. More accurately, in Abraham Maslow's terms, Ringling had reached the stage of self-actualization. In the vernacular, he could do whatever he liked. He could begin to function as he had aspired.

The main focus of John Ringling's adult life was providing entertainment for people. Pleasing them had made him rich, a powerful lesson that he was never to disregard. In Sarasota, his attention turned to seeking ways to attract, to entertain, and to please a growing throng of buyers (rather than speculators). One feature of his great plan— building entire communities of houses that would be designed by a prominent architect—never came to fruition. Those idealized subdivisions, like his land sales schemes, were aimed at the moderately well-to-do buyer, the type of family that was acquiring a somewhat larger share of the national wealth in the post–World War I economy.

Ringling and others like him could easily see that land development alone was not enough to bring a new population to Sarasota. The city was a remote appendage of Manatee County, its citizens increasingly aware of the neglect that severely limited its improvements in roads and schools and the other amenities of a modern community. As long as the city and its environs were part of Manatee, little could be expected from the county power structure. Sarasota city leaders were aided in their drive for separation by the *Sarasota Times,* for the editors fanned public discontent by publishing figures to show how little return their tax dollars seemed to bring. The rural and cattle ranching interests opposed separation from their long-established place in county politics. Ultimately, lines were drawn in a compromise that satisfied both the Sarasotans and the ranchers who remained within the Manatee County limits.

On 1 July 1921, following legislative approval, Sarasota County was established by Governor Cary A. Hardee. Community leaders now had a new power center that could smooth the way for development through the issuing of bonds for improved roads and schools. Public demands for a larger police force could be met from county revenues.

Unlike the smaller Gulf coast communities, Sarasota was continually urged by its leaders to increase its population, its winter colony, and its commercial shipping facilities. Once the constraints of war were removed, the prospect of building attractive resort hotels promised improved tourist accommodation. Still, Florida's glamour remained on the Atlantic coast, centered firmly on Palm Beach and Miami, with Miami Beach just beginning to join the older resorts. In the faster pace of the 1920s, Florida's resorts were continuing to sort themselves according to the differing appeal that attracted winter residents and visitors to one or the other. Palm Beach was firmly entrenched as the haven of inherited wealth. Miami was preferred by those with newer riches and by some celebrities of good or bad repute. Sarasotans wanted a share of the postwar wealth, but few of the city's leaders had connections or influence that reached into the world of the newly rich. If anyone could deal with this new market, it was John Ringling.

The coming Florida land boom was only one of several excesses that occurred nationwide in the next years: spasms of industrial disorder in the North, the conspicuous antics of the newly rich, and the fatal combination of politics, law enforcement, and corruption that from time to time captured public attention in a number of cities. These forces brought their own violence and social disruption, engendered largely by the evasion of Prohibition. Little of the turmoil or the irrational fears of Bolshevism fanned by the Harding administration or the wealth generated in the underworld ever reached the Gulf coast. Quiet resorts from St. Petersburg to Boca Grande and Fort Myers were fashionable in their restrained privacy. Their appeal was a more sober brand of affluence that did not attract exciting but dangerous characters such as "Scarface" Al Capone, Chicago's powerful leader of organized crime. The pattern of winter migration to the Gulf resorts, generally from the Ohio valley and the upper Midwest, remained much as before. Although eastern financiers began to appear in Sarasota, they came to inspect the investment potential, but not to stay.

The unique social character of the Gulf coast resorts became a developer's advantage as the postwar social order overturned the pattern of urban life that had persisted since the close of the Civil War. There was a new freedom and mobility in America, but with it came the anticulture, corruption, and violence that was provoked by the rule of Prohibition. Sarasota's society had its own mannerly way of dealing with the supply and demand of illegal liquor. A prominent citizen became an elite bootlegger who kept the social scene supplied with spirits. The third-floor vault of the Ringling home routinely held a large supply of wines, spirits, and liqueurs procured and delivered regularly without the risk of raids. The poor and rural population, which had to make do with hidden stills and their nameless products, was forced to suffer raids, injuries, and even deaths for such flagrant disregard of the law.

Clearly, more than a restless nature and surplus funds led Ringling to begin a program of development in Sarasota. He was in a position to observe the accumulation of new wealth in the East, the wealth of finance and industry. He could not fail to see that one rail line after another became the victim of overextended economies in the wheat and cotton states, and his own western holdings no longer held his interest. His oilman in Oklahoma, S. Tide Cox, kept meticulous accounts for the two corporations and other sundry leases that remained outside the companies. Cox remained loyal to Ringling interests for the remainder of John's life.

The end of the war in 1918 was a time for serious reflection on the place of the circus in the nation's entertainment industries. Alf T., Charles, and John decided to combine the Ringling Bros. Circus with Barnum & Bailey, forming one super show. The decision marked their awareness of the declining level of public appetite for circus entertainment, and of competing claims for public attention and loyalty. By 1919, small-town and urban America was generally served with year-round entertainment through films that could be shown in any type of facility. Moreover, formerly isolated families now owned automobiles, relieving them from dependence on railroads. With their new mobility, these people could travel at will to central towns and cities. Before long, many preferred to stay at home and listen to their radios.

The Ringlings publicly cited logistics as their reason for combining the two historic shows. True, the burden of transport was doubly complex during the war years, followed by the turmoil of labor disputes after the peace. Henry Ringling North, who came to know some details of his uncles' decision, found that the changed social conditions of the nation presented more compelling reasons.[42] Then too a circus was a highly labor-intensive operation, dependent on low costs for labor and materials to retain its profitability. The 1918 season had been the hardest since their early wagon show days. Emergencies and delays disrupted the rail schedules. Troop trains, food, and materiel had priority; the draft was snatching away the younger workers faster than they could be replaced. When the shortage of personnel was at its worst, Charles called upon all hands, whatever their regular task, to help with the job of dismantling the big top after evening performances. Those who volunteered to help were paid seventy-five cents for the three-hour job.[43] The Ringlings soon found that the day of cheap labor, materials, and subsistence had vanished with the war.

J. M. Kelley was an expert on the history of the circus in America. In 1923 he examined the record of several hundred wagon and rail shows; he found that none had lasted more than one generation of management. This was a critical issue for the Ringlings, who knew the history of many of those smaller shows. Prospects for a second generation to operate their shows were dim.[44] Richard, who inherited one-third of the circus from his father, Alf T., in 1919, was mainly interested in life on his Montana ranch and in New York during the winter. He had no desire to return to the circus after his one brief experience with it.[45] Charles and Edith had one son, Robert, who was on his way to a career in opera.

As they assessed their prospects in 1918–19, Charles at age fifty-five and John at fifty-three may have believed that they would live longer than their elder brothers and would perhaps have many more years to operate the family shows. The circus was truly an organic part of their family, something they could never share with outsiders. Their true family, the surviving Ringlings and their sons, was growing smaller. John's hopes may even then have been placed on John and Henry North, the two sons of his sister Ida.

One advantage to the merger of Ringling Bros. and Barnum & Bailey was that a single crew of experienced and able managers could be formed from the two organizations. They included Fred Bradna, Pat Valdo, and a few others who had the forceful, even powerful personalities that could handle the volatile stars and the rough, transient work force. The combined show was safely organized and its senior managers in place before Alf T.'s death in October 1919, which left only John and Charles as partners with their nephew Richard. With able men at the top and Charles devoting full time to the combined show, John was less constrained to share their routine supervisory roles. When he was with the circus or negotiating its affairs, he gave it his single-minded attention; but he could now give time and energy to other interests where he saw opportunities developing.

No one can now say which came first: John Ringling's perception of Florida's opportunities or the influence of his many visitors from the North who represented the business environment in which he wished to share. Many came as guests. Among them were S. Davies Warfield and other officers of the Seaboard Airline Railroad, who brought their plans for expansion through southwest Florida; W. T. Tyler, director of operations of U.S. Railway Administration, who was familiar with the railroads taken over by the government during the rail strikes;[46] and David Knapp, sheriff of New York County and a future hotel builder in the Florida boom. Hotel owners such as London Wallick and Albert Keller (of the Ritz Carlton) as well as other financiers and investors came in turn. These people and others like them were always alert to potential opportunities. Ringling could not have had more astute advisers to help him shape his plans for Sarasota.

Typical of those whom Ringling found congenial was George Mooser, then a vice-president of Goldwyn Studios in Hollywood. Mooser played a minor role in the development of Englewood, a community south of Sarasota. As a buyer of Ringling property on the keys, he was one more voice urging John to move into resort development. He was courted by the *Sarasota Times* because of his motion picture connection, for some Florida entrepreneurs hoped to supplant California as the nation's motion picture center. Mooser, who was sufficiently alert to notice that a distance separated Ringling from the local establishment, felt that the city did not appreciate the value of such an important friend. When Mooser borrowed and six years later repaid a small loan, Ringling never cashed the check—a gesture indicative of his little-known generous impulses.[47]

Ringling did not burst onto the Sarasota real estate scene. He started slowly, more as a speculation than as part of a concerted plan. His first land purchase was the defunct Yacht and Automobile Club. Members had fallen behind in their dues, and the club was foreclosed by order of the sheriff. With the club came a string of lots on the Cedar Point peninsula, adjoining another undeveloped area that belonged to Owen Burns, whose plans for a hotel were halted by the lack of financing during the war years. Ringling and Burns had occasion to travel to Chicago together in 1918. Soon after that they became associates in Sarasota development.

Ringling could not work alone in Sarasota; he needed a local associate. His frequent, often long absences meant that he required someone he could trust and whose advice was sound. Owen Burns not only met those conditions, but he was also an established leader in the community. Working with Burns could end the invisible social barrier that for a decade had made Ringling an outsider. His experience with seawall construction and dredging made Burns a versatile and skilled entrepreneur. For Burns prospect of a succession of large-scale projects in association with Ringling was not without the lure of future profits. Yet Burns knew Ringling only superficially. He knew nothing of what it meant to work with him. Ringling was always the autocrat, accustomed to giving orders. Because of his sporadic presence in Sarasota, few could have known much of his business personality, of his unusual work habits, or of the strange hours he kept when he worked at night and slept all day. Burns must indeed have been a man of infinite patience, for he would need it.

As Ringling's concepts took shape, Burns was to be the agent for realizing much of the program. Their association would be a colorful and sometimes exciting combination of personalities and wills. It was not altogether gratifying, as matters did not always run smoothly. True to his usual practice, Ringling treated Burns as an employee with no share in decision making. Most of his messages were telegraphed instructions, peremptory in tone and often demanding an immediate response. For example: "I notice you drew $2000 last week. Let me know what for. I have not received a statement on dredging. . . ." A few days later he again had a complaint. "Regarding the seawall—I had no idea you were going ahead so extensively with it . . . wire me cost running foot."[48]

Correspondence between the two was most often by telegram. Only occasionally did it take the form of more detailed letters. As Ringling's local concerns became larger in scope in the mid-1920s, he came more often and spent more time in Sarasota, where he needed to be more visible and active in the local power structure. Even then, Burns was often his proxy in bringing pressure on the city or county. In later years he and Burns conducted more of their business in conversation at Burns's real estate office, which was shared by the Ringling Isles enterprise. Hence, they left few records of their joint projects and still fewer of their disagreements.

In their first joint project, Burns contracted to build a seawall to extend the size of Cedar Point. There were no immediate plans for a hotel, even though the old Belle Haven and the popular Bay View were the only ones on the bay. The start of the Ringling-Burns combination was perceived in Sarasota as the beginning of a great future for the resort. The persistent wish for a lavish hotel led the *Sarasota Times* to press Ringling for details of his plans, but repeated efforts failed to reveal anything of his intentions. Around this time he was promoted in the press to more prestigious-sounding descriptions. In 1922, when his dredge-and-fill contract with Burns had been signed, Ringling was "the well-known showman who has a winter home near the city." A year later, when he arrived in his private railroad car with a group of potential investors, he was "the New York and Sarasota capitalist."[49] The yacht *Zalophus* was brought from Fort Myers especially for the VIP passengers on that occasion. The dock at the Yacht and Automobile Club had become Ringling's personal embarcadero.

When the real estate enterprise was incorporated, Ringling named himself president and treasurer, Mable a vice-president, and Burns (with a 25 percent share) a vice-president and secretary, the usual distribution of titles in a small organization with the minimum of three officers. The charter of John Ringling Estates, Inc., was far from modest. It included electric power and water services, hotels, golf courses, and steamboats.[50] In effect, the company embraced all the essentials for a well-founded resort. Clearly, from the outset, the two developers planned a far more complex program than they were ever able to achieve. The charter is now the only documentation that defines the extent of Ringling's vision.

The one somewhat novel feature in the arrangement was the inclusion of Mable Ringling as an officer of the company. His inclusion of

Mable in the workings of his business affairs was altogether contrary to Ringling's beliefs about the role of women. He needed a third member of his firm, yet he did not have enough confidence in any other Sarasota businessman to share even a limited knowledge of his financial affairs. His nearest associate and friend was Ralph Caples, but Caples was not a developer. His primary interest was in his advertising agency, which had branches in several cities. If asked, Caples would surely have refused, for he was something of a loner. Like Ringling, he was more accustomed to having authority than sharing it.

Mable, without an established role in Sarasota, needed to become more active in the community. Excessively reserved, she was too reticent to seek social prominence. The answer, Burns decided, was Mable's genuine interest in gardening; she should become the head of a garden club.[51] Conveniently, a newly forming Sarasota garden club provided the opportunity. Sponsored by Mrs. Owen Burns and Mrs. Ralph Caples, Mable was not only welcomed; she was elected by the founding members as the club's first president. She soon found how pleasant Sarasota society could be. Before long, her two sisters, Alma Ried and Dulcie Schueler, were included in some invitations, as were Edith (Mrs. Charles) Ringling and Ida Ringling North when she moved from Baraboo to Sarasota with her family.

Both John and Mable were at last part of the Sarasota establishment and they were enjoying it. Mable was always among the most elegantly dressed in a community that had become quite cosmopolitan. She was steadily active in holiday dances, parties, and card luncheons, yet she retained that characteristic silence about her origins and early life. She was never interviewed or photographed for the Sarasota press. This was her own choice but was also consistent with the absence of publicity in the *Sarasota Times* for local society. There were no publicized hostesses visibly seeking first place on a social ladder.

John Ringling's new press image as a "capitalist" was a recognition of his more recently acknowledged role as an entrepreneur. While the circus was one source of his wealth, it was by no means the only one. The circus was earning for him $300,000 or more each year; his oil leases and royalties produced about the same or even more.[52] Various other investments, largely in bonds, brought their share of dividends and interest. His total income approached $1 million a year during his initial years as a Sarasota developer.

When the *Sarasota Times* ceased to identify Ringling as "the well-known circus man," he was pleased. He had never been apologetic about his circus career and wealth, but his activities in Sarasota required a change in emphasis. Until 1927, there were no visible signs of Ringling Bros. and Barnum & Bailey in Sarasota. There was only the millionaire entrepreneur. His beautifully landscaped estate, opulent yacht, and Rolls Royce limousines could not fail to impress upon the Sarasota community that this was a man of consequence.

At that time, Florida's most recent disaster was the hurricane of 1921, a terrible storm that brought death and destruction to entire communities. In Sarasota there was one public benefit. Nature had swept away in one great surge many of the ugly fish houses on the bayfront, destroying the fishing village look that Owen Burns so often derided. A stub of the Seaboard Airline Railroad dock remained, but its useful days were finished. Calvin Payne, a Sarasota millionaire, offered to build a new terminal for the fisheries at Hog Creek, north of the city. His generous gesture greatly improved the appearance of the city's waterfront.

Sarasota's boosters hoped and believed that Ringling and Burns would use their adjoining space on the bay at Cedar Point to erect a large resort hotel and an array of fine homes. Ringling had other plans. His view of the future was based on the keys, not on the mainland. Burns had made his plan to build a hotel contingent on selling some New York City property. He was ready to proceed on his own, without waiting for a joint effort. Ringling responded to questions merely by saying that other considerations made the idea of a mainland hotel impractical.

In 1921–22 Ringling was forced by violent and prolonged rail strikes to turn his attention to the circus and to leave the future of Sarasota until later. A number of marginal circuses were forced into bankruptcy, but the Ringling combined show managed to avoid the worst effects of the strikes. John and Charles had many important, useful acquaintances, including W. T. Tyler, who operated the federally controlled rail lines. Other rail executive friends of Ringling lent their influence to keep the huge circus moving.

From long experience, John knew that a strike leading to disruption of railroad service meant dislocation in many other industries, resulting in smaller pay envelopes for many workers. The rail strikes indirectly caused investors and bankers to add caution to their customary prudence. In his new role as a Florida entrepreneur, Ringling found the time appropriate for accumulating property but not for building, particularly since Florida was heavily dependent on rail transport for building supplies. Florida's ports were of minimal use because there were few roads for intrastate transport and not enough trucks to haul supplies from ports to distant sites.

Pleasure spending, however, was not curtailed in the Ringling households. Both John and Charles added major luxuries, including new yachts that were delivered to Sarasota. Charles' *Symphonia,* built for him in Port Clinton, Ohio, started south via the Hudson River before the ice had cleared in the spring. John's *Zalophus,* built for him at Staten Island, New York, cost $200,000.[53] The two Ringling yachts were by far the most splendid among those docked at Sarasota's city pier. Because the Shell Beach homes were in shallows, the yachts had to remain at the city pier or at the former Yacht and Automobile Club dock, where *Zalophus* was equipped with telephone connections to the Ringling home.

Zalophus was the ultimate symbol of John Ringling's success. It resembled John Wanamaker's *Pastime* of Palm Beach—in other words, it was a duplicate of a boat owned by a man of great wealth and social position.[54] What more could the boy from McGregor, Iowa, aspire to possess? Except for the cabins for maids and valets, all the rooms on *Zalophus* were spacious. The furnishings and decor were lavish enough to satisfy Ringling's taste for opulence and fine detail; some guests might have found it just a little bizarre.

The interior was paneled in fine woods. Space for the owner and guests was provided in six staterooms. Each room was fitted with a brass bedstead, a chest of drawers, a dressing table, and a large wardrobe. Five baths completed the owner-guest quarters. The long deckhouse was reached by a mahogany companionway. Cruising radius was rated at 5,000 miles at fourteen knots.[55] Nevertheless, the craft was heavy and more ponderous than graceful, best suited for cruising the warm coastal waters of Florida.

Zalophus was ready for delivery in December 1922. It was sailed by a crew of ten, first headed by Captain Arthur Rowe and later by Al Roan. The maiden cruise was a leisurely voyage from Jacksonville, south to the Keys, and then along the Gulf coast, with a full complement of guests. Charles and Edith, secure in the knowledge that their new *Symphonia* was nearly as large as *Zalophus,* made their first voyage a fishing trip to Fort Myers and Lake Okeechobee.[56]

Zalophus represented more than John Ringling's riches. For nearly a decade he entertained on board a procession of guests who were pressed to become investors, backers, and buyers in the skillfully planned developments on the Sarasota keys. The island properties could only be visited by boat until the causeway was completed in 1926.

John and Charles were elected in January 1923 to be directors of the Bank of Sarasota.[57] The bank was then controlled by the Taliaferro family of Tampa, organizers of the first bank south of Tallahassee in 1883. The Ringlings were being courted as rich entrepreneurs with connections to potential investors outside Florida; hence their presence on the board had a certain public relations value. Their appointment granted them an inside place in local banking, which was important for their own interests.

In the same month that he was elected to the bank board, Ringling began to convert the former Yacht and Automobile Club into an apartment house. The project was entrusted to Mable, working with Owen Burns as the contractor. The apartments were to be rented furnished to winter visitors. Much of the furniture came from surplus items in the various Ringling homes. Burns also planned to dredge around the point, which would greatly increase its size, and then enclose the whole with a seawall. Ringling now held a large, open space facing city hall and the county offices, which invited frequent speculation about his plans for development.[58]

The expanse of empty ground at Golden Gate Point (formerly Cedar Point) and the conversion of the old Yacht and Auto Club could scarcely be interpreted as a grand gesture leading to a fashionable metro-resort. But any development seemed encouraging. Tampa's *Suniland* was quick to credit Ringling with having moved sleepy Sarasota into the present: "John Ringling of Sarasota; there is a name to charm. For Sarasota, what she is, wonder city that she is to become, owes and will owe to John Ringling her sudden leap into prominence, unique in the annals of the country and her place among the man-made paradises of this earth." Those were strong words of praise from an observer who had first seen Sarasota at about the same time Ringling began to buy island property. *Suniland's* writer had found it a "self-satisfied little seaside town . . . but for the most part it was held that its destiny would unfold itself in due time, nothing would be gained by trying to hurry nature."[59] That was the way others perceived Sarasota in the early 1920s. John Ringling, with his far-flung connections and rail-hotel friends, seemed the most promising prospect to energize the self-satisfied community.

Ringling was clearly prepared to lead Sarasota into the next stage. Soon the capitalist, financier, and promoter would be calling Sarasota his home, a city that he intended, through his own efforts and those of others who would join him, to transform into the most beautiful city in Florida. This was a large order, but it was one well suited to Ringling's personality and his apparently boundless energy.

The Florida Gold Rush

HE FLORIDA BOOM took off when throngs of unwary buyers raced to join with speculators to spin the real estate market out of control. "Florida fever burned so hotly in the veins of some of the 'migrants,'" wrote Kenneth Roberts, assuming the role of social critic, "that they roared and banged their way southward all through the one-time silent watches of the night. Although the Florida climate can accomplish many startling cures," Roberts added, "it cannot change a stupid man into a sensible one."[1]

Gullible buyers and rapacious sellers provided Roberts with ample material for satire. But he chose to stress the negative side of a postwar phenomenon. The surge of wealth and industry that World War I engendered was felt in many parts of the nation. In Florida, some of this new wealth fed the excesses of the land boom. At its worst, it was one of those aberrations that occur when avarice is coupled with a false sense of urgency.

While the boom lasted, roughly from 1922 to 1926, a roller coaster effect offered a thrilling ride to many who took part and to many more who were only spectators. What started as a healthy increase in land sales was followed by a ruinous spiral of unregulated trading. There were certain benefits, such as improved infrastructure and genuine land development.

Once a movement such as the Florida boom gathers irrational force, its initial cause, if known, is often lost from view. Many other forms of wealth have become the objects of uncontrollable waves of speculation—tulips in the Netherlands, overseas investment in the South Sea Bubble. In Florida, land was the available commodity. The attraction of a mild climate and the potential for a comfortable life on farms and near citrus groves proved to be an irresistible combination. The notorious land promotions addressed to the uninformed investor were only one aspect of the state's burgeoning economy.

The impact of the boom years was pervasive. Migration into the state increased the population by several hundred thousand each year.[2] Rail expansion made Jacksonville one of the nation's largest terminals. The Florida East Coast Railroad rushed to build double tracks to increase its capacity, lending force to the boom, which was most extreme in southeast Florida's Dade County.

On the Gulf coast, always less publicized than the Atlantic shore, investor development helped to generate boom conditions, but with somewhat less excitement. In 1925 the Seaboard Airline Railroad added another step in its long march from Tampa to Miami by laying track from Venice, just south of Sarasota where its line ended, to Fort Myers, thus increasing buyer demand. In late September 1925, would-be buyers stood in line all night to buy lots in Fort Myers that were about to be put up for sale. Within an hour after opening, sales of $1,380,000 were reported.[3] Around Tampa Bay and in St. Petersburg, the new causeway provided access for the eager buyers and settlers who preferred the Gulf coast.

Sarasota, too, was to have its share of speculative fever, but the number of such incidents amounted to only a minor episode in the general stampede. In and around Sarasota there was not much available land in large blocks for clever speculators to acquire and subdivide into house lots. The eastern area of Sarasota and Manatee counties was held primarily by ranchers who were content with their large tracts of land. Palmer interests controlled even larger acreage of farm and ranch land. The Brotherhood of Railroad Engineers held most of the land in Venice. John and Charles Ringling jointly owned 66,000 acres of eastern Sarasota County, undeveloped land that they did not propose to sell to speculators. Consequently, in-town commercial property and Sarasota house lots became the target of boom sales. City lots caught up in the spiral of resale, sometimes on the same day, rocketed upward in price, only to fall later to their previous level. City tax rolls became cluttered when the boom ended, leaving whole pages of listings with unknown owners. "Sidewalk cooties" sold land for "binders" too fast and too often to pause and register the owners.

Amid these changes caused by the boom-inflated economy, Sarasota's business community was in agreement that the city was destined for a great future. But its members could not agree on how to participate in the opportunities presented by the boom. There remained a strong, lingering belief from the 1880s that Sarasota should become a major deepwater port, welcoming shipping from the Panama Canal and from South American ports, and functioning as a transfer point from freighter to rail through a bayfront terminal. Looking back, one could recall the early days of sail transport from Sarasota to Key West and Havana, and the first steamers from Tampa in 1895. Boosters in the mid-1920s also welcomed the prospect of large resort developments for homes and hotels without recognizing the conflict of the two ideas. Sarasota might prosper as a resort or as a freight-handling port, but not both.

John Ringling cared not a flick of his cigar ash for visions of large freighters unloading at Sarasota docks. His plans were aimed exclusively at resort and metropolitan growth. Once his own plans were well advanced, he wished to prevent industrial and commercial projects from damaging the elegant appearance of the properties that he and Owen Burns were promoting.[4] In his desire to turn Sarasota into a tourist haven his two important allies were Owen Burns and S. Davies Warfield, president and later chairman of the Seaboard Airline Railroad.

Burns was eager to work with Ringling, whose views of Sarasota's future were similar to his own. The association with Ringling was clearly advantageous for the continued employment of Burns's dredging and building supply firms, two entities that he had formed several years earlier.[5] The two developers were in full agreement that Sarasota's future (and their own) lay in resort development for the moderately rich winter visitor and settler.

While Burns served as the local associate that Ringling needed, Warfield represented the establishment of eastern railways and financial power. Warfield was a man with influence among financiers, as well as the head of a rail line that had special plans for the Gulf coast cities. His company had ties to lines reaching into the Atlantic coast states and the Ohio valley. Warfield was the kind of influential friend that Sarasota needed, a man with the resources to create useful publicity in the Northeast and a company that could help to strengthen Sarasota's economy by stimulating tourist travel. With Burns and Warfield as allies, Ringling gained the support of both local and national figures who focused on the essential industries of building and transport, two key features of any successful development program.

The Ringling-Burns consortium had started with a project to dredge, fill, and erect a seawall around Ringling's Cedar Point property. The project added twenty-two valuable acres to Cedar Point.[6] Burns had already laid out house lots on his share of the point. He introduced two novel ideas: homes must be priced upward from a minimum amount, and no commercial buildings would be permitted. Ringling made no move to market his land, now protected and expanded with its new wall. The city council offered inducements if Ringling would build a hotel—free water, free electric power, and no taxes for ten years—but he would not be moved. His rail and hotel friends visited and consulted with him; their advice seemed to have favored delay. Among them was Albert Keller of the Ritz Carlton hotels, who was even then looking over the area. Keller would have perceived at once that a view of the Gulf was essential for an elegant resort hotel, which meant choosing a location on the keys rather than on the mainland. Ringling curtly informed Burns that the idea of a hotel on the mainland was not feasible.[7] Burns was not convinced; he determined to go ahead on his own.

Ringling was not only entertaining visitors to seek advice for his own plans; he also brought friends and acquaintances to Sarasota as potential investors or buyers of property for winter homes. His first arrangement for a sale brought with it consequences that extended far beyond any he could have imagined. He persuaded Samuel W. Gumpertz to buy two lots from Burns—one for a home and the other to be transferred to another buyer. The Gumpertz house, like the Ringling home that was then in the planning stage, was to be pretentious, with ornate chandeliers and other relics from dismantled buildings in New York. A number of its rooms had fine mahogany doors; the knobs were ennobled with the initial "A" for Astor. The house was one of the first in Sarasota to include a central heating system.[8]

Among the many who were associated with Ringling in his long career, none was to have such a strong and enduring impact upon his fortunes as did Sam Gumpertz (1869–1952). Ringling never permitted a close, confidential relationship to develop with any business colleague, even among those he knew well, but Gumpertz was partially exempt from this rule. Ringling trusted him, something that he would later regret. The two had been friends for many years before they became neighbors in Sarasota; both were conspicuous figures in celebrity circles in New York. Sam's wife, Evie, was warm-hearted and blessed with a generous nature. She was a congenial companion for Mable on the Ringling yacht or at Palms Elysian, where Sam and Evie were winter visitors each year before the Gumpertz house was built. Like Sam, Evie had grown up as an entertainer. She first teamed with Sam's sister in a vaudeville act, and later with the famous duo Weber and Fields.

Gumpertz had become rich from his amusement enterprises. Like the Ringling brothers, he knew from early years the relentless, turbulent life of the traveling circus—but he knew it only as a performer. At the age of nine, after three years of school, he began to perform in an acrobat troupe.

The act, headed by his mother, broke up after her death, and Sam moved on to become a rough rider with Buffalo Bill's Wild West Show. In 1893 he switched to managing theaters and shows, a career in which he soon excelled. It was Gumpertz who introduced Florenz Ziegfeld to the world of the theater. Among his clients was Harry Houdini, the magician and escape artist. After developing the world's largest entertainment park, Dreamland at Coney Island, he moved to Brighton Beach, where he brought amusements to crowds for more than twenty years.[9] In Manhattan, he was the owner of the famous Garrick Theater.

Gumpertz, like John Ringling, was adept at making friends with people of consequence. As president of the Coney Island Board of Trade, Gumpertz came to know city and state officials. He was influen-

tial in New York City's Democratic Party apparatus and a strong supporter of Mayor Jimmy Walker and Governor Alfred E. Smith.[10]
Through Gumpertz, Ringling got to know these popular New York
political figures. While he may have encountered them on his own, his
friendship with Gumpertz was a useful advantage in becoming well
enough acquainted to invite them to visit Sarasota.

During Gumpertz's Brighton Beach years, he and Ringling were
often together. Both traveled in Europe, sometimes together for similar
purposes: Ringling sought new acts for the circus, Gumpertz wanted
novelty acts and grotesque sideshow figures for amusements at the
beach. Among Gumpertz's less seamy acquisitions was the highly popular Czechoslovakian National Band, which played for Gumpertz at
Brighton Beach in the summer and came regularly to Sarasota for the
winter season. Ringling hired them often to enliven parties at his home
and for daily promotional concerts in the keys.

Sam Gumpertz had the showman's outgoing nature, and his easy,
friendly manner made him popular in the Sarasota community. Moreover, he quickly became a leading philanthropic figure. He was as
generous to Sarasota charities as he was in devising ways to promote the
city as a resort. Perhaps recalling the hardships of his own childhood, he
was especially concerned for the welfare of children. Among his larger
gifts were a children's ward for post-surgery recovery at the hospital and
a gift of valuable land to the Boy Scouts.[11] During the mid-1930s, when
he was allied with Edith Ringling in the circus, Gumpertz worked to
establish a retirement village for ex-performers. The idea was taken up
by the Circus Saints and Sinners organization, but it failed to generate
enough response, one more victim of the Depression that caused so
many generous impulses to wither.[12]

Gumpertz was at least partly responsible for two events of lasting importance to Sarasota's city life. One was the decision by John
McGraw, manager of the New York Giants, to bring the team to Sarasota for spring training, adding another tourist attraction. Major league
baseball was an ideal pastime for the vacationers, campers, and "tin
can tourists" who needed recreation and diversions to fill their days.
McGraw became Gumpertz's neighbor in a home on the adjoining lot
in Burns's subdivision.[13] In later reflections, Gumpertz claimed that he

also persuaded Ringling to bring circus winter quarters to Sarasota from Bridgeport, Connecticut.[14]

Gumpertz and McGraw were examples of the new Sarasota elite— northerners with money or status. Unlike local boosters, their primary interests were elsewhere, yet their presence and activities brought certain social and economic benefits to an expanding community with varied interests. During the season they entered the social life of the city, and they were also alert to the potential for sharing in the gathering boom. McGraw would have been wiser to stick with baseball and stay out of speculative real estate. His ill-fated Pennant Park subdivision, with its streets named for winning teams, fell victim to the collapse of the land boom in 1926. His image in Sarasota was irreparably damaged as losses were suffered by those who had, in good faith, bought house lots from him.

Sarasota was growing fast in the early 1920s. The city was starting to attract investors, developers, and builders who could sense from afar the expanding market for homes and apartments to house the wave of new residents. Builders found opportunities for homes close to the bayfront on Siesta Key (the only island with access by a bridge) and north of the city. Charles Ringling would soon invest in the area on the eastern, inland side of the city; John Ringling was to capture the islands. Sam Gumpertz joined associates in New York to form the Prudence Bond Company; he opened their Sarasota office to lend money on first mortgages. Company officers William K. Greve and Frank Bailey announced that they would finance large projects, such as apartment houses and hotels.[15] In time these three would become the enemies of both Owen Burns and John Ringling.

Sarasota, so long without rail service, was not to have not one but two trunk lines. The Atlantic Coast Line planned to move its Tampa Southern Railroad south, starting with an extended line from Bradenton to Sarasota. Another route was to connect Tampa with Miami, tying into ocean shipping from there to Havana and the Bahamas. Two competing lines would bring about lower freight rates, while the heightened activity would mean employment and enhanced property values for the city.

Sarasota was to provide the railroad with a right of way into the city and access to tidewater at the Payne Basin, provided by Calvin Payne,

Standard Oil heir, millionaire, and philanthropist. The Atlantic Coast Line also demanded exit to the south from Sarasota at a point near the golf course owned by Charles Ringling. That exit was to become the route extending the line to the Charlotte Harbor region, thence across the Everglades, along the Miami Canal, into Miami and the port. Once more the vision of a deepwater port for Sarasota seemed practical.

John Ringling was now among a small, select group of local power figures. For a decade, he would be represented when decisions were made. Now, when the Atlantic Coast Line made its position known, the Chamber of Commerce appointed a committee to negotiate the city's share in the agreement. J. H. Lord, a longtime promoter of the city and often an agent for the Palmer interests, was chairman. The Palmer Bank was represented. Owen Burns, John Ringling (now described as "the millionaire circus king"), and E. A. Smith added wealth and prestige to the panel.[16]

The public announcement of the new railroad plan came almost a year after John and Charles Ringling purchased the huge Woodward tract in eastern Sarasota County. Each bought 33,000 acres. This was isolated wilderness; its cost of around one dollar per acre was perhaps its principal attraction. It proved to be too far to the east of Sarasota to benefit from the new rail line. Shortly before the announcement of the railway, John Ringling bought a smaller tract, less than 1,000 acres, in an area known as the "sugar bowl," south of the city astride the Tamiami Trail, the long-unfinished highway from Tampa to Miami. Burns had urged the speculative value of the deal, certain that the demand for open acreage would increase when the railroad plan was made public.[17] The sugar bowl was once considered ideal for growing sugar cane, but the industry had moved farther south in search of frost-free winters.

While the Woodward tract lacked the potential for rail and highway development, there was an even chance of some future profits as ranch land. Timber, both live and fallen, was a marketable commodity. In April 1924, Burns arranged a contract for fifteen cents for each dead tree removed from the entire tract—scarcely a timber king's fortune, but it may have repaid a good share of the initial cost.[18] Rich "muck land" (a surface made from decaying vegetation that is ideal for farming) was thought to cover much of the tract.[19] The land, however, was so densely overgrown that in those days of open range, cattle foraging into the tract were often lost. Hunters, not cattlemen, occasionally recovered lost stock as game.[20]

These large real estate purchases, sometimes reported in the *Sarasota Times* at prices far in excess of their actual cost, added to the altered image of John Ringling as a rich investor in Sarasota, no longer the remote circus magnate. In 1923 another gesture helped to give him a new image as a benefactor who worked for the good of the city. A city bond issue to finance the new recreation pier had failed dismally; only $5,000 of an issue of $75,000 had sold. Ringling bought the entire remainder.[21] He quickly became "the well-known capitalist" instead of the "well-known showman" in the *Sarasota Times*. In announcing the two Ringlings' election as directors of the Bank of Sarasota, the *Times* described the brothers as "noted capitalists of unlimited wealth."[22] Thus began the popular misconception about the extent of John Ringling's riches. Few would know that he was often in need of cash, which was frequently borrowed or contrived from manipulating movable assets.

An important part of Ringling's real estate strategy, begun while he was still accumulating land for his Ringling Isles program, was to invest in grandiose landscaping projects. From a nursery on Longboat Key, he moved hundreds of palms and exotic plants to his own estate and to his other property on the keys. His intent was to give his estate and the keys a thoroughly tropical appearance as an inducement to northern buyers. Prospective buyers were not asked to visualize a "someday" Florida community; they were to see carefully planned landscaping already in place. Sarasota was to be promoted as an "almost tropical" resort, welcoming all who wished to escape from the cold northern winters.

While John Ringling preferred to buy and develop property into beautifully landscaped homesites, his nephew Richard decided to turn his estate north of Sarasota into a dairy farm with Holstein cattle from his Montana ranch.[23] Richard was still a young man, only twenty-five in 1923, but already owner of some 80,000 acres of ranch land in Montana, where he had started with a few thousand acres purchased from his Uncle John. Richard was always a favorite with John and Mable. He and his bride, Aubrey Black of White Sulphur Springs, Montana, had spent part of their wedding journey on the Ringling yacht. In their one joint enterprise, Richard and John were partners in the oil lease scheme that had failed to secure federal approval on Indian lands.

These varied ventures demonstrate the debate over the course of development and underscore the absence of a consensus regarding the economic future of Sarasota. Some promoters clung to the vision of a deepwater port. Others—Ringling among them—saw the future of Sarasota as a thriving metropolitan resort. The new city could attract great numbers of people who would bring their wealth with them. The remainder looked to their traditional farming and ranching interests, led by the Palmer family enterprises. The three groups continued to drive the city and country forward. As conditions moved with the times, one or the other ascended in the local power structure. One element of a truly composite economy was absent: there was almost no industry in Sarasota, nor was any likely to move there. South Florida was then at the end of the rail lines—a fact that became increasingly obvious to northern freight traffic managers. The climate was not suited to factory work, nor were the traditionally self-reliant Floridians a likely labor market for industry's monotonous assembly-line tasks.

These competing interests did not deter Ringling from building his island empire and going his own way. His influence in local affairs was growing; moreover, he was free from competition on the keys, for none of his holdings were accessible except by water. Only one island was connected to the mainland—Siesta Key (once Sarasota Key), where other developers had preempted much of the property. Once he began to accumulate island property, Ringling, with Burns's assistance, kept up a steady pace until he held all the other islands between the mainland and the Gulf. Just as the boom was starting to escalate land prices, Ringling made a handsome profit when he sold his share of a Shell Beach parcel that he and Ralph Caples had bought together shortly after Ringling's move to Sarasota.[24]

Ringling had been able to buy acreage at moderate cost after the hurricane of 1921, the most severe storm in many years. It had swept over Longboat Key and ended the short life of the island as a specially favored farm area that was always free from winter frosts. The entire island was then in private hands; all federal homestead ground had long since been transferred to the farm owners. The major difficulty in the

1920s was to acquire enough land without resorting to a checkerboard pattern. Ringling wanted all of St. Armands Key, the Lido, and as much of Longboat Key as he could get.

Some parcels fell easily into Ringling's hands; other owners held out, demanding $200 per acre, which he refused to pay.[25] By the end of March 1923, he had about 1,500 acres on Longboat Key. Only the large Palmer property at the island's southern tip remained unavailable, held by Berthe Palmer's brother Adrian Honoré. Then, unexpectedly, Honoré offered to sell, even at a loss, hoping to move the entire 400 acres at once.[26] With that purchase, Ringling lacked but one small piece, which was essential to the whole project. Its ownership was traced to heirs somewhere in Oregon or Idaho; an attorney was dispatched to find them and secure title deeds.[27]

A few days after the Palmer-Honoré property was added to Ringling's empire, a headline story in the *Sarasota Times* described the splendid future that would soon "electrify" Florida. The *Times* rated Ringling as the seventeenth richest man in America, a popular fiction based on an expanded estimate of his actual fortune. However, the grand scheme attributed to him at that time was not much different from his actual plan: a causeway from the mainland, a grand boulevard to run the length of Longboat Key, a great hotel, a bathing pavilion, smart shops on St. Armands Key.[28] Owen Burns, vice-president of the newly formed Ringling corporation, was never mentioned in the press accounts of Ringling's projects. In the Ringling Isles venture, the real estate was held by the corporation; the purchase money came from Ringling's own resources of accumulated capital. He held a mortgage on the company-held land. Over the years of their association, Ringling and Burns resorted to a number of varied, often arcane arrangements. They never clearly sorted out their degrees of participation or respective personal rights to selected parcels of the island properties.[29] Burns was a builder and a land developer, but not a financier. His personal traits of loyalty and integrity were not wholly suited to the shrewd practices of his partner.[30] There was a fundamental honesty in John Ringling that was part of the Ringling Bros. concept, but he was not averse to taking advantage of others when it was convenient and resorting to sleight-of-hand tactics in a crisis.

Burns was not long in discovering that he was tied to a man whose freewheeling methods defied understanding. Largely as a result of Burns's efforts, the Ringling Isles firm acquired all the land needed to make the keys a single domain before the worst excesses of the boom drove prices beyond reason. The entire cost of the land was but a fraction of the development costs that would have to be met before the land was salable for homes or suitable for hotels and shops. Probably the worst flaw in Ringling's business sense was his indifference to the concept of cost as a serious issue in accounting. Haphazard approaches to accounting were common in the Ringling Bros. Circus history. Cost was money spent each day; the remainder of the circus admissions was considered the profit. For many years, the total was divided by five (a fifth to each partner) and sent to the Bank of Baraboo in Wisconsin. In his dealings in Sarasota real estate and his other enterprises, John Ringling was equally casual. He failed to record initial outlays of his own funds, nor did he keep any independent records that could be used to reconstruct his costs.[31] He tended to avoid any action that would permit others to gain access to knowledge of his private affairs.

Fortunately, before the island property records were confused beyond redemption, a local accountant was engaged to manage the office. James A. Haley, later to become an official in the circus and, still later, a congressman from the Sarasota district, was recommended to Ringling at a meeting with the directors of the Seaboard Airline Railroad. As lots were sold or set aside for specific purposes, title and mortgage data were necessarily recorded at the county courthouse, a formality that could not be disregarded. However, Haley could not recover lost data, nor could the CPA firm of auditors later engaged by Ringling's executors. A state of Florida auditor later concluded that the multimillion-dollar investments credited to Ringling were greatly inflated in the publicity that followed his grand proposals.[32]

While Ringling was indifferent to the techniques of cost accounting, he was deeply interested in what he was creating on the islands. For the successful promotion and development of the island, he needed access from the mainland by causeway and bridges. Mable offered a novel suggestion. Since it might be desirable to have a railroad on the causeway, she reasoned, why not start from the point on the mainland where the Seaboard Line extends to Dixon's fish house, some distance out into the bay? The advantage seemed obvious. The start of a rail line was in place; the water was shallow all the way to the first channel marker going out to Big Pass.[33] The plan sounds as though Mable visualized something similar to the rail line that crosses the lagoon from Mestre on Italy's mainland to Venice. Another advantage to Mable's plan, Ringling noted, was that the route would bypass his Cedar Point. No salable land would be disturbed and the view would remain unspoiled.

Ringling and Burns used every opportunity to promote the island causeway route, lobbying public officials and building public opinion. The townspeople responded well. Burns was certain that 98 percent of the city favored the railroad route. This may have been an exaggeration, but before long, public opinion became moot. All the plans fell apart when the Selby family publicly opposed the route and were joined by the residents whose homes faced the bay. Burns and Ringling also failed to recognize a new force in local affairs: the League of Women Voters, which had successfully urged the city to form a planning commission. Its first priority was a mandate for the removal of rail lines near the bay.[34] The day when rail lines were tolerated in or near upscale residential areas was nearly over. The causeway reverted to Cedar Point, where it had begun.

John's brother Charles was also entering the Sarasota development scene, but in a much less flamboyant program than the one planned by John. Choosing the less fashionable east side of Sarasota between the two railroads, he organized the Sarasota Home Building Company and planned to build 150 modest homes. At the same time, recognizing the close ties between real estate and banking, Charles formed the Ringling Trust and Savings Bank. He became its president; his son-in-law, Louis Lancaster, was named vice-president. Not long after, Silas Juliar, one of the Ringling cousins from the Juliar circus family, became a member of the staff.

While Charles was busy in Sarasota, John divided his attention between his interests in Sarasota and those in New York. Working with his longtime associate Tex Rickard, he was helping to put together a scheme for a new sports arena in New York City. The old Madison Square Garden designed by Stanford White had opened in 1890. The massive structure was a vivid expression of White's enthusiasm for the Italian Renaissance. In 1908, Ringling, Rickard, and the other directors decided to sell the building. By then some of the more prominent millionaire directors had left, including J. P. Morgan, Sr., and Charles Crocker; they had lost interest in a venture that consistently failed to turn a profit. In 1916, the New York Life Insurance Company bought the site. No changes were made until 1924, when the owners announced that the building would be razed and replaced by an office building. Demolition was delayed until after the 1924 Democratic National Convention, the Garden's last major event. In August the portico was removed prior to the widening of Madison Avenue.[35]

During that year, the search for a new site had begun. A syndicate headed by Ringling and Rickard first negotiated for the Seventh Avenue car barns, but they abandoned the idea when the threat of prolonged litigation dimmed the prospects of major financing. In July, the two were joined by Richard Hoyt, of the investment firm of Hayden Stone, and Eugene L. Garey, the largest shareholders. Garey and Ringling now renewed their acquaintanceship, which had begun many years earlier in Chicago when Ringling was a client in Garey's law practice there. The team acquired for $2 million a site on Eighth Avenue between 49th and 50th streets. There they would build the new Madison Square Garden, the largest building in the world devoted exclusively to entertainment. A rival group then bought the Seventh Avenue site and announced plans for a building to take the place of the old Garden, but their competition soon faded.[36]

The new Garden opened in late 1926. Ringling continued as chairman and Tex Rickard as president. Among the other directors were Kermit Roosevelt, several bankers and businessmen, and Richard Fuchs, Ringling's private secretary. The building was designed to seat about 25,000 spectators. Beneath the exhibition hall on the lower level was ample space for the entire circus, including all its equipment and animals. It was entered by a broad ramp that would permit the largest circus wagons to turn easily when entering or leaving the building.

Once arrangements for the Garden were safely under way, Ringling turned his attention again to Sarasota. The causeway under construction, minus the rail line, was a highly popular project. The bayfront owners were mollified by the altered route, which was the one Ringling had originally proposed to use. Mable's railroad idea turned out to be hopelessly outdated; in fact, the bayfront owners, led by Marie Selby, had helped Ringling to avoid a shortsighted folly. Since all members agreed on the preferred route, the city council granted permission and gave Ringling the authority to start "from such point on Cedar Point as he may desire." Ringling and Burns jointly bought a huge dredge capable of meeting all the demands of the project. Burns was steadily urging his colleague to move faster to overtake their rival, Andrew McAnsh, who was selling lots almost daily on Siesta Key, lots that Burns argued were worth much less than those on Ringling Isles.[37]

In planning for the causeway construction, Ringling continually sought small economies—a lifelong habit, as many circus workers would testify. In this major decision, his insistence on using cheaper material—pine instead of cypress—resulted in a greatly shortened useful life for each structure. Once that decision was made, work rushed ahead. Ringling agreed with Burns that they must begin an aggressive sales campaign while money was still plentiful in Sarasota.[38]

Ringling was now ready to advance his resort plans, having made certain that the causeway would be in place. He was soon able to pass on some of the forthcoming costs to others while they, in turn, helped to further his interests. An opportunity arose that was made to order for a typical Ringling gesture. In May 1924, city leaders and golfers organized an association to find ways of acquiring a new golf course. J. H. Lord, the wily operator who held many pieces of property in and around Sarasota, offered a tract about five miles south of the city. His price was about half the current value of the land. When the group met to consider Lord's proposal, Ringling rose to say a few words. He offered to *give* 130 acres for a new country club, on either Longboat Key or St. Armands Key. Ringling was his customary, reserved, soft-spoken self, "no fireworks, no blurb, no verbal trimmings about 'dear old Sarasota'—merely handing over a property worth no less than $100,000 as another would pass a cigar to a friend."[39] He casually added, "I will give you a causeway to the key." At the next meeting, he was met by the assembled group, standing and applauding.

Ringling's dramatic gesture gained him several advantages. The golf club members were almost certain to see that public money would become available to build a bridge to connect the islands, saving Ringling a substantial outlay. Members were also to assume the expense for club facilities as well as for engineering and building the course. Without seeming to have upstaged his fellow Sarasotan J. H. Lord, Ringling's gesture made certain that the elite center of Sarasota would remain on the west side, on one of his islands. His community standing was enhanced and he would soon come looking for a favor in return by calling upon the city leaders to buy shares in his planned resort hotel.

Important as they were, Ringling's causeway and golf course schemes were still isolated features in need of a cohesive program. Both John and Charles were aware that new hotels and golf courses would not create or sustain a thriving city economy. A larger population of all classes would be needed. Mechanics and craftsmen were required as builders, and homes for their families had to be built. If building was to become a major industry after tourism—and that seemed to be the likely future of Sarasota—then inducements were needed to bring new residents, particularly for the building trades, to the area.

To attract new residents of all classes, the Ringlings had immense resources for advertising: circus posters and programs. Their audience was nationwide. In 1923 more than three and a half million spectators, three-fourths of them adults, attended the circus. That amounted to one in thirty among the country's entire population. Countless others saw the Ringling Bros. posters. The new campaign promoted Sarasota's seaside charms and sports attractions: "Spend a Summer this Winter in Sarasota." On placards in hotels, terminals, and store windows—in any public place that would permit them—the Ringling message was broadcast. Few could match the circus organization in the sweep of its advertising. For the first time, much of the nation became aware of Sarasota and the then-developing Florida dream. Such publicity attracted people with money and leisure; it must have also influenced many more to believe that Florida was a good place to live and work.

🎭 The central feature of Ringling's island plan was St. Armands Key. The much-discussed causeway was designed to lead into a circle, while exits would lead south to Lido and north to Longboat. A boulevard 100 feet wide was to extend the length of Longboat Key, provided that Manatee County would start building from its end. To the Manatee business community, Ringling presented a splendid prospect. He asked them to imagine a continuous ribbon of fine homes. Houses would extend from Bradenton and south Manatee County along the Tamiami Trail to Sarasota, across the causeway, then loop back along the length of Longboat, and finally along Anna Maria Island to the Cortez Bridge, already in place.[40]

Ringling was especially proud of the elegant design of St. Armands, for it promised to be a model of resort elegance, a fitting rival to the best of Florida's east coast resorts. Planning, engineering, and landscape design were entrusted to John J. Watson, who had gained his reputation from his success with an entire township near Toledo, Ohio, for the Willys Overland Motor Company. In Florida he had done the same for some 3,000 acres near the Gandy Bridge of St. Petersburg.[41]

To ornament St. Armands, Ringling spent with a lavish hand. Imposing Italian statuary was starting to arrive from Ringling's purchases in Venice, Rome, and Naples. Harding Circle dominated the island. One of the presidential boulevards fanning out from the circle was also named for Warren G. Harding. It led to the former Worcester home on Bird Key, which Ringling now proposed for a winter White House.

Locally, Ringling was credited with being a friend of President Harding, though it is not certain that Ringling and Harding ever met. The connection, if any, was through their mutual friend Ralph Caples. An Ohioan like Harding, Caples managed the campaign train in the autumn of 1920 that helped Harding defeat James M. Cox. Afterward, Caples and his wife, Ellen, were guests of the Hardings when the president-elect vacationed on the east coast of Florida. Ringling was better acquainted with some of the figures in the Harding administration who gained a measure of notoriety as a result of their manipulation of oil lands and government-owned leases.

The site chosen for Ringling's Ritz Carlton Hotel adjoined the new golf club on Longboat Key, where members were already raising funds. There were enough signs of actual development to make the hotel a plausible though still invisible entity. Caples took up the role of advocate. From his Sarasota office he issued an appeal to Sarasota investors to match Ringling's share, then about $400,000. The Caples letter was equivocal, if not intentionally deceptive.

> I feel confident that it will be a source of gratification to you as it was to me to know that Sarasota could secure a Ritz Carlton hotel, they being willing to erect and operate one of their famed hostelries here, provided we show some spirit of cooperation ourselves . . . made possible through . . . John Ringling . . . who has donated 20 or more acres. The Ritz Carlton people will then come and possibly spend from one and a half million on a building that will be unexcelled anywhere as a tourist hotel. It is planned to have this hotel in operation by December 1, 1925, it then becoming one of a chain of these internationally known hotels.[42]

The reader might easily believe that the Ritz corporation was to be builder and operator of this hotel for which local participation was asked. That impression was not wholly removed by the later suggestion that after the building was completed, the Ritz would come in and make it its own. It does seem unlikely that Caples would risk his own integrity for such a deceptive manipulation.

The business community of Sarasota was accustomed to such appeals; money had recently been solicited for a large hotel on the mainland. But in early 1925, the prospect of such a glamorous resort hotel was particularly attractive. They were told by Caples that the hotel would cater to the "ultra exclusive . . . the best, the richest people of the nation." That idea of being somehow associated with the superrich was also used by Addison Mizner to bring buyers to Coral Gables. He too was working with the Ritz Carlton Hotel Corporation to franchise the name for a luxury hotel that he had designed. Warren and Wetmore of New York, the architects who were engaged for the Ringling Ritz Carlton, were commissioned to plan and execute the interior of Mizner's Coral Gables Ritz.[43]

For the next several months, propaganda about the splendor of the Ringling Isles was spread widely. Trade papers, such as the *Industrial Record* published in Baltimore, ran releases (sent from Sarasota) that were then reprinted by the Sarasota press. Ringling's investment during the summer of 1925 was reported to be $10 million; the expected return in four or five years was placed at $100 million. There was a local story about the Harding memorial at the center of St. Armands, to honor Ringling's "warm personal friend." Another reported that Ringling had donated $1 million for the memorial.[44] In fact, Ringling himself was becoming part of the boom propaganda, freely supplied in *This Week in Sarasota*, propaganda masked as a newspaper and frankly addressed to potential investors in other parts of the country.

Driven by the boom, the year 1925 was more active in new developments and building than any yet in Sarasota. In the first six months, no less than $19 million in real estate transfers were recorded in this community of just 5,500. John and Charles Ringling were by no means alone, but they were certainly the largest investors to capitalize on the growing demand for homes and business property. Owen Burns, who continued as vice-president of the Ringling Isles firm, was handling all the island development and the building of the causeway and John Ringling's new palazzo home. Burns still managed to start several projects for his own interests. One was a cluster of small, Mediterranean-style homes designed by local architect Thomas Reed Martin. Several of the homes were occupied by Ringling associates, among them Richard Fuchs, John Ringling's aide. Another was for a time the home of John Ringling North, one of Ida's sons.

After long hesitation, Burns finally ventured into the hotel field, putting much of his own fortune into El Vernona, named for his wife. The opulent and distinctive El Vernona became a symbol of Sarasota's boom and then of its bust. It opened with minor fanfare on Labor Day 1925. A grand opening awaited the new year and the return of the city's social leaders. The heavy masonry walls, concrete, tile-covered roof, and absence of woodwork were the architect's ideas of adapting to Florida's climate.

The architect, Dwight James Baum, had come from New York to supervise the building of a new home for John and Mable. In this massive, Mediterranean-style hotel, most rooms enjoyed an unobstructed view of the bay. On the roof, two bungalows surrounded by colorful gardens offered privacy and particularly elegant rooms.[45] Ceiling decorations painted in the public rooms by skilled young decorator Robert Webb were among his finer works. Baum, who chose him for a number of his commissions in Florida, including the Ringling home, was then heavily favoring Spanish and Italian design. The Ringlings were helping to give Sarasota a new, Mediterranean-inspired appearance with the buildings designed by Baum and others who followed his lead. Sensing the opportunities in a growing city, Baum opened an office in the Burns-Ringling office building and designed many public and residential buildings in the city, on the Ringling islands, and in other parts of Florida. From Milwaukee came the firm of Clas, Sheperd and Clas, architects of the new Charles Ringling mansion. Like Baum, they stayed in Sarasota only until the boom went bust.

Burns's El Vernona was large and distinguished, but a fatal flaw in its operations came from an unfortunate choice of manager. More than a year earlier, Ringling had introduced Burns to Harry Griswold as a personal friend who was one of the best hotel men in America. Burns accepted Ringling's recommendation and leased the hotel to Griswold for five years. In less than a year, Griswold departed quietly without having made a single payment on his lease.[46] Ultimately the hotel failed, and the mortgage holder, the Prudence Bond Company, foreclosed. Sam Gumpertz, speaking for his associates in the company, announced that there would soon be a new owner, John Ringling. The Ringling-Burns relationship could not survive this blow.

Penalties like this for the excesses of the boom were not far off. For a few more months in early 1926, however, the Ringling Isles Corporation enjoyed some fruits of its costly development program. On 1 January 1926, John Ringling's dark green Rolls Royce limousine was the first automobile to cross the finished causeway, just one year from the day he announced his plan. Work continued until an hour before his crossing, when the last nail was driven into the planks of the draw span. For its time, it was an expensive venture for private capital, unsupported by public funds for engineering or construction. The causeway, built on concrete piles with a roadway laid on pine timbers, extended one and three-fifth miles. Its construction was thought to be as strong as human ingenuity could devise. Its life, proclaimed the *Sarasota Herald*, should be measured in centuries. The writer could not have been more mistaken. It lasted less than ten years.[47]

For the moment, prospects seemed unlimited. The Ritz Carlton name promised an alluring aura of riches, elegance, and exclusive clientele. The prominent guests who visited the Ringling home and the accompanying publicity helped to promote Sarasota as a rival to Miami or Palm Beach as a resort for the chic, cosmopolitan set. One of Ringling's celebrity guests, Mayor Jimmy Walker of New York City, generously agreed to appear one evening at the Sarasota Kennel Club, where he and John Ringling acted as judges for the dog races. Some of Sarasota's older elite may have regarded Mayor Walker as a somewhat tarnished representative of 1920s celebrity, more appropriate for Miami than Sarasota, but many would contend that he might introduce a lively note to Sarasota's sedate life-style.

Ringling was beginning to need all the evidence he could find to show that his expensive hotel scheme was a sound investment. He was deeply committed, not only in his personal investment but also in complex ties to his real estate enterprises. The builder's hotel contract was assigned from one entity to another.[48] As he was prone to do, Ringling was again following a convoluted course, one that might conceal the trail of assets and ownership from prying examiners or creditors. In the following years, the practice became almost an obsession.

Most of Sarasota's leaders knew little of John Ringling's idiosyncracies and his unorthodox accounting practices. The *Sarasota Herald* always loyally supported promotion efforts when a new local facility was in the offing. By unfortunate coincidence, however, in March 1926 the subscription drive for the hotel shared front-page space with reports of the most severe stock market failure since the armistice of 1918. Heading the Ritz Carlton appeal was the line "START WORK SOON AFTER STOCK SOLD." Next to it appeared the chilling report "STOCKS CRASH AFTER A TIDAL SELLING WAVE." Never before had the ticker fallen so far behind, nor had so many shares been sold in a single day's trading at the New York Stock Exchange.[49] There was a general, well-founded feeling in Sarasota that real estate prices would tumble when the speculative market ended. Near the end of the drive, with Caples in charge, Sarasotans were urged "to beg, borrow or steal money to subscribe . . . it will advertise Sarasota to people who will bring wealth and prestige." Wealth and prestige were admittedly goals of the Ritz Carlton project, but Sarasota's leaders were becoming aware that a small city could not thrive on wealth and prestige alone. Real growth required a balance of classes, occupations, and industries. There was a note of desperation in that last appeal for hotel financing suggesting that if this project failed, Sarasota's future was threatened.

In an attempt to help overcome Sarasota's limited income base, the Ringling Bros. Circus was again called to bring tourists and new residents to the city. John and Charles agreed that the publicity director for the Chamber of Commerce would travel with the circus through the United States and Canada. His assignment was to promote Sarasota all across the nation and to report Ringling Bros. Circus news to Sarasota—the first suggestion that Sarasota ought to know more about the circus.

Nine million patrons and spectators saw this latest publicity of Sarasota, which was proclaimed from every parade wagon, each tent pole, and the sides of each elephant. The official program sold at every performance contained a page of good news about the land and its climate: "Sunshine and balmy breezes tenderly lengthen the days of the aged. . . . Here life is joy."[50] While this message was aimed at retired Americans with modest incomes, the general publicity was especially directed to the still active working population who made up most of the circus patrons.

The circus promotion was a broadside approach, aimed at tourists and those who might consider moving to Sarasota to live and work. In effect, circus advertising targeted every individual as it touted Sarasota and its place in the Florida dream. The moneyed buyer to whom the island properties were marketed would be suitably impressed by the quiet elegance of St. Armands, by the model homes designed by Dwight Baum and Thomas Martin, and by the proximity of a fashionable golf club and luxury hotel. By contrast, the daily concerts given on St. Armands by the Czechoslovakian National Band seemed somewhat common in that rarefied atmosphere of upscale living. Ringling, however, knew that a band stirs its audience and he had many house lots to sell. Not all could go to the rich and the moderately rich.

Sarasota was reaping a barrage of publicity and promotion, much of it the work of John Ringling. Prospects for continued growth and prosperity seemed assured if one measured only the first months of 1926, when bank deposits increased by 25 percent. The largest construction projects in Sarasota's history were underway or at least under permit. The Ritz Carlton, rated at more than $3 million, was the largest permit ever issued. The two Ringling mansions and the county courthouse were equally positive evidence of material progress. The *Sarasota Herald* noted the array of millionaires whose fortunes were at work in Florida, among them John D. Rockefeller, Jacob Ruppert, Cornelius Vanderbilt, Jr., Otto Kahn, John Ringling, and Thomas Sinclair.[51] Another member of the famous Rockefeller family, Percy Rockefeller, purchased 33,000 acres in Pasco and Hillsborough counties in the autumn.[52] The impression grew that nothing could stop the destiny of this splendid state.

In Sarasota the consequences of this uncritical view were many, although not all became apparent as the boom began to fade. In the early flush of excitement, voters had agreed to expand the city limits to about sixty-nine square miles, including that part of Longboat Key that lay in Sarasota County. In another move that combined sound and unsound decisions, the Florida Power and Light Company offered to buy the city-owned power plant, which was no longer adequate. The Ringlings favored the sale, knowing there would be a more economical, professional operation. The city council agreed upon a price of $1 million. The money could be used for a deepwater port, according to City Attorney Burket, because the city had authority to use its funds for the public good.[53]

The perennial dream of a deepwater port was near realization. Supporters envisioned that within a few months oceangoing ships would bring cargo and passengers to the city, giving employment to thousands. The *Sarasota Herald*, caught up in the excitement of the moment, saw massive ocean commerce fast approaching: "Then will the dream of men such as Edwards, Ringling, Thompson, Lancaster and Day and others with foresight and vision come true. The Sarasota of the future is too glorious to contemplate. The favored of cities, Queen of the new Mediterranean will be her name."[54]

In 1925 the major rail lines declared a boycott on Florida, where there was so little industry that freight cars by the hundreds would sit idle after coming south, because northbound freight was almost nonexistent. In view of the railroad boycott, local pressure for an ocean freight terminal seemed reasonable. Cost estimates were prepared by engineers for a ship channel and a turning basin. The expected benefits of a busy port clouded much of the public thinking; buildings, rail lines, cranes, and the usual structures that surround a port would have to be built. There was one presumed advantage: Sarasota was located *on* the Gulf, while New Orleans was 110 miles up the Mississippi and Tampa 38 miles inland along a twisting entrance to the bay. Sarasota appeared to be the port of easy access, a city that could flourish from transshipping from ocean to rail. Funds were spent, channels were dredged, an island was raised, but only one ocean ship came, for there was no commerce to be served.

The hasty action that consumed the million dollars gained from selling the power plant could not be recalled, but the expanded city boundaries were vulnerable to second thoughts. By the autumn of 1926, the glow had faded from dreams of rapid growth and prosperity. Those citizens whose land had become part of greater Sarasota discovered to their dismay that city taxes were higher than in the county. Moreover, bridges and highways were county and state issues, and these were matters of prime importance to Ringling with his large island properties. In agreement with his brother Charles, Ringling decided to pressure the city authorities to force a return to smaller city limits.

When the boundary topic was first discussed publicly, work was halted on the Ritz Carlton. Charles Ringling bluntly informed city officials that work would be resumed if the vote for boundary reduction prevailed. Nevertheless, the vote overwhelmingly supported the city leaders' decision, 965 for and 66 against relimiting the city boundaries. Once again Sarasota became a small city of only twenty square miles. With that action, the county gained responsibility for the bridge and draw span over New Pass, the extended Longboat Key boulevard that would meet up with the bridge, and another boulevard on Anna Maria Island.[55] In effect, Ringling was starting the long process of withdrawing from an overextended position and transferring some of the public-use facilities from private to public funding. It is clear from his agreement with the city that he had decided not to abandon the Ritz Carlton. But in the interval, while work was stopped, he used the occasion to cancel his contract with the builder.

In a parting gesture to the city council, Ringling pointed out that bonds to be issued by Sarasota County for completing the bridges on the keys would sell at par, considerably better than Florida bonds were then achieving on the market.[56] He could make that statement because he intended to buy the entire issue.

Another component of John Ringling's island program was just then ready to take its place in the overall production. He made it an event of circus proportions. With much publicity and a program of sports and social activities for all ages, Lido Beach was opened to the public. The first-day crowd of over 2,000 visitors was more than one-third of the entire city population. A new pavilion and bath house, built with the combined efforts of Ringling, Burns, and Gumpertz, offered residents and tourists an attraction directly on the shore. Lido Key, a name assigned to the island by Ringling developers, was a smaller, less exclusive subdivision than the St. Armands part of the Isles complex. Lot prices were lower, mainly to attract families to build beach houses or permanent homes. Deed restrictions were less demanding; houses costing as little as $4,000 could be built on Lido lots.

The opening, with fun and games for everyone, free bus rides from downtown, a pie-eating contest, and other crowd pleasers, was true Gumpertz and something of the old circus showman Ringling. A festival, even a brief one, would help to overcome the effect of the unusually harsh posture that Ringling had adopted to force the boundary decision. He might have had what he wanted for less, for the majority of outer city residents had voted to reduce the city limits.[57]

Late in September, Florida experienced its second major hurricane in five years. The most serious loss of life in 1926 occurred in the southeast, where several hundred lives were lost. Property damage was also more severe on the east coast. First estimates placed Sarasota's losses at about $1 million; the figure fell by half when a less hurried survey was possible.[58] For many boom time buyers, the storm ended their interest in Florida. Intense efforts in advertising and promotion would be needed to revive Florida's image. Confronted with falling land values and a slowing economy, Sarasota, like other cities in the state, lost the exuberance that had accompanied the boom years.

When important civic decisions were to be made, in Sarasota a panel of leading citizens convened to advise the city council on ways to deal with a developing crisis. In November 1926, a group headed by Owen Burns recommended that all property values be reduced by 50 percent. This move would forestall the fiscal crisis that was arising from unpaid taxes and would restore property values to a more realistic level. The idea was in tune with President Calvin Coolidge's tax plan but for the opposite reason. Having found that the national treasury showed a substantial surplus, Coolidge announced a 10–15 percent tax refund from 1925 taxes. His shocked cabinet quickly persuaded him to recant.

The rapid turnabout from boom to bust, coupled with a devastating hurricane, panicked many speculators who watched their prospective clients disappear as fast as they had earlier come looking for something to buy. The collapse created highly unstable conditions in Sarasota as well as in the rest of Florida. The altered circumstances made it prudent for one or both Ringlings to be on the scene, for they were now bankers, developers, and builders—vulnerable to any sudden shift in public confidence. The signs of retrenchment in Florida cast a shadow from the Atlantic coast as far west as Ringling Isles on the Gulf of Mexico. Fortunately for John and Charles, the circus was having a fine season, playing to unprecedented crowds. Charles, although he seemed to recover from an illness during the spring, did not regain his strength and vigor of past years. He loyally supported the Chamber of Commerce throughout the city boundary affair. He did, however, start to reduce his personal commitments, beginning with the sale of his title and mortgage company, which served as an adjunct to his bank and real estate interests.

While men like the Ringlings were concentrating on retaining their hold on selected market segments, an entirely new tourist class, generally known as "tin can tourists" because they often camped and carried canned food with them, was beginning to play a part in the economy of Florida. The importance of this ever-increasing winter population was generated by changes in the times. The auto industry was producing small, reasonably efficient trucks capable of carrying an early form of the motor home. Other types of equally primitive homes were hauled as trailers behind family automobiles; many were the owners' own handiwork. Improved roads nationally, some of them in Florida, enabled thousands of these tourists to spend the winter months in Florida, bringing their temporary homes with them.

Tin can tourists were part of the great annual winter migration into Florida that began around 1920. As an organization with an annual "convention," the Tin Can Tourists were first established in Tampa in 1919. Made to feel unwelcome in Tampa, they removed to Arcadia and in the mid-1920s brought their hundreds of members to Sarasota. Mayor A. B. Edwards, who welcomed their spending, greeted them and invited them to make Sarasota their headquarters. At first, campers and trailer residents in large numbers created problems for Florida cities unprepared for their unique demands. Crowded conditions and inadequate facilities in the camps threatened health and well-being.[59] Once the worst problems were resolved, the next phase, as in Sarasota, was to establish trailer parks, offer police protection, and provide water and sewer facilities. Space and opportunities for recreation followed, which made their areas largely self-contained entities within, but not part of, the community. The Tin Can Tourists, on their part, were satisfied with their acceptance by the municipality. They did not seek social acceptance in Sarasota but retained their own identity.

One conclusion that emerged from this phenomenon had little precedent in the social fabric or the economy. Highway access was visibly overtaking rail access as a major tourist concern for Florida. Sarasota, astride the Tamiami Trail, was to benefit. Its boosters and officials had been calling for intercity roads since the first surveys for the Tamiami Trail were made in 1914.[60] The boom years helped state officials to abandon their indecision and to support Governor John Martin's drive for a road building program. During his administration, Florida advanced to rank twenty-seventh in the nation in its spending on roads and bridges in 1925. The Trail had shown little progress in its first decade. In 1916, the Highway Commission voted to change its route so that it followed the Gulf coast, rejecting the proposed eastern swing that would have taken it to Myakka and Arcadia farther inland.[61] Also in 1916, the Miami end of the Tamiami Trail was begun and in about a year was within sixty miles of Naples. Private interests in south Florida demanded faster action and were led by Barron G. Collier, whose immense landholdings were locked in without adequate road access.

Collier invested funds from his own millions for road building, but progress still lagged. Governor Martin took the Trail under state control in 1924. At Caples's invitation, Martin came to Venice, where he promised the railway brotherhood a completed Tampa-to-Miami highway in the following year.[62] In about eighteen months the road was opened. Ceremonies included the usual motorcade; about five hundred vehicles made the trip to Miami. At a meeting of the Tamiami Trail Association, John Ringling was elected president. The organization and its board had little function except publicity and promotion.[63]

The highway and the tourist influx helped to transform Sarasota into a more diffuse community. A new element found its place in the social order. The motor home tourists added several hundred winter visitors, and the number increased to nearly two thousand during the time of their annual gathering. Among the transients who passed through town on the new highway was a mysterious flow of high-powered motor cars—Stutz Bearcats, LaSalles, Pierce Arrows—that rushed bootleg booze from Key West to Chicago.

Outside Florida, several spectacular figures made exciting reading. Aimee Semple MacPherson was on trial in California for concocting a kidnapping story, with occasional fights in the courtroom and tears showering the witness stand. Daddy and Peaches Browning and the sensational Hall-Mills case added a measure of spice to daily news of Florida bank failures, bankrupt enterprises, and other less entertaining events nearer home.

The Teapot Dome scandal engulfed Harry F. Sinclair and former Secretary of the Interior Albert Fall. John Ringling and his nephew Richard had counted on Fall in 1921 to approve Crow tribal land oil leases, only to be outmaneuvered by richer, more powerful rivals whose claims had greater validity.

At the New York State Democratic Convention in September, Governor Alfred E. Smith was nominated for a fourth term, amid signs that he would soon be the party's choice for president. Sam Gumpertz was active as a speaker at the convention, for he and Ringling were ardent supporters of the governor, better known as "the happy warrior."

Back in Sarasota, the death of Charles Ringling on 3 December 1926 ended the forty-two-year collaboration of the Ringling brothers. Their unique concept of collective management had survived for more than forty years, lean and affluent ones alike. Charles had been ill for much of the year. For the first time in his life he had failed to travel with the circus for half the season. His short, final illness ended a long career with the circus to which he was passionately devoted and a later, brief career as a financier and builder in Sarasota.

For John Ringling, Charles's death marked the beginning of a new stage. He was alone in his command of the circus organization. Despite his great energy and abilities, the demands of his other ventures, added to his sole control of the circus, presented a formidable combination. He responded by increasing his reliance on hired managers to head the circus. He could not have known that a carefully contrived tax fraud had been in progress for several years and was to continue within the circus until it was exposed nearly a decade later after a two-year federal investigation.[64] By then nearly $4 million had disappeared. Such unscrupulous conduct, alien to the Ringling ethic, was one of the hazards of absentee ownership.

Charles Ringling never learned of the crime and its scandal. He died greatly respected for his remarkable skill in administering the circus organization with its volatile characters and frequent crises. Moreover, he was held in the warmest regard and even affection by a host of current and former performers and many hundreds of workers to whom he was always "Mr. Charley." John and Charles were often seen as competing with each other, but, as May Wirth, their greatest equestrian star, had discovered many years earlier, they competed to bring the best talent into their show. Their personalities were markedly different, but at no time were they estranged.[65] However they differed, they were wholly alike in maintaining the high standards that had been established when the five brothers organized in 1884. Those standards meant giving quality performances, maintaining a decent character in their entire enterprise, and letting no employee be cheated from a promised wage. While such standards might seem no more than routine in many industries, in the circus they were nothing less than astounding.

Sarasota's public mourning was a clear measure of its genuine sense of loss. On the day of Charles's funeral, banks, businesses, and city and county offices were closed, their flags at half-staff. The American Legion placed flags, again at half-mast, at intervals along city streets. In a profusion of eulogies, Charles Ringling was admired for his character and credited with his efforts to develop and advance the city and its quality of life. His death was the first among that active group of businesspeople who, from about 1910 when their influence first became visible, initiated and pressed forward the transformation of Sarasota. Unlike his brother John, he made no grand gestures; he was a prudent man, honest and dependable. He died peacefully with his fortune intact, secure in his splendid marble mansion, his image unscathed by adversity.

Whatever feelings the loss of Charles may have aroused in him, John did not share them with those around him. Probably only Mable and their sister, Ida, knew the true state of the relationship of the two brothers. A change in the last years had introduced a note of acrimony; the burden of running the unwieldy circus organization had fallen more heavily on Charles as John spent more time on his other burgeoning interests. Charles's resentment grew as his brother did less of the work but still maintained his domineering attitudes. This discord did not become public, although some in Sarasota and in the circus sensed the tensions below an amicable surface. The two adjoining mansions were equally splendid and costly, though totally unlike; the two yachts were nearly the same size. Circus profits were divided equally among the partners. John's name always seemed to gather the national and public acclaim, though Charles was more popular with the people of the circus and in Sarasota. Charles and Edith would not have been human if they had accepted the obscurity of second place without feeling some resentment.

Mable and Ida were surely aware of the moderating influence that Charles exerted upon his more volatile partner. John's overweening self-confidence was both an asset and a liability. Without Charles beside him, John was now *the* circus king. While Charles lived, John was shielded from the destructive forces of envy and jealousy. The signs of trouble were present, but John failed to see them. Throughout Charles's last day, John waited downstairs most of the day and was finally summoned to see his brother. Afterward, John crossed the wide lawns alone, past the house Charles and Edith had built for their daughter Hester on the site of the Thompson residence, to his Italian palace. At age sixty he was now the last of seven brothers.

Life in the Grand Manner

BY THE EARLY 1920s, the John Ringlings began to discover how delightful it was to be rich. At mid-decade, gains generated by Ringling Isles, Inc., started to replenish the initial large cash investments that had gone into the purchase and development of island properties. These gains added to the wealth that already flowed from various business interests in Sarasota, New York City, and Chicago. Much of the money still came from Oklahoma oil wells and, of course, from the circus.

For Mable and John Ringling, their pleasure in costly surroundings not only celebrated success in several business ventures beyond the circus but also marked their complete escape from the struggles of earlier years, now relegated to a dim reminder of life without wealth. Both Mable and John came from exceedingly modest homes. John certainly could not have forgotten the crowded cottage in McGregor, Iowa, and Baraboo, Wisconsin, where he had shared his childhood with Ida and Henry, the youngest members of the Ringling family.

John and Mable grew accustomed to living amid the trappings of wealth. Strangely, they surrounded themselves in greater splendor when traveling than when they were at home. A succession of private railway cars, richly appointed yachts, and uniformed chauffeurs and footmen provided the appearance of regal grandeur, yet the Ringlings' residences before 1926 were actually undistinguished. Even though the aging Sarasota house was gradually encircled with beautifully landscaped grounds, the house itself was old, comfortable, and unpretentious. Their estate at Alpine, New Jersey, shared a corner of its rose garden with the state police.[1] The Fifth Avenue apartment in New York City was basically a business convenience.[2] (When sold years later, its furnishings barely brought enough to pay the arrears of rent.[3]) In the mid-1920s Mable and John began seeking to increase the elegance of their surroundings. The fruits of this quest were soon visible in their palatial new home, Ca' d'Zan (in Venetian vernacular, "House of John"). To their earlier acquisitions they added an array of paintings, art objects, and jewels, which they had gathered on their extensive journeys or purchased in the salesrooms of New York and London.[4]

The Ringlings enjoyed their pursuit of pleasure and glittering display of wealth among the newly rich and beautiful people in the 1920s. Travel to Europe was essential, preferably aboard the socially prestigious ships, the *Mauritania* and the *Aquitania*. Each summer, the John Ringlings, the Charles Ringlings, and their neighbors, the Ralph Capleses, joined the ranks of first-class passengers bound across the Atlantic.

For many American travelers, the cosmopolitan life-styles, extravagant homes, and elegant possessions of Europe's noble and gentry classes offered a tantalizing model, if not an educational experience. Postwar Europe proffered new standards of aesthetic taste and fashion. Many of these trends were soon absorbed into diverse aspects of American culture, including architecture. Regional preferences emerged in the American rush to build homes that emulated styles seen in England, France, and Italy. While half-timbered English Tudor houses with oriel windows appealed to many in the North, Italian and Spanish Mediterranean-styled residences were favored in California and Florida.

Back in Florida, the grand but very private world of inherited wealth continued in its established patterns, lived out by a select few in their great houses and in the hotels on Palm Beach. Worldly travelers and some of the more notorious figures of the Prohibition era preferred to frequent Miami, with its greater panache and its proximity to Havana. The comparatively sleepy tempo of Sarasota attracted neither the widespread violence nor the serious corruption reported in other parts of the country.

After Berthe Palmer's death in 1918, no one from the world of high society journeyed to Sarasota—not that Mable and John desired to move in those social circles. Why should they risk the kind of rejection they had encountered in Tarpon Springs fifteen years earlier? Instead, John assumed an increasingly prominent role in the commercial and political development of Sarasota. His associates and friends expected him to transform the Ringling Isles, and thus Sarasota, into a huge, elegant resort that would rival anything the east coast of Florida could muster.[5] He pressed toward that goal with a zeal matched only by his commitment to the circus.

It became essential to the Ringlings that they cultivate a highly visible posture in local society. (Interestingly, one local resident observed that although John was often seen in the Ringling real estate offices and in downtown Sarasota, he spoke to everyone and talked with no one.) Friendly relations with local residents in business and banking circles were crucial to the progress of Ringling's affairs, the public approval of his plans, and securing the necessary financing for his buyers. The Ringlings began to entertain more extensively, and the need for more space to receive guests became evident. For some time they had dreamed of a grand new home to replace the old Thompson house. John wanted a mansion that would express the same qualities he saw in the great houses of Europe: power, wealth, and hospitality.[6]

The house that he built, Ca' d'Zan, eventually gained significance beyond its repute as the curiously ornate mansion of a rich showman. A certain kind of great house holds a lasting historical importance that stems from the life that took place within it, not merely the splendor of its appointments or its architecture. The new house would reflect his achievements and his aspirations as a money and power broker. Mable's interests, more limited than John's, focused on her home and the local society of Sarasota. Her wish for an Italian palace was to be gratified by the generous heart and open purse of her husband. Together, they

Ca' d'Zan under construction, May 1924. Owen Burns, the builder, noted that construction of the foundation had begun before plans were delivered from New York. Courtesy of Lillian Burns.

would create a great house, where they would assemble an almost continuous stream of guests, most of them useful to John in his soaring plans for Sarasota's future.

The Ringlings had gained a fair knowledge of what a great house should look like on their lengthy trips to Europe, particularly Italy. Their decorating tastes, never clearly defined, were influenced heavily by the aesthetics of seventeenth-century Italy, as demonstrated in their search for Italian architectural and sculptural pieces for St. Armands and the Ritz Carlton and the beginnings of their substantial art collection. The ornate, colorful decor of Venice and the architecture of Rome in the age of Bernini figured prominently in their preferences. The more restrained and excessively formal English adaptations of villas by Andrea Palladio lacked the warmth and rhythm that appeared to John and Mable. They found the proportions and grace of Venetian palazzos more suited to the location and kind of home they envisioned for themselves.

By definition, a Venetian-style residence must stand at the very edge of the water. And while John Ringling cared little for sailing and even less for sport fishing, Sarasota Bay itself was important to him. He once remarked to an interviewer, "Florida is a nice place. You ever been there? You ought to see it. Blue water, and green and lavender in the bay. Lovely at sundown. Beautiful light and air."[7] His staccato speech and waving cigar added emphasis to each image. The natural beauty of the bay and its barrier islands formed the foundation of his vision for Sarasota and defined his personal empire. The relation of the new house to the bay became a critical factor in the image that must impress itself upon visitors and friends. The *Sarasota Herald* predicted that it was to be the forerunner of scores of fine homes that would grace the shore of Sarasota Bay and the Gulf: "Some day Florida and the nation will awaken to the fact that Sarasota on the gulf is the most splendidly and aesthetically built city in America. Today we are but in the days of pioneers. It scarcely appears what is to be our future. But the erection of the beautiful home on Shell Beach gives us a slight intimation of it. It is the first glimpse of the morning's dawn of a new day. It will not be long until the full splendor of that day bursts on us and we shall see Sarasota in all her glory."[8]

The Ringlings wanted the new house to be built on the same site as their Palms Elysian home, which they had continually enhanced over the years with formal outdoor decorations, extensive plantings, and avenues for strolling.[9] The existing house had to be either torn down or relocated. They chose to move it to a spot close to where a guest cottage was later built. Once moved, the house was left to decay and crumble into ruin, not unlike an abandoned circus wagon. John Ringling had no interest in preserving the past.[10]

A balustraded seawall, connected by a short walk to the old house, already lined the bayfront. The construction of a new seawall, extending farther into the bay, would allow space for a terrace and a dock, even though only small boats could enter the shallows.[11]

The Ringlings' first requirement was that the house be large. Although John protested that he would be satisfied with a small place and that it was Mable who insisted on a grand one, his correspondence with Owen Burns revealed his intention to build a "pretentious house."[12]

When he demurred at the projected cost, it was not the price of the house but the fee for an architect's services that he found excessive.[13]

The new home was a long time in the planning stage. In the summer of 1923, when they were staying at Alpine, New Jersey, Mable was ready to have architectural plans drawn. During that summer, she discussed her ideas with a New York architect who frankly admitted that he wanted the job so he could spend the winter in Florida for his health. Interviews in Sarasota with the father-and-son architectural team of Thomas and Frank Martin left Mable doubtful that the Martins could meet their needs. Still undecided, Ringling asked Owen Burns to make additional enquiries. Meanwhile, John sent messages to Frank Martin. Since the Ringling home would be an imposing structure, might he be willing to reduce his rate to get this important commission?[14] In plain words, Ringling wanted to know, "What is the lowest commission fee you will accept?"[15] Burns learned that Martin was more than eager to obtain the commission, but he refused to accept the blatant request for a reduced fee. The standard fee of 5 percent was not negotiable.[16]

When questioned about Martin's abilities, Burns evaded a direct response. He noted that the Ringlings had interviewed Frank Martin on several occasions and should be able to judge for themselves.[17] Mable made a hurried trip to Sarasota, and the discussions ended. Ringling abruptly rejected Martin's terms.[18]

Eventually the Ringlings wisely decided to put their trust in Dwight James Baum, a popular and highly successful architect whose portfolio of fashionable but thoroughly conventional residences attested to his ability to please rich clients. Known for his versatility, Baum had demonstrated great ability in several styles, ranging from English Tudor to adaptations of villas from the Italian Renaissance.[19] One of the more successful eclectics of his time, Baum did not try to be innovative. He was at his best when he served clients who wanted a fine home but not one so original that it might startle their neighbors. These clients, including the John Ringlings, could not have afforded the monumental splendor that was created for the super-rich by such earlier firms as McKim, Mead and White.[20]

The Ringlings brought more enthusiasm than knowledge to the task of selecting a design for Ca' d'Zan. Intellectually, both were products of

Aerial view of Ca' d'Zan under construction, 1925. The island in foreground was formed from sand dredged by Owen Burns to create a yacht channel for John and Charles Ringling's yachts. Courtesy of Sarasota County Department of Historical Resources.

their time and the culture in which they lived. They were unlikely to break with the 1920s and to demand an authentic reproduction of an earlier taste in architecture. At about the time when designs for Ca' d'Zan were complete and the building was underway, new and more sophisticated influences were creating major changes in John's ideas and perhaps Mable's as well. Albert Keller and his friend Julius Böhler, the Munich art dealer, helped them to make the great leap in imagination that became visible in the contrasting architecture of the art museum just three years later.

Baum's work on Ca' d'Zan clearly showed a highly professional approach to building American homes with a European air. Matlack Price (one of Baum's associates), in his analysis of Baum's work, stated his views: "Our houses, seldom attempting scholarly accuracy in their renderings of European precedent, are adaptations and as such should fairly and properly be called 'types.'" Baum's practice, he said, was to build a house that "in plan, methods of construction, in materials and in interior equipment is as different from an Italian villa as it is from an Eskimo's igloo."[21] In effect, Baum constructed American residences that merely appeared Italian on the exterior. He quite correctly judged that a truly Italian style would be wholly unsuited both to the climate of North America and to the culture of its people.

In designing the Ringling mansion, Baum and his assistants, Lyman Dixon and Earl Purdy, essentially modernized a mid-nineteenth-century tradition that had infiltrated American taste from England. In domestic architecture, the stately Italian Renaissance villa captured the imagination of architects and clients alike. The more lavishly ornamented Italian Renaissance palace became popular for public buildings. Still another style, Victorian Gothic, was added to this mélange, with further embellishments popularized by aesthetician John Ruskin, who had a fascination with Venetian Gothic. Numerous American structures, some dating to the middle of the nineteenth century, were adaptations of these Italian models and thus were clearly dated by the aesthetic preferences of their time. Stanford White once refused a commission to reproduce the Doge's Palace for a client. Another architect, Peter B. Wright, inspired by Ruskin, designed a version of that famous Venetian palace and as a result received the commission to design a new building to house the National Academy of Design in New York City.[22]

Baum had ample opportunity to study examples of all these styles. After a trip to Italy in 1924, he began to utilize the Italian villa in his own designs. In the mid-1920s, during Sarasota's building boom, his work advanced an architectural movement toward Italian- and Spanish-style construction. Several of Baum's Mediterranean-inspired buildings in Sarasota were recognized for their restrained exterior decoration.[23] In contrast, he produced for the outer walls of Ca' d'Zan an unusual decorative scheme of brightly colored glazed tiles that was never copied in his later commissions.[24]

Baum's ultimate design for Ca' d'Zan proved more authentic than some of his modified Italian villas in the Riverdale suburb of New York City. Whereas his northern clients desired the grace and charm of an Italian villa, they also intended to utilize their homes in a thoroughly domestic manner. Mable Ringling, however, demanded the added feature of a palatial appearance, in scale and decoration as well as in exterior design. The general style and structure of her house would not essentially differ from the villas she had seen in Tuscany. In this major respect, her home was unique among those Baum designed, and it ranked among the important houses of that day because of its novel features.

Mable Ringling may have had little knowledge of architectural traditions, but she was instinctively moved by her love of the beautiful houses she discovered in Italy. Moreover, she was building a home, not a museum or a copy of any historic building. The house was already under construction before the Ringling collection of Venetian and Florentine paintings was seriously begun and was not designed to house the collection, as might be surmised. The specifications were determined by Baum's own perception of what suited the Florida climate and the special features and circumstances required of a house placed almost at the water's edge.[25] He also planned it as a winter home; hence, there was a greater provision for light and sun than in a year-round residence. He included in the final design extensive areas of window and little blank wall space for hanging works of art.

In the exterior of Ca' d'Zan, he merged two distinct types of Italian architecture: the elaborate detail of Venetian Gothic and the irregular, asymmetrical outline of the Italian country villa. To achieve a harmonious combination he emphasized separately the Gothic and villa styles in the design of the west and east fronts. On the west (appropriately, the water side), the building's central block has a fully detailed Venetian facade. The tall, pointed arches on the first floor and a series of smaller, ogival windows above are characteristic of many palazzos on the Grand Canal. In contrast, on the east front as seen from the entrance drive, outlines of a series of rectangles break the long facade into six areas. A tower, the mark of an Italian villa, stands prominently on the east side and recedes when viewed from the west. By the careful and uniform use

Entrance to Ca' d'Zan, designed by Dwight James Baum of New York and
Sarasota, c. 1927. Courtesy of Henry Ringling North.

of decorative detail, Baum retained the essential unity of the whole,
balancing the west and east fronts to convey a single impression.[26]

Each striking feature of the house's exterior was devised to herald the
power and wealth of its proud owner. Guests would arrive at Ca' d'Zan
by an impressive approach. The long avenue of palms adorned with
statues and urns was calculated to heighten the impact of elegance.
Dwight Baum fashioned an exterior design with that most desirable of
all features: it pleased his clients.[27] Ironically, Baum and his staff were
never certain that they had produced a house of true architectural
beauty. While they sensed that Ca' d'Zan reflected a contemporary
American trend in its pursuit of novelty, the house embodied few actual
innovations.[28] Its size, shape, and floor plan were thoroughly conventional for a mansion of its style and elegance.

Ten years later, Baum said that he had worked on the creation and
execution of this house for several years and that he regarded it as an
important achievement.[29] But at the time it was built, his feelings were
ambivalent. Perhaps he was uncertain about the reaction of his peers.
He may also have believed that certain economies he was forced to
observe had compromised the entire concept. Although such publica-

tions as the British monthly *Country Life* gave feature space to the house, Baum never publicized the Ringling commission; he did not include it in a published collection of his Florida designs.

Baum began his commission under the popular assumption that Ringling, whom he scarcely knew, was an immensely rich man. Only after his work was well along and a general configuration of the house plan was presented to his client did Baum discover that Ringling's fortune was not limitless. Parts of the plan were too expensive. The structure could not be as large as originally intended. Ca' d'Zan records do not reveal how much was deleted to save money, but the unexpected need to economize clearly deprived Baum of satisfaction and pride in his achievement.

Mable could contribute little to the exterior design of her new home, but the interior was another matter altogether. She had definite ideas about the creation of a gilded backdrop before which guests and friends could enjoy the leisurely, gentle dance of social mingling in surroundings of the extravagant style favored by the newly rich of the 1920s. She differed with Baum and his staff on many points and was never intimidated by his professional training and experience. The changes she demanded were made. The living room Baum commissioned became a large foyer; the interior patio became the court/living room; and the billiard room disappeared, making the ballroom spacious as well as beautiful with its Asian teak floor. A useless balcony and loggia on the bay side were removed, incorporating the Venetian facade directly into the structure of the court.[30] The glancing light of the bay could now reflect the colors of the stained-glass windows on the white marble of the floor.

In the end, compromises on the functions and arrangement of the ground floor rooms minimized the early design's worst features. An aura of dignified wealth remained but in a way that was neither forbidding nor ponderous. At the same time the house gained real distinction by the extension of the seawall to make room for a huge terrace, paved in varied Italian marbles. In sum, Baum created in Ca' d'Zan the effect of life in the grand manner on a scale that provided space without overwhelming a small company of family, friends, and acquaintances.

The house was designed for expansive hospitality, proclaimed by the arrangement of the rooms. Unlike the country houses of England and the palaces of Europe, it contains only "state apartments" for entertaining. Separate areas for family use do not exist. The entire house was laid out for the convenient movement and comfortable entertainment of numerous guests. At Mable's direction, exotic birds and seascapes were painted on the inside of closet doors in the guest rooms to surprise and amuse her guests.

Only the court or living room is actually imposing in size, yet it does not dwarf guests or furnishings. In place of an arcaded corridor on the upper level, as in a Venetian palazzo, Baum included a cantilevered balcony, which relieved the appearance of excessive height. All the other first-floor rooms were scaled to human proportions, a feature that compensated for the formality of the entire house. The unpretentious size of these rooms is noteworthy. John Ringling, essentially a private person, favored small gatherings. Although Mable was apparently given complete freedom to plan their home, she did so with John's preferences well in mind.[31]

When plans were at last agreed upon, Baum sent his assistants, Lyman Dixon and Earl Purdy, to work with Owen Burns as the structure began to rise on the site of the old house.[32] In the planning stages, Mable was the one who negotiated with the architects. Once construction was under way, Ringling was persistent in his attention to the smallest details. He sent a stream of telegrams loaded with questions and peremptory orders addressed to Burns.

Ringling, Baum, and Burns agreed that the entire structure—foundation, floors, walls, and attic roof—would be built of masonry. A minimal amount of wood was specified throughout. Even the teak floor in the ballroom was screwed to a concrete base. One exception, the ceiling of the court, was constructed from pecky cypress below a steel frame. The cypress was calculated to withstand heat and moisture for many decades. Robert Webb, the decorator, stenciled figures from Venice's past in dim colors on the cypress ceiling. To compensate for the lack of framing, walls were built from hollow clay tiles. Stone would have been authentic for a Venetian home, but its massive weight would probably have posed a risk so close to the water's edge on sandy soil. Besides being fireproof and lighter than stone, the tiles were of a density that repelled moisture, and they were easily covered with plaster on the inside and stucco on the outside. After putting in the foundations, Burns worked rapidly. Work progressed night and day as an oversize concrete mixer maintained a continuous pour of concrete. Such large pours of concrete were not altogether new in Sarasota. A similar "monolithic" pour, free from seams and their inherent weaknesses, had been employed in pouring the floors for the Mira Mar Hotel a year earlier. However, poured concrete walls such as those of the massive lower level of Ca' d'Zan's tower were perhaps the first used locally.[33]

An enormous amount of glazed, brightly colored terra cotta was featured in the extensive decoration of the interior and exterior, the most spectacular being in the cornice of the great hall, on the walls of the gate house, and on the tower belvedere. Mable had seen terra cotta utilized in this way in Italy. Quite by chance, she discovered the exact type of tile she wanted on the walls of St. Bonaventure's Monastery in Buffalo, New York. Only one other building in the nation possessed similar tile work: the West Side YMCA in New York City. Ca' d'Zan thus became the third. After a lengthy search, Mable located the producer, O. W. Ketchum of Crum Lynne, near Philadelphia. She summoned Dwight Baum to the plant to observe the process of baking tiles and to settle specifications for making them.

Careful research into Venetian architecture preceded the final drawings for the house. Mable collected masses of sketches and drawings and Baum added still more notes to her file following his research trip to Venice. Sketches from Baum's office show the front and bayside facades much as they were finally built. By incorporating the artistic devices of a fourteenth-century adaptation of Byzantine and Gothic architectural styles, Baum produced a striking resemblance between the west, or bayfront, side of Ca' d'Zan and two Venetian landmarks: the famed Ca' d'Oro and the canal view of the Bauer Grunwald Hotel.[34] There are also reminders of Venice's Hotel Danielli in Baum's interior design. Equally striking is the similarity between the house's entrance and that of the Arrowhead Inn in Riverdale, New York, which Baum designed at about the same time as the Ringling home.

An astonishing amount of detail is on the exterior of the house. Lending authenticity to the balconies and the balustrade of the dra-

Belvedere atop the tower at Ca' d'Zan. Longboat Key is in the background, 1927. Courtesy of Henry Ringling North.

matic terrace are carefully executed but inconspicuous colonettes, or little columns, derived from the fourteenth century. Specific features, such as the corner window on the second floor, came directly from models found in Venice. And, as in many Venetian homes, lower floor windows, nearly square in shape, are guarded by strong iron bars.

Pierced copings on the roof facing the bay imitate those of Ca' d'Oro and its greater precedent, the Doge's Palace. Even the wall that hides the service area is mounted by a decorated coping that was closely duplicated from several dating from the fourteenth century.[35] The small bas-relief figures in poured stone are emblems of Venice—crowned seahorses entwined in pairs—arranged with acorns and oak leaves to signify male strength and courage. Small urns in bas relief filled with fruit echo the themes of hospitality and welcome in the larger, gaily colored vessels of glazed terra cotta that adorn the walls above.

Perhaps excessively generous with decoration, Baum exercised restraint in avoiding unnecessary structural detail. He added no portico or porte cochere to mar the east facade, even though they were status symbols in American homes. He also placed the tower off center, showing disregard both for Victorian symmetry and for the rural Italian preference for locating the tower directly at a corner. This decision has been attributed to Mable's sudden impulse to copy the Spanish tower of the old Madison Square Garden, but the tower actually resembles a type found in many Italian villas of the 1800s.[36]

As a prominent feature of an Italian country house, the tower once stood as a warning that a defending force of retainers resided therein. Long since a purely decorative feature, the tower still distinguished a home of wealth and status; campaniles were incorporated into Osborne House for Queen Victoria and Prince Albert. At Ca' d'Zan the tower retained certain functional as well as decorative purposes. Baum realized that the true Italian villa reserved all its points of interest for the interior and showed virtually blank walls to the passerby. Placing the tower on the east front helped to relieve the potentially monotonous 200-foot facade. He also covered the walls of the tower with colored terra cotta tiles arranged in a diagonal, or diaper, pattern authentic to Venice. Without this lavish decoration, which might have seemed excessive mounted on a smaller structure, the entire appearance of the mansion would have been too severe. Ca' d'Zan's purpose—to express outside as well as within the charm of an enchanted time and place— would have been obscured.

Like the rest of the house, the tower was virtually fireproof, with its thick concrete base and terra cotta tiles.[37] In the 1920s, electrical and bottled gas systems were still dangerously unreliable, and fire remained a constant risk for homes located far from municipal firefighting facilities. Every precaution was taken to reduce the risk of fire in the mansion. The threat of ocean storms and hurricanes presented still another danger. Few Sarasota residents had forgotten the destruction of the 1921 hurricane that battered the Florida coast. Should the rest of the house be damaged by a similar storm, the tower was a five-story fortress that seemed sure to withstand any challenge. The third-floor vault within the tower's twenty-inch-thick walls was thought to be storm-proof. Behind a massive steel door, hidden by a false wall, there was space for the more valuable objects of the household: liturgical objects and other fine works of art from the Emile Gavet collection, Mable's jewelry with her collection of unset cameos, and John's collection of wines and spirits.

The interior decoration and furnishing of Ca' d'Zan were handled by the Ringlings themselves. No hired decorator devised a plan for a consistent style or color scheme. John and Mable's taste in colors focused on red and gold. They purchased all their furniture at auctions following the dissolution of many of New York's exquisitely appointed mansions of the 1880s and 1890s. John Ringling had a lingering affection for the elegance of seventeenth- and eighteenth-century Europe, perhaps gained from his association with Stanford White, who had gathered innumerable treasures for the homes of his clients.

Other items were obtained from salesrooms and auction houses in New York, Venice, and Rome. After the excitement of bidding had passed, some purchases were difficult to justify. For example, Mable bought an enamel telephone valued at ten dollars at the George Jay Gould sale at Georgian Court. Her winning bid was seventy-five dollars. She emerged the heaviest buyer at the sale.[38]

The result of these frequent excursions to sales and auctions was a miscellany. A few of Mable's purchases were antiques, but most were reproductions. Some were stored for years, awaiting a new home. The New York apartment and the house at Alpine, New Jersey, overflowed with the tapestries and furnishings that accumulated. Ca' d'Zan was soon filled to overflowing, conveying a thoroughly 1920s appearance.

The formal dining room's dark paneling, composed primarily of walnut, walnut veneers, and pine, cannot be traced to any original home. The carvings decorating the panels have been attributed to a wood carver from Baraboo.[39] The dining table with fifteen leaves obviously came from a much larger room, one with space for a table of such extraordinary size. The twenty-four chairs were part of the Emile Gavet collection. These chairs are distinguished by the eighteenth-century machine-made embroidery that decorated the red velvet covers. An imposing console table, twelve feet in length with a veined black marble top and heavy gilded base, served as a buffet here or in the family dining room. Ringling bought it in 1924 at a sale of George Crocker's effects held at Mahwah, New Jersey.[40] Before the art galleries were built, some of the finer works of art were hung at Ca' d'Zan. Over the dining room mantel hung the *Portrait of General Benvenuti* by Giovanni Battista Moroni. A portrait of Dona Mariana of Austria, second wife of Philip IV of Spain, attributed to Velázquez, was placed at the dining room's entrance from the foyer.

Typical of the 1920s, the ground floor rooms were filled with a fashionable surfeit of splendor; the ballroom best exemplified Mable's own tastes. Its teak floor was protected with a large antique oriental rug, predominantly mauve with red figures. Walls finished in troweled plaster were a light biscuit color, which enhanced the tapestry hung across the entire length of one wall. Dark venetian blinds and heavy red silk drapes screened the room's six windows. Gilded or Venetian-glass framed mirrors adorned the walls. A pair of seven-light candelabra, each towering more than eight feet in height, illuminated the room.

Mounted in the panels of the ballroom ceiling were *Dancers of the Nations,* a series of paintings on canvas created by Willy Pogany in his New York studio and sent to Sarasota for installation. Pogany commented that the colorful and sometimes humorous dancing couples, representing more than twenty cultures and times, were all moving to the same rhythm.[41] The diverse figures positioned within the ceiling's gold leaf framework immediately suggest Pogany's avocation as an illustrator of children's books. He was perhaps better known as a set designer for the Metropolitan Opera and for Ziegfeld productions.

To complement this festive mood, arranged around the room were a settee, six armchairs, and two matching stools, all gilded and upholstered in a red-and-cream brocade. A three-panel folding screen with a gilt frame, brocade and tapestry panels, and a round insert of beveled glass was placed near the arched entrance from the reception room.[42] Such screens were in fashion, and Mable was fond of them and used them throughout the house. Some were made of fine tapestry and needlepoint work in heavy carved frames.

Another purchase of some interest was the furniture in Ringling's bedroom. Dwight Baum mistakenly recalled seeing a report that documented it as belonging to Emperor Napoleon III at Fontainebleau. Whatever its origins, Ringling bought the ponderous suite of Empire furniture at an auction in New York. Napoleon's suite now belongs to the palace of Malmaison in Paris.

Baum later said that Ringling paid $35,000 for the nine pieces, which were of French manufacture. In 1938, the appraisers valued it at $50,000. Since Ringling spent much of the day in this room, he must have enjoyed its kingly style, down to the gilded crown mounted at the head of his bed. The huge sofa was well proportioned for his 250-pound frame; in his later years, after his stroke, he only felt comfortable sitting in the small armless chair, resting his arm on a cushion. According to Baum's estimates in 1937, the furnishings for Ca' d'Zan cost the Ringlings about $400,000, excluding paintings and tapestries. He included in that figure the cost of the ceilings decorated by Pogany and Robert Webb. Without knowing which pictures and tapestries remained in the house in 1937, Baum wisely refused to estimate the total value for the estate.[43]

❧ John and Mable continued to entertain guests while the house was being built. The old house, on its new site, was provided with amenities, but guests were more often housed on the *Zalophus*, away from the noise and confusion of construction. Two prominent New Yorkers were among their visitors in early 1926. Mayor Jimmy Walker, the quintessence of the sophisticated New Yorker, stayed for several days, accompanied by a large party of newsmen. The mayor, Ralph Caples, and Ringling were scheduled to arrive at the city pier from St. Petersburg in the early evening of 22 March 1926. Dense fog delayed the yacht by almost three hours. By then, the band and most of the reception party to greet Mayor Walker had given up and left the pier. Walker declared on arrival that having viewed the beauties of the bay and islands, he intended to buy property in Sarasota for a winter home. The mayor was referring to fog-shrouded land belonging to the Ringling Isles Corporation.[44]

Another esteemed visitor who stayed on the *Zalophus* was Edward F. Albee, owner of the B. F. Keith circuit of vaudeville theaters and a widely known investor in the field of live entertainment. His vocation perhaps did not altogether impress Sarasotans, but in the exotic world of theater stars and entertainers he was indeed an important figure. Albee echoed Mayor Walker's sentiments in answer to a reporter's question about his reaction to Sarasota's beauty and added that John Ringling's "vision and construction work are doing more toward making Florida's gulf coast the beauty spot of the world and Sarasota an international port of call, than any other individual." His remarks about Mable's work on the new home sounded more sincere: "She is a genius in planning, building, and furnishing the most beautiful home in America as she is doing."[45]

Like Albee, Ringling ranked among the true professionals of the entertainment field, including the motion picture industry, who had attained wealth and status. His business acquaintances from New York City politics and the world of big name entertainment filled the social strata he knew and understood best. This nascent class of rich Americans responded positively to the promise and potential of Sarasota. In them, Ringling saw a ready market just waiting to be tapped. Florida was the *in* place to be, before Americans discovered the French Riviera. These people wanted to enjoy the sports, warm winters, and undiscovered beaches of Florida but in surroundings that conveyed an air of luxury and affluence. His island empire at Sarasota could offer visitors and buyers precisely that combination of attractions: romantic, exhilarating Florida without the closed society of Palm Beach or the overly popular appeal of Miami. His misfortune was that this dream was all too soon shattered by events that were approaching.

Just as he and his brothers put together their unrivaled tent shows, Ringling was setting out to assemble the components he needed to entice buyers and rich hotel guests to come to Sarasota. Ca' d'Zan formed an important element in his perception both of himself and of his status in the community. It served as the stage setting for his role as the great developer of Florida's western shore, the nearest thing to Henry Flagler and Addison Mizner the Gulf coast had ever seen. To borrow a phrase from England's Blenheim Palace, Ca' d'Zan was Sarasota's greatest house for its greatest man.[46] For three winter seasons, the Ringlings' life in Sarasota pivoted around this grand mansion.

In addition to the spectacle of its novel architecture and opulent furnishings, Ca' d'Zan held a meaning that only John Ringling could savor. To him, this house represented ultimate success. He not only overcame his unpromising start to become an admired figure of national repute, but he was also the proud owner of the most magnificent residence in a growing city he was helping to build. Opinions about the house have differed widely as the years have passed. A. E. Austin, the museum's first director, was uncertain what his professional and artistic friends might say, so he retreated into quoting opinions voiced by others. Some, he said, found the house ludicrous, even laughable. By contrast, Hugh F. McKean, president of Rollins College and a member of the state-appointed board named to survey the museum, once said of Ca' d'Zan, "The total effect inspires interest, fascination, admiration, and awe."[47]

After the Boom

LIKE MANY ANOTHER Florida community, Sarasota found that municipal growth slowed, then halted with astonishing finality in 1926. The heady excitement of the boom days vanished. In its place came a disquieting sense of uncertainty. The experience of a continually rising real estate market over several years left the people of Florida wholly unprepared when prices fell. The prices of Sarasota city lots dropped to sums that were low even before the boom. The collapse of real estate prices stopped the growth of many newly expanded Florida settlements. The receding economic tide took with it much of the out-of-state capital that was sustaining local growth. Numerous bank failures and losses forecast the national depression that was soon to come.

Sarasota faced an unpalatable dilemma. Shortfall from unpaid or uncollectible taxes on hundreds of properties demanded immediate retrenchment on city and county budgets. Yet the impact of such actions could lead to still greater losses by depressing the incentives for tourist and winter visitor seasons. A citizens' budget committee headed by Owen Burns recommended a drastic 40 percent reduction for Sarasota's 1927 city budget.[1] To a city that had been dreaming of a great ocean port and a magnificent metro-resort, this was a harsh dose of reality, in spite of the forced optimism of official and press publicity. Moreover, it was feared that the departure of the speculators coupled with the wide path of destruction caused by the September hurricane would lead to a decline in tourism. Two intensely interested partisans, Florida's governor and the chairman of the Seaboard Airline Railroad, hastened to publish full-page newspaper advertisements. Northern readers were assured that storm damage positively would not interfere with their pleasure visits to Florida. However, some of the magic was gone. The reality that emerged showed Florida to be less than perfect, and, like other regions, no less prone to the follies of humankind and the aberrations of nature.

The established corps of winter residents were not part of the problem. They saw no reason to abandon their usual practice of passing the winter months at their Florida homes, particularly on the Gulf coast, where storm damage was less severe. In addition, the anticipated losses in the transient tourist business did not materialize. The seasons of 1926–27 and 1927–28 were among the best ever. There were, indeed, some lasting gains from the less frenzied aspects of the boom. Sarasota now offered tourists new, attractive resort hotels—the Mira Mar and Owen Burns's El Vernona—as well as several smaller ones. Ringling's Lido gave pleasure to the beachgoers. A sense of equilibrium returned to Sarasota with its area reduced to an appropriate size. Locally, the Sarasota Chamber of Commerce, headed by Charles Ringling until his death in December 1926, tried to interest investors in the city's potential for growth. But a city without industry other than the building trades could not provide alternate employment to the workers displaced by the boom's collapse.

In these same seasons, Ringling's Ca' d'Zan and its Byzantine splendor seemed to upstage its owner. A procession of social, business, and entertainment figures came almost every week to the new Ringling home, adding well-known names to the roster of Sarasota's winter visitors. Through their newly adopted share of civic and social activities coupled with the substantial investments of John and Charles, the Ringling colony became firmly established in the small circle of Sarasota's social elite. Thanks especially to Owen Burns and the Ringlings, the city changed materially in appearance. It now housed a larger business-

The Worcester mansion (1912) on Bird Key in Sarasota Bay, purchased by John Ringling in 1922. Ida Ringling North later made her home here until her death in 1950. Courtesy of John McCarthy.

commercial class, yet the traditional social order changed little. Most of the newcomers found a social niche that did not quite reach into the invitation lists of the older, affluent families. The lines were more visible in the evening. Whereas the afternoon social life of bridge and woman's club activities embraced a larger circle, evening entertaining in Sarasota's homes tended to be less open to newer residents.

That well-established social pattern probably helped Sarasota survive the social pressures of the boom without losing its character or reputation, established over the years. Neither the accelerated expansion in the 1920s nor the more restrained growth in the previous decade seemed to alter the framework of Sarasota society. An enduring character of southern life, which began with a strong Methodist influence, continued into the post–World War I stage of resort development. Patterns were too firmly fixed to be overturned by the infusion of a new moderately affluent population. The richest winter residents continued to be best known for their generous philanthropy. Their wealth was not reflected in a conspicuous life-style, but rather in its restraint. Since these families chose not to be social leaders, the patterns of Sarasota society continued to be those favored by the local elite. They were

Crescent Beach, Siesta Key, Sarasota, connected to the mainland by a bridge in 1917. Siesta was the only island accessible by automobile until 1926. Courtesy of John McCarthy.

joined by winter visitors who enjoyed the life of a quiet resort. Sarasota was not forced to compete with the glitter of the east coast resorts, for its attractions brought a winter and tourist population who liked its more restrained character.

At the worker's end of the social scale, conditions were less favorable. The end of the boom meant the end of employment for many. The largest single employer was John Ringling. The threat of hard times offered a challenge to Ringling, who was often at his best when large, dramatic gestures were called for. He would have to come up with some elaborate schemes to revitalize the local economy, in which he, more than anyone else, held a material interest.

By the standards of his day, Ringling was a rich man, but despite popular misconceptions he did not have uncommitted millions at his command. He did have intangible, personal assets of good will and repute built up over the years, which could now be drawn upon. He had access to circles where financial decisions were made. As a businessman who headed nearly a dozen enterprises, he had respectability among financiers. He was briefly a director of the Chatham and Phoenix Na-

Sarasota waterfront, c. 1927. The Sunset Apartments, remodeled by Mable Ringling from the former Yacht and Automobile Club, are in the background. The private dock of the apartments shows John Ringling's two yachts, *Zalophus* and *Zalophus, Jr.* Note the collapsed seawall on Golden Gate Point (upper left) after 1926 hurricane. Courtesy of Florida State Archives.

tional Bank in New York.[2] Among financiers, his rail, oil, and real estate holdings counted for more than the circus. A seat on the board, even in a minor bank, conveyed a status that no circus, however large, could equal. As evidenced by history, a circus was one of the most fragile of enterprises. Nearly every circus ended sooner or later on the auction block. After forty years on the road, the Ringling circus was still a big moneymaker, giving John a substantial income; but his other, more stable interests gave him status.

The increasing pressures of Ringling's expanding Sarasota interests forced some changes in his routines. The pattern that he had followed in recent years was to winter in Sarasota; in summer, circus business found him in New York or Alpine, or on trips to Europe. In 1927 he found it necessary to make frequent trips to and from New York to consult with attorneys and bankers. On other occasions, a number of Sarasotans made the journey to meet with him in New York—so urgent was the need to talk with him that even the telephone was not near enough.

A significant change in this way of life emerged over several years, implicit in his decision to make Sarasota the personal focus of his business interests. For over forty years, Ringling had been accumulating hundreds of acquaintances—government and political figures, functionaries, officials, sports and entertainment promoters, financiers—a rich cross-section of the nation's social and economic life. Each individual was reminded of him as he sent out several hundred New Year greetings.[3] The lists of names for telegraphed greetings represented a band that reached from New York to Los Angeles. When Ringing began to devote his capital and energy to Sarasota, his circle of contacts became smaller as his travels about the country became less frequent.

The consequences of Ringling's absence from the circus did not become manifest for several years. Shuttling between New York and Sarasota, he attempted to manage the circus singlehandedly, a task five brothers had once shared. In the circumstances, it is remarkable that he survived so long without serious challenge. The results of his divided attention were disastrous. In time, he lost the confidence of several key staff members, who then joined his adversaries. For several years, he was assisted in his convoluted financial deals by Richard Fuchs, his

Main Street, Sarasota, Armistice Day parade, c. 1920. Courtesy of Sarasota County Department of Historical Resources.

harried aide and confidant. Ringling unwisely failed to bind his loyalty.[4] Ringling's excessive demands and peremptory manner, combined with an appearance of ungrateful indifference, exasperated Fuchs, who not only quit but accepted an offer from Ringling's creditors in the Prudence Bond Company.

All of these actions lay in the future and were an unfortunate result of Ringling's personal nature. He did not properly appreciate that a man in his position needs the loyalty of close associates. But Ringling was incapable of seeing the value of such gestures. In the near future, this flaw would be fatal to his career.

Ringling was immersed in his own plans for Sarasota. In 1927 the prospects were dim, but scarcely alarming. The heightened activity of 1922–26 had made a substantial improvement in the appearance of Sarasota. Land was cleared, roads and facilities extended, even the mosquitoes were less of a menace, thanks to newly drained areas that were improved during the boom days.

In early 1927, Ringling, Caples, Gumpertz, and others pressured some of their capitalist friends to show support and confidence that

The Sarasota municipal pier and arcade building. Ringling purchased the bond issue to finance the new pier; *Zalophus* is at left, Charles Ringling's *Symphonia* at right. Courtesy of Sarasota County Department of Historical Resources, Stanley Bartlett Collection.

would help to reverse the flight of investors and builders from Sarasota. New York bankers were invited to visit Ca' d'Zan and cruise on the *Zalophus*. Ringling's own immediate need, fast becoming critical, was to prevent a debacle in his island kingdom. Backers for the stranded Ritz Carlton could still rescue the ill-fated hotel, but its stalled appearance was a formidable obstacle to investor interest. The stoppage at the hotel was damaging the image of the entire Ringling Isles concept.

The Sarasota Building Exchange—composed of resident real estate people casting about for help in any form—voted to draft Ringling into a civic office. The Chamber of Commerce needed a president to fill the post, vacant since Charles Ringling's death, and Ringling accepted. In 1927, the Chamber of Commerce needed influence among outside investors, and influence was something that Ringling had. Perhaps his influence was less than his local supporters believed, but still he had access to investors with financial resources. There were richer people in Sarasota, such as the Paynes and the Selbys, but none who were active in the business community or who possessed the name recognition that Ringling enjoyed.

Most of the new development money to restart Sarasota's building trades would have to come from outside, from conventional moneylending sources. Ringling and his colleagues made several attempts to revive the moribund real estate market. Ringling and Gumpertz brought their Prudence Bond Company friends from New York to see for themselves that Sarasota was still a viable entity. Prudence officers traveled to Sarasota in their private car, aptly named *Advance,* and were hosted on arrival by the Gumpertz and Ringling households. The quid pro quo came almost at once. From their New York offices Prudence Bond Company announced its great faith in the future of Sarasota. The company promised to demonstrate that faith by financing mortgages. But there was a qualifying phrase: Prudence would finance mortgages only for buyers of lots in the Ringling Isles.[5]

A more conventional group of financiers arrived next. They came as a result of influence exerted by Sarasota's Chamber of Commerce, especially Ringling and Caples (who had been nominated as a member of the national board of directors for the Chamber). Following a directors' meeting in Havana, they were persuaded to make a brief stopover at Sarasota, where they were given VIP treatment.[6] A similar effort was arranged for the nation's realtors, who had convened in Miami; a motorcade from Fort Myers brought 375 of them to Sarasota. The *Sarasota Herald* saw in these visits a resurgence of confidence in the city. (However, their description of the Prudence Bond Company as one of the most substantial and wealthiest in the United States suggests blatant flattery or a lack of knowledge.)[7]

An exciting diversion from the recessionist economy now appeared on the scene. Oil was fast becoming a magic word in Florida. In the Sarasota area many residents conceived great expectations of riches from the encouraging reports of experienced oilmen and of others who were not.[8] The investor-promoters avoided publicity, preferring to have one spokesman, a professional oilman. Kenneth Hauer, president of the

Owen Burns (left) and Dwight James Baum in the court of the Burns office building, 1927. The building and adjacent El Vernona Hotel were designed by Baum, also the architect of John Ringling's home, the county courthouse, and other structures in Sarasota and Tampa. Courtesy of Lillian Burns.

Associated Gas and Oil Company and head of the Biscayne Oil Company of Miami, was engaged to oversee the arrangements for exploration and drilling. Hauer answered all questions by saying that until drilling was accomplished, no one could tell if oil was or was not present. Yet he followed such cautions with renewed assurances of geologists' favorable opinions.[9] He soon had the whole city in a new fever even more exciting than the land boom.

Participants in the oil venture included Ringling, Owen Burns, and J. H. Lord, joined by the Palmer interests. They were quietly backing the venture, meeting costs estimated at between $45,000 and $100,000. Hauer warned eager Sarasotans against unsound schemes and the blandishments of outside promoters. Then he encouraged them further: "If oil is really found there will be glory enough and money enough for all, it means another reawakening for Florida. It means untold prosperity."[10]

A mass meeting of more than 500 citizens gathered at the new courthouse. The site geologist, Captain B. F. Alley, assured the crowd that he expected huge quantities of oil to be found within the next ninety days: indeed, "The real estate boom was a mere shower compared to the cloudburst of money that is coming into this section with the oil boom—and that boom is coming just as sure as we are seated here." He assured his hearers that he "could almost see the oil."[11] The excited citizens formed a committee, charged with chartering a community oil corporation. Next they moved to put into this highly speculative oil stock the unused funds that had been subscribed a year earlier for a resort hotel on the mainland. Unlike Ringling's Ritz Carlton, this one was never started.

Ringling's "sugar bowl"—33,000 acres east and south of Sarasota—formed the largest individually owned tract in the county. His entire acreage, together with another nearly 33,000 acres belonging to Edith Ringling, was leased to the Associated Gas and Oil Company. Robert E. Ellis of El Dorado, Kansas, arrived to take up the job of site superintendent.[12] Experienced oil workers, enough for two day crews and one night shift, were brought in to work the drill. J. M. McCawley came from Ringling's Oklahoma oil fields to boss the derrick and rig. Ringling and the others qualified their publicized expectations with warnings of the relative chances of success or failure, but the unwelcome negative issues were never clearly stated. The geological evidence seemed to be strongly in favor of finding commercial quantities of oil. The oil fever

John Ringling inspecting the "sugar bowl" area where oil exploration was being conducted at Well No. 1, 1927. Courtesy of John and Mable Ringling Museum of Art.

was sustained in various parts of Florida by the promise of a state bounty of $50,000 to be paid to the first finder of commercial quantities of oil.[13]

The Ringling test site, named Well No. 1, was located beside the Tamiami Trail, about ten miles south of the city. Opening day, 12 March 1927, was celebrated like a true carnival: free cigars, refreshments, balloons, entertainment, music.[14] Traffic jammed the trail. Sarasotans came to watch Rogers Hornsby, captain of the New York Giants baseball team, set the apparatus in motion by breaking a bottle, as if christening a ship. This would surely be known later as the happiest day of the entire oil well episode, which ended without success. Although the Humble Oil Company later claimed the state bounty, commercial quantities of oil never became a viable resource in Florida.

❧ Ringling had made a public promise not long before the oil diversion claimed local attention. He had said that if certain conditions were met, he would start again on the Ritz Carlton. As the dreams of new riches faded, the hotel became a major concern in the city once more. While under construction in the boom days,the hotel had employed several hundred workers. When finished, it promised to bring a substantial flow of dollars into Sarasota. The *Herald* reminded Sarasotans that big hotels on Florida's east coast were the main cause of its growth and wealth.[15] Ringling's first condition was met when the residents voted ten to one to reduce the city boundaries to more rational limits. There remained the unfinished bridge from St. Armands to Longboat Key and the boulevard that was to run the length of Longboat—part of it in Sarasota and the remainder in Manatee County. A bond issue of nearly half a million dollars was required to build the missing pieces.

Largely as a token demonstration of his promise, Ringling put a work crew at the hotel site on the day of the boundary vote—primarily to clear away the accumulated debris and prepare the site for builders to start work. Developers the world over have resorted to this familiar charade. The place had to look busy and active to present a viable appearance for visiting financiers. A completion date of late 1927 was held out as the aim of the renewed activity, but no construction work could begin until the bond issue was approved.[16]

Approval was voted with little dissent. Ringling hated to break a promise, and he was publicly committed to finish the hotel. However, he still had no assurance of capital financing. The corporate health of Ringling Isles was suffering from the precipitous fall in the real estate market. He decided to attempt a remedy that would gain wide attention and create some favorable, free publicity. In a blare of advertising, he announced a "readjustment" program. Lot prices in Ringling Isles were reduced by two-thirds.

The greatest gain would go to those who already purchased lots. Buyers whose payments equaled the new price would receive deeds to their lots, free from any further obligation. The readjustment plan was not original; it had been proposed elsewhere in Florida. It was a generous gesture; but on the other hand losses to the developer would be greater if purchasers sacrificed their down payments and abandoned the property. Then the developer would have the task of repossession after long delays and legal fees. Locally, the publicity was generous. The *Herald* used a full-page editorial to describe the plan: "He (Ringling) has shown a wisdom and magnanimity that has seldom, if ever, been exemplified in the business world on so large a scale . . . . John Ringling has placed the entire state of Florida tremendously in his debt."[17] Despite this extravagant praise, the newspaper staff probably had few illusions about Ringling's motives.

Ringling replied in a full-page interview, "There is to be no fanfare, no loud trumpets, no loud or blatant promises. It is my intention to have my performance of intentions speak more loudly than advance promises. . . . the moment the work on the bridge and draw span is completed . . . the work on the Ritz Carlton will be pushed to completion."[18] For the first time he also revealed a new development for Longboat Key to be called Ritz Carlton Park—a colony of several hundred bungalows to be built in collaboration with architect Dwight James Baum. This, he said, would be the most unique and beautiful bungalow colony in America.[19]

The *Sarasota Herald* pinned hopes on Ringling to restore confidence in the city. "His project will involve millions, the fact that he has the millions gives us assurance."[20] The assurance was premature, for Ringling did not have the millions. Several major firms looked over the Ritz Carlton structure and the plans for its completion, but none came to an agreement.[21] For the short remainder of its unhappy life, construction was to be financed by raiding the treasury of the Ringling Isles Corporation.

Owen Burns had been pressed by Ringling to start the hotel even though subscriptions failed to reach the starting level. In the hard times of 1927, Burns became angry as he saw the all but bankrupt Ritz Carlton devouring the assets of the still-solvent Ringling Isles. Given the uncertain state of his own real estate ventures, he was unwilling to trust the schemes that Ringling seemed to enter upon so freely. Their collaboration had survived for nearly ten years. It was about to end in lawsuits and recriminations.

Ringling's long experience with American and Canadian railroads had exposed him to many examples of developer schemes. From his cruises and travels along the Florida coast, he knew well how a resort that started with a few rich visitors could grow into a community of homes and attractions, while those, in turn, brought still more visitors and more buyers. The rail and hotel combination had worked well for the biggest Florida developers. However, by 1926, the mass of travelers

Ringling's causeway, facing Sarasota. The surface of the road was heart of pine. Courtesy of Lillian Burns.

was no longer so dependent on trains for visits to Florida. Ringling's outdated idea of bringing a rail line to the Sarasota keys had been forestalled by local homeowners, but his causeway offered a ready access to travelers who came by road. The fault in the Ritz Carlton lay not in the idea of a great luxury hotel spawning a resort, but in the timing of the scheme. Ringling came too late to benefit from the postwar surge of new wealth that had swept into Florida. By the time he had the causeway in place and enough land developed to sell the hotel idea, his project fell before the looming economic collapse. More than twenty years would pass before the Depression and World War II were followed by another boom. By then the Ritz Carlton was beyond redemption.

The failure of the local subscription campaign was an early indicator that the plan was doomed. Ringling still chose to go ahead, forcing Burns to agree unwillingly in writing that the real estate corporation would finance the hotel's completion.[22] Their disagreements sharpened as the hotel floundered. Whereas Ringling had major sources of income far removed from his Florida interests, Burns was heavily invested locally; severe losses in Sarasota could demolish his entire fortune. Well into 1927 and still holding on, Ringling wanted to keep his promise.

Although many Sarasotans questioned his sincerity, believing he was primarily loyal to his own investment, Ringling actually had developed a loyalty to Sarasota and its people that was second only to his devotion to the circus. Realizing that the workers would suffer from the day he halted the project, he kept the hotel alive a few months longer, but without any backers. He had put more than $400,000 of his own money into the skeleton structure, and he never acknowledged defeat. The unfinished building diminished steadily in value. Its ultimate indignity came when the Florida governor's cabinet and the Ringling executors established its worth at $25,000. Materials to be sold from unused supplies included several thousand clay tiles, eight hundred doors from the old Waldorf Astoria (all in poor condition), a few old-fashioned toilets, and some damaged light fixtures.[23] Ringling had kept the doors insured and paid a watchman to guard the piles of useless materials.

Ringling was the ultimate salesman; before a failure became a public humiliation, he was ready with an even more exciting diversion, one that would give him a whole new stature in the community. He decided that the time had come to move the winter quarters of the circus to Sarasota. The impact on the city was almost instantaneous; the announcement of the move aroused a rush of energy, enthusiasm, and a new confidence in the future that had been moribund for months. It was an act that changed the character of Sarasota for a generation.

The idea of a move was not new, but it never seemed to offer enough advantage to justify the upheaval of the cumbersome circus establishment at Bridgeport, Connecticut. When questioned about it several years earlier, Ringling had said that no thought had been given to such a move, either by himself or by Charles. He pointed out that Sarasota was far from New York City, where the circus opened each year. After Charles's death in December 1926, Ringling was free for the first time to act on his own. His new partner, Charles's widow, Edith, was not then prepared to demand an equal role in making decisions. Alfred's son Richard Ringling, who spent most of his time on his immense Montana ranch, left circus affairs to his uncle and collected his one-third share of the profits, which then totaled close to $1 million a year.

There were several good reasons for leaving the circus where it was. The Bridgeport quarters were firmly established with all the necessary

The unfinished Sarasota Ritz Carlton Hotel on Longboat Key, 1926. Built by Hageman and Harris of Tampa and Chicago and designed by New York architects Warren and Wetmore. The skeleton structure was demolished in 1962. Courtesy of John and Mable Ringling Museum of Art.

John (in yachting cap), J. J. Watson (standing on wagon), Mable (next to Watson), and friends on an impromptu visit to Ringling Isles in 1926. Watson designed the development plans for St. Armands and Longboat Key. Courtesy of John and Mable Ringling Museum of Art.

facilities in a location close to New York. The site was on a trunk line, ideal for the annual journey to Manhattan for the opening. For the safety and well-being of the animals, this was an important issue.

Bridgeport had been the circus home for more than fifty years, begun by the Barnum & Bailey show before the Ringling purchase. Following the merger in 1918–19, even hometown Baraboo was abandoned by the Ringling Bros. half of the combined show. Bridgeport became home for many performers and even more of the work force. But it was a northern city with winters that were often severe, a hardship for many animals that were brought from the tropics. Forced to remain indoors for the entire winter, the animals became tense and restless. Sarasota was more than 1,200 miles from Madison Square Garden, but it offered the mild winter that animals and performers in training would find an advantage. Still, that long, expensive journey was an uncertain tradeoff for the Florida climate.

There was a long tradition in the circus of using animals as performers and for exhibition. A menagerie had been part of traveling shows since the eighteenth century in England and Europe, where rare and exotic animals were exhibited at fairs and pubs. The Ringlings' first caged animal was a blind hyena, billed as one "that in the dark of night when no hand was there to stay him, robbed the graves of the dead . . . and whose laughter chilled the bravest heart."[24] As the Ringling circus grew, so did the number and variety of animals. In addition there were the 350 valuable riding horses for the bareback and acrobatic riders.

The earliest trained, performing animal acts had used dogs, geese, goats—generally domestic animals and birds. Later came the wild animals—lions, tigers, and other large cats. John and Charles were never certain that they wanted to accept the liability of using such powerful and dangerous animals. Trainers in the ring knew and accepted the personal risk of injury or even death. But the circus owners were always nervous about the specter of an accident such as a tent blown down with the animals loose in a hysterical crowd. Moreover, public criticism of cruelty to animals was growing, and the Ringlings were quick to sense the pressure of adverse publicity. In 1925 they dropped those thrilling acts from the show. Humane societies applauded the decision to remove the acts from the program, and parents were relieved that humans and ferocious animals were no longer exhibited together in cages.

Charles was usually perhaps more willing than his brother to cut out a controversial part of the show.[25] When the decision about moving to Sarasota was his alone, John reconsidered the wild animal acts. As with the high wire acts, animal trainers were presenting feats that were visibly dangerous and publicly billed as such. The fearsome attraction of possibly witnessing death, the spectator's ultimate thrill, brought throngs to the Flavian amphitheater and, more recently, to auto races and similar events. The circus could never revert to the outdated acts with trained domestic animals whose appeal was more comic than exciting, especially in view of the recent and somewhat unexpected finding that three-fourths of circus patrons were adults, not children. Eventually he decided to reinstate the wild animal acts.

In 1927, Ringling began to plan an alternative home for the circus animals—an immense zoological park with natural habitats. It was to be a Sarasota tourist attraction, a forerunner of the theme parks. He formed a corporation for this purpose, but never followed up on the proposal. All the animals stayed at the circus winter quarters on the Sarasota County fairgrounds.

The time was right to move the circus to Sarasota. The local depressed conditions for the building trades and the alarming fall in real estate activity had severely damaged Sarasota's economy, aggravating the retreat of northern buyers and posing a further threat to Ringling's island empire. Had oil been found in Well No. 1 on Ringling property or even elsewhere in the area, Sarasota would have been gloriously rescued. But it was becoming increasingly evident that oil was not going to flow. The community had no alternate hope for recovery; some were already talking about a depression. Ringling could expect maximum concessions that would lessen the expense of moving the circus to a new home.

He was astute enough to speak only of benefits to Sarasota, and thus camouflage his intent to develop renewed interest in his real estate holdings. When the circus move was announced, Sam Gumpertz quickly claimed that he had been pressing for the move for the past two years. Later he would say that it was through his efforts that the circus came to Sarasota.[26] James A. Haley, who had become the office manager at the Ringling Estates, claimed that he, too, had a part in urging Ringling to act.[27] Gumpertz and Haley may have done as they claimed, but Ringling never acknowledged that he had been urged by anyone to bring the circus to Sarasota.

Having made his decision, Ringling staged the announcement to gain the most dramatic impact. This occasion, perhaps more than any other during his island development program, brought the interests of the city to coincide with his own. It was an act of genuine public service that served his own ends equally well. Sam Gumpertz initially suggested the possibility of moving the circus at a directors' meeting of the Sarasota Fair Association. Within minutes a committee was named, and inside the hour its members called upon Ringling at his office (where he rarely could be found at midafternoon). They secured his unqualified assurance that the move would take place. The Fair Association was neatly maneuvered into *inviting* Ringling to bring the circus to Sarasota. He graciously agreed to their request.[28]

Ringling permanently altered his posture in Sarasota by this one action. From that time, he would become circus man first and entrepreneur-developer second in the mind of the community. The image that he had cultivated for a decade was overtaken by reversion to the circus man—except this time he was not a circus man who was a newcomer but the millionaire-entrepreneur who had come to the rescue of Sarasota. For more than a year after the March 1927 gesture, which was widely publicized as a step taken to help the city, Ringling continued to thrive on his returns from western oil and the circus. His status as a man devoted to the city was reaching its peak. He was roundly cheered in public, a sound that he loved to hear.

The immediate effects of the circus move were expected: new jobs constructing buildings and rail lines at the old fairgrounds, the influx of a winter crew, and the attraction of tourists. In the following decade, as many as 100,000 visitors came each winter. But there were other more subtle effects. The circus brought an alien culture for this southern town. Sarasotans found themselves living among performers and families (many of them European) whose traditions and customs contrasted, sometimes vividly, with local life-styles. Recalling those first years, the *Sarasota Herald-Tribune* observed that while the circus had by no means ended the Depression, it had certainly made the times more lively.[29] Of course there were citizens who did not welcome the circus. They regarded this new population as déclassé and had the fear of foreigners that is common in provincial towns, a mistrust of anyone who is different in culture, language, or appearance. However, the minority made little public airing of their views, so thoroughly had the community power structure embraced the novel idea of becoming a circus town.

Sarasota could not afford to reject the boost to its economy, even if it meant welcoming southern Europeans, an ethnic group that was becoming increasingly unpopular in Florida. However alien they might have seemed, the circus performers were spared much of the hostility that immigrants normally would have encountered. Circus people came with preestablished identities, and many of their names became familiar in press accounts of the circus and its crew.

The city council rushed to offer inducements to the circus. An increase of nearly 2,000 new residents, work for many mechanics and laborers, and spending for materials and supplies promised a surge of benefits to stimulate the faltering economy. Ringling found it prudent to contradict some of the most glowing, unfounded expectations. Experience would soon show Sarasotans that circus contracts were mostly seasonal and that many performers and a great percentage of the work force faded away at the close of each season. Many families would be moving to Sarasota, but in the hundreds, not thousands. A greater, less visible benefit was to come from the tourist and winter crowds of spectators who would pay to visit the circus grounds. Still to come were the end-of-season festival days made colorful with circus trappings.

After the initial announcement came the carefully worded offers and tradeoffs. Ringling made his plan contingent on finding suitable land at a reasonable price. He knew from Gumpertz (a board member) that the Fair Association would transfer its land in return for relief from a debt he promised to pay off for the association. The city council could do no less. In return for the expected advertising value of the circus presence, the city agreed to rebate to the circus a sum equal to its city taxes on grounds, personal property, and equipment, less $500; the offer was to extend for ten years from 1927. The city was well advised to be both prompt and generous: notice of the council's resolution shared page one with reports of foreclosures against two local enterprises.[30] In Palm Beach, three banks had closed their doors.

A liability that accompanied the circus was the mass of transients known as "trailers" who followed the circus. They became a new underclass, something Sarasota had not known since 1886, when workers were brought in to build for the Florida Mortgage and Investment Company. The trailers were not part of the circus work force; their livelihood depended on whatever they could cadge or steal. When the circus moved, many of them traveled under the freight cars or in other vacant, unguarded spaces. In Sarasota, minor disorder, thievery, and occasional violence placed an unaccustomed burden on the county sheriff and the city police. Arrests and thirty-day jail terms were about all they could do to control the menace during the winters.

Ringling was reelected to head the Chamber of Commerce, a post to which he willingly lent his name, but little if any of his time.[31] In early 1928, the shareholders of the Seaboard Airline Railroad elected him to the board of directors.[32] The rail line and Ringling had many common interests in working for a return to more rapid development on the Gulf coast. But his election was perhaps equally a recognition of the profitable association between the line and the circus train; the circus, without common carrier status, paid maximum freight rates.

Ringling's election to the chairmanship of the Bank of Sarasota was of more local concern. His election followed the death of the previous chairman, T. C. Taliaferro of Tampa, a founder of the bank who had helped to guide it from modest beginnings as a branch of the Bradentown bank to rapid boomtime growth, when dividends had increased fourfold. The directors now owned 80 percent of the stock.[33] Ringling and his colleagues borrowed the money for the stock purchase from a winter resident. He now held a position in two Sarasota banks. From his viewpoint, both were primarily sources of mortgage funding for buyers of Ringling Isles property.

City council members and voters, eager to cooperate with Ringling, allowed him to divest himself of the causeway that had cost him nearly $700,000 by giving it to the city. This gift was accepted willingly by the city, for it opened valuable new areas to the city tax rolls. The one piece missing from his island plan was a causeway draw span connecting Longboat Key to Anna Maria, the island north of the Sarasota keys. That too was funded in a March vote. In midsummer it seemed likely to be in place by the year's end.[34] Finally, building materials could be delivered by trucks rather than boats.

The island empire looked as though it would survive. All that Ringling appeared to need now was a new wave of local and Florida prosperity to regain his momentum as a major developer. He had secured his main objectives from city and county. His real estate empire could easily survive a temporary recession, but he still needed the Ritz Carlton to attract the richest visitors. Their prestige and glamour would draw lesser but equally welcome buyers. Ringling had watched the same idea succeed at Coral Gables. While he was urging the people of Sarasota to restrain their expectations of what benefits the circus would bring, he also suggested that extravagant circus pageants would become part of the springtime scene, larger and more splendid than any other in the nation, bringing throngs of visitors, filling all accommodations, pouring money into local shops and businesses. It was possible, if not likely, that the prospect of a nationally popular event might interest one or more investors in the great white skeleton on Longboat Key.

Ringling was beginning to look like a traditional Chinese figure—the man holding down nine fleas with his fingers while trying to catch a tenth. He borrowed money to pay for his shares in the Bank of Sarasota, yet he purchased an entire county bond issue for $450,000. He contracted for the building of a large, expensive art museum and he was buying paintings to fill its galleries as soon as they could be made ready. He was starting to manipulate assets that sent his associate Owen Burns into the courts to stop him. Concrete for the footings of the museum had scarcely set before Ringling was forced by sudden money constraints to halt further progress and dismiss his contractor. The new home, Ca' d'Zan, was finished but it too had been truncated by the need to reduce spending. Again and again through 1927 he tried to raise money for the hotel, but none of those who came to look were willing to back him.

Late in the autumn of 1927, the circus ended its season at Tampa. A new custom for Sarasotans began with the Tampa closing. All who could manage a day off went to the closing show—truants, runaways, and a throng of workers dismissed for the day's outing. For many of Sarasota's younger elite, the new routine became de rigueur: an auto or train trip to Tampa, shopping at Maas Brothers, and a pleasant leisurely luncheon before the afternoon performance.

The winter quarters of the circus were finished. An entire complex of buildings and rail lines on the transformed fairgrounds was the work of the contractors Chase and McElroy. Three barns, each with stalls for 400 horses, were ready, as well as dormitories, shops, and menagerie houses. The old fairgrounds had disappeared, and the unpaid Fair

Association debt faded from view; Ringling was not one to be troubled by a need for haste in dealing with those obligations.

The social impact of this migration was not so immediate, but it became widespread and enduring. The outer fringe of rich winter residents who lived on or near the Gulf were personally unaffected. Moreover, the small, old-time Sarasota elite had largely receded in influence, giving way to the commercial-professional class that had come to dominate the city. The latter welcomed the infusion of new residents and their role in the local economy, knowing that the city and county were both burdened with heavy bond interest payments and redemption costs, and that the tax base was badly battered. Ringling was popular, if not particularly well liked personally, in the business community. Sam Gumpertz was another who gained materially in public favor. In the transition from the reserved air of Sarasota to the almost carnival air of a circus town, Gumpertz, who had been a master promoter at Coney Island, was gaining visibility.

Ringling tried to preserve the special elegance of Sarasota in the winter quarters. He had the circus grounds made as attractive as landscaping could make them, welcoming visitors with an avenue of coconut palms leading from the entrance to the animal houses, large car shops, stables, and rail yards. And the tourists did come; as many as 3,000 came in one day on the Wednesday and Sunday openings. Of the total circus population of about 1,700 in 1927, about 300 were working at the grounds. Many performers, after spending the winter in other shows, would return to practice in the two rings before the next season. Sarasota was getting a much-needed boost in spirits and in funds, and the popular misconception of John Ringling as a man of limitless wealth grew apace. Throughout Florida, developers had slowed or halted their projects, but he seemed on the surface (and few could see beyond that) to be unaffected. This was indeed an illusion. One needed to look no further than the Ringling Isles to see that Ringling's capital was stretched thin in 1927.

It was the first year of life in the grand manner at Ca' d'Zan. With the exception of some interior work, the great house was ready for entertaining. The initial housewarming combined with a Christmas celebration was a scaled-down family gathering, coming soon after Charles Ringling's death.

Mable, whose beauty and sense of fashion were part of her Sarasota image, was about to realize her dream. She would be like a *principessa* in an Italian palace, but without the pride and arrogance that often accompany a climb to riches. She now began to dress in Paris couturier fashions, purchased during summer visits at the Ritz Hotel in Paris. She chose to buy from several of the smaller designers rather than from the world-renowned fashion houses.[35] Entertaining now meant large musicales and afternoon parties for bridge. The number of dinner and evening guests was more limited, usually not exceeding the number conveniently seated at the Ringling dinner table. Arriving gentlemen were given small envelopes, "Compliments of Mr. John Ringling." Inside, the card read: "Will you take _____ in to dinner." Judge Edwin W. Cummer, whose father was one of Ringling's business associates, recalled seeing a uniformed servant (as in royal households) behind every two guests seated at dinner.[36] His recollection of service on gold plates was perhaps inspired by Mable's blue and gold service plates and her gold-plated sterling silver flatware.

Life in the two great mansions built by the Ringlings began within days of Charles Ringling's death. Charles had left most of his estate to Edith, which placed Edith on an equal footing with John as a one-third owner of the circus. And Edith, more than Charles, had always resented John's flamboyant career and his manner, at once breezy and authoritarian.[37] Edith and John were also now owners of one-half the sugar bowl tract where oil drilling was to be attempted, and of Metropolitan Velodrome, a bicycle racing arena in New York City.

Charles and Edith's new home was finished only a short time before Charles's last illness. Just as the house rivaled Ca' d'Zan in cost, it too mirrored the personalities of its owners. Its pink marble structure was as conventionally American as a Wisconsin clergyman's daughter could desire. The interior and the furnishings were unmistakably products of the 1920s. Charles built a home only slightly less splendid for his daughter Hester and connected the two houses with an arcaded walk.

Edith and her daughter Hester entertained very much as Mable did, welcoming the women of Sarasota at bridge, garden club meetings, and occasional evening dances. (Circus people, however, were rarely among the guests at the John Ringling home; for example, Merle Evans, leader of the circus band,—whom John addressed as "Merley"—often led a dance band for John and Mable's guests. Yet his wife had never seen the estate or the house.) The Ringling women—Edith, Mable, and Ida, John and Charles's sister—were regularly among the guests at similar afternoon events hosted by Sarasota's elite. Hester entertained younger friends at pool parties and dances. Mable's sisters, Alma Ried and Dulcie Schueler, were on an outer fringe, never freely admitted to the more select circle. However, during the few years when these five sisters and sisters-in-law all spent the season in Sarasota, their relations apparently were not marred by jealousies or disagreements.

The brothers generated a cult based on hyperbole, and in time they became fantasy figures. The line between fact and fiction was never clear, and their stories about them were full of anecdotes that were a mix of ballyhoo and little, if any, truth. Shortly after Charles's death, a reprint (its source unidentified) appeared in the *Sarasota Herald.* The writer freely mixed the attributes of John and Charles. He assigned John's New York apartment to Charles and gave a bizarre description of the Sarasota home.

In his own right the late Charles Ringling was one of America's twenty-five richest men. With a very red face, a gold watch chain across his prosperous stomach, he was seen from time to time on Fifth Avenue, perhaps entering his apartment at No. 636.

His friends speak of him as a kindly man, vain, charitable, shrewd in business, passionately fond of the circus. Its atmosphere was all about him. He carried it into his Fifth Avenue apartment, setting off the carefully planned Louis Quatorze furniture with circus posters, Yale banners and glaring paintings of bareback riders and trapeze artists.

This home was a huge duplex affair with four enormous drawing rooms on the lower floor, the chef d'oeuvre of which was a very small grand piano, enameled white. On it was painted a complete circus menagerie. A toy bulldog which opened its mouth and wagged its head invariably stood upon it.

Charles Ringling's real pride, however, had been his winter home built a year or two ago at Sarasota, Florida. He and his brother John owned 500,000 acres of land on the west coast of Florida . . . .

The interior of the house was Italian, its hall cluttered with art treasures wedged between huge cloisonné jars which were kept in meticulous order by Arab servants with flowing mustaches and turbans.

Charles' supreme effort went into the design of his own bedroom. It was oval in shape with walls of green marble . . . .

In the center of this stood the bed. It was a huge one with no footboard, and was covered by a spread of old Italian embroidery. The ceiling of the room was painted to represent sky and clouds and the lighting of this was controlled by an elaborate electrical installation.[38]

❦ Prospects for better times were making Sarasota's future look more promising. The economy seemed to be slowly recovering. Nationally, President Coolidge presided over a complacent administration. Early 1928 was the time of Ringling's unchallenged glory as Sarasota's first citizen, benefactor, and leader of his chosen home city. His friends and associates, apparently inspired by Sam Gumpertz, gave him a grand testimonial after the circus closed at Tampa and moved to Sarasota for the winter. The stag event for nearly 200 men of affairs, including Governor John Martin of Florida, was a solid evening of praise, testimonials, and cheer after cheer for his many contributions to Sarasota and, more broadly, to the nation: "A man whom the people of Florida and the entire nation hold in high honor."[39] The occasion demonstrated with high visibility the public recognition of Ringling's achievements. That night it seemed as though Sarasota's progress had been wholly generated through his own energy, acumen, and fortune. He passed by the opportunity to share some of this acclaim with Owen Burns, the companion developer who had helped to turn his vision into reality, or Ralph Caples, civic activist and promoter of Ringling ideas.

In the pleasant 1928 winter season, John and Mable hosted a series of spectacular events. Ca' d'Zan's largest gatherings, arranged by Mable, were not organized to impress some moneyed guest or political figure whose influence was needed. They were events where Mable could share her Italian palace with Sarasotans whose company she enjoyed. Guests at luncheon might be as few as 50 or nearer to 100. She sent invitations to 375 for her largest afternoon musicale, at which two bands played for dancing. Merle Evans, leader of the circus band, led one group in the solarium for dancers in the ballroom. The famous Czechoslovakian Band was seated on the upper deck of the *Zalophus* at the landing stage, playing for dancers on the huge marble terrace. An oriental tent for tea occupied one end of the terrace. The entire grounds were part of the display, for they were crowded with an immense variety of blooming tropical plants and trees spread throughout the beautifully maintained lawns. Guests strolled through the formal, Italian garden among the many marble statues and whimsical cast-stone figures from folk tales and fables.[40] On another day Mable offered her guests a tour of the exotic plants and trees in the Ringling nursery on Longboat Key, then luncheon on the terrace of the unfinished Ritz Carlton Hotel—the only meal ever served at that ill-fated reminder of Ringling's ambition.

On another occasion officials of the New York Central Railroad and the Big Four lines arrived on two private cars. They were met by the Ringling Rolls Royce limousines and given a tour of the city, the circus quarters, and of course, the Ringling Isles. At dinner in the evening, Governor John Martin joined the group at Ca' d'Zan—an indication that these northern railway executives[41] were still important to Florida, in spite of growing indications that roads were replacing rail lines for many Florida travelers. Events such as these were typical of Ringling entertaining. The afternoon parties were Mable's, while the evenings were often for the smaller, VIP guest lists, people important to John Ringling's business interests.

The 1928 season closed with the Sara de Sota festival, three days of carnival events and promotion for the city. The local presence of the circus gave the festival the promised colorful pageantry that made it unique. Sam Gumpertz organized and ran it smoothly and professionally, enhancing his own reputation as a skilled impresario. A spectrum of events, some with broad public appeal and some more formal and exclusive, made the festival the publicity success that the city needed.

Ringling hoped to use the festival as a vehicle for venturing into the arts, making Sarasota a home for ballet, opera, and his own art museum. He often took visitors to view the massive structure of the museum as it slowly took shape at the south end of his estate. He brought his friend Otto Bartik, the ballet master at the Metropolitan Opera, from New York to work out a plan for a ballet, which never materialized because of the oncoming Depression. Bartik was a friend of both Charles and John Ringling, occasionally a visitor at Ca' d'Zan when ideas for the circus spectaculars were being considered; in 1928 they produced one called "The Tourney of the Jewels," staged by 800 performers. Bartik hoped that a ballet would become a regular event at the Sara de Sota festival. Moreover, he told an interviewer that Sarasota would soon become the art center of the South, with not only ballet but also opera, staged by local talent with visiting soloists.

John and Mable left for New York and the opening of the circus in March. In the summer, when they were traveling in Europe, Mable was hospitalized in England with pneumonia. After her recovery, she went to one of the elegant spas at Carlsbad in Czechoslovakia and from there to a mountain retreat in St. Moritz, Switzerland, for additional rest. John returned to New York alone. Mable was back in New York by late summer in 1928.

In the autumn, the circus was once more scheduled to end its season in Tampa, but this time, instead of closing out, the entire show moved to Sarasota for two performances on Saturday, 27 October. The newspapers were filled with descriptions of the show, with its five rings, several platforms, and a staff of 1,800, including such glamorous stars as Lillian Leitzel and a sensational new high wire act from Germany, the Wallendas. Special trains from south and central Florida brought hundreds of people to Sarasota for the one-day event.

For Ringling, having the circus quarters nearby was a great convenience. He was almost entirely dependent on hired managers, and it was no longer possible for a member of his family to be present at all times when the show was on the road. For business conferences with key circus officials, Sarasota rather than New York became a convenient meeting place. On occasion, but not often, a few of the most trusted met with Ringling at Ca' d'Zan—George Meighan from the Chicago office, manager Fred Bradna, and ringmaster Pat Valdo.

The yacht *Zalophus* ready for delivery, 1922. The houseboat style (shallow draft and square windows) was patterned after the Wanamaker yacht at Palm Beach, which Ringling chartered after the sinking of his *Vidoffner II.* Courtesy of Henry Ringling North.

In the winter of 1928–29, Ringling once again entertained important visitors. Former Democratic Governor Alfred E. Smith of New York was the first of the new year. Sam Gumpertz was the closer friend of the "happy warrior," but Ringling took the role of host. Governor Smith's unsuccessful 1928 campaign for the presidency had been marred by virulent anti-Catholic sentiment, particularly in the South, where the establishment was almost wholly Democratic but in large part fanatically anti-Catholic. Now that he was no longer a candidate, Governor Smith was welcomed to Sarasota with a great flourish. His party was met by a civic reception committee, the ever-present Czechoslovakian Band, and a throng of curious citizens.

At the moment of arrival, Smith had an opportunity to show that he was not openly bitter about the southern rejection that had probably cost him the election. A woman among the spectators rushed forward to shake his hand, saying, "I want you to know that I voted for you." Always ready with an apt response, the governor replied, "Madam, I am glad to find out where I got that vote from down here."[42]

The party moved at once to the El Vernona Hotel from a private rail

Saloon on the Ringling yacht *Zalophus*. In 1930 the yacht struck an underwater object and sank. The entire ninety-foot deckhouse was swept away by Gulf currents. Courtesy of Henry Ringling North.

car, the *St. Nicholas,* owned by wealthy manufacturer William Kenney and used by Smith in his presidential campaign. The first day at Sarasota included a large civic luncheon attended by most of the business and political figures of southwest Florida. Many Democrats were once again eager to prove that they were loyal to their party. Clearly, Gumpertz had planned the Sarasota visit to showcase a little public healing of the campaign's wounds. That evening, dinner for a small group at Ca' d'Zan brought a few select Sarasotans to meet the distinguished visitors. The following day, before moving on to Miami, the party was given a cruise aboard the *Zalophus.*[43]

This was a time of self-actualization for John Ringling. Nearly 2,000 acres of the island he could see across the bay from his house belonged

Ringling with President and Mrs. Calvin Coolidge and a friend's child at the circus in Washington, D.C., May 1924. When Ringling called at the White House to deliver his invitation, the president remarked that since the boys were not there, he lacked an excuse for attending the circus, but he was going anyway. Courtesy of John and Mable Ringling Museum of Art.

John and Mable at the Ringling tropical plant nursery on Longboat Key, 1925. Courtesy of John and Mable Ringling Museum of Art.

to him. Rich and important people came to his home as his guests.[44] His real estate ventures were not regaining momentum, but Ringling was a manipulator as well as an investor. He was ever the optimist, never without a scheme for ad hoc solutions to the most vexing problems; lesser ones he could ignore.

The day before John and Mable were to leave Sarasota for New York and the 1929 circus season, county officials arranged for the Ringling limousine bearing John, Mable, and Sam Gumpertz (now Sarasota's second most honored citizen) to be the first to cross the just-finished bridge that connected two keys, Lido–St. Armands and Longboat, across New Pass. The draw span was lowered for their car to cross slowly and return.[45] The following day they left in their private railroad car, the *JoMaR*.

꧁ Owen Burns had decided that he must halt the maneuvering that Ringling was using to keep alive his ill-fated Ritz Carlton. Burns filed suit against Ringling personally and against the Ringling Estates Corporation. Burns was convinced that the continual use of Estates Corporation money to finance the hotel or to pay off its obligations meant ruin for the real estate enterprise as well. The latest device Ringling had used was indeed devious. He had recorded a mortgage made by the John Ringling Estates, Inc., to himself for more than $700,000, mortgaging all the real property of the corporation. By this move he became owner of 75 percent of the corporation (Burns owned 25 percent), and the corporation owed him $700,000. In addition, there was another loan.

Burns looked upon the entire scheme as a device to underwrite loans to the hotel company until the crippled real estate firm was insolvent. In those circumstances Ringling could then foreclose the mortgages and take possession of the land and all assets of the Ringling Estates. By so doing, Ringling would also preempt Burns's 25 percent share of the company, a share then worth several hundred thousand dollars. Burns asked that a receiver be appointed to guard the firm's assets of more than $3 million. Even in court, however, he was unable to thwart the moves of his erstwhile partner.

Burns had worked in Ringling's interest for more than a decade. His construction company had built the causeway, Ca' d'Zan, the Sunset apartments; he had done all the dredging and seawall work on Cedar Point and at Shell Beach, plus all the land development for St. Armands and Longboat keys. He was heavily in debt to the Prudence Bond Company of New York through Sam Gumpertz. He had also recorded an agreement in which he unaccountably and without any consideration released John Ringling from any outstanding claims for all work ever performed by him by the Burns enterprises. Probably Burns had been promised certain lots on the keys in return for abandoning his claims for payment, but no such recompense was named in that strange document of release.

Ringling was manipulating the corporate finances in a highhanded manner as though they were his own private possessions, and Burns

Ringling and Captain Arthur Rowe collecting coconuts at Cape Coral,
Florida, 1926. Sprouted coconuts were planted to start palms for the
Ringling Isles development. Courtesy of Sarasota County Department of
Historical Resources, Arthur Rowe, Jr., Collection.

could not casually accept the risks. He saw Ringling threatening what
fortune he still possessed, and he was ready to accept the unpleasant
consequences of open conflict with his longtime colleague. Ringling
had decided even earlier to sever their working relationship. In his view,

he was the aggrieved party, for he believed (or pretended to believe) that Burns had not dealt fairly with him when the causeway and the El Vernona Hotel were being constructed at the same time.[46] Their mutual trust, always fragile, was not strong enough to meet a real crisis in their mutual affairs.

In the early summer of 1929, Ringling's personal life was disrupted in a way for which he was wholly unprepared. After the Ringlings had settled in New York in June, Mable became seriously ill. She was moved from their Fifth Avenue apartment to the LeRoy nursing home on East 61st Street. Within a few days her condition became critical, and on June 8 she died from diabetes and Addison's disease.[47] The few remaining Ringling family members were summoned to her brief funeral at Alpine, New Jersey. John and Mable had met in New Jersey. They had both loved their summer home at Alpine on the Hudson, with its shaded lawns, its dramatic overlook, her long, well-tended rose garden.

John Ringling could not accept this final disruption of their life together.[48] Their marriage had begun when he was deliberately breaking away from the limitations of his first, successful celebrity image in the road show industry. It had flourished for twenty-five years, through all the changes his wealth had brought.

In the 1920s, Ringling had two public images, the capitalist-entrepreneur and the circus man who lived like a king. In contrast to the steady flow of publicity about his business and circus affairs, he had made certain that his domestic life remained altogether private. Through the Sarasota years Mable had given their home a stability that endured, one that sustained their relationship. Without Mable, his life became devoid of intimacy and before long, he was further alienated from many of his friends by disagreements and distrust.

The Art Collector

THE REMARKABLE FEATURE of the life of John Ringling was neither his ability to accumulate wealth nor his egocentrism, but rather the inner complexity of his personality, formed by nature and experience, together with a quickness of mind that enabled him to grasp and assimilate new elements into a life already richly filled. He reached the age of fifty-nine in 1925, the last full year that he shared the circus with his brother Charles. His Sarasota ventures and investments were increasing rapidly. That same summer, at the close of a business trip through Italy, where he bought a shipload of architectural relics for his Ritz Carlton Hotel, he casually told a friend that he intended to collect Old Master paintings and build a museum.

Any one of his occupations—circus proprietor, resort developer, art collector—could have consumed his attention, yet he addressed all three with equal enthusiasm, moving confidently from one activity to another. He approached the art world aggressively, building a fund of knowledge to help him find his way among the intricate and sometimes devious ways of art market professionals. He had made several earlier sorties, apparently beginning shortly before his 1905 marriage to Mable. They made purchases here and there, but with no particular purpose or knowledge, as they traveled in Europe each summer.[1] Whatever he bought (possibly mid-nineteenth-century French salon works), he made no mark as a collector, nor did he attract any attention as a buyer. He became dissatisfied with his undistinguished purchases, then, after a lapse of several years, once again took up collecting, this time more seriously.

The long transition from his first untutored experiments with art purchases to becoming a collector of museum-quality works and a respected amateur connoisseur began about the time that he moved the center of his interests from Chicago to New York. That symbolic move was finalized in 1906, when the Ringling Bros. bought Barnum & Bailey, a maneuver that gave national status to the Ringling name.

There was far more to Ringling's complex nature than a superficial public image. Among other features was a wish to participate in some of the intellectual and artistic pursuits that lay beyond the popular culture of the circus. Several influences helped to form his tastes; the opportunities to indulge them were afforded by his wealth. He came to know Stanford White, the prominent architect and socialite, when both were major shareholders in Madison Square Garden, which White had designed a decade earlier. Ringling became a regular at a card-playing club that met at White's Giralda tower rooms atop the Garden.[2] Another in that elite group was Augustus St. Gaudens, whose weathervane statue of Diana was poised at the top of the Garden's tower. Ringling began to assimilate some of his new companions' ideas as he admired their elegance and style. Later he considered naming the museum's largest gallery for St. Gaudens but abandoned the idea, perhaps because he did not own significant works by his friend.

Stanford White was an adherent of a new and intense nationalism, a sort of collective self-worship, that developed in America around the turn of the century. It became popular as great industrial fortunes were being amassed and the power of financiers grew unchecked. There occurred a subtle shift in the power of wealth from Europe to America, and treasures of Western culture—some from impoverished churches and empty palaces—began to move to the New World. This early twentieth-century migration of art was one result of the conviction that a nation that was growing so rich and strong was the rightful home for the finest creations of humankind. J. P. Morgan was perhaps the foremost example of collectors who believed and acted upon that doctrine. Though far less wealthy than Morgan, White acquired many European art objects for the homes of his clients.[4] Many years later, Ringling followed a similar pattern more modestly, when he bought Italian relics for Sarasota; a few select pieces from White's estate ultimately found a new home in Ringling's museum.

In the mid-1920s, as England and the Continent were gaining a false sense of stability after World War I, works of art flowed steadily from London, Paris, and Berlin to New York. Each year, greater numbers of paintings, sketches, and drawings from prominent collections were sold in London. Their number reached nearly 9,000 in 1926 and rose to 11,000 in 1927.[5] Many were immediately shipped to the United States. American financiers who scorned the Old World as effete and decadent were nonetheless eager to acquire some of its finer works for their homes or for gifts to perpetuate their names in glory, inscribed on the walls of municipal museums.

When Ringling decided to enter this art market in 1925, several new acquaintances were influencing his thinking, much as White had done in their card-playing days nearly twenty years before. Two important figures were indirectly brought into Ringling's circle through the Sarasota Ritz Carlton Hotel project. Albert Keller, operator of the Ritz in New York was a Swiss national who became president of the Ritz Hotel corporation in American in 1928 and was a key figure in planning and designing Ringling's ill-fated Sarasota Ritz venture. Keller was a discriminating art collector who had decorated his home with elegant European furniture and paintings by Frans Hals, Adriaen Isenbrandt, Jan van Goyen, and other Dutch and Flemish masters. The Kellers often entertained Julius Böhler, a prominent Munich art dealer, at their New York Ritz apartment. John and Mable were also frequent guests at the Keller apartment in 1922–23, when plans were being drawn for the Sarasota Ritz Hotel. The same group occasionally gathered in Sarasota as visitors at the Ringling mansion. Böhler soon became Ringling's mentor and the principal agent in the process of assembling the collection for the Ringling Museum.

In preparation for decorating the hotel, Ringling started to collect furnishings and decorations for the public rooms that he believed would convey an air of elegance and upper-class taste. He wanted to replicate the splendid ambience of the New York Ritz and its Paris model. The winter months in New York were an ideal time for attending auctions where furnishings from dismantled houses and estates (both antiques and reproduction pieces) were offered in rich profusion.

At first his interest focused on accessories. From auction catalogs, he selected marble and stone pedestals, carved figures, lighting sconces, tall candelabra, and torchiers. Few of his purchases at these sales were either rare or costly. In November 1924, at the McMillin and Crocker sale at Darlington in Mahwah, New Jersey, he acquired a number of trivial items, such as silk cushions with arms embroidered in gold and silver bullion thread. (Ringling noted in his catalog: "Buy if cheap.") Nevertheless, he was also starting to buy objects of genuine worth. At that same sale Ringling chose two fine seventeenth-century German carved wooden figures of missionary saints. He also bought several paintings, including a family group portrait by Sir Peter Lely, *The Children of Lord Craven*.[6] For his home, he obtained an immense Georgian-style console of mahogany and gilt with a top of black and gold marble. He was learning; but he was still an amateur. His new friends would later convince him that there was no future in random buying from estate sales.

In a similarly unstructured vein, Ringling began to buy tapestries, most of them intended to adorn the walls of the Ritz Carlton. However, he continued to buy them after the hotel became an acknowledged failure. Subsequent purchases were selected for his New York apartment and Sarasota home, and were later placed in the museum. The twenty antique tapestries in his estate cannot be described as a collection, for the term implies an ordered and purposive selection. Ringling never followed a systematic approach, nor did he buy only from established dealers whose tapestries would be accompanied by documentation. Just as there was no apparent pattern to his purchases, there was inevitably an uneven quality of artistic merit. What preference led him to select one item and reject another in the same sale cannot be ascertained from his markings in sale catalogs. Unlike his later studies of paintings, he did not master the technical knowledge of weaving methods and colors and the complex history of weaving that would have qualified him as a connoisseur. He seemed content to enjoy the richness of large tapestries, coupled with the realization that they had come from homes of distinction.

Flemish tapestries often attracted Ringling's bids, suggesting that he preferred the softer, muted colors and the styles of Brussels, avoiding the more vivid roses and reds of the eighteenth-century French Gobelins and Beauvais. Two were chosen for their relation to the Rubens and studio cartoons he bought when the art museum collection was forming—the *Fides Catholica* and the *Triumph of Faith.* There were other unusual pieces, such as two fine seventeenth-century Brussels tapestries from the sale of Vincent Astor's home and its contents. Ringling's winning bid of more then $10,000 made them the most expensive objects in the entire sale.[7] Three historically important tapestries came from the McMillin sale, part of a famous series known as the *History of Alexander the Great,* designed in part by Jacob Jordaens and woven by Jan Leyniers.[8] They had passed through several great Italian families to an American collector who, in turn, presented them to General Philip H. Sheridan. The *History of Alexander the Great* pieces were exceedingly popular in their time and a number of sets were woven as cartoons passed from one workshop to another.[9]

When Ringling acquired his tapestries, he did not pause to establish designer or provenance (previous ownership), or to search for documentation beyond whatever was stated in the auction catalogs. Moreover, he did not preserve or protect them; this was not so much a matter of indifference as a result of his habit of plunging into a new activity before he had learned enough about it. The penalties for neglect were not immediately apparent, but Ringling's somewhat cavalier treatment of such fragile antiques encouraged the disapproval of critics who saw in his collecting only a passion to own the splendid objects enjoyed by the rich.

The Ringlings were gaining experience with the special language and techniques of auction buying, although this did not altogether prevent John and sometimes Mable from bidding up things they could not use. Some of those hasty purchases encumbered storage rooms at Ca' d'Zan and the museum.[10] In spite of some impulse buying, however, their auction purchases showed a rising level of sophistication.

The Ringling homes became furnished in the style of upper-class houses of a previous generation.

In less than six years, Ringling added more than 400 paintings of major and minor artists, bringing his collection to 625, and several times that many art objects.[11] The sheer number of his purchases and the astonishing speed of buying led some onlookers to question whether this was anything more than a shallow, uncritical fancy.

His critics aside, John Ringling was enjoying an exciting challenge. He had quickly discovered the rewards and satisfaction that made art collecting attractive to many like himself who could afford fine works of art and in return found gratification in ownership. It was part of living in the grand manner, but it was more than that. He perceived himself as the builder of a monument that surpasses any stone memorial.

The artistic memorial that Ringling was building became part of his Sarasota program. "Culture" came to be an integral part of his marketing strategy. Ultimately his program led to an endowment of the city with a cultural character that was unique in the resorts of Florida. Although many others had a part in forming that character, Ringling's museum and accompanying art school were crucial to it.

As the museum neared completion, there was much public curiosity and conjecture by the press. "It is quite natural," *ARTnews* explained to its readers, "that great scale should become one of the foremost attributes of Mr. Ringling's museum; huge galleries, enormous canvases, great names."[12] Only a few had been invited to see the Ringling collection. Sarasota was remote from the nation's art centers, known to few art professionals and visited by fewer still.

Aware of a certain prejudice against the circus man-turned-collector, *ARTnews* wryly commented, "The number of men who are active both as heads of art museums and of circuses is somewhat limited. There are scholarly gentlemen whose candle trembles as the calliope roars past, who may contend that a great chasm exists between the two fields." Whereas Ringling's defenders have often tended to isolate the circus man from the art collector to forestall criticism, *ARTnews* adopted the opposite view, suggesting that the same gifts of showmanship and vitality that made the circus thrilling were excellent qualities in an art collector.[13]

Many of Ringling's detractors were misled by their failure to realize that the collector of 1925 was far more discriminating than the newly rich buyer of a decade or two earlier. As he became more experienced, Ringling came to know (and learn from) prominent dealers such as Arthur Newton in London and Sir Joseph Duveen in New York and London; many of his purchases came from these two. Among museum directors, Edward Forbes of the Fogg Museum at Harvard was perhaps the most prominent with whom he became acquainted and whose respect he gained. Most often it was Böhler who discovered many of the paintings that entered the Ringling Museum, but at no time did Böhler make the selections alone, as did so many agents who acted for rich American collectors. In consequence, the Ringling collection retains the stamp of his personality. Few others can be so closely identified with their owner.

Moreover, Ringling was less inclined than many rich Americans to "worship the certificate," the warranty of attribution to a great master as the ultimate criterion of worth. In that respect he was wise indeed, for in those years many a spurious certificate misled buyers not only as to author but as to provenance as well. This practice flourished particularly in America, where collecting was much in vogue among those with money but little experience. Journals of the art market contained a barrage of scholarly warnings to alert the unwary buyer. Sir Joseph Duveen offered an unequivocal judgment. "Moral number one—an expert's certificate is not worth the paper it is written on."[14] Robert Benson, owner of one of Britain's foremost collections of major Italian schools of painting, stated in his catalog: "To know what you like instead of saying 'amen' to what the world says you ought to like is to have kept your soul alive."[15] *ARTnews* put the same idea in more mundane terms: "The happiest collector and the most successful forget the market and buy to please themselves. Their rewards are certain for they will have the enjoyment that only pictures can bring."[16]

Certainly Ringling was impressed by great names; he was particularly attracted to the works of Titian and others of sixteenth-century Venice, yet he did not make such artists the only object of his search. He bought more by Rubens, Tintoretto, and Giordano. He did feel a certain awe when confronting distinguished provenance. His multiple purchases, which ranged up to twenty or more, came from the collections of rich and noble families. Perhaps he mistakenly saw in princely ownership a surer guarantee of attribution. Some of those collections were already dispersed when he started to buy. For example, the collection begun by the first marquess of Westminster around 1818 was auctioned by the second duke in 1924. From 1926 to 1930 Ringling bought no fewer than eight paintings from that sale after several years of searching, among them Rubens's *Pausias and Glycera,* another oversize canvas.[17] Ringling never ceased venerating the world's elect and their proud possessions. He found a special satisfaction in owning paintings from the great mansions and palaces of England and Europe, from owners whose names could be found in the *Almanach de Gotha.* Collecting brought him into the company of dukes and princes in a way that no other avocation could have done.

His penchant for buying from noble collections was one manifestation of Ringling's lifelong fascination with rank and wealth. And, as he had done in other aspects of his career, he now sought the acquaintance of people who were important in art and museum circles, at length gaining admission to this select company by proving that he was not merely a circus man but a knowledgeable amateur collector and connoisseur. However, an essential difference set him apart from scholarly museum specialists. Ringling was a proprietor, the sole owner of a museum. During his lifetime it remained a rich man's private domain rather than becoming a public monument. In contrast, the heads of the nation's major museums were professionals, serving under trustees and governors. Ringling failed to understand, or more likely chose to ignore, this difference and its implications. He became respected as the builder of a splendid gallery, but as long as he remained its proprietor, his museum stood outside the mainstream. In 1928 he sought to overcome this barrier by naming a panel of world-renowned figures who were to become directors of his museum, but he never carried out the promise.[18]

Ringling may never have realized how much he owed to his friend Julius (Lulu) Böhler for helping him to gain admission to the circles of world-class collectors and to develop certain tastes. Böhler was a greatly respected dealer in Munich, the owner of a first-rank collection and a palatial gallery inherited from his father. In New York, Böhler was associated with the prestigious Reinhardt Galleries until he opened his own establishment at the Ritz Carlton Hotel.

In the course of their friendship, which lasted through Ringling's lifetime (although it diminished in later years), Böhler became the link between his client and the art market. Ringling, of course, was only one of many collectors who bought through Böhler, who came to New York several times each year, sometimes as the courier of valuable paintings for his clients. His few surviving letters show a warm and genuine affection for Mable and John, who were friends as well as clients.

Böhler was a true friend in the sense that he understood Ringling's position and encouraged him to adopt a practice that was followed by many European collectors who could rarely afford the finest works or the greatest names. Such collectors frequently purchased good, even superior works produced by artists who were less exalted—and therefore less expensive—than those of the first rank. Paintings were selected for their artistic quality, and it was this principle that Böhler stressed. He did, however, tend to overlook or disregard damage that might have dissuaded Ringling from buying in some instances. Another feature that helped to cement their relationship was Böhler's genuineness; although extremely well known for having secured important paintings for many of the world's greatest museums and collectors, he was never arrogant. Böhler understood perfectly what Ringling wanted: that he wished to assemble a large collection to fill his museum and that he wished to do so speedily and in a certain price range.

Böhler soon learned what pleased his energetic client. He guided Ringling toward styles and periods that he liked and that were then selling for prices far below their range a generation earlier—some because the artists were no longer in vogue, others because buyers of the 1920s preferred smaller canvases. Examples were Rubens, Poussin, Murillo, artists whose works were often being auctioned for about one-third of their former selling prices.

Not only buyer preferences, but also circumstances of the time uniquely favored Ringling's aims. Many rich Americans were no longer living in the huge mansions of the 1880s and 1890s. The new generation of buyers favored smaller paintings for their city townhouses and apartments. Out of favor were the large Baroque canvases of many seventeenth-century Flemish and Italian artists, paintings of monumental figures that had been produced for the palaces or villas of nobles, princes of the Church, or family chapels in churches. Post-Renaissance patrons had favored works that reflected the new religious fervor of the times, with a new dynamism and animation that was a rejection of Renaissance devotional images and more recent mannerist extremes. These qualities of complete naturalism, so popular in the seventeenth century, were features that Ringling found compelling. His collection was developing an emphasis, and he was beginning to assemble an outstanding representation of Italian Baroque.

As he bought against the tide of fashion, Ringling's developing tastes fell conveniently into a pattern that fitted neatly into general conditions in Europe. German postwar politicians and bankers had first stimulated and then manipulated the country's rampant inflation to serve their own ends. In 1923 Hjalmar Schacht was charged with stabilizing the mark. His draconian method was to introduce the Reichsmark, and to exchange old marks at a rate of one trillion to one. For the first time since the war had ended, Germans were required to pay taxes. One consequence was that many a discrowned prince, including several Hohenzollerns, was willing to turn family treasures into hard currency.

In Mussolini's Italy, chaotic conditions were concealed beneath Il Duce's Fascist system, where order was maintained by his increasingly repressive police. Ambitious businessmen and aristocrats alike rushed to join the regime through conviction or fear. Some recognized the signs of approaching disintegration; they quietly prepared for the future by moving assets into cash or real estate outside the country. Once again churches were surrendering their altar pieces and side-chapel paintings to pay for repairs and restoration.

With the Treaty of Locarno in 1925, surface tensions subsided enough so that a peaceful era seemed at hand. Europe appeared to be regaining its equilibrium, and the later 1920s became a pleasant time for travel, for leisurely visits to museums and churches to inspect the works displayed in the salesrooms and galleries. This was an ideal time to be rich and to buy art. (There had been other periods in Europe's history when similar conditions brought works of art flowing into the market. For example, the grand tour of British nobles in the eighteenth century started many collections that grew with the dislocations of the Napoleonic wars.)

Ringling and Böhler brought to this scene of opportunity a combination of enthusiasm, shared knowledge, and ready money. In London, where much of Ringling's buying took place, the economy was less shattered by the war, but a number of major owners had placed their collections on the market. Taxation was especially severe for families in which wartime deaths had threatened the dissolution of great estates through a succession of death duties. Some owners no longer had any direct heirs. Others saw omens in the uncertainties of the times and decided that the time for keeping large, private collections was ending. Inflated prices for fine Renaissance and even earlier works made selling more attractive to those who preferred to hold more liquid assets.

Connoisseur skills at that time were essentially those of close observation and study of available sources that helped to document many unsigned works. X-ray techniques were challenging the conventional experts, but few seemed to realize that in all instances, the result of analysis by whatever means was still an opinion and therefore subject to revision. Bernard Berenson, speaking ex cathedra from his villa in Florence, was the best-known arbiter in this intensely competitive field. He authenticated many attributions under contract with Sir Joseph Duveen.[19] Such authoritative opinions (which later turned out to be worthless, according to Duveen) had a profound impact, causing the market price of paintings to soar when a first-rank artist was named. Yet opinions were only verifiable by a second expert. In consequence, collectors were vulnerable to misjudgments and even deliberately false claims. Given the state of the art, Ringling was probably as safe with his own judgment backed by Böhler as he would have been with any other authority.

The summer auctions at Christie's in London offered splendid opportunities for Ringling, but there were risks of error in these sales. Many great houses held paintings that had been purchased in Italy in the eighteenth and nineteenth centuries. Attributions made so long ago would soon be exposed to critical opinion. Many might not stand careful scrutiny, but nevertheless were placed on sale bearing their traditional authorship. Ringling placed his trust in the noble titles of the owners. In the seasons of 1927 and 1928 a flood of famous collections came intact to the auction rooms. In their enthusiasm and eagerness to share in the bonanza, Ringling and Böhler were perhaps too ready to accept established attributions. Ultimately, some gave way; others proved to be valid, and still others proved to be the works of artists even more distinguished.

John Ringling knew that he was a novice in a field where he needed all the knowledge he could gather. He brought to his study of art a remarkable memory for detail, just as he had once amazed his brothers with his capacity to memorize masses of railway timetables. The books and journals on the shelves in his room at Ca' d'Zan works included Johann Winckelmann's *History of Ancient Art* (1763), Bernard Berenson's *Florentine Painters of the Renaissance* (1909), monographs on Rembrandt, Rubens, and many Italian artists, gallery guides, and private catalogs of major collections. Eventually he owned several hundred book and journals that became the foundation of his art library.

Notes that Ringling made in the margins of art journals offer clues to his pursuit of authority. He was particularly interested in commentary about works attributed to Titian, and focused on newly discovered facts about Titian's original vivid tones and the ways they had become darkened or discolored. The more perceptive researchers were coming to recognize that when a painting is obscured by thick, yellow varnish, the varnish may have been added to hide damage from overcleaning or even abrasion of the original surface. Among these researchers was Baron Detlev von Hadeln, who came to Sarasota to view the Ringling collection. The baron was then publishing his study of several Titian canvases. Studies of this sort were among the tools used to assess authenticity, and for Ringling they became sources of information that helped him to make purchases. Ringling was by no means an innocent among predators, but even when misrepresentation was not an issue (as in his purchases of paintings attributed to Titian), inexpert opinion misled him. His Titians, which gave him so much pleasure, ultimately were reattributed to studio painters after closer study—but only after his death.

Ringling left no memoir, nor even any correspondence, to disclose his thoughts and feelings about his collection and his study of art history. Whatever correspondence Böhler may have kept was lost from his files in Munich in the chaos of World War II.[20] Hearsay, anecdotes, and a few interviews are about all that remain to explain Ringling's passion for buying paintings. The anecdotes must be viewed with skepticism, for Ringling was always a showman, never averse to embroidering a story to suit the occasion. One account reports a conversation between Ringling and a Sarasota neighbor, the Princess Cantacuzene of Russia. The princess, the former Julia Grant, was a granddaughter of President Grant and a niece of Berthe Palmer. When she expressed surprise at Ringling's sudden interest in fine art, he replied that he had started many years ago buying inexpensive pictures. Upon being told by the director of the Chicago Art Institute that they were worthless, he said, he had discarded them and started studying art books.[21]

In a 1928 interview for the *Christian Science Monitor*, he mentioned that he had been buying paintings for twenty-five years, and that more recently he had started to acquire bronzes and sculptures. This was a particularly curious remark, for it is unlikely that he then owned any bronzes or original sculptures. (He may have been speaking of the bronze copies of Greek and Hellenistic sculptures that he bought in 1925 for the Ritz Carlton Hotel.) He also recalled that at one time he had bought some French pictures: "People were buying French pictures in those days. I was very pleased with them at first." Ringling's next reflections are among the few that offer any insight into his feelings about his collection:

But I was looking about and I discovered the Old Masters. It seemed to me that I had been wrong about my first purchases. They lost meaning for me so I gave them away. When I began to learn, I did not want any one school, or no school at all. My own viewpoint and tastes were shaping, and I wished it to be toward liberalism and universality. I must keep the broad view, I thought. By degrees I learned of Titian and Giotto, Romney, Velázquez, and Michelangelo. I was pleased when I obtained Velázquez' portrait of Mariana, Queen of Spain, wife of King Philip IV. [This painting had special meaning for him, for he always kept it in his home.] It made me happy to have Titian's *Queen of Cyprus* and Tintoretto's *Young Lady with a Dog* (described by

Robert Benson as a "noble ruin"). Everything new gave me something I had not had before; those things are hard to define; you know for yourself when paintings give them to you but it is not easy to tell anyone else.

When he spoke of the origins of his idea for a museum, Ringling refused to be drawn into speaking of his purpose or motivation except in a rather casual way: "Well, you know from time to time I have found some fifteenth-century doors and pillars I liked, I have bought them. The doors are bronze, three pairs of them. The museum garden has an arcade, and some columns I found too, will go there; they belonged once to beautiful Italian renaissance structures. I had to have a permanent place to put those things; I was wanting to build a beautiful memorial. It seemed to me it was time, and what better place could the doors and pillars have?"[22]

On another occasion he offered an interviewer an explanation of his initial interest in fine art that differed from what he had related to the Princess Cantacuzene. It was the only public statement in which he connected his circus experience to his interest in art:

You see, every year when I was planning our poster campaign, I had artist chaps in conference to design the posters, circus posters. Of course, they made sketches. As I looked them over it seemed to me that every now and then they missed something in the action of a galloping horse, something that missed the grace and spirit of a lion at bay, the Hogarthian line of beauty in the pose of a feminine gymnast. And you see, I didn't know what to tell them. I was not an art critic, I felt there was something wrong or something lacking, something that I wanted to see, and something that I felt other people wanted to see. So I got together some little books on art and studied them. They had pictures, illustrations from famous canvases. Rosa Bonheur's *Horse Show*, things like that. And I found things in the little books to which I could turn and say, "Make it like that as much as you can."

He decided to see the originals, he continued, and found them even more fascinating than he believed they could be, so he said to himself that he would just collect some of them.[23]

This explanation seems too facile, particularly the reference to little books. But it was typical of Ringling's manner. His tendency to oversimplify in speaking sometimes reveals a hint of the pride that feigns humility. Speaking of their visits together in the winter of 1922–23, Böhler later recalled that neither John nor Mable showed any interest in discussions about painting—a contradiction of Ringling's story about his pursuit of little books and pictures.

In 1925 Ringling and Böhler went to Italy for a shopping expedition. In Venice Ringling bought tons of statues, columns, marble doorways, and other fragments of buildings and had them shipped to Sarasota. At the Chiurazzi foundry in Naples, Ringling bought a bronze casting of Michelangelo's *David*, one of several produced in 1874 by artisans at the foundry. Other purchases at Naples included the bronze copies of Green and Hellenistic sculptures that were to ornament Harding Circle and the boulevards at St. Armands, and later the court of the museum.[24] At the end of the trip, Böhler recollected, he heard about the museum for the first time:

> The last day in Naples I was sitting alone with Mr. Ringling when he told me that he and Mrs. Ringling had been pondering over what they could do for Sarasota that would perpetuate their names. They had finally decided to build a museum and to collect pictures and other works of art. I was thunderstruck, especially when he said that he already had engaged an architect to make sketches, and that he hoped I would soon go to New York to give my opinion. Furthermore, he asked me to buy for him two pictures I had talked about during our trip, without thinking for one moment that he would buy them. . . . so after he left I bought those pictures and took them along to New York.[25]

In time, the most unflattering stories about Ringling's motives were dispelled. One story, claiming that he had turned to art collecting at the urging of his wife, solely to gain social esteem in New York, was clearly false, since neither John nor Mable had any pretensions to a role in New York society. Some said he went about buying up job lots, hoping to find something of value among them. Still others scoffed at his collection, claiming that he had bought nothing but copies. Somewhat more mean-spirited were the reports that he proposed to use his paintings for exhibition with the circus—a sufficiently plausible story to arouse ill feelings, even a reluctance to sell to so déclassé a buyer.[26]

Those reports and others in the same vein were intended to harm his standing in the community of honorable dealers and museum professionals. When he bought particularly large canvases he was accused of measuring artistic merit in square yards, though his largest, *Diana's Hunting Party* by Hans Makart (about fifteen by thirty-two feet), was purchased at a Metropolitan Museum sale.[27] Makart was an Austrian (1840–1884) whose work was displayed in many of the national galleries of Europe. But it did not matter; Ringling never escaped his circus image. Upon the dedication and opening of the Ringling art school in October 1931, *Time* noted that "Ringling's taste in art is authentic. . . . he did select his own pictures. But [referring to the large Rubens cartoons] his taste still runs to circus poster size."[28] However, *Time*'s comments were without malice, and by that time Ringling had established his place among serious collectors.

The initial purchases that he and Böhler negotiated in Naples had scarcely been delivered to New York in December 1925 when Ringling was ready to send him searching after more. There was no space for hanging or even storing such treasures; Böhler's first deliveries were kept at the Reinhardt Galleries.[29] Early in the new year, Böhler was commissioned to bring still other fine canvases on his next trip to New York. Ringling telegraphed his delight to Mable; for Böhler had produced a "wonderful Titian, the greatest bargain in the history of Titians, and then a few days later, a fine Velázquez."[30]

The traditional summer journey across Europe now had an added purpose and a new excitement for John and Mable. Wherever Ringling and Böhler traveled together from city to city, Ringling was always the eager scholar, learning as much as he could from their visits to major and minor museums. Among the ones he came to know well, he always found the greatest pleasure at the Alte Pinakothek in Munich, Böhler's home city. His new knowledge of particular artists and schools of painting would prove valuable at auctions, where competition was often keen and a hasty or mistaken judgment could be costly to an unwary buyer.

At first Ringling was without a pattern or focus. After his first few selections, he turned to buying portraits. He bought two of uncertain authenticity from Böhler, one attributed to Tintoretto and another, *Portrait of a Gentleman,* attributed to Titian. Upon later scrutiny, the latter was judged to be the work of assistants and only *perhaps* partly from the hand of Titian himself. It was renamed, first *Palladin and Page,* then later *Portrait of a Nobleman in Armor and Red Hose.* (The unnamed nobleman appeared to be Duke Guidobaldo II, a member of the Della Rovere family, elevated to be the duke of Urbino by Pope Julius II, who was a Della Rovere.) Next came several German princesses (two sold by displaced Hohenzollerns); all were eighteenth-century court portraits by Anton Pesne, a French painter who was popular at the court of Frederick II of Prussia. Attractive as these portraits were, the coming vogue was for British portraits in the Van Dyck style and the works of Gainsborough and Reynolds, which were already commanding record prices.

Scarcely five months after his 1925 purchases in Naples, Ringling concluded a deal that permanently established the focus and the central core of his collection. The previous autumn Böhler had told him of four exceedingly large Rubens cartoons (patterns for tapestries) that were awaiting a buyer. The cartoons, from a larger series titled *The Triumph of the Eucharist,* were by Rubens and his assistants (1625–28). The series had been commissioned at Brussels by the governor of the Spanish Netherlands, the Archduchess Isabella Clara Eugenia, to commemorate the Spanish victory over the Dutch at the Battle of Breda. The cartoons went to England in 1803 and by inheritance became part of the duke of Westminster's collection; three were placed with Christie's for auction in the summer of 1924. They were withdrawn from the sale when the total bids at $10,000 amounted to only a fraction of the duke's reserve price. He was now offering the same three, together with a fourth, for about $100,000.[31]

In May 1926, Böhler bought the four somewhat reluctantly, claiming that the asking price (ten times the total auction bids) was excessive in view of the oversized canvases and the current disfavor for Rubens's high Baroque style. He then sold them to Ringling, who was delighted with their dynamic energy and the monumental size of the figures.[32] His museum was then only in the planning stage and he was able to include a gallery designed especially to hold them. The result, said Ringling, would be to make his museum look like the old museums of Europe. Böhler later conceded that he was right: the cartoons gave the museum an air of uncommon splendor and authority.

Just before the *Triumph of the Eucharist* deal, Böhler and Ringling had attended an important event, the auction of the contents of the Vincent Astor mansion. Only a few of the more than one hundred paintings sold that day merited Böhler's nod. Some were at best minor works, the rest mediocre. Most of the collection hung salon-style in the great gallery-ballroom, filling the walls frame to frame. The prices averaged about $300; in some instances, the value of the frame exceeded the auction price. However, Ringling paid some of the highest prices of the sale. He bought three large French works, including Van Marke's *Dans les Landes,* which showed masses of sturdy cattle in a meadow, halting as though posed for the artist; for many years it had been the centerpiece of the Astor ballroom.[33] A more important selection was J. B. E. Detaille's *Le Campagne en Russie.* It has since been identified as a scene from the Franco-Prussian war of 1871, a major work of this artist-historian who used his powerful realism to document many of France's major battles.

Astor's great chateau in the style of Henry II was itself a work of art. Ringling purchased many of its opulent appointments to decorate interiors at his museum. He also bought the inner entrance gateway, which eventually became the main entrance to the Ringling Museum. It was a superb wrought-bronze set of double doors with fixed side panels and a fanlight that extended across its nearly thirteen-foot width.

The Astor home was built in 1893–95 for Mrs. William Astor. The architecture was closest in style to late sixteenth-century French, also showing Italian influence and still more of the influence of its own day. The richly crowded rooms were filled with reproductions of court furniture from the periods of Louis XIV, XV, and XVI—precisely the sort of splendor that John Ringling admired.[34] At minimum cost he acquired two entire rooms (reproductions of seventeenth- and eighteenth-century French salons) and transported them to Sarasota. Although he debated buying a third salon paneled in white and gold, and the marble-walled dining room, he perhaps recognized, for once, that too many period rooms would be unsuitable for the Italianate museum he was building.

The great bronze doors of the William Astor home, New York. Ringling purchased the doors for the front entrance to his art museum. American Art Association auction catalog, April 1926.

The documentation of the two salons remains incomplete. The Astor mansion was designed by Richard Morris Hunt, known for his ostentatious taste. The southwest regency salon—richest of all in the great house—contained walls, mirrors, and over-door painted canvases provided by Jules Allard et Fils of Paris and New York. The marble fireplace was sold separately but the leaf-scrolled over-mantel mirror with "J.J.A." medallion cresting was included. The walls were finished in cream lacquer, embellished with gilded molding, hand-carved rococo medallions, and festoons of flowers and trailing ribbons. Each panel was further decorated with festooned shell motifs, strap carving, and trophies of arrows.[35] The arrows, echoing the Rothschild symbol of bunched arrows, are an example of efforts to emulate what had become known as "le gout Rothschild."[36]

The southeast salon was paneled in dark oak with parcel gilt decoration, a gilded molding, and hand-carved shell, leaf scroll, and floral ornament. The room was originally Colonel J. J. Astor's dining room. When Astor renovated in 1910 and added a new marble-walled dining room, the original became a library. The eighteenth-century Dutch arcadian scenic canvases on the wall panels were removed, and the walls were hung with tapestries and portraits.[37] When the room was installed at the museum, Ringling had the canvases remounted on all the panels. Although he bought an oval ceiling painting from a third salon, Ringling never had it installed in the museum.[38]

Ringling emerged from the Astor sale as probably the most successful buyer, and without question the biggest spender. Although he had not abandoned his plan for the Ritz Carlton, he was starting to think of transferring some of his hopes, and his art objects, from the keys to the mainland and his planned memorial. He went once more to Europe that summer of 1926, buying more columns and fragments, though he must have known that the Ritz Carlton was destined to become a huge, ungainly liability that could not be saved. While in Genoa he found a small Rubens, *Head of a Monk* (now considered studio work), and Fra Bartolomeo's *Holy Family and the Infant Saint John* (now ascribed to Mario Albertinelli with little of Bartolomeo's work).

On his return journey Ringling stopped again in London. There he bought an important work, Francesco Granacci's *The Assumption of the Virgin*. The Virgin, borne aloft by angels, lowers the Santissima Cintola ("sacred sash") to the hand of Saint Thomas, who is one of a number of saints and apostles at the tomb.[39] The Granacci held special interest because Giorgio Vasari, a Florentine biographer who sometimes made doubtful assertions, describes and praises the picture at length, suggesting that Granacci's friend and colleague Michelangelo perhaps had a hand in the kneeling figure of St. Thomas. Both artists were pupils of Domenico Ghirlandajo, and Vasari's suggestion carries a measure of plausibility, though he cites no evidence other than the quality of the work. The previous owner of the painting, R. Langton Douglas, whom Ringling came to know well, was a leading Renaissance scholar and authority.[40]

In the following year, with greater self-confidence, Ringling acted on his own initiative. He bought Rembrandt's *Saint John the Evangelist*, one of several purchases from the Charles C. Stillman sale. About this time, through Böhler, he made his most costly single purchase, Frans Hals's *Pieter Olycan*, at a private sale in England. (Hals had also painted the young Olycan at age twenty-nine, many years earlier, now in the Mauritzhaus in the Hague.) At about $100,000, the Hals equaled the price paid for the four Rubens cartoons, but Sir Joseph Duveen offered him three times that amount when he saw it in New York.[41] Intense interest in this sale brought more than 1,200 dealers, collectors, and spectators to the auction room. Joseph Duveen paid $285,000, the highest auction price ever at a sale in America at that time, for Rembrandt's *Titus in an Armchair*. This was substantially more than Ringling's $76,000 for *Saint John the Evangelist*. The difference was in part due to the subject, Rembrandt's son; moreover, it was an earlier work and more finely executed. There was also a sentimental reason; Duveen had owned it once before. Also at the Stillman sale, Ringling bought the rococo *Madame de Bourbon Conti*—then attributed to Van Loo, later to Carl Antoine Coypel—and Giovanni Bellini's *Madonna and Child* (now attributed to Rocco Marconi, a pupil of Bellini).[42]

Ringling had moved into a higher echelon with his purchase of the Rembrandt and the Hals, although he never again bought such expensive single works. The 1927 season in London brought onto the market a flood of important paintings. One of the foremost private collections in England, that of the late Sir George Holford, was auctioned in a series of sales. For two generations this collection had graced Dorchester House, Holford's London home, a great Italian place with its own picture gallery. Several hundred works of art had been assembled by Robert Holford and inherited by his son, Sir George, an official in the household of King Edward VII and again in that of George V. The senior Holford had assembled the collection in the middle of the nineteenth century; many of his paintings had come to England's earlier collectors as part of the 1790–1815 art migration from the Continent.

The Holford sale presented a dilemma that was common with many well-known nineteenth-century collections. Few of the hundreds of canvases in Britain's noble homes had been examined by modern methods; their repute was based on long-standing attributions to some of the greatest painters of Western culture. Although the Holford collection held some real treasures, many works would not stand up to newer authentication techniques. The *Times* cautiously rated them "important and otherwise," a correct assessment since not more than a dozen among more than 100 works were first-rate. But the sale was a spectacular event. A throng of more than a thousand sightseers, collectors from abroad, and dealers from nearly every notable gallery in England, Europe, and America were present.

Böhler seemed to be as excited as his client. "The second sale is on July 15th and is very important for us! There are big Caraccis of wonderful quality; there is a marvelous Andrea del Sarto also very big but one of the finest. This might bring money, but this we ought to get."[43] Del Sarto's *Vision of Saint Matthew* did not fall to Ringling at the sale, but to a dealer from whom Ringling eventually bought it. Böhler had probably based his opinion on a photograph. (Holford's brother-in-law Robert Benson rated it as a copy, a later version of the one at the Prado in Madrid.)

The large, seventeenth-century Italian canvases, the proto and early Baroque that had been so popular in the first half of the nineteenth century, aroused almost no buyer interest other than Ringling's. Works by the Caracci, Carlo Dolci, and others of their kind sold for under $500. The larger the canvas, the smaller the bids.[44]

Among the high prices were several for paintings attributed to Titian. Böhler bought one that gave Ringling singular pleasure. It had been in Lucien Bonapart's collection that was dispersed in 1819— exciting to Ringling both for artist and provenance. Now titled *A Sultana of Venice*, it was one of two portraits of the same title in the Holford collection. The subject, favorite wife of the Grand Turk, was earlier known as Catarina Cornaro, Queen of Cyprus; Titian's daughter was presumed to have been the model.[45]

At the second sale were three works by Velázquez. Ringling was top bidder on the most important—a full-length portrait of the young Philip IV of Spain in campaign attire.[46] Robert Holford had bought it from the Alton Towers sale in 1853, when it sold with doubtful attribution for one-tenth of Ringling's price. The painting had not been seen publicly since 1877; its reappearance was a matter of some interest as an obscure work of Velázquez, who had painted his royal patron's portrait no fewer than twelve times, allowing nearly every important museum in Europe to acquire one.

Ringling also bought *Holy Family with a Donor* (early 1520s) by Gaudenzio Ferrari, often regarded as the finest northern Italian painter of his time.[47] It was in astonishingly fine condition, including the panel, which retains its pristine form. Another find was a full-length figure of Francesco Franceschini, purchased as the work of Romanaino but now thought to be Veronese's earliest inscribed and dated portrait. The obscure sitter's one claim to distinction was having his portrait painted by so prominent an artist. Another extremely fine canvas, in the early Baroque style out of fashion in Ringling's day, was *Susanna Surprised by the Elders.* It has been attributed at various times to each of the Caracci (Ludovico, Agostino, and Annibale) and more recently to Sisto Badalaccio. From the first Holford sale, where he was represented by Böhler, and the second a year later, which he attended himself, Ringling acquired altogether twenty-eight pictures, and five more later from galleries that bought at the auction. Of these, six were later determined to be the work of the presumed artist's workshop or were copies of the original work. Four were thought to be too badly damaged for restoration.[48] Such were the hazards of collecting in the 1920s, when historic collections were first exposed to critical analysis.

The unusual number of important sales in 1927–28 helps to explain how Ringling could acquire such a large collection of significant works in a short time. Among the sales, Robert Benson's was perhaps the most spectacular. Like his brother-in-law Holford, Benson owned more than one hundred Italian paintings. His were more recently collected, many of the finest rank, divided among six prominent Italian schools of painting. Böhler found the presale photographs even more exciting than the Holford sale. Sir Joseph Duveen was negotiating to buy the entire collection for $2.5 million and had promised Böhler not to sell any until Ringling had made selections. Duveen succeeded in his plan—the price may have been higher—and brought the whole to America, where he promptly recovered nearly half his investment in the sale of four Duccio altar panels.[49] John Ringling bought at least two canvases from this splendid collection.

Ringling's next major purchase, early in 1928, brought him in one gesture a great miscellany of art and fine furnishings. Sir Joseph Duveen had brought to his New York studio an outstanding assembly of paintings, furniture, decorative arts, and liturgical objects from the collections of Emile Gavet, a rich French industrialist of the nineteenth century. The collection and its privately printed *catalogue raisonné* (analytical list) purchased by William K. Vanderbilt, then later placed with Duveen for sale. Ringling bought the entire offering. Two of the finer works in it were Piero di Cosimo's *The Building of a Palace* and, by the Master of the Lathrop Tondo, *Madonna della Cintola*. This version of the Assumption of Mary was a favored subject in Florence, for the sacred *cintola* ("sash") was among the treasures of the Cathedral at Prato (a neighboring town), brought from the East by a crusader as part of his wife's dowry. Other notable objects in this collection were several sixteenth- and seventeenth-century clerical chests, Renaissance watches, jewels, and historic vestments.[50]

Ringling found another opportunity to buy en masse at a sale of Cypriote archaic and antique objects. Robert W. DeForest, then director of the Metropolitan Museum, arranged with the Anderson Galleries to place for public auction a large surplus of Cypriote and other classical antiquities that were in storage. At two sales in March and April 1928, hundreds of items were auctioned, most of them from the collections of Luigi Palma di Cesnola, an Austrian adventurer who came to America to serve in the Union Army. In 1865 he was made a major general in a New York regiment. When peace returned, he was named U.S. consul on the Turkish island of Cyprus, where he also acquired the title of Russian consul. Cesnola was an avid collector but not an archaeologist; hence he left only weak documentation of his many excavations. In ten years of aggressive collecting, he assembled the largest and richest hoard of objects reflecting the unique encounter of civilizations, religions, and archaic art on the island, before its culture moved on to Greece.[51]

Ringling had no special knowledge of this field, but he bought with confidence stemming from the authority of Metropolitan ownership. He bought more than 1,000 objects, guided in his selections by Karl Freund of the Anderson staff. No less than three-fourths of the entire offering became his; sixty other collectors and museums accounted for the remainder. A few rival bidders were able to acquire some select pieces, but Ringling drove the prices up and made them pay handsomely for their successes. In one swift action he had become the owner of enough archaic and antique relics to found a museum of ancient art. The Metropolitan sale remained his one excursion into the ancient world.

Such a lavish purchase so far afield from the rest of his collection may have had the appearance of speculative, impulsive, or superficial interest. But Ringling clearly considered these objects of great significance in the movement of Western art from its remote beginnings to the more familiar expressions in the painting and sculpture of Western Europe. His Cypriote collection formed the largest assembly of archaic Greek art in America outside the Metropolitan. The unfinished "round gallery" under the bridge between the two wings of the museum became the storage area for the stone, pottery, and glass relics. Ringling intended to house them in a separate building, but he was never able to carry out this plan. Nor did he have access to anyone capable of selecting, arranging, and preparing it for display.

He made only one more mass purchase. When he went to Europe in July 1929 after Mable's death, he went to the sale of an important British collection belonging to the earl of Yarborough. Many of the earl's pictures had been brought from Italy more than a century earlier when his ancestor was British Resident at Venice. Among them was Il Guercino's *Annunciation,* a dramatic painting in two irregular panels that had hung over an arch in a church at Reggia Emilia until 1803. The auction house cast doubt upon its authenticity, and Ringling bought the two panels for fifty-six dollars. Later certified as Guercino's work, they gained in value enormously. The purchase was typical of Ringling's willingness to buy a painting on his own judgment, because he liked it or perhaps trusted its noble provenance. This was either an example of perceptive connoisseur opinion or else it was a lucky guess.[52]

The Yarborough collection offered several other works that were destined to outlive the temporary eclipse of the Baroque period. Ringling's spectacular selection from that sale was Nicolas Poussin's *The Holy Family.* Its quiet, contemplative, elegant pose is typical of Poussin's special power, its composition not unlike that of his *Holy Family* at the Hermitage in St. Petersburg. Ringling also bought a remarkable series by Sébastien Bourdon, *The Seven Acts of Mercy.* The seven large and important seventeenth-century canvases show damage that could have been the result of unskilled cleaning or a chemical change in the composition of the paints, thus allowing the sienna ground to show through.[53]

His selections from the Yarborough sale show how far Ringling progressed in a short time. With just four years of experience he had become a sophisticated buyer. The excitement of the first years was followed by a more sober but still enthusiastic search for art. Between 1929 and 1931, he bought more widely in various schools and periods, seeking to achieve what he had once called "universality" by avoiding concentration on one particular school. He bought more in New York, adding a few nineteenth-century American works to give balance to his collection. There and in London he bought several British portraits but did not compete for the elegant Gainsborough figures that were then commanding the highest prices, pushed through the half-million-dollar barrier by Duveen. During these few years he also added nearly fifty Dutch paintings, many of them expressing the quiet tranquility of the northern Netherlands in contrast to the dynamism of Flemish and Italian Baroque works. To broaden the scope of his collection, he bought examples of Gothic, earlier Flemish, German, and several fine pre-Renaissance Italian works; the earliest was an arcane allegorical representation of the Crucifixion dating from about 1350.[54] The high Baroque era was still shunned by buyers who based their selections on fashion, leaving collectors such as Ringling to acquire major artists' works at noncompeting prices.

Individual artists also experience the rise and fall of fashion. Among those no longer in vogue was Rosa Bonheur, whose animals Ringling particularly admired. His purchase of her *Labourage Nivernais* for forty-six guineas ($230) was a vivid example of how an artist falls from favor. This canvas, painted in 1850, represented the unity of the French peasant, his land and nation, and the labor of his oxen—a tranquil scene in the turmoil of the 1848–50 upheaval when France was torn by revolution and strife. It was a huge canvas (four by nine feet), one of several reproducing an earlier version that hung in the Luxembourg Palace until moved to Fontainebleau. (Although Ringling was a keen admirer of Bonheur's horses, his other Bonheur purchase was a painting of highland deer.)

The precipitous fall of prices for Bonheur and her British counter-part, Landseer, led A. C. R. Carter, the art critic for the *London Daily Telegraph*, to review the history of *Labourage Nivernais*. In 1866, when French salon paintings were in high favor, Lord Wimborne bought it for $10,000 (about $200,000 today). It was sold to the 1929 owner, W. H. Smith, for $23,000 in 1888. Carter added that he was probably the only survivor of that 1888 sale who was present in 1929 to witness the turnabout in buyer favor: "The fact is that the day of the big wall-spacer is over. There is no room in the ordinary house for a huge canvas, and the public galleries say they have all the Bonheurs and Landseers necessary." The *Daily Telegraph's* critic ended his comments: "The modern market was inured to this depreciation and nobody shed a crocodile tear when the last bid for this huge Bonheur picture was only forty-six guineas."[55] This was but one example of changing fashion; a John Charlton canvas of the same size, admired in the Paris exposition of 1890, brought only three guineas in London in 1929.[56]

Ringling spent freely in 1930; a good circus season had insulated him from the first blows of the Depression. However, as he went on buying, he chose less expensive works, already responding to the pressures of the deflation that was sweeping the United States and would soon spread to Europe. Pictures bought at auction had to be paid for promptly. Only with dealers whose galleries allowed regular buyers to establish credit would Ringling be permitted to carry an account. When he bought through Böhler, he paid promptly. At New York's Chatham and Phoenix National Bank, Ringling kept deposits particularly to pay for his art purchases. His 1930 checkbook (one of the few records that escaped the Internal Revenue Service sweep of his personal papers) shows a rush of purchases that year, when his museum was nearly ready to open. In January, he bought several paintings from Julius Weitzman, including an unnamed "Italian Portrait," Sebastiano Conca's *Vision of Aeneas in the Elysian Fields*, and Isaac Luttichuys' *Portrait of a Gentleman with a Spear*, all for $1,400. (This last work was reunited with its pendant portrait of the sitter's betrothed, *Lady with a Rose*, thanks to a donor's gift to the museum in 1981.) In July he acquired a group of three from William Sabin, eleven from J. Leger and Son, plus several from Christie's summer sale.[57]

By autumn 1931, Ringling had ceased buying. He made a single, mediocre purchase in 1932, doubtfully attributed to Marco d'Oggiano. With that he ended his brief but rather heady career as a buyer. Böhler and others familiar with Ringling's history later agreed that his mounting misfortunes prevented him from further refining the quality of his collection. Böhler believed that his client bought rapidly to fill his galleries; once that aim was met, he would have begun to trade and sell lesser works to improve the standard.[58] Of course he was consistently short of cash after 1931, his second marriage was foundering, and his illness was developing. All these and the financial problems that threatened to topple his business interests brought an abrupt end to the free-spending years.

In this last phase of his collecting, two important pictures seem never to have entered the collection. At the Yarborough sale he bought a supposed Rembrandt (later proven to be a copy) titled *A Woman with Folded Hands* and, on another occasion, an El Greco. Given the uncertain state of Ringling's finances by this time, both paintings could have come and gone quietly without leaving a trace. Later, Böhler recalled that around this time Ringling sold two Niklaus Manuel-Deutsch works from the Gavet collection for $40,000.[59]

Throughout his years of intensive buying, Ringling was also acquiring especially fine frames, both in Europe and in New York. This was an area in which he was one of the few active collectors. Some of these antique frames added much to the appearance of the museum; others

were stored. Among them was an unusually fine French frame desig-
nated for the Poussin *Holy Family.* An appraiser rated an antique from
Seville as the most spectacular in the museum; in his opinion no frame
in the National Gallery was equal to this one.[60]

Ringling's hope for a catalog of his art collection was never realized
in his lifetime, nor were all his pictures assembled in one place to make
possible a complete inventory. Most, of course, found their way to the
museum. A few, such as the Frans Hals portrait, remained for a time in
the New York apartment; some were hung in Ca' d'Zan; still others,
including the Hals, were pledged for loans and impounded in locked
warehouses. About twenty more adorned the public rooms of the John
Ringling Hotel in Sarasota. Shortly before his death, Ringling permitted his friend Hazen Titus, manager of the hotel, to borrow whatever
pictures he wished from Ca' d'Zan to make the hotel look elegant for
the 1936–37 season.[61]

The Great Depression exacted its toll, and Ringling stopped buying
art as he wrestled with the financial problems that threatened to over-
whelm him. His second wife, Emily, actively opposed his art purchases,
and he believed that she regarded the art collection with acute disfavor
and would have liked to have it sold. Later, in court, he said that she had
coveted a pearl necklace that cost about $250,000 and had said it could
easily be purchased from the proceeds of an art sale. She had urged in
her strongest language that the collection should be sold; if not, it
should be moved to Palm Beach, where it would be appreciated.[62]
Several times during the following years the collection was at risk for
payment of debts. In the remaining months of their marriage, Emily
tried to help fend off the predatory adversaries whose demands threatened the very existence of the collection.

An overview of Ringling's picture-hunting years discloses the diversity of his collection—its range of schools, national cultures, and periods. There was a profound difference between the selections of his
earlier and later stages of collecting. Only after he came within Böhler's
orbit was he able to move from the indiscriminate, untutored buyer to
the rank of a recognized collector in the professional art market. The
discovery that enabled Ringling to gain a niche among the world's
buyers and sellers was one that he was unlikely to have expressed and
perhaps did not recognize: he found that noble art is wealth in itself.

For about twenty years he bought what was in vogue, only to discover that he had made poor choices. He realized that following fashion without regard for quality was a useless guide, that it often led to buying bad and valueless art. His concentration on seventeenth-century Baroque proved to be a shrewd decision even though Baroque was no longer popular. He learned that with or without the nod of fashion, quality art gives its owner lasting pleasure; it exists in limited supply; it is transferable. Those principles formed the basis for his museum collection and they continue to define its enduring and unusual value. Employing the criterion of artistic quality, Ringling acquired many superior works by artists whose paintings were not then found in the routine choices of many American collectors.

✤ Like the design of Ca' d'Zan, the planning of the museum seemed to invite ideas and proposals from all who came within John and Mable's Sarasota circle in 1925–26. One feature was agreed upon from the outset: the museum must be of Italian design. It would have to stand alone on the estate in a parklike setting close to the bay. Rome's Villa Borghese, although lacking a waterfront, seemed an apt inspiration: a palace within a city, set apart in spacious grounds. The building would need to meet the requirements imposed by its location; it would be the first art museum in the nation placed on the edge of the sea in a subtropical climate.

The selection of John H. Phillips as the museum architect seemed almost a matter of proximity. Phillips and his wife were occasional visitors of Ralph and Ellen Caples, whose home adjoined the Ringlings'. Early in 1926, Phillips was commissioned by Caples to design an Italian-style home. Mable then promptly engaged him to design a guest house close to Ca' d'Zan. He made it a minor outpost of Venice.[63] Phillips was a man of considerable artistic talent and engineering skill. He had studied in Italy, where he too became enamored of the grace and rhythms of the Renaissance. He had designed many public buildings in Chicago and New York, and had won the commissions for the Grand Central Station entrance, the central section of the Metropolitan Museum, and the Massachusetts Institute of Technology campus on the Charles River in Cambridge. These credentials were important, but equally important was the fact that he and John and Mable liked each other; these three and Böhler made an unusually compatible team. It may have been Phillips's earlier work for McKim, Mead, and White that convinced Ringling to select him. Phillips once suggested that he got the job because he, too, came from Wisconsin. Whatever the reasoning, their arrangement began with a typical Ringling proposal: "Well, I want a museum built to put my art collection in, how'd you like to design one for me?"[64]

Ringling and Phillips walked around the accessible parts of the property. Phillips made some notes about the terrain and the many scattered Italian relics that were once intended for the Ritz Carlton Hotel. He went back to New York but soon returned with sketches and a cardboard model. Böhler was visiting at the time and expressed his delight; he also suggested some ideas for the loggia around the court.[65] Ringling was so excited by the concept that he commissioned Phillips at once; his plan had a restrained elegance that contrasted with the novelty and exuberance of Ca' d'Zan but did not conflict with it. John, Mable, and Phillips had already established their working relationship; it never faltered, even when the flow of money was so reduced that sharp economies were needed just to keep the project going. Occasionally, when Phillips lapsed into the jargon of his profession, Ringling would slow him down: "Now, Jack . . . when you speak to me, use English. It's all right when we're showing visitors around for you to talk like that, but I want to know what you are doing."[66]

What Phillips was doing was converting the Ringling vision into reality. Their first task was to select a site. With approximately thirty-seven acres, the estate was surely large enough to hold the museum without crowding. They finally settled on the south corner of the estate, almost up to the Caples line—swampy ground that was home to various forms of Florida wildlife, including snakes and a large alligator. Two ponds were drained and filled with shell taken from the bay. By late June 1927, the preliminaries were finished, site preparation complete and construction begun by Hageman and Harris of Tampa. A financial crisis halted activity and the contractor was dismissed. For a time, nothing moved, then the crisis passed and Ringling's friend Lyman Chase from Alpine, New Jersey, became the new builder. The ground was deeded to the museum on 7 September 1927 by John and Mable.

East front of the John and Mable Ringling Museum of Art under
construction. John H. Phillips, architect; Chase & McElroy, builders,
1927–28. Courtesy of Maxine Baylor.

(After Mable's death, wishing to make the deed free from any possible
challenge, Ringling granted the property again in 1930. The directors
named in the charter, recorded on 7 September 1927, were John,
Mable, and Julius Böhler, who was also named curator.[67])

Looking back on his work, Phillips remarked, "I loved Rome, Venice
and Florence especially, and of course I was delighted when I found
myself in Sarasota where buildings in the mood of these cities fitted into
the landscape. Also, it was great to be working for a man who loved Italy
as much as I did." Phillips's fascination with Renaissance Italy is apparent in the design of the museum, which resembles the villa of a noble
Italian family. The arrangement of the columns around the court, while
not a copy, was apparently suggested by the cloisters of various
churches. The design embraced Böhler's suggestion for placing statues
on the roof of the loggia and twice enlarging the size of the building.[68]

Phillips had set to work believing that this client possessed unlimited
wealth, an impression encouraged by Ringling himself. But it was soon
apparent to him that Ringling lacked the money to build the museum as
planned and that some retrenchment would be necessary. One major
cost-saving device was the employment of 300 members of the winter

circus crew, many of whom were skilled artisans and decorators. In spring, when the circus moved out, as many as 80 local workers took their place. In these pre-Depression days, Ringling was the largest single employer in Sarasota.[69]

Bringing in the circus labor still did not reduce the cost enough. Ringling was willing to settle for a smaller and less costly building; Phillips argued against that, saying anything less than the original plan could never be regarded with pride. Mable, too, insisted they must not settle for half-measures. Their principal saving of half a million dollars resulted from abandoning the plan for a large extension of the north wing beyond the picture galleries to house a school of art and student dormitories. Both John and Mable were committed to forming a school and only reluctantly accepted the fact that they did not have the money to build student housing. As a temporary measure, they decided to use the attic story of the front or east wing as a school, without a planned dormitory.[70]

Phillips proposed several innovative ideas to meet the unique conditions of the local climate. He was particularly anxious to install an effective lighting system after rejecting the Ringlings' request for gallery skylights. (He feared that severe summer storms and hurricanes might shatter a glass roof.) He proposed long windows on the outer walls, spaced so as to prevent shadows from being thrown on the paintings. The problem with this plan was that windows admitted glaring light that might harm the paintings. (They were installed but were later bricked over.) His highly original scheme for artificial light called for lighting to be installed in the jambs of the windows to give the effect of daylight coming from the windows at night. Ringling refused (because of the cost) and over Phillips's objection insisted on conventional indirect lighting even though the exposed fixtures conflicted with the atmosphere of the galleries. He agreed to Phillips's plan to make the museum one of the first public buildings planned to be heated by electricity,[71] but the system was never installed.

There was no disagreement among the three principals on the appearance of the east front facing the street. It is like an Italian villa—large unbroken surfaces with three round arches forming the central entrance. The cornice over the arches is supported by caryatids of pure white marble, somewhat small in scale for the dimensions of the entrance. Above the arches, Phillips placed figures symbolic of Music, Sculpture, Architecture, and Painting. The loggias that form the sides of the court and give the whole its strong Renaissance flavor were paved with pink marble and framed by arches supported by pink stone pillars. Although these slender columns were new, they were then believed to have been taken from pre-seventeenth-century buildings. Cast-stone bases (composed of marble dust and a binder) effectively masked the varied height of the columns.[72]

Within the court a formal Italian garden, designed to conform to Mable's wishes, was arranged in three descending terraces. Phillips laid out each level in squares ornamented with a maze of small shrubbery. He left space for the bronze and cast-stone figures initially intended for the Ritz Carlton Hotel. Phillips objected to the Caribbean pines that stood in the court because they did not conform with the Italian motif. Mable insisted that they should remain. The pines stayed.[73]

Two additional design tasks were later added to Phillips's initial contract. One was for a gate at the entrance and another was for a crypt and catacomb. The gate consists of stuccoed pillars supporting a large wrought-iron gate.[74] A local German craftsman, Albert Roehr, created a work of art in the European tradition, giving a graceful, almost airy pattern to the strength of iron. Roehr set up a small forge at the entrance and fashioned the gates where they were to stand.

The crypt would be in a vaulted section of the passage under the bridge connecting the two wings (a space then being used for storage of the Cesnola antiquities). An original sketch was prepared by C. R. Renshaw, a young assistant in Phillips's New York studio. Phillips recalled that Ringling had been most enthusiastic about it, "as both Mr. and Mrs. Ringling had long dreamed of their resting place that had been decided upon in the early stages. A dramatic incident occurred shortly after Mrs. Ringling's death while I was walking with Mr. Ringling in the court toward the statue of David. He said he would like for me to design the tomb for the resting place of Mrs. Ringling and himself."[75] The idea of being buried in the museum was perhaps suggested to Ringling by a similar chamber in Sir John Soane's classical Dulwich College gallery in London. But Renshaw's design for the

Italian court of the John and Mable Ringling Museum of Art, under
construction (above, looking east) and completed (below, looking west).
Courtesy of Maxine Baylor.

Ringling tomb is more nearly medieval. Within a mosaic-lined chamber, partly hidden behind an elaborate perforated alabaster screen are
two sarcophagi mounted with sculptured reclining figures similar to
those in a tomb in the Church of Santa Maria del Popolo in Rome—

funerary splendor usually reserved for kings, queens, and princes of the Church.[76]

Ringling took no action on the plan. Upon his second marriage, the idea of a tomb for Mable and himself became a somewhat awkward issue; yet, after his separation and divorce, Ringling never revived the idea. In time, he lost his desire for such a tomb, a decision he made known to his nephews, John and Henry North. He then decided to be buried outside the museum in a tomb located on the grounds of the estate. He sent for Lyman Chase, the museum builder, to discuss an alternate plan for such a tomb, but never finalized this decision either.[77] His and Mable's caskets were not interred on the grounds of Ca' d'Zan until 1992.

Like the exterior and the garden court, Phillips's interior design, which comprised twenty-one galleries, was responsive to Ringling's wishes. Phillips was exceedingly proud of his design, especially the lighting. He wrote in the *New York Times,* "Experts have been unanimous in expressing the opinion that the Ringling Museum . . . has the most perfect lighting of any museum in existence."[78] The major galleries in the front or east wing, the two Rubens galleries, are lighted by a clerestory. The first holds two tapestries woven by Jan Frans vanden Hocke (with a design attributed to Rubens), *Fides Catholica* and *The Triumph of Religion over Ignorance and Blindness.* The second gallery displays Ringling's proudest possessions, the four great Rubens and studio cartoons from the *Triumph of the Eucharist.* At the opposite end of the entrance foyer is the large auditorium, at first called the St. Gaudens Room; it is decorated at the cornice with a marble frieze supplemented with sections made from plaster, surrounding the 100-foot gallery.[79]

Phillips gave special attention to the Rubens gallery, where the cartoons were to hang. There he placed two door frames with Solomonic columns strikingly similar to those depicted in two of the cartoons. Ringling's taste for gilded, twisted (Solomonic) columns seems to have been acquired from Stanford White, who often used them for decoration. In the third, the Italian gallery, Phillips installed the blue and gold entrance and wainscot panels that had come from White's estate. This historic wainscot was taken from the Villa Palmieri in Florence on one of the many occasions when the building was remodeled; its most famous tenant, Boccaccio, wrote his *Decameron* there. Over the cornice of the door frame was a large bas relief (now lost) showing Saint Anne washing the newborn infant Jesus while Mary is attended by servants.[80]

In late December 1929 the building was essentially complete, but the galleries were largely empty on Mable's last visit to the museum in March 1929. The opening was scheduled for February 1930—later postponed to March—and several important tasks for the collection had yet to be accomplished. There was no catalog. Ringling knew that achieving status in the museum community would require one. The editor of the *catalogue raisonné* of the Gavet collection, Emile Moliniere, wrote, "A complete catalog (of) objects establishes their genealogy and their title of nobility which are more lasting, however great the collector. . . . One can perceive almost at once upon seeing a collection what were the dominant sentiments of the possessor—whether one is in the presence of one who is a man of taste or one who is merely curious."[81]

Preparation of a scholarly catalog was postponed, but an art photographer, V. Sakayan, was commissioned to photograph 350 pictures for an eventual publication. About the same number (352) were later listed in the Rembrandt Corporation inventory when Ringling formed the company in 1932.[82] The exclusion of a substantial number from his more public records suggests that even then Ringling was separating out works of lesser worth and some of uncertain attribution.

Apparently selected by Julius Böhler, Arthur Fischer, a gallery owner from Lucerne, Switzerland, was engaged to organize the collection, arrange the selections in each gallery, and place the statues in the court. Fischer chose to place the paintings in most of the galleries according to the artists' nationality. Some were devoted to a particular style or period, as in a large vaulted gallery where he arranged a mixed group classified as "primitives"—making a striking impact on viewers, but having a theme that was difficult to follow. In the gallery used as an auditorium, a Gobelin tapestry hung at the rear of the stage and the paintings were of epic themes and heroic size.[83]

Finally, in early 1930 Ringling could view the splendid Renaissance palace filled with the collection that he personally had assembled—the realization of his long-held vision. *Art Digest* described it as "a museum

John and Mable Ringling Museum of Art. Above, Rubens tapestry gallery, showing *The Triumph of Religion* from the series *Triumph of the Eucharist.* Below, Rubens cartoon gallery, showing *The Gathering of the Manna* from the same series. From Ringling's own collection of photographs that appeared in the 1931 bulletin of the art school.

of architecture," praise that would surely have pleased Mable, for she had wished the building to do more than merely house the collection; she had hoped it would enable students to learn something of the history of architecture.[84] The *New York World* gave high praise: "On the northern edge of this little Florida town, John Ringling, who used to drive a circus wagon, has built one of the finest museums of art in all the world."[85]

There was still no professional administrator for the museum. It was not open to the public on a regular basis. In the next few years, Ringling received countless offers from unemployed specialists who asked only token salaries. Some he considered, but he failed to take action. He might have scraped up enough for a small salary, but he would have had to reveal his precarious position; he was holding his collection only at the sufferance of money lenders.

John and Mable had planned to found a school of art as part of their initial concept of a museum. Unlike many self-educated men, Ringling did not scoff at formal education. He believed it was essential for the professional artist. That view, which Mable shared, stemmed from a realization that much more was needed than mere training in the craft of drawing and the skillful manipulation of paint. He believed that artists would be barren, however talented, unless they understood the culture and civilization in which they lived. To provide that kind of education as well as training, the Ringlings were determined to establish a broadly based school and join it to the museum.

There were several reasons for this. John and Mable saw the museum as a locomotive, drawing in its train the school, a colony of resident artists, and the community of Sarasota. They expected it to attract artist-teachers whose instruction would bring forth a new generation of promising artists. And the museum was to be their laboratory, providing inspiration as well as objects of study. The interaction of school, museum, and community would create a rich cultural environment. That environment, in turn, promised to give character to Sarasota as the city continued to grow into the kind of metro-resort that Ringling envisioned—and that vision, of course, also included his exceedingly large real estate holdings waiting to be sold.

Ringling did not limit his school plan to college-level classes. At one stage, before the lack of funds forced him to narrow his concept to a minimal program, he even included a place for instructing children. He reasoned, "Not all the Old Masters were painters when they were young. Some became settled in metalworking, some beat gold or worked in precious stones, long before they were able to turn to portraiture for their freedom and full expression. I want the school to be a place where children interested or talented or just inclined may go directly to painting, to sculpture, and design, instead of roundabout."[86] This idea may have been one of Ringling's expansive flights of fancy, but it suggests the range and diversity of his thoughts about his art school. Taken together, the ideas of John and Mable clearly manifest their resolve to endow the future of Sarasota. The very splendor and lofty dimensions of the architect's drawings for the school wing convey the broad measure of those ideas, with its grand proportions and great sculpture court re-creating the magnificence of the Italian Renaissance. (Neither Phillips nor Ringling seemed to be aware that such veneration of the past was wholly out of step with the work and ideas of contemporary artists in America.)

While the museum was being built, plans for Phillips's elegant school were abandoned, a victim of the limits set by lack of funds. While Phillips accepted the reality of Ringling's erratic cash flow, Böhler found it difficult. A decade later he still regretted the downward revision, saying that the museum was only a torso, not what it was meant to be. Not long after the school wing was deleted from the plans, Mable's unexpected death in June 1929 further disrupted all hopes for the school.

Without Mable to help him and to restrain his tendency to rush ahead, Ringling seemed to be adrift, unsure of how to convert their common wish into a practical plan of action. Astute man of business that he was, Ringling was about to enter a field in which he had neither knowledge nor experience, handicapped by his habitual refusal to attend to details. Fortunately he found an associate who could attend to the minutiae of organizing a new institution. The long struggle to form a viable school took little from Ringling because he expended neither time nor energy on it. As the autumn of 1929 unfolded, with its national and local calamities, he was soon caught up in other affairs that demanded his entire attention.

He had scarcely completed negotiations for purchase of the American Circus Corporation before the first losses of the Depression engulfed the national stock markets. Investors were sent running for cover, too late for most of them to salvage much from the ruins. His immediate financial losses did not cause Ringling to abandon the idea of founding a school, but he was forced to reduce its scope still further.

Now without a plan for a building to house a school, he decided to move ahead with the formation of a school within an existing college. He found an admirable and willing associate in Dr. Ludd M. Spivey, who since 1925 had been president of the Methodist-supported Southern College in Lakeland, Florida.[87] By March 1930, Ringling and Spivey were at work devising a plan for a combined school of art and junior college. Southern College was to be moved to Sarasota. It would retain its existing organization and trustees, but its new name was to be the John Ringling University. Spivey wrote to Ringling in New York: "You could not do a finer piece of service for the world than to establish the John Ringling University."[88]

Spivey presumed Ringling to be an exceedingly rich man. The museum and its collection stood as a convincing proof of his fabled fortune and his resolve to benefit the community. Spivey was an able administrator and educator, but he was too readily convinced that the impractical university scheme was feasible. His hopes were short-lived. The plan was scarcely drawn up when Ringling wired, regretfully postponing it. His words would be repeated a number of times during their association: "I deem it unwise to attempt anything at this time."[89]

Spivey tried again a few months later. This time he had a glowing prospectus for schools of art, music, journalism, business, and education. The trustees had been summoned to approve a plan that needed only Ringling's signature to set it in motion. Again Ringling refused, leaving Spivey to deal with the peevish trustees and the curiosity of others who heard something of the plan from stories circulating in New York.

Ringling's responses grew more evasive as Spivey pressed him for a specific answer. On 17 May, he wired Spivey that there were many things in his business that demanded attention; he was uncertain when he could come to Florida, but as to the university, he could do nothing definite.[90] Spivey had already borrowed money, enough for the first year, on the strength of Ringling's promises, and his position was becoming embarrassing. The college trustees were losing patience and calling for a decision; Ringling was no nearer to making a commitment.[91] He seemed incapable of saying "yes" or "no."

For six months or more, the entire project halted. In June 1930, the State Bank in Lakeland closed. The college was solvent, but barely so. Spivey had unwisely placed his hopes on a profitable art school within a new university as a means of keeping the college from going under.[92] Reluctantly, he at last faced the realization that there was never going to be a John Ringling University.

Once the university concept was abandoned, Ringling and Spivey were able to work out a compromise. They agreed to form a school located in Sarasota under the auspices of Southern College at Lakeland. It would include a junior college program that would enable graduates to teach in Florida schools. Ringling's long experience with artists, he said, had taught him that many of them needed to be educated.[93]

In March 1931, the formation of the School of Fine and Applied Arts of the John and Mable Ringling Museum of Art was announced. The school was not to reside in Renaissance splendor on the museum grounds. Instead, Ringling arranged to lease a defunct hotel about a mile from the museum, promising to pay for alterations or to see that they were done by the owner.[94] Spivey recruited the faculty for the first semester, scheduled to begin in October 1931. Verman Kimbrough from the Southern College faculty was to head the operation at Sarasota; Spivey as director was to remain at Lakeland. Several well-known artists were hired on contracts, among them George Pearse Ennis as head of the art faculty and Benjamin Turner Kurtz as instructor in sculpture. Altogether, fifteen faculty members offered courses not only in art but in journalism, biology, sociology, and education. Ringling specified only that the school catalog must contain illustrations of his paintings by Titian, Rubens, Tintoretto, Tiepolo, and Hals.

Spivey astutely made concessions to his Methodist trustees. Every student was required to attend daily devotional services. On Sundays, each must attend Sunday school and a preaching service at a church of the student's choice.[95] No provision was made for non-Christian students and their religious preferences. (Spivey later learned that these requirements were not enough for some of his more conservative Methodist colleagues. In his enthusiasm he could not resist showing off his new school to a group of trustees, who were shocked to observe a class where nude models were sketched by the students. The complaining clergyman offered to forego proceedings against Spivey if he would promise that no such practice would be resumed.)

The dedication of the museum and the opening of the art school were combined and made into a great occasion on 2 October 1931. Sarasota businesses were closed so that the entire local establishment could be present. Spivey coached Ringling on the wording of invitations, wrote his speech for him, and generally made sure there would be an impressive array of guests and speakers. By now Spivey had come to know his associate-benefactor quite well and, a few days before the opening, wrote to remind him: "Governor Carlton will be the main speaker; I am planning on your making a brief address, I will have it ready for you. Please do not fail me now, for it's necessary for you to be present."[96]

Spivey's efforts were successful. The dignitaries were flanked by a parade in academic regalia. Using his prepared speech, Ringling spoke briefly, just long enough to exchange compliments with Spivey and to welcome the students. Although the governor had cancelled, Senator Duncan U. Fletcher and Congressman H. J. Drane spoke at some length. John Phillips, the museum architect, described the splendid court as a natural amphitheater, which he said was its planned function. Massed choirs sang for the 2,000 guests seated in the loggias.[97]

Despite this grand ceremony, the future was highly uncertain. The large number of art schools already seeking to attract students, especially in the northeastern cities, would seem to have saturated the market. Many were small proprietary schools while others were open for summer classes only. Neither Spivey nor Ringling thought of consulting with other schools, independent or within a university, to determine their financial status in a time of severe economic depression. There was some advantage for a school that was joined with a college offering degrees, but scarcely enough in 1931 to meet Spivey's expectation of enrolling 300 students. *Art Digest,* which gave considerable space to art education and to contemporary artists, welcomed the new school. The *Digest* pointed out that the location, offering something of the nature of a winter resort, tended to attract students from the North. The publicity emphasized landscape and marine painting, for which George Ennis, the leading faculty member, was particularly well known.[98]

On the opening day of the academic year, more than one hundred students registered for the three semesters. In 1932, the second year, the Depression brought disaster to its unfunded financial structure. With a shrunken enrollment (only four students a few days before opening) and with no endowment, the school seemed bound to fail. The only uncertainty was how soon it would close.

The uncertain alliance of Ringling and Southern College was strained to its limit. Ringling was soon too ill to assume any significant role in school affairs, and both partners were in poor financial health.[99] No help could come from Lakeland. Like other small private colleges, Southern College was in a crisis that was becoming acute. At the art school, Kimbrough urged faculty members to move into vacant dormitory space, thus assuring themselves and their families a home and food. At Lakeland, faculty salaries were reduced by 40 percent. Even at Winter Park's Rollins College, reputed to be a rich school, faculty were being asked to return one-third of their salaries.[100]

Tension between the Sarasota faculty and the Lakeland administration mounted until finally there was a faculty demand for reorganization. Sarasota faculty members feared that they could be held personally liable for the Ringling school debts, as the school was not incorporated. Spivey was deeply disappointed by the manifest failure after what had seemed so promising a beginning, and he was particularly hurt to find himself abandoned by Ringling when the entire school was falling to pieces. By then Ringling was seriously ill. His finances were in a state of chaos. Signatures on his letters became more and more tremulous through 1933 as his illness took more of his strength.

Failure was now inevitable. Spivey saw that financial backers would not come forward so long as they mistakenly believed that the school was financed entirely by Ringling, whose financial empire was tottering. Accordingly, he proposed that the school should be given a new name. He appealed to Ringling, Sarasota's mayor, E. A. Smith, and other civic leaders to help by recruiting a board of trustees who would not be asked for money but who could help in a search for new funding.[101] His appeal, tied to the now locally unpopular name of John Ringling, failed to arouse a response. The city's power structure was already distancing its members from a fallen leader. Ringling was already dealing with others in Spivey's place. On 15 May 1933, a corporation was formed to organize a new school. On that day the original school ceased to exist. Funds in the school account amounted to $32.97; a check for $34 failed to clear.[102] Ringling, harassed on all sides, could spare little time for regrets. He wrote a one-sentence finale: "I fully appreciated that you worked hard for the school and I am sincerely sorry that it was not a success."[103] Thus ended Ringling's personal role in the art school bearing his name; it was now owned and operated by an independent corporation.

Ringling's farewell left Spivey to deal with clamoring suppliers of fixtures, desks, textbooks, and school supplies, all looking to Southern College for payment. Requests became more peremptory as many of the suppliers neared insolvency. Spivey advised them all that the college was not responsible, and that he could not pay. At first he alluded to Ringling's illness and his financial straits as typical of many other businessmen.[104] Before long, frustrated and pressed by problems of the college at Lakeland, he merely replied to dunning letters by saying that Ringling was broke.

Spivey was an able administrator and could handle the arcane politics of the academic world; but he was naive in the rougher tactics of the marketplace. He succeeded in keeping the college going until better times returned, but the art school defeated him, for it lacked the guidance of trustees in their traditional function. The union of a school of art and a church-supported college was perhaps fated to dissolve, as Spivey's experience with some of his less liberal clerical colleagues attested.

The new Ringling School of Art and Design was structured on a faculty cooperative plan. Once the school broke away from Southern College, its future was placed in the hands of Kimbrough. He managed to survive the 1932–33 academic year and to keep the new school solvent. In his second year after the reorganization, Kimbrough began to negotiate with Ringling for land on the museum grounds where a new building could house the school. Ringling promptly agreed to donate the land. He recommended that the school adopt a building plan drawn by John Phillips. This time, Ringling prudently left matters entirely in the hands of Phillips and Kimbrough. The dream of a magnificent center of teaching and learning seemed to become once more an attainable goal. But again, the idea faded and the scheme was dropped for lack of funds.[105] The school continued to grow slowly at its original site in the old hotel, through the lean years of the Depression. It flourishes there today, with several other buildings added over the years.

While the art school was struggling, the museum was attracting attention locally and among some professionals in American art circles. Published stories stressed its imported treasures: columns from classical and Renaissance Europe, iron lanterns from Spain, woodwork and rooms taken from their original settings and built into the new museum. Comparisons often mentioned the Corcoran Gallery in Washington as the nearest in size and splendor; Ringling liked to tell people that his was larger, second only to the Metropolitan. As more and more private visitors were permitted to see the galleries and as the two brief public previews in 1930 and 1931 revealed the extent of the Ringling possessions, interest in a formal opening became intense. True to his longstanding promise, Ringling opened the museum permanently to the public on Sunday, 17 January 1932.[106] In the first three weeks, 14,000 visitors toured the museum; by the end of February the number had increased to more than 20,000. Auto tags from thirty-eight states and six foreign countries were counted in the parking lot.[107]

The twenty-one galleries seen by these visitors were arranged to display works by artists from a particular country or region. A contemporary description of one gallery exemplifies the way the collection was perceived:

> The last room of the north wing which is Gothic in design, is admirably suited to house the fine collection of Italian, Flemish and German primitives and works of the late fifteenth century and early sixteenth century. Here hang works by Carpaccio, Mazzola, Catena and Gio-

vanni Bellini, early Venetian masters. A splendid small group by Raphael Santi is flanked by an exquisite Filippino Lippi (son of Fra Filippo) and the *Judgment of Paris* by Domenico Beccafumi, one of the last of the fine Siennese masters. Here too are a pair of priceless panels in the manner of Fra Angelico. Three battle scenes by Paolo Ucello, known as the father of modern perspective add greatly to the richness of this room, as do *A Descent from the Cross* by Adriaen Isenbrandt, a *Madonna and Child* by Quentin Massys, a tryptich by the Antwerp Master, and a world famous *St. Jerome* by Lucas Cranach, the elder.[108]

In time a number of these initial attributions would be disproven by more precise analysis. Several of the great names were not authenticated—in the room of primitives alone, Carpaccio, Raphael, Bellini, and Ucello. These discoveries were not marred by the exposure of falsely claimed copies or fraud as many of Ringling's critics had claimed. Instead, the questioned works were correctly attributed to artists who themselves merited recognition. Unfortunately, much of the local publicity that surrounded Ringling's collection emphasized the number of works attributed to artists of the first rank. When so many of those well-known names were withdrawn, the repute of the museum dimmed accordingly. Ten years later, the museum came under professional direction. Only then did art professionals learn the true scope of the Ringling collection.

In the end, the central theme of Ringling's life was manifest in his bequest to the people of Florida. For decades, that theme was effectively masked while he pursued the company of rich and important people. Yet he felt an equal attachment to the millions who lined the streets to watch the circus parades and passed through the turnstiles to attend the more than 40,000 performances of the Ringling Bros. shows. For more than fifty years he and his brothers had brought popular culture to the towns and cities of the country. With the gift of his estate he added another dimension of culture, one of lasting dignity and splendor, and he addressed an audience composed essentially of the same people who had delighted in the greatest circus of them all.

A Long Farewell

"Farewell, a Long Farewell to all my Greatness."
—Wolsey to Cromwell, *Henry VIII*, act 3

FTER THE SUMMER of 1929, Ringling began to encounter new obstacles. As these obstacles became more formidable in the last years of his life, his capacity to deal with them diminished. Ringling's decline was slow at first, apparent only to those close to him—his family and a few associates. In July 1932, he experienced his first serious illness, followed by another at the year's end. As misfortunes seemed to pile one upon another, he lost much of his famous ebullient nature and his ability to thrust aside the problems of the moment. However, the Great Depression, his illness, and his domestic crises—an unmanageable combination—could not wholly account for Ringling's misfortunes. Pride and willfulness on his part share responsibility for his fall.

In Sarasota, the public approval that he had enjoyed a few years earlier faded and then vanished as reports of his bad financial deals began to circulate, beginning in 1932. During the following two years, the ever-increasing pressure of money problems, the chaotic state of his home life, and his illness left him embittered and increasingly sensitive to criticism. In the midst of his business and financial disarray, he rashly quarreled with the local newspaper. He demanded that reporters bring everything they wrote about him to the Ringling office for review before publication,[1] a damaging error in public relations.

Ringling's fall from grace was but a part of Sarasota's faltering economy. As the Depression tightened its grip, the city's overdependence on the building trades became a liability. New construction slowed still further, marked by the foreclosure on the fashionable Mira Mar apartments and the Whitfield Estates subdivision that stood on the former Alf T. Ringling estate. As the Depression deepened, developers and promoters not unexpectedly lost influence as their ability to control events diminished. In their place, Palmer farm-ranch interests ascended. Outside the city limits, the county was largely sustained by ranches and agriculture. There, unemployment was less devastating than in the city. People throughout the county suffered: 20 to 30 percent of the population needed assistance. Rural families stretched fifty cents' worth of beans to last two weeks.

In the pre-Depression year of 1927, when Ringling had brought the circus quarters to Sarasota, he had formed a charity to offer relief to needy families and schoolchildren. From the time the circus quarters were opened to the public, admission money was set aside for the John Ringling Community Chest. The fund was started to offer relief to the working class following the collapse of the land boom. The Chest idea might well have been Sam Gumpertz's suggestion, typical of his genuine concern for those less fortunate than himself. The sums involved were small, unlikely to drain circus finances, and the publicity value was significant. In 1929 the fund could not keep up with the need. In reply to a private school's appeal for funds, Ringling explained: "The Community Chest is out of funds as the Chest advanced the city $8,000, and $10 a week to the Salvation Army for a year, eighty bottles of milk a day for the poor children of Sarasota. There is no way of telling what the receipts would be this autumn and winter to provide milk for the poor."[2]

Public relief was not then available. In general, Florida's economic depression, brought on by the boom's bust, was months ahead of the nation's. General Hugh S. Johnson, head of the controversial National Recovery Act (NRA) under President Franklin D. Roosevelt, described the condition of Florida in a style peculiarly his own: "The economic whoopee in land and lots was all her [Florida's] own. It left as much local wreckage as the 1929 fantasy and disaster. Before she could recover from that, the world-wide business typhoon struck her."[3]

Early in 1930, local reporters in Sarasota tried to find signs of an upturn, not realizing that this typhoon was only the start of the Depression. The *Sarasota Herald,* with little evidence, turned to praising local agriculture for leading a turn for the better and heaped thanks for improved conditions on the efforts of the Palmer Estates.[4] Before long, the Palmer Bank was the one remaining commercial bank that was still solvent. The *Herald* espoused the positions and views of Palmer interests, particularly on the disputed issue of bond refunding. Many city businesses strongly opposed that regressive step, arguing that it would have a still more devastating effect on real estate values and the burden of taxes. City leaders and residents alike became convinced that the county administration was heavily influenced by Palmer interests, which did not always coincide with the best interests of the community.[5]

The decline in cotton and wheat shipping meant a troubled economy in the Southwest. Ringling's once profitable Wichita–Eastland Falls (Texas) Railroad was plagued by falling revenues, while interest payments continued to consume its funds.[6] He had already sold his first rail line in Oklahoma to the giant Santa Fe Railroad. The half-million dollars worth of gold bonds that he had received from the sale were soon impounded by the federal government in complicated tax disputes; they remained impounded until long after his death. This was a substantial loss, one that he could ill afford, but he was astute enough not to engage in a costly court battle to recover his bonds. Meanwhile, the Internal Revenue Service sent resident examiners to Sarasota to study tax returns filed by the Ringling Estates, Inc., for the past several years.[7] Federal authorities looked with increasing disfavor on the freewheeling operators of the 1920s, and Ringling's affairs were not entirely aboveboard.

Upon his return from Europe in August 1929, Ringling found that the circus demanded his immediate attention. The new management of Madison Square Garden had changed the terms of the traditional Ringling circus contract for a month's engagement in the spring of 1930. There would be an increase in rent, and a key clause permitting the circus uninterrupted use of the arena was deleted. Ringling's longtime friend and associate Tex Rickard, who had managed the arena for many years, had died. William Carey, the new manager, insisted on reserving Friday evening each week for the Garden's highly profitable boxing matches, claiming that the financial loss from suspending the Friday-night fights for a month would cost the arena $60,000. Tex Rickard's accommodating policy had given way to a new emphasis on management for the shareholders.

Ringling objected loudly to the proposed change. He publicly stated that this was an ethical issue, that the circus and boxing were on altogether different planes. "My business means too much to me," he said, "for me to allow it to be mixed with prizefights. Money? Money is hardly important enough for that."[8] Ringling never opposed boxing in principle. In fact, he helped to promote an arena in Tampa for championship fights. But he had no illusions about how clean a sport it was then, or about how its audience differed from the circus audience. In the Garden corporation, Ringling was still an officer and a director, but he was no longer a major shareholder. The major shareholder was now a brokerage firm.

Ringling insisted that he had not been present when the directors announced the executive committee's unanimous agreement on the terms of the new contract. When he refused to sign, the same contract was at once offered to the American Circus Corporation's Sells-Floto and Hagenbeck–Tom Mix combined show. The owners accepted promptly and closed a deal for four weeks in April 1930.

When questioned about his plans, Ringling hinted that he would have more to say shortly. He then added, "At present I have nothing to say other than that I will not mix my circus with prizefighting."[9] He was not ready to reveal that he had already decided to buy out the entire American Circus Corporation.

By taking the dispute to the public press, Ringling succeeded only in demonstrating that he could no longer treat the Garden as his private preserve. His high-sounding statements would have carried greater conviction had he not signed the rejected contract when Carey presented it again the following year. Under its terms, the circus was to vacate the arena by 7:00 P.M. each Friday, leaving the space free for boxing.[10]

One of the early signs of spring thus disappeared from New York City in 1930: posters of the Ringling Bros. Barnum & Bailey Circus.

Each year in March, the genial Dexter Fellows, head of circus press relations, came to New York from Bridgeport, Connecticut, in his black-and-white plaid overcoat to announce that spring and the circus were on the way. He found the winter-bound city "like an old man with the grippe, forced to work all day when he should have been in bed with a steaming toddy."[11]

Ringling had three options: he could buy out the competition, he could sell, or he could find another arena.[12] He knew his adversaries, and they knew him. The three owners of the rival firm were longtime competitors and friends of the Ringlings. Jeremiah Mugivan was the key figure; his two associates were Bert Bowers and Ed Ballard. Together, they owned a group of small survivor shows that had managed to outlive nearly all their contemporaries, combined under the American Circus Corporation umbrella. These circus names had been advertised on barn walls for most of the century. The Mugivan group had a firm contract for April 1930 at Madison Square Garden and knew they were in a strong position to negotiate. Mugivan even refused to meet Ringling in New York, forcing him to come to their offices in Peru, Indiana, at the beginning of September. There, a deal was worked out. Without consulting his circus partners, Ringling bought the entire operation, including five circuses, equipment, show names, and quarters in Peru and Denver. The price was $2 million. A face-saving gesture for Ringling was the agreement to sign the deal in New York.[13]

The Garden contract issue had so enraged Ringling that he allowed it to cloud his judgment.[14] In the name of the Ringling Bros. Barnum & Bailey Circus, he borrowed $1.7 million and gave his personal guarantee for the note. He had lived and dealt this way for twenty-five years, but never had he borrowed at that level, nor had the circus ever before been placed at risk. The purchase came only days before the stock market crash, which cut off his plan to charter a public corporation and to market the shares. His independent decision, taken without consulting his partners, was especially resented by Edith (Mrs. Charles) Ringling.

The deal may have been hasty and ill-considered, but it was the largest circus deal that had ever been made. The scope of Ringling's purchase—he had devoured the competition in a single bite—was worthy of the circus king. The 1929–30 season was the last that Peru, Indiana, was known as "Circus City." Ringling's near monopoly led one of the remaining rival show-owners to bring suit, charging Ringling with conspiracy to violate antitrust laws.[15]

For the continued vitality of the circus in America, Ringling's decision may have been the correct one. Only three months later, in December 1929, Jeremiah Mugivan was dead. Without its forceful leader, the corporation that he headed might easily have foundered in the Depression years that followed. For circus entertainment to survive as an institution, possibly only the Ringling organization could have saved it. Ringling Bros. standards of quality were expressed not only in superior performances, but in every aspect of the show. When either Charles or John was with the circus, one or the other stood at the entrance of the big top to check the appearance of each performer.[16] Such standards extended beyond the capability of shows that were barely able to fend off the bailiffs.

While Ringling was in New York trying to negotiate the 1930 Madison Square Garden contract, his yacht *Zalophus* sank in the Gulf of Mexico on the evening of 4 February 1930. Sam Gumpertz had borrowed the yacht to take some friends on a cruise, planning to sail along the Gulf Coast on an overnight voyage south to Useppa Island. At about 3:00 A.M., the yacht struck a submerged object a mile off Lido Beach. No lives were lost or endangered as the craft slowly settled in about twelve feet of water.[17] New York City Mayor Jimmy Walker and his friend, actress Betty Compton, were taken to Fort Myers. From there they took the next train to Miami and discreetly faded from public view. Three days later, Mayor Walker arrived alone for a much-publicized visit at Ca' d'Zan.[18] Walker was reported to have come from a leisurely cruise on board the yacht of multimillionaire Barron Collier.

A day after the sinking, only the smokestack remained above twenty feet of water. Portions of the upper deck and a truckload of furnishings washed up at Cortez, almost twenty miles north of Lido Beach. Within a few days only the engines were worth the cost of salvage. The hull was badly torn and the seventy-foot-long deckhouse was gone, wrenched apart by tide and currents. Everything that could break away had floated to the surface.[19] The names of the mysterious passengers, if in fact they were ever on board, were never revealed.

Ringling and friends on board *Zalophus*. Courtesy of John and Mable Ringling
Museum of Art.

The wreck was not a total loss, however. Ringling collected nearly $100,000 from his insurance, about half the initial cost of the nine-year-old craft.[20] He had never personally cared for sport fishing or cruising, finding those pastimes useful only for entertaining important guests. For that purpose there still remained *Zalophus Junior.* The smaller fifty-two-foot craft was of an unusual but rather rakish design, its narrow beam suggesting a smart, fast boat not unlike an admiral's barge. For the short cruises most appropriate to the bay and islands *Junior* was much better suited than the large, clumsy *Zalophus* had been. While it lacked the opulence and splendid appointments of the bigger craft, it had the advantage of needing only a crew of one or two.[21] Ringling was better off without having to support the eleven-person *Zalophus* payroll. Not long afterward, when money was badly needed, Ringling agreed either to sell *Zalophus Jr.* or to charter the boat through a New York and Miami yacht broker. However, like many of his half-formed plans, this too was allowed to lapse with no decision.[22]

The *Zalophus* incident was soon forgotten, thanks to the generous insurance settlement. His huge, newly purchased circus resources were another matter altogether; he could not afford to leave that investment idle for long. He was soon ready to consider a novel plan for bringing indoor entertainment to Sarasota to enliven the winter season. Like other Florida resorts, Sarasota needed new attractions, any stimulus that would restart the flow of money into the economy. The idea of a Sarasota entertainment arena came first from Sam Gumpertz, always alert for opportunities in the entertainment field. He found a willing group of local investors—Edith Ringling, Ralph Caples, and A. E. Cummer—who were intrigued by the idea of a large arena seating around 20,000 spectators.[23] John Ringling found Gumpertz's plan attractive as a lure for tourists and visitors. Despite his refusal to mix his circus with boxing, Ringling now proposed to bring boxing to Sarasota. Boxing was the real moneymaker for Madison Square Garden, and, at that time, the sport could be enjoyed in Florida only occasionally at Tampa or Miami. He also suggested that he would introduce a spectacular rodeo starring Tom Mix.[24]

In effect, this arena scheme was to be a southern version of Madison Square Garden, large enough for conventions, such as those of the

Ringling's small yacht *Zalophus, Jr.* After *Zalophus* was sunk in 1930, *Zalophus, Jr.,* continued to provide island sightseeing for prospective buyers who were being shown the Ringling Isles. Courtesy of John and Mable Ringling Museum of Art.

political parties and the American Legion. The plan for raising capital was unusual, a typical Gumpertz proposal. Only preferred stock would be issued to earn a fixed dividend. Profits were to be used for a new children's hospital.[25]

Despite the apparent potential for a sports arena in Sarasota, the timing was wrong. Edith Ringling initiated the action by making land available from property left to her by Charles in 1926. But as the investors began to commit, the size of the arena grew smaller and smaller. The original plan to seat 20,000 spectators was soon reduced to 4,000. It fell to 2,000 before the first concrete was poured. Once the arena was completed, events were scaled to its modest size; it hosted American Legion–sponsored boxing and occasional social events. Ultimately it was converted into a restaurant.

While the arena was still in the proposal stage, Ringling announced another plan that would focus more of his interests in Sarasota. He appointed Alice J. Moynihan to be chief accountant and auditor of the six circuses and all his other activities—a total of fourteen corporations of which he was the operating head.[26] The broad assortment of businesses were experiencing varied degrees of fiscal health. In organizing his convoluted, scattered assets and obligations under a centralized structure, Ringling was breaking the habits of a lifetime. Intense scrutiny by the Bureau of Internal Revenue may have influenced his decision.[27]

The new fiscal arrangement improved matters somewhat, but Ringling had moved alone through so many deals and counterdeals in the past two decades that only he could disentangle their many threads. The closest that he had ever come to permitting another to share in his most confidential business affairs was with Richard Fuchs. Fuchs, who had been with Ringling since 1919, was more than a private secretary; he was Ringling's confidential man of business. Yet even he was part of the tangle; he was paid not by Ringling but from a pro forma position in the Rockland Oil Company in Ardmore, Oklahoma, where he was listed as an officer of the corporation.[28]

Some of Ringling's problems were more damaging to his public image than to his corporate affairs. Twice in 1930 he found himself in court, facing conflicts with Mable's sisters. First, he sued to regain possession of bonds that Mable had placed with her sister Alma, assuring her that "they will take care of you and Mother." Ringling contended that only the interest was intended for the Burtons, while the actual bonds were to remain in his possession. He lost his suit in a courtroom scene in which both attorneys were fined for contempt, so noisy and acrimonious was their exchange.[29] Subsequently, in a New York court, two of Mable's sisters applied for appointment as administrators of Mable's estate, claiming that she had been a New York resident and that she had died without leaving a will. Ringling summoned two friends to testify: Mayor Jimmy Walker of New York City and Mayor Frank Haig of Jersey City. Both attested that the Ringlings were residents of Florida. The judge agreed and rejected the sisters' application.[30]

In Sarasota, Owen Burns had filed suit against Ringling in 1926 for moving funds from their healthy island real estate enterprise to the ailing Ritz Carlton Hotel. A series of adversarial actions began from the time Burns first questioned Ringling's handling of finances in companies he controlled. Those actions lasted for the remainder of Ringling's lifetime. Some he won; others he lost; many were pending at the time of his death. The cases that arose early in the 1930s were only the start. By 1936, almost every attorney in Sarasota was engaged in a suit for or against John Ringling.[31]

There had always been a contrast between the long-established reputation of the Ringling circus for honest dealing and the only slightly shorter history of manipulation that characterized the personal business affairs of John Ringling. Incidents—some minor, others more important—continued to accumulate, eroding his image in the business community. One device he used to bolster his financial position was switching ownership of assets to increase apparent net worth or to shelter assets from creditors if a deal turned out badly. Ringling was not alone in using such evasive techniques, but perhaps he resorted to such tactics more often and on a larger scale than his Sarasota colleagues. On one occasion, Burns refused to "lend" Ringling some land. Ringling accused his colleague of failure to trust him (which was true)[32] and promptly attempted to foreclose on mortgages he held on the land owned by the Ringling Isles Corporation. He changed the organization name, dismissed Burns (who held a 25 percent share) as vice-president, and replaced him with George Schueler, Mable's brother-in-law. Burns successfully halted the action, which would have allowed Ringling to regain personal possession of all the land on the islands held by the company.[33]

As Ringling's affairs started to unravel, he took a public relations step that was welcomed with great enthusiasm in Sarasota. He announced that twenty-one galleries in the museum would be opened to the public for one day.[34] A crew of forty workers rushed the final construction to make the facility ready for its first preview. Ringling then telegraphed from New York and authorized Sam Gumpertz to open the museum for one day. This was a typical Ringling gesture carried out by proxy, without ceremony. He wished the people of Sarasota to have an opportunity to view the paintings and the building that had been a topic of speculation and publicity for five years. Some 15,000 visitors thronged the museum on a Sunday afternoon in January 1930. There were no more public days until a second preview a year later.

His major expenditures on behalf of Sarasota ceased as Ringling's circumstances began to reflect the pressures of the advancing Depression.[35] The first bank failure in the county was the Bank of Englewood, which was soon followed by the closing of every commercial enterprise in Englewood except for one small shop. In Sarasota, the proud El Vernona Hotel was an early casualty, scheduled to be sold at the demand of the Prudence Bond Company, the mortgage holder. In a separate sale, John Wanamaker's of New York repurchased the hotel furnishings it had sold to the El Vernona, for the balance of unpaid bills.[36] At a foreclosure sale, the hotel sold for a fraction of its cost, leaving Owen Burns with a loss of about $500,000. The new owner was Burns's former friend and associate, John Ringling.[37] It was renamed the John Ringling Hotel.

More devastating than these first blows of the Depression were the traumas in Ringling's personal life. For a year following Mable's death, Ringling seemed unable to face the reality of her loss. Nor could he find a new pattern of life as a widower. He must have realized that few women could fit so happily into his unusual life-style—that he might never find another who could make his home at once publicly elegant and privately congenial. He chose a new wife whose domestic style proved to be a total contrast to Mable's. The two domineering personalities soon found living together less than harmonious, even in the thirty spacious rooms of Ca' d'Zan.

During the summer of 1930, while he was in Europe, Ringling met an attractive American divorcee, Emily Haag Buck. She was thirty-four by her own account, or forty-five according to Ringling's estimate; he was then sixty-three. They met, Emily later recalled, at a Fourth of July party in Amsterdam. When Ringling returned to the United States, he renewed their acquaintance with frequent calls and messages.[38] By late November, they were engaged to marry.

Emily Buck was an attractive socialite—exceedingly chic, tall, and blonde. They were both sophisticated, worldly-wise people—he after twenty-five years of domestic accord, she after one brief failure—yet neither developed an understanding of the other's nature or character.

The marriage was arranged to take place in Jersey City on 19 December, following two highly charged events that would reverberate through their years of marriage and far beyond. Ringling borrowed $50,000 from Emily just four days before the wedding. Emily probably had several hundred thousand dollars of her own, but far from a large fortune. She agreed to the loan without protest. His second request, made at the last minute, was that she sign a prenuptial agreement in which she waived all dower rights, particularly to the art collection and the museum. Ringling's purpose was to protect the art collection from becoming part of any possible dower settlement; under Florida law, the dower right claimed one-third of a total estate. The provisions of the agreement long remained unclear. As time went on, Ringling placed greater emphasis on the separation of the art collection from his personal estate by telling Emily that the paintings had been collected by Mable. Neither he nor Emily really believed that to be true. Ringling later conceded in court that he had purchased nearly all the paintings, but Mable had cooperated readily with him and had in fact purchased a few of them herself.[39]

Each member of the wedding party later recalled a different scenario of the wedding day. Sometime during the afternoon of 19 December, Emily went from her home in the Barclay Hotel to John's Fifth Avenue apartment. In midafternoon Ringling showed her the prenuptial agreement. The document had arrived not long before from the office of the circus attorney, John M. Kelley. Before they left for the marriage ceremony, John and Emily signed the agreement.

While they were en route to Jersey City, accompanied by old friend Frank Hennessy in Ringling's limousine, Emily asked for the document. Ringling handed it to her, and she kept it. At Mayor Frank Haig's office before the ceremony, she showed it to the other witness, Thomas McCarter, a friend of many years who was then president of the Public Service Company of New Jersey. McCarter was heard to say, "You should not have done it."

After the marriage and the signing of the register, the wedding party returned to New York. At some point Emily returned to her hotel, and John went to his office—not the most romantic evening for the newlyweds. Emily destroyed the agreement that she had signed only a few hours earlier. John, Emily, and Hennessy recalled the event differently, but the most graphic was Ringling's account: "I asked her for the paper. . . . I was suspicious that she had torn it up. Emily said, 'You will never see that again!' She told me that she put it in the toilet and pulled the chain." Ringling believed he had made certain that the art museum would not be sacrificed in his estate; Emily was content in believing that she was no longer bound by the hated agreement.[40]

On the surface, the episode did not seem to mar their initial marital bliss. John and Emily hurried their journey from New York to Sarasota, stopping only briefly at Palm Beach on the way. Ringling once again enjoyed the satisfaction of having a companion, one whose sophisticated style promised to enhance his social life in New York and Sarasota. Emily supposed herself married to a man of substantial wealth, with just a shadow of doubt introduced by his need to borrow from her. Yet she was to be mistress of a fabled palace, the grandest house in Sarasota, and she had lots of friends to whom she could show it off.

John and Emily's arrival at Ca' d'Zan was initially upstaged by the first event of their stay. On Christmas Day at an evening ceremony, John's niece Salomé North Stratton and Randolph Wadsworth of Fort Thomas, Kentucky, were married in the court of Ca' d'Zan before a small group of family and friends. Salomé, always loved by John and Mable, had been especially welcome in their childless home and had been showered with gifts as a young girl. Her wedding was the first social occasion of the reopened house, and the first occasion when the new Mrs. John Ringling was its hostess.[41]

Both newly married couples were listed among the passengers traveling from Tampa to Havana for a Latin New Year.[42] Shortly after their return, Edith Ringling introduced Emily to Sarasota society. The occasion was as splendid as Emily could have wished. The music room of Edith's elegant marble mansion was cleared for dancing to an orchestra, and a smaller room was set aside for those who preferred to play cards. A midnight supper was served. For a day, the *Sarasota Herald* put aside its growing coldness toward Ringling and offered what might seem excessive praise. Emily was described as the beautiful member of an old New York family: "She has held a socially important place in society on both sides of the Atlantic and is equally at home in high circles on the continent and in the simple social affairs in Sarasota. . . . She has captivated everyone she has met with her simplicity and charm."[43]

It was the beginning of 1931, a dark year early in the Depression. Sarasota society was unsure of how best to handle the austerity that came with such hard times. In France, one would say, "If the poor are to eat, the rich must dance." In Sarasota, country club members were offered such diversions as a Depression dance with the theme "How to have fun though broke." Costumed as the poor might dress, the revelers succeeded only in looking tasteless and ridiculous. Emily Ringling, who was a member of the dance committee, appeared in a native Cuban costume and a necklace of new potatoes.[44]

If the poor were to eat, more than dancing was needed. By mid-March, Sarasota County was nearly broke. Only 30 percent of county taxes were paid, giving the school fund a balance of $1,350. Teachers received half-pay for January, and nothing for February or the first half of March. Elementary schools closed on 3 April; the rest stayed open until the end of April. By late summer, most of the school year salaries were paid,[45] but a year later, the public schools were officially closed, open only to children who paid tuition.

Even in the height of the season, Sarasota lacked enough excitement to entertain Emily Ringling. The newlyweds did not remain long in Sarasota. They were off to New York and Miami, "where the fun is," said Emily. In New York they stayed at the Ritz Carlton, avoiding the apartment, where the rent was overdue. Ringling asked Emily to lend him $60,000, the amount needed to pay off a note at the Madison National Bank. Emily refused, claiming that she did not have the money.[46] However, lack of funds did not stop their pursuit of pleasure. When they were at Ca' d'Zan, the house was usually filled with guests. Almost daily parties and dinners filled the reception rooms. Gone were the small, quiet dinners with conversation turning to investment opportunities. Sometimes, oldtimers such as Frank Hennessy were among the houseguests, but most were Emily's friends from New York and Miami. One of John's friends who qualified as a thoroughly dashing visitor was Gould Dietz, an Omaha banker. In his more romantic avocation, he was a real lion hunter, reputed to hunt and train lions in their native regions and then bring them back to the United States to jump through hoops of fire in the circus.[47]

In March of 1931, Ringling and the Norths were saddened when

Lillian Leitzel, one of the greatest aerial performers in circus history, was killed in a fall at an indoor show in Copenhagen during the off season. Leitzel had joined the circus ten years earlier and was the highest paid aerialist at Ringling Bros. She was as popular with the Ringling family as she was at the circus, and she was generous with the bandsmen, especially the drummers, whose rolls and flourishes conveyed to the audience the thrill of her appearance. Her tips often exceeded the drummers' weekly pay, and on one occasion she presented Merle Evans, the band leader, with platinum cufflinks.[48]

When the 1931 circus season ended, Ringling and his bride departed for New York and Europe. On the surface, he and Emily continued to enjoy the forced gaiety of the 1920s with its class of postwar, newly rich arrivistes; but Ringling's affairs were starting to disintegrate. His partner Edith watched with increasing concern lest the worsening Depression bring disaster to the debt-ridden circus.

Across the nation, the autumn of 1931 and the spring of 1932 brought soaring unemployment and workers who still held jobs were placed on ever shorter hours. President Hoover in his last months in office proved wholly incapable of intervening in what he regarded as natural market behavior. Florida had its own set of calamities. On 31 August 1931, Flagler's East Coast Railroad went into receivership. An invasion of the Mediterranean fruit fly placed the citrus industry in a year of quarantine,[49] a devastating blow to the already floundering economy of the state. John and Emily had spent the summer in Europe, returning in time to learn that his nephew Richard Ringling had died less than three months after his mother, Della, the divorced widow of Alf T., had died at Baraboo. Richard's widow, Aubrey, was now an equal partner with John and Edith Ringling. The two women soon formed an alliance of two-thirds ownership that became known as the widow's voting trust.

Despite the Depression, early indications in 1932 promised an unusually good season for the circus. Signs of record attendance were watched closely in Sarasota, where the duration of the season was a key factor in the livelihood of the many circus families and of the town's merchants. Although John Ringling's personal reputation was suffering, the circus was very important to Sarasota's economy. Amid general evidence of worsening conditions, the circus opening in New York attracted what seemed at first to be the best-ever crowds and high gate receipts. The best seats were selling fast at $3.50, although advance sales of the cheaper gallery seats were lagging. The encouraging start was not sustained through the season. The tour was shortened; it closed at the first of October. Sarasota welcomed the homecoming performers, the menagerie, and the money that came with the move to winter quarters.[50] The uncertain season convinced Edith Ringling that her interests were not safe under John's sole management. She summoned Aubrey from Montana and her son Robert to Sarasota to consider strategy for the future of the circus.

The winter months of 1932 were full of depressing news. The proud Mira Mar Hotel, one of Sarasota's showplaces, suffered the indignity of foreclosure on its furnishings. The *Chicago Tribune* reported that Sarasota was "a ghostly town with its poor, empty skyscrapers," although Sarasota had few skyscrapers. One ten-story building stood empty; there was only one other, the Sarasota Terrace Hotel, which was kept solvent under the skilled management of Hazen Titus, a longtime friend of both John and Charles Ringling.[51] However, only 25 percent of city taxes for 1931 were collected by the end of March 1932. Seventy-five properties were to be auctioned for unpaid 1928 taxes.[52] There were a few bright spots in an otherwise gloomy spring. The first Ford V-8 arrived in Sarasota on 3 April, marking a new era in automaking. Contract bridge had become the game of choice among the elites of the country. In early April a number of Sarasotans, including Ida North, competed in the international bridge olympics.

Earlier this winter, Ringling had made another of his magnanimous gestures: the permanent opening of the museum. Even for this momentous event, he once again chose a proxy to make the announcement; Dr. Ludd Spivey as head of the Ringling art school declared that the museum would be open beginning on 17 January. No formal ceremonies would mark the occasion. Public admission was free, but a parking fee would be collected. John Ringling had at last achieved his and Mable's noblest ambition for their city. Several months later, Southern College conferred the degree of doctor of law upon Ringling, citing his career as a great builder and a discriminating patron of art. Dr. Spivey was absent from the event, mourning the death of his seven-year-old son Alan.[53]

The museum was overwhelmingly popular with residents and tourists alike; in its first seven weeks, there were about 20,000 visitors. In reviewing the city's attractions, the *Sarasota Herald* named the museum "a great landmark to travelers, something that no one of taste and culture can afford to miss." That, along with the area's beautiful beaches and homelike city atmosphere, made Sarasota an obvious candidate to participate in the forthcoming Century of Progress Exhibition at the Chicago World's Fair of 1933, which was confidently expected to reinvigorate the nation and drive away Depression gloom.[54]

In March John and Emily left Sarasota with the circus. Emily found the circus distasteful, but the comfort of a private train car made the journey to New York bearable. In May, John suffered the first of a long series of illnesses. While John and Emily were in Washington with the show, a seemingly minor infection began to trouble him, causing him to hasten to New York for medical attention. The condition was diagnosed in late May as blood poisoning, apparently caused by an injury incurred several months earlier when someone had stepped on his foot while he was dancing at the Gasparilla Ball in Tampa.

His condition was not made public until after the more serious effects had been corrected by surgery; it then promptly became a topic for speculation and contradictory stories. The United Press International wire service reported that he was critically ill in a hospital in Seagate, New York, where both his legs had been amputated in an effort to save his life. The UPI even circulated an obituary for its subscribers to have ready if he should die.[55] Ringling's servants offered their version, and newspapers contradicted one another. Finally Ringling spoke to the press in a message from Sam Gumpertz to Charles Sanford (husband of Hester Ringling) for the *Sarasota Herald:* "John is feeling fine. No truth in report. Kindly notify *Herald.*" The *Chicago Tribune* also printed an emphatic denial of alarmist reports on the same day. Ringling was staying deliberately out of sight at the Half Moon Hotel on Coney Island, one of Sam Gumpertz's properties.[56] Although his illness was not as serious as the wire services had reported, it was by no means the trivial infection that he pretended. Emily had either visited or stayed at the hotel each day; Ida North came from Sarasota to be near her brother. At Emily's insistence, a heart specialist was summoned from New York City to join Dr. Ewalt, the attending physician.

Meanwhile Ringling was being constantly harassed by his circus creditors, who were then preparing to move against him. He was like a captive at Gumpertz's hotel, possibly to conceal the plans of his creditors and isolate Ringling from competent legal help. Richard Fuchs, the aide who consulted with him every day, stated that these adversities and the daily attention they demanded caused him great mental agony.[57] Throughout the period of crisis that followed, Ringling was isolated from his attorney. He had already lost the loyalty of John Kelley, the circus attorney, who was working with his partners and soon-to-be adversaries, Edith and Aubrey.

In July 1932, the widely dispersed Ringling empire was effectively dismembered. This personal disaster was partially concealed by Ringling's illness, which occupied the attention of the press. The step-by-step marauding of Ringling's assets and his corporate positions was carefully hidden from the public and probably from friends and acquaintances in the business and financial world—particularly from any who might have consoled him or helped to avert some of the most damaging actions of his adversaries.

Ringling's illness had thoroughly alarmed his circus creditors, and on 14 July they moved to protect their interests. Not every Ringling asset was visible, and some were probably uncovered with the help of betrayed confidence. He was pressured to sign a collateral pledge. Under its terms, almost his entire estate outside of Sarasota was pledged in security to the circus loan that had enabled him to buy the American Circus Corporation in 1929. The reasons for the exclusion of the Sarasota properties still remain in question; perhaps even his most grasping enemies preferred to leave him a survival stake. Another possibility is that Sam Gumpertz did not wish to see Ringling destroyed in Sarasota, particularly since Gumpertz would ultimately be shown to be one of the principal figures in the capture of Ringling's assets and his removal from authority in the circus. In the space of a few days in late

July, Ringling was placed in a position from which he was never to escape. Moreover, from then until his death he was continually under the care of physicians, and for most of the time he was assisted by a nurse in constant attendance.

More than his physical condition, his impaired ability to reach decisions was the most damaging to his interests.[58] This debility prevented him from being able to grasp his few opportunities to reassert control of his affairs. Indecision, inaction, and intractability helped to ruin him. Despite their sometimes violent disagreements, Emily tried to protect him from some of the worst invasions of his assets. Nevertheless, he persisted in regarding her efforts to intervene as "stealing his papers" or demanding that she be allowed to bring in another attorney whom he would not see. For fifty years the Ringling women had had no direct involvement in family business matters, and John kept insisting that she knew nothing of his affairs and hence could not have an opinion.[59] This quarrel continued through all the crises with his creditors. He could not accept the fact that Emily, his adversary in so many domestic matters, wanted to help him.

At the center of Ringling's problems was the Prudence Bond Company and its two subsidiaries: New York Investors and Allied Owners. In 1929, when Ringling was searching for funds to purchase the American Circus Corporation, William Greve, the central figure of this network, offered to advance the needed funds. The hand of Sam Gumpertz was not in evidence at this point, but he was intimately associated with the group. The circus purchase price was $2 million. Ringling found about $300,000 in cash, most of it from another loan. Greve arranged for the Central Hanover Trust Company of New York to advance the $1.7 million on a personal promissory note signed by John Ringling, endorsed by the New York Investors. Later, Allied Owners purchased the note from the bank without Ringling's knowledge. In consequence, New York Investors, as the parent company, acquired an interest in the loan. That note ran for only six months, unsecured by any Ringling collateral. Ringling, trusting in Sam Gumpertz (who had introduced him to these financiers), believed he was among friends. New York Investors agreed to obtain renewals, and the extension of the note provided that Ringling must pay the interest and reduce the principal by $200,000 a year.[60] Half the stock in the five newly acquired circuses was held in trust by New York Investors.

A year later Ringling could not meet the first payment of interest and principal, due 6 September 1930. Falling ever deeper into the net, he borrowed another $200,000 from Greve's firm, assigning two substantial New Jersey property mortgages.

At about the time when Ringling became ill in the spring of 1932, another installment of interest fell due on the circus note. New York Investors then held the funds from the New Jersey mortgages; the interest due was about $20,000. The creditors now had the opportunity they expected and for which they had prepared. They elected not to apply any of the mortgage money to overdue interest. Greve and his colleagues, increasingly dissatisfied with the note because it was unsupported by collateral, declared the circus loan in default. Thus New York Investors pushed Ringling into a position where he was compelled to make ruinous concessions.

In July, when Ringling was forced to sign away his assets, Emily urged him not to agree to their demands, which she rightly believed would leave him broke. She tried without success to bring in an attorney whom she trusted. Emily perceived, as Ringling did not, that Kelley, the circus attorney, was pushing the interests of the circus as he saw them and that he was supporting Edith Ringling. She saw clearly that Ringling was without an ally within the circus. For too long he had plunged ahead, indifferent to his partners Edith and Aubrey and brushing aside all who questioned his total command.

Ringling would not listen to Emily, now the only voice urging him to resist. The creditors' threat of closing down the circus with a foreclosure so alarmed him that he took a fatal, irrational step without the guidance of an attorney. At that final moment, rather than allow the circus to be shut down, he chose personal ruin. With competent advice he might well have turned aside some of the outrageous demands of the moneylenders. His new agreement with Allied Owners contained 165 pages of conditions and terms. The Ringling partnership was dissolved; in its place was a Delaware corporation that had the same Ringling

Bros. name but was controlled by Allied Owners. Ringling became the personal endorser of the new circus note, pledging most of his assets as collateral.[61]

New York Investors also gained the right to sell off any Ringling property (even that not pledged as collateral, including the Sarasota properties), whether or not there were any default in payment of the note. A bonus of 10 percent of the stock in the Ringling Bros. circus and the smaller circuses meant that for the first time in its history a share of ownership was held outside the Ringling family. Among the directors of the new corporation were Edith and Aubrey Ringling. John Ringling was retained as president, his salary reduced from $50,000 to $6,000 a year. Sam Gumpertz became general manager[62] of the Ringling Bros. Barnum & Bailey Circus.

The terms of these complex arrangements seem so outrageous that they defy understanding. A bizarre combination of circumstances had abruptly placed all the advantages in the hands of Ringling's adversaries. On the one side stood the creditors, the holders of the circus note. Their own enterprise was reeling toward financial collapse; hence, this capture of substantial assets might yet save them from ruin. They were joined by Edith Ringling, who was impatient to see John Ringling removed from his position of authority. With much less eagerness the third partner, Aubrey Ringling, followed Edith's lead. Aubrey was reluctant to forsake the bond that had once existed among John, Mable, herself, and her husband, Richard, John's nephew. Sam Gumpertz stood to gain by supporting the actions of the creditors, who were his associates, and the two Ringling partners.

Much more was to come. The July attack on Ringling's remaining personal fortune began with the formation of the Rembrandt Corporation to manage the art collection. At its first meeting on 26 July 1932, the board of directors elected the company's officers. Ringling was unanimously chosen president. The charter called for two vice-presidents and a treasurer. These three positions were filled by officials of the Prudence Bond and New York Investors combination: William Greve, Francis Pender, and Sam Gumpertz.[63]

In their next step, the new officers acted on a letter from Ringling to the corporation, in which he offered to "sell, transfer and deliver" to the corporation all paintings listed in an inventory of his art collection plus all of his other pictures and art objects. In return, the corporation would issue to him all the authorized shares of stock—100 shares.[64] On that same day, however, the entire issue of stock was recorded not to John Ringling but to the New York Investors.[65] The paintings were, by agreement, to remain at the John and Mable Ringling Museum of Art, where they would be shown and protected. Five of the more valuable works were noted in the inventory as subject to an existing mortgage; they were the five paintings named in the bill of sale that Ringling had executed for Emily as security for her loan of $50,000 four days before their marriage. Three others were in a New York warehouse, pledged to the Manufacturers Trust Company. From that day, Ringling could not sell a single painting or art object without his creditors' permission.

Within a few days the grip of the Prudence Bond group tightened still further. Ringling was forced to sign transfers that named New York Investors as proxy with the power of attorney for his interests in eight corporations, among them some of his major assets.[66]

Crushing as they were, these blows did not wholly destroy Ringling's health or his courage. By late September, he left behind the distressing scenes at the Half Moon Hotel and returned to Sarasota, apparently in restored health. He appeared with Emily at the second-year opening of the art school, held in the museum courtyard. Arriving at the ceremony, he was greeted with gratifying applause from the audience. In his brief address, Ringling stressed once more his belief that this collection of paintings and other objects had been brought together for the good of the community and the cultivation of artistic knowledge.[67] For a few hours he could forget the battering he had received from New York Investors and bask in the warmth of sunshine and praise.

During his brief stay in Sarasota, he opened negotiations with the state controller, Ernest Ames, in an effort to find a formula that would permit the Bank of Sarasota to reopen. After weathering the worst storms that followed the land boom, the bank had succumbed following the Roosevelt bank holiday. In addition to his shareholdings, Ringling had nearly $100,000 on deposit, funds that he could scarcely afford to lose. The attempt to reopen was a failure, for the bank's assets were insufficient to justify a loan.

The bank closing was one more symptom of the worsening conditions in Sarasota. Because publicly funded relief programs did not yet exist, the Sarasota Welfare Association urged citizens to donate food, which was then offered to all who could work—a day's food for a day of work, with greater amounts of food given to those with dependents.[68] Help was on the way as the Roosevelt administration set its plans in motion, but it did not reach the local level fast enough. Meanwhile, the Parent-Teachers Association joined in public appeals for food to help with a school lunch program for poor children. The Welfare Association reported that just under 30 percent of the population needed help.

The Ringling circus was ending its 1932 season. Thanks to its good start, the season's receipts were better than expected for a Depression year. Offering performances on Sundays, which was contrary to the Ringling custom, had helped. Meanwhile, the new directors were stripping Ringling of his authority. They were able to keep secret the maneuvers that created the voting trust and the bylaws that placed Gumpertz firmly in control.

When the circus opened its stand in Chicago, Edith Ringling announced in an interview that she was now the manager. "It's nothing," she said. "I mean that anyone who has been with the circus as many years as I have should be able to run the show." The New York office promptly denied that John Ringling was out. Not until November was there a clear picture of what had happened. The *Sarasota Herald* took its story from *Billboard*, where the story first appeared, naming Sam Gumpertz as the new general manager of the circus.[69]

The public statements framed by Edith and others stressed that Gumpertz's role was of great assistance to John Ringling, whose health was said to be no longer equal to the immense task of managing the massive organization. *Billboard*, the voice of outdoor entertainment, focused attention on the approaching fiftieth-anniversary season of 1933–34, when Gumpertz's great skill and experience would be so valuable. A fantastic spectacle, "The Durbar of Delhi," was promised to be the greatest display of pageantry that America had ever seen.[70]

The fiction that Gumpertz was Ringling's personal choice to take his place was still maintained when the circus train left Sarasota in April of

Hand-drawn poster advertising the Ringling hall show in its second season, 1883–84. From this small beginning came the great Ringling Bros. Barnum & Bailey show with its nearly 2,000 performers and workers. Courtesy of Lillian Burns.

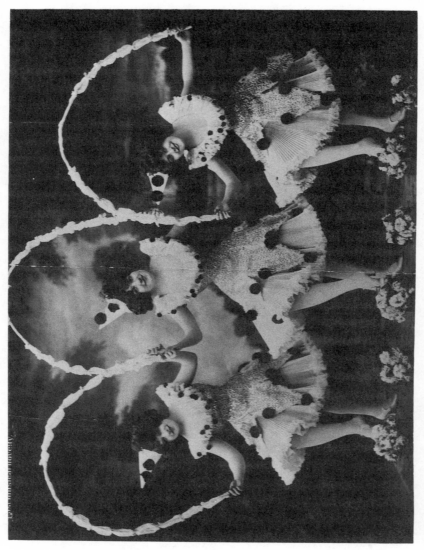

The Grona Sisters photographed at Berlin, 1916. During the first years of World War I, many performers sought contracts in America. Ringling Bros. or Barnum & Bailey contracts were the most prestigious. Courtesy of Lillian Burns.

1933 to open its anniversary season. As the city turned out in force to watch the departure, the scene was poignant. A parade to the train station was formed, led by an open car bearing Sam Gumpertz, his wife, Evie, and Edith Ringling, smiling and waving to the crowds. John Ringling stood alone at the Seaboard station platform to see them off. The first train carried the performers, animals, and equipment for the stand at Madison Square Garden. At the end, the last car to which Ringling waved farewell was the splendid private car of Sam Gumpertz.

In truth, Ringling and Gumpertz were now enemies, except in public. Ringling regarded his long-trusted friend as a conspirator, a man who had colluded with the New York Investors and the other two Ringling Bros. partners. The little remaining harmony within the Ringling family had vanished forever. In the following two years, rumors circulated that John Ringling was disposing of his circus shares, that he was not voluntarily retiring from active management, that he had been pushed out. For the most part, the Sarasota press avoided the sensitive topic of a breach between the Charles Ringling family and John Ringling. An unfortunate casualty of the family estrangement was its extension to the friendship of John Ringling and Ralph Caples. Believing (perhaps correctly) that Caples had taken Edith's side in the circus infighting, Ringling broke off this friendship of nearly thirty years. Caples ceased to visit his friend at Ca' d'Zan.[71]

In December 1932, John Ringling had learned that he was forbidden to make any further commitments in the name of the circus. He was in New York, preparing a contract for the Cristiani family to join the circus from Italy, when Gumpertz notified him by telegram that he must cease all such actions. On the same day, still at his office, Ringling had just finished signing some real estate contracts when the pen fell from his hand and he fell back from his desk.[72] He was assisted to his home, where Dr. Ewalt diagnosed a severe thrombosis, which caused partial paralysis of the right side of his body. For several weeks he was in critical condition, attended by two nurses. One of them was Ina Sanders, who remained with him for the remaining four years of his life.

From the time of that attack until the spring of 1933, Ringling, once a physically imposing figure, was confined to bed or to a chair, unable to rise or turn over without assistance. Even so, the pressure of his unraveling business affairs was so great that daily sessions with his aide were resumed as soon as the doctor allowed.

Added to the frustrations of his paralysis and the compelling problems of his financial affairs were the rising decibels of domestic discord. While Ringling was immobilized, there were frequent, almost daily cocktail parties at the Park Avenue apartment. When the guests reached a state of noisy, friendly intoxication, many would insist on visiting him in his room. Against all medical advice, these scenes continued amid reports that even Emily was ordered to stay out of his room; her visits usually ended with his blood pressure and pulse rate soaring. Fortunately, his condition started to improve, and by March 1933 he was ready to return to Sarasota. Emily protested that she disliked Sarasota and would be happy never to see it again. In her view, the move to Florida in late March, when the winter vacation season was nearly over, meant that the fun in Palm Beach and Miami had ended for the year. To Nurse Sanders, she said that she supposed she would have to take him down anyway to bury him.[73]

Soon after their return to Ca' d'Zan he had a second attack of thrombosis, which affected his speech as well as his freedom of movement. For several months, his home life matched the chaos of his finances. Domestic scenes grew more and more noisy and disturbing. Emily's once rich and vigorous husband had changed into a fretting invalid, one who could not assert his own interests, let alone afford or participate in the good times in Miami and Palm Beach that she enjoyed. His financial straits meant that even common household bills went unpaid, an embarrassment for servants as well as for the unhappy mistress of the house.

For several months there seemed to be no acceptable solution. Ringling was never left unguarded by his nurse, who tried to shield him from the tension of quarrels with Emily. Emily's sister Alean Kelly, who spent much of her time with them, sometimes tried to act as peacemaker, without success. (To complicate matters, Alean's husband brought suit against Emily for having alienated his wife and son from him with favors and money.) Emily seems not to have discussed the possibility of divorce from Ringling in her conversations with Alean. She could, as she later did, stay alone in the New York apartment, but lack of funds finally made that solution impractical. Moreover, Emily precipitated the conflicts by accosting John in his room several times a day. Ca' d'Zan was large enough for her to live apart to herself if she chose, but she could not keep silent.

In late spring, the turmoil in Ca' d'Zan increased when Ringling experienced another severe attack of thrombosis. At one stage, Ringling's Sarasota physician, Dr. Joseph Halton, despaired of saving his patient, but again Ringling's strength slowly returned.

Ringling would need all the strength he could summon as his financial and marital troubles redoubled in intensity. New York Investors were again demanding concessions. The Madison National Bank called in an overdue note for $60,000. There was a real danger that one creditor would start an action against him, which might instigate a rush among them all. So far, Ca' d'Zan had remained unencumbered. Ida North agreed to hold a mortgage on the home, and papers were drawn up; Emily refused to sign. The house, she said, was almost the only property still free from debt. If that were lost, her dower would be empty.[74] She was mistaken; there were other properties not then obligated. But she remained adamant and the mortgage was never signed.

Ida, who had only modest funds of her own, would probably have assigned the mortgage, although she was able to lend money to her brother from her own resources on several occasions. She later said, "All I had—all of the money I had was at his disposal." Her loans came to about $90,000, secured by a mortgage on the furnishings of Ca' d'Zan and shares of Ringling Isles.[75] That collateral was an example of Ringling's questionable tactics: his paintings and art objects (at any location) had already been transferred to the Rembrandt Corporation, whose shares were in the hands of New York Investors. While this suggests duplicity (either out of habit or desperation) even in dealing with his sister, a bond of affection and loyalty was clearly apparent in the willingness of each to come to the aid of the other. Sometime later their positions were reversed. Ida was short of ready funds and John sent her $300, saying that it was the best he could do: "It is all I can do to keep my head above water."[76] The sum was small, but it testifies to Ringling's affection for his sister.

In late July 1933 Ringling filed for divorce in the circuit court of Sarasota. By a mischance, Emily was served with a summons not at home, as he intended, but in a shop on Main Street. Confronted with that unexpected blow in a public place, she became visibly ill. Even in the comparative freedom of life-styles in the early 1930s, there remained a social stigma for women whose husbands divorced them. When she recovered from the initial surprise, Emily decided to halt the action or somehow prevent it from coming into court.

A month of wavering indecision and expensive negotiations with their attorneys followed. The outcome could scarcely be called a reconciliation. In the end, two documents were signed, defining and extending the relationship for a short time longer. The prenuptial agreement of December 1930 was reaffirmed, but its terms were more limited. Emily disclaimed her dower rights only to the museum and art collection. No other properties were specified. The $50,000 note for her loan to John just before their marriage was renewed. It was to run for four years at 6 percent interest. Emily gained the right to foreclose if the note went to default. She could then sell the five valuable paintings for which she held a bill of sale. At Emily's insistence, the note was recorded at the Sarasota County courthouse; this time she was taking no chance of a lost or destroyed document. On the following day, the petition for a divorce was withdrawn.[77]

The truce in domestic bickering brought relative peace to Ca' d'Zan, so Ringling could give his attention to his affairs in New York. In November, Ringling's principal creditors, New York Investors and its subsidiary Allied Owners, were declared bankrupt, and court-appointed receivers assumed the management of their tangled affairs. Among the assets were the two Ringling circus notes, one for each corporation, and Ringling's own collateral agreement. Ringling was called to testify several times about the assets he had pledged, including the shares of the Rembrandt Corporation. He insisted that he had been victimized by a conspiracy to take away all his assets while he was too ill to resist the pressure brought by his creditors. Emily, too, was summoned to testify about the five paintings, since her claim subtracted a substantial sum from the total value of the collection. She managed to evade the summons by escaping over the rooftop of their apartment house into an adjoining building (John's idea); she remained out of reach for three days. There was no longer any way to conceal the fact that creditors had possession of the Rembrandt Corporation stock. At issue was the actual ownership of the paintings and whether or not such ownership rested with Ringling while the creditors held the shares as collateral. The museum was a separate entity, but the collection was clearly at risk if it became entangled in legal battles for possession. The most threatening feature was the provision in the July 1932 agreements that allowed New York Investors to sell *any* Ringling asset.

Sarasota city officials were alarmed enough to take action at the prospect of losing the museum and collection. The only apparent defense was quickly adopted. In a concerted effort, federal, state, county, and city tax liens were placed against the museum. A total of some $6 million in past taxes from 1930 to 1933 and more for 1934 were assessed. Federal claims were based on delayed customs and import charges, state and local taxes on real and personal property.[78]

Museum contents were assessed for $5 million, but because they were used for educational purposes, no tax had ever been collected. The legal opinion of the city attorney now held that by pledging the works of art as security for a loan, Ringling had placed them in a commercial status. The charge for admission that had been imposed in 1933 presented an additional argument for tax liability in 1934.[79]

Since tax liens took precedence over private debts, the tax seemed large enough to give protection against a foreclosure sale. While the county tax assessor did not expect that any tax would ever be collected, the expected court battle would leave the museum intact for several years, time enough for a solution to be found. The issue attracted a barrage of litigation, court appearances, and public attention that continued for years. The principle of a tax-free institution retaining or losing its status was of vital interest to many educational institutions. The attorneys who fought the tax claims for New York Investors Corporation ultimately collected their fee from the Ringling estate.[80]

Less than a month after the museum crisis began, Ringling decided that the situation in his home was no longer tolerable. He left New York for Sarasota on 23 December 1933. Emily protested strongly, but he refused to let her accompany him. In effect, the marriage had ended, after three years and fours days. Emily's sister Alean and her son, who had been living at Ca' d'Zan for a year, returned to New York. Ringling suffered another attack of thrombosis shortly after he arrived in Sarasota. Dr. Halton found him near death, his chances of recovery most uncertain. Yet he did survive, summoning reserves of strength from his once powerful constitution. Freed from the tensions of marital conflict, he continued to improve slowly through 1934 and 1935.[81]

Once again, moderately improved health and strength enabled Ringling to cope with financial demands, but only to the point of averting further disaster. Debts large and small were a constant drain on his disposition and his income. Until their separation, Emily had paid some of the most persistent claimants. Early in 1934, Florida Power and Light Company delivered a disconnection notice for Ca' d'Zan and two other buildings where power was charged to Ringling personally. His New York office and apartment rents fell behind again. Grocers, Rolls Royce rental agencies, and other New York suppliers were growing impatient with the evasive answers they received to their dunning letters. A loyal friend and colleague, Tide Cox at the Rockland Oil Company in Oklahoma, sent money to pay the rent of the Madison Avenue office.[82]

In early 1934 Ringling became aware that his adversaries in New York Investors had captured the loyalty of Richard Fuchs, his aide for more than fifteen years. In response to Ringling's letter of dismissal, Fuchs left his service on two days' notice to accept an attractive offer from New York Investors.

In a long polemic, Fuchs spelled out in colorful detail information that he was certain would lead Ringling's creditors to sell out his collateral in a rush to get whatever they could. Furthermore, Fuchs added, "From the moment I cease to work for you, I shall feel under no obligation to withhold any knowledge I have of your dealings, either with the United States government, the New York Investors, Mrs. Ringling or anyone else who may be interested. You may be sure they (Bureau of Internal Revenue) will receive exact information both as to amounts and where each item may be located."[83]

Fuchs believed he had been badly used and that Ringling did not appreciate his years of service and the long, irregular hours that he had worked. In many respects, he was right, for Ringling was not one to value loyalty in others. But their parting was inevitable once Fuchs came under the influence of Ringling's adversaries. He was offered more money and a position in what seemed like a more solvent operation, and it was clear that he was bitterly hostile toward his former employer:

> I have written you that the Internal Revenue Bureau is inquiring into your affairs. I have, thus far stalled them off, but as a private person I intend to have no such false idea of what you might term loyalty to you. Therefore, when questioned, [I will] be very frank and open with the government, maybe they will think my information of some value, though you believe it of no consequence. . . . this will no doubt precipitate a nice scramble of your creditors, I think a receivership for your estate is inevitable and you won't need a secretary or anyone else in your employ.[84]

However, nothing came of Fuchs's hope of being interrogated and his promise to reveal what he knew. In truth, the Bureau of Internal Revenue did not need him. The officials of the Bureau had collected the data they required and were content to wait for an appropriate time to file their claims against Ringling through his estate.

For the five years during which New York Investors held control of the circus no dividends were paid to the shareholders, even though the circus grossed more than $20 million. Only $300,000 was paid on the circus note.[85] The 1934 season was disrupted by a robbery and murder on the train as it traveled through Indiana. In midseason an outbreak of typhoid killed several members of the circus and sent seventy-seven of the crew to a hospital in Detroit. Among the victims was Baby Ruth, fat lady in the sideshow. She lost more than 200 pounds during her illness and retreated to Sarasota to regain her weight and title.

Without his circus dividends, Ringling was becoming desperate for cash. Between 1934 and 1936, his New York attorney acted for him in no fewer than thirty suits in New York alone.[86] The dire forecast that Fuchs left as his parting wish for Ringling failed to elicit any exposure of concealed assets, and federal investigators did not uncover any hidden sources of income.

Ringling's nephew John North became his business aide, scrambling for every dollar to meet the most demanding claims for payment. In 1934, North stayed at the Ringling apartment and gave up his job with a brokerage firm to give full attention to his uncle's affairs. He assumed many of the duties that had been assigned to Fuchs. Acting on his own initiative, he was able to assist his uncle in some of the many searches for funds to stall the smaller but no less persistent demands for cash.

Fuchs had become Emily's ally, taking her side in the Ringlings' continuing domestic conflict. After his hasty departure, Ringling seemed more sure of himself, more able to cope with daily routines. In March 1934, almost immediately after Fuchs left, Ringling returned to the Sarasota circuit court, where he filed a second time for divorce, under charges of extreme cruelty.[87] This time there would be no bargaining that could lead to a dismissal. The process took more than two years, with testimony that sometimes became profane. Emily fought the action in Sarasota, Bradenton, Tallahassee, and New York. The contest dragged on until 6 July 1936, when Ringling finally won a divorce decree. Even then it did not end. The case was reopened after Ringling's death, and Emily sought to have the decree set aside, a conflict with the executors that lasted another five years.

In early 1934 the Madison National Bank, holding a note for $55,000, demanded payment. John North raised the money after a furious night-and-day effort, but at a terrible price. For a loan of $30,000, Ringling became obligated to a private moneylender at an outrageous rate of interest.[88] Ever suspicious, Ringling believed that North had taken a kickback from the lender. Ringling withdrew his trust and never again had any confidence in his nephew.

Many more claims followed. Almost everything Ringling owned in New York had a lien on it, even the old Rolls Royce, the wine cellar, and the bourbon whiskey. In Sarasota scrap steel was sold, as were the wine and whiskey, and valuations were quietly obtained in preparation for selling some of the paintings. Sarasota properties were swept up in Ringling's storm of adversity, but first all those curious transactions that clouded ownership had to be unscrambled before his Sarasota real estate, such as the El Vernona Hotel, St. Armands, and the sugar bowl lands, could be readied for marketing new owners.

Throughout 1934, when there seemed so little prospect of avoiding receivership, Ringling's attorneys labored over the mass of details to assemble a file that set forth the entire truth of his situation. With this in hand they approached several prominent banks, finance companies, and individuals in negotiations to finance John Ringling in a complete restructuring of his debts and assets. Charles Allen and Company nearly came to an agreement. They offered an entire plan and financing schedule, fully in accord with Ringling's expressed conditions. Had their offer been accepted, the remaining history of John Ringling and his financial interests might have been profoundly altered. However, Ringling delayed his response and then attempted to impose new conditions. Allen and Company withdrew its offer. Thus had Ringling's illness impaired his judgment and his ability to reach and act upon a decision. He found it impossible to admit that he was no longer in the role of leader, even in his own affairs. This had been his last opportunity. The futile exercise cost him $140,000 in legal fees, a charge that remained for his executors to settle.[89]

Meanwhile John North was fending off marauding tax certificate buyers who scanned city and county tax rolls looking for properties that might fall into their grasp. For his Sarasota holdings, Ringling's taxes were somehow paid, at least within time limits to avert the certificate sale.[90] Some relief for depositors at the Bank of Sarasota arrived in the form of a loan from the Reconstruction Finance Corporation. The loan, somewhat smaller than Ringling hoped to get, was to pay depositors a fraction of their lost funds. The conditions of the loan forbade any further payment to depositors until the loan was repaid, a condition that the bank could not overcome.[91] It never reopened.

Ringling had ceased to be the man whom Sarasota publicly honored. That place was occupied by Sam Gumpertz, while two negative issues kept Ringling's name in print. His protracted divorce action was treated as a celebrity case and reported in the national press. For example, the *American Weekly* claimed, "Wife number two gave him more pulse-quickening thrills in his Florida palace than any under the big top."[92] The coverage must have been painful to Ringling, who has scrupulously avoided the antics of many other celebrities. The second issue, the museum tax dispute, dragged on. Ringling incurred heavy public disapproval for placing the museum at risk in his dealings with moneylenders.

To counter some of the unfavorable publicity, he resorted to writing letters to the *Sarasota Herald* in which he oversimplified the issues of ownership of the museum and the Rembrandt Corporation. One lengthy letter was revised (probably by Henry North) to soften some of its statements about the unscrupulous people who were trying to ruin him. Ringling's latent anti-Semitism, which only surfaced when he gave way to ill-tempered remarks, was carefully edited out of the letter.[93] Henry, Ida's younger son, had become Ringling's companion and chauffeur. Henry lived at the Bird Key house and spent much of his time with his semi-invalid uncle. Their relationship eventually became somewhat strained as Ringling became increasingly hostile toward Henry's brother, John.

With all his myriad embarrassments, Ringling still enjoyed a measure of peace that he had not known while Emily shared his home. He was limited to one cigar a day, a severe restriction indeed. But that one cigar was smoked to less than an inch. When it became too short to hold, he would call to Henry North, "Get me a toothpick, Buddy." Together, Ringling and Buddy attended movies regularly, traveling to theaters throughout the area in the old limousine.[94] Life at Ca' d'Zan was quiet, in complete contrast to the entertaining in Mable's time and in Emily's. Now he met occasionally with Sarasota friends. A newcomer, Karl Bickel, retired head of the Associated Press, was using the remodeled Burns-Ringling office building as his home. Bickel became a staunch supporter of the museum and of Ringling's interests as he perceived them.

Ringling's quieter home life, free of emotional conflict, helped to lessen the tensions that had kept him ill so long. As noted above, Eugene Garey, his New York attorney and Madison Square Garden colleague, recalled that toward the end he had a good prospect of recovery in health and financial condition. But the events of those few turbulent years had had an impact on Ringling's character and his resolve. His pride was battered, and his spirit was mortally wounded by the betrayal and conspiracy of the circus takeover.

In November 1935, Ringling signed a codicil to his will, which had been drawn in May 1934, a short time after his second suit for divorce. Eugene Garey, Ringling's New York attorney, was summoned to New

York's Ritz Carlton Hotel, where Ringling had spent much of the year. Late in the afternoon, Garey arrived to find the chauffeur with cap in hand, already standing in the corridor outside the Ringling suite with piles of luggage, ready to drive Ringling and Nurse Sanders to the station, where they would take the early evening train to Florida. Inside the suite, Frank Hennessy and Nurse Sanders were making final preparations to leave. Garey asked them to withdraw. In the privacy of the sitting room he then learned that Ringling wished to attach a codicil that changed his will only in two respects; first, John and Henry North were to be cut off from any participation in his estate so they could receive nothing that belonged to him; and second, his sister Ida, their mother, was to receive not more than $5,000 a year.

Since Garey had not seen the will, he knew nothing of its provisions. He insisted that it would be difficult to draft a codicil to a will that he had neither seen nor drawn. "I urged that he return with the will," Garey later said, "and then we would draft a codicil." Ringling replied, "No, I want it now."

Garey wrote the codicil in longhand on hotel stationery. It was never converted to a more formal, typewritten document. Hennessy and Sanders were called into the room as witnesses. Sanders assisted Ringling to cross the room to the desk, where she held the paper for him to sign. All signed, then left the suite and descended in the elevator. At the hotel entrance they separated; Sanders and Ringling entered the limousine and started their journey to Florida. The codicil was among the accumulation of papers that Ringling kept in his possession. A year later, on the day after Ringling died, Sanders and her assistant, Nurse Canivan, took the codicil from the apartment and gave it to Garey at his office. Garey promptly sent a copy to the Florida attorney general because of its importance to the state as principal beneficiary.

Garey did not know that in the will the Norths had been named executors of the estate and trustees of the museum. Had he been able to raise the issue and discuss it with Ringling, years of litigation might have been avoided. As it was, those provisions remained unaltered; only the specific bequests were changed.

Garey recollected that when they drew up the codicil Ringling spoke with harsh intensity, saying that John North had conspired against him.

(When asked to repeat Ringling's specific words, Garey refused, saying that he had used unprintable "circus profanity.") Later, when the codicil was offered for probate, the witnesses were not in agreement about Ringling's feelings toward John North. Sanders, increasingly hostile to the Norths as time passed, later testified that they laughed and joked during Ringling's dying moments. Ringling's intent regarding the Norths as executors was fought over for ten years.[95]

At a still later hearing, when the status of the executors was again in question, Sanders and Garey even more adamantly declared that Ringling had a strong and abiding antipathy for John North, even including Ida North.[96] Yet family correspondence in 1935, the year of the codicil, points to a warm, even affectionate concern for Ida and her family, with the possible exception of John North.[97] Although the codicil had the appearance of a last-minute decision, impulsive action was never one of Ringling's traits. He was unquestionably angry and resentful toward John North, and according to Garey feared him. Those same bitter feelings may have spilled over into his attitude toward his sister Ida and her younger son, Henry North.

The fate of his art collection might have been his main consideration. By late 1935, Ringling had regained some physical strength, but his finances were in a permanently chaotic state. Given the tight grasp of his creditors, the ill will of his circus partners, and the uncertain outcome of his divorce action, the survival of an appreciable estate was by no means certain. If his estate were forced into receivership, there would be no way to save his art collection. Ringling's principal concern was to preserve the collection and the museum intact as a public bequest. Its preservation could not be a certainty, but the state of Florida was the most likely beneficiary to force its way through the host of thorny issues that would arise upon his death. The balance of his assets, while greatly diminished, might be the incentive to persuade state officials to fight for the museum and its contents.

The world was rapidly nearing its greatest upheaval. In 1936, war in the Far East was overshadowed by two new conflicts: Mussolini's open attack on Ethiopia and the Spanish Civil War. For some in the United States, the Depression was over. A growing momentum would now carry the economy to greater strength as the world moved with seeming indifference toward greater wars.

Economic upturn in Sarasota brought a moderate revival of building and growth. The other major source of income, tourists and winter visitors, also improved. For Ringling, a modest increase in land sales indicated that perhaps the worst was over. But if better times permitted Ringling to relax slightly, his hostile feelings about the circus takeover continued unabated. Ringling smarted as he watched what he regarded as amateurish management ruin the show and the organization.[98] He continued to quarrel with Edith and Sam Gumpertz, as the organization was clearly foundering. Edith's son Robert, whom she had brought in to share director responsibilities with Gumpertz, was unable to turn things around.

Ringling's New York attorneys quietly proposed to New York Investors that they abandon Gumpertz and in a friendly move reinstate Ringling. As badly as Investors needed the circus debt repaid, they were already in too much trouble to disturb the precarious state of the circus corporation. Gumpertz had perhaps heard of the attempt to oust him, because he would allow Ringling no voice in circus affairs. So bitter was the conflict that Gumpertz would not even permit Ringling to mingle with the crew. In the spring of 1936, when Ringling attended a performance in Brooklyn, orders from Gumpertz forbade any member of the show to greet him, to approach him, or to talk with him. Not everyone obeyed the order. Some old friends insisted on greeting "Mr. John."[99] It was the last time the circus staff would see John Ringling alive.

Other loyal employees had also disappeared from Ringling's life. Sophie Collins, the cook at the first Sarasota home and later at Ca' d'Zan, retired after twenty-five years. John Russos, who served John and Mable for nearly as long as head houseman, at both Sarasota and Alpine, New Jersey, retired and died a year later. Charles Kannely, for many years private secretary to John and Charles at the circus, was another whose death meant a break with the past. Two more recent employees remained: Nurse Sanders stayed, although she had been unpaid since the end of 1933; James Haley, manager of the Sarasota real estate office, worked without pay for half of 1936.

Apart from the North family, John's only remaining contact with his family was with his niece Marjorie Ringling, who lived in New York and had recently married Jacob Javits, who was just beginning his distinguished political career.

The 1936 season was not a happy one for the circus. In Washington, D.C., a violent storm tore loose several support poles, causing a panic as the big top fell; one young girl was killed. Gumpertz's authority was further eroded by a federal grand jury that indicted twelve executives of New York Investors.[100] After a two-year investigation by the Bureau of Internal Revenue, a federal court action in New York revealed that a tax fraud (unknown to the Ringlings) had been instigated by circus officials in 1918. The case ended with convictions and prison sentences for several circus staff members, tax consultants, and former Internal Revenue aides.[101]

In the autumn of 1936, Ringling was physically able to move about, and Eugene Garey was encouraging him to believe that his financial health was improving. Then, in early November, came the federal court order for the forced sale of Ca' d'Zan.[102] The house had been the very essence of John and Mable, the material expression of their two personalities. Its impending loss turned out to be a final blow.

Ringling fell ill with pneumonia while in New York in mid-November and died on 2 December 1936. Ironically, a journalist reminiscing about an encounter with him had recently written: "You learn from John Ringling that Sarasota is the one place on earth that has never known a case of pneumonia. That's important to old people, they die of pneumonia often, and so many other diseases run into pneumonia. Besides, says Ringling, 'the wise people are moving to Sarasota from everywhere.'"[103]

John Ringling's threescore and ten ended in a ceremonious farewell scene. His great gold bed was surrounded: the North family, his servants, Nurse Sanders, his physician, and one friend, Frank Hennessy. In his last moments, he called repeatedly for his sister, Ida. Age seventy was old for a Ringling. In a career of more than fifty years he had met the world's standards for success. He had accumulated a fortune, controlled a monopoly, and lived in a palace. Although the last years of forced retirement had dimmed his celebrity image, the change was more apparent in Sarasota than in the world at large.

Eulogies followed, in newspapers from Sarasota to Ardmore, Oklahoma, and in trade magazines of the entertainment industry such as *White Tops* and *Billboard*. They emphasized recollections of circus life in its greatest years, and expressed affection for the brothers who had created a national institution. Ringling's public career thus began and ended as the circus man, the role that had earned him the most respect. His art collection was pledged to the moneylenders who also held a firm grip on all his corporate assets. Even the grand museum was starting to show damage from Florida's climate. He had stopped collecting five years earlier, and the art world took no notice of his death.

The driving ambition that fueled John Ringling's career obscured his diffidence and lifelong rejection of close relationships. The few whose lives were closest to his seemed no more successful in penetrating his reserve than strangers. Charles and Edith, Sam Gumpertz, Ralph Caples, and Owen Burns were all excluded. In his reminiscences, Charles, a gentleman who always avoided giving offense, permitted himself only one burst of indirect candor to describe his brother. He had written on an early circus roster next to John's name: "(ME, ME, ME)." That one lapse tells much.

The sole exception to Ringling's inability to achieve intimacy was the unqualified felicity of his marriage to Mable. Within their home he put aside the coarse language, the flaws in character that marred his circus and business image, and the haughty facade that he presented to the world.

John's imperious, temperamental manner was not formed by status and wealth. One of the first circus employees, remembering the 1880s, said that he got along with all the brothers except John, who was too domineering. Ringling's aide, Richard Fuchs, testified after they parted that his employer was a man of violent temper, of such habitual profanity that he was unaware of his own constant swearing. Among Sarasota's elite he was accorded the deference that acknowledged his wealth, but no warmth or affection. Although they appreciated his public-spirited gestures, Sarasotans generally found him distant, arrogant, and bent on using the city to enhance his own fortune. They felt little sadness or regret at seeing him brought low.

This image is scarcely flattering, yet it may have missed the complete picture of John Ringling, whose egocentricity overshadowed his finer qualities. His refusal to share center stage with his partner-brothers was equally apparent when he turned from the circus to other interests. In each small corporation that he controlled, he was the head; in Sarasota affairs, he stood foremost among his colleagues. While he did not seek to gain a major shareholder's position in a trunk railroad, his short lines placed him at the top of several small pyramids. Similarly, in Oklahoma oil, he was a sole owner, answerable to no one. In his one Montana sortie with the Crow Indians, the unassailable power of big oil promptly drove him from the field. As a Florida developer, he chose a west coast city and its islands, where there were no competing moguls such as Merrick of Coral Gables or Mizner of Boca Raton to dispute first place.

Once he gained first place, Ringling was able to indulge generous impulses. In company with Sam Gumpertz and many others, he showed his willingness to help when employees suffered misfortune or hard times. His unpublicized charities were numerous. Like most people, he was inconsistent in his prejudices. In good health and prosperous times, Ringling cultivated important and useful people. His good humor and companionable ways were shared with those whom he regarded as his equals or superiors. Lesser folk often found him inclined to be peremptory, quick to anger but also quick to cool down.

One of Ringling's famous contemporaries, David Lloyd George, prime minister of Great Britain in the later stages of World War I, complained that his fate was to live on, to see his successes turn to failures and public adulation turn to hate. In a small arena, John Ringling suffered a similar fate. At the end of his life unfriendly reports about him circulated in Sarasota; malicious relatives and friends joined to destroy his place in the circus. Then, on the day following his death, family, friends, and adversaries learned that the people of Sarasota and Florida were to inherit his entire estate.

Ten Years in Probate

HE FUNERAL of John Ringling was attended mostly by relatives, circus friends, and business associates. The relatives included his sister, Ida North, with her sons John and Henry and her daughter Salomé. Seated beside them were Marjorie Ringling, Henry Ringling, Jr., and Aubrey Ringling, who represented all the original Ringling brothers and their families. The Charles Ringling family was absent. Sam Gumpertz also had the grace to stay away. There were many longtime circus associates, for whom this last rite for the last of the Ringling brothers meant a final break with the past. Among them was Dexter Fellows, who for many years headed press relations for the Ringling show, and many present and former performers and managers, including Bert Cole, Carlotta Goertz, Clifton Sparks. Eighty-seven-year-old Sophie Collins, cook to John and Mable for twenty-five years, brought memories of the earliest days at Sarasota. Apart from the North family, the Hazen Tituses were the only Sarasotans present. Titus was the manager of the John Ringling Hotel and one of the few mourners, like Frank Hennessy and S. T. Cox of Ardmore, Oklahoma, whose friendship reached well into the past, before the days of status and riches gained and lost.[1]

The *New York Times* printed an obituary-cum-circus history and a lengthy editorial. Without alluding to the altered circumstances of his last years, the *Times* reminded its readers of the modest start from which the great Ringling organization developed; then, using this success story as a stick for beating the Roosevelt administration, the editorial went on to blame new taxes for having deprived Americans of the chance to develop great corporations from small beginnings: "our concept of America as a land of opportunity must not be sold for a bowl of Quaker Oats."[2]

Ringling had left behind a twofold legacy of issues to be resolved. In what proved to be a gross understatement, one of the estate attorneys described them as "financial entanglements of unprecedented complexity."[3] The executors were well aware of the staggering number of obligations. Of still greater concern than the sum of those obligations was a second issue: the knotted mass of improvisations that were made necessary by Ringling's precarious standing since the summer of 1932. There was no certainty that even with the greatest skill and diligence, the estate could be brought to an orderly state of solvency.

A cast of characters quickly assembled to take part in the ensuing drama, for which the county court of Sarasota was the principal arena. The court, in haste to keep the whole matter a local concern, immediately qualified John North and Ida North as executors. (In court documents, John North was generally cited as the "acting" executor, distinguishing him from Ida, who assumed a minor role in the events that followed.) John and Henry North and Randolph Wadsworth (husband of Salomé North) were appointed as trustees—all so named in Ringling's will of March 1934. Next came the state of Florida, named as principal beneficiary to receive the art museum and the residence. The state was also to receive the income from one-half the remainder of the entire estate. Under the terms of the codicil, which was not sent to probate for another eighteen months, the state would take all (including Ringling's one-third share of the circus), except an annuity of $5,000 for Ida. One other beneficiary, Emily Ringling, was to receive $1.[4] In the event that the state failed to inherit, the city of Sarasota was to be the contingent beneficiary.

A small legion of Ringling's creditors, seventy-one in all, soon gathered. Their claims ranged from $3.25, owed to the *Sarasota Herald*, to something over $13 million, demanded by the Bureau of Internal Revenue. Last in line came a hastily organized faction of relatives calling themselves "heirs at law."[5] They persisted for a decade in demanding dismissal of the court-appointed executors. In addition they sought an interpretation of the will in their favor; the art collection, they claimed, belonged to them.

Tumultuous times lay ahead for the executors; the interests of the various claimants did not often coincide. The state of Florida sometimes acted as a colleague, then as an adversary of the executors. The state's legal officers could not be convinced that the Norths were the intended executors. In consequence, Florida's suit for a decision on the construction of the will outlasted the settlement of the bequests. In the most difficult times, the attorney general refused to deal with the Norths.

One of the first to move against the estate was Emily Ringling. A few days after John's funeral, she began the first of many actions to establish her dower rights, asking the Sarasota court to set aside the divorce decree and the provisions of the will and give her one-third of the whole estates. The divorce petitions, appeals, and counteractions provided frequent diversion for the readers of the *Sarasota Herald.* Much of Emily's small fortune was consumed in the fruitless procession of court actions, and her character was maligned in the negative publicity. Interestingly, in later years Emily (who had disliked and resented the circus during her marriage) attended many of its performances at Madison Square Garden as a guest of the Norths.[6]

There seemed only a dim prospect of salvaging the estate. The executors were confronted with a barrage of obstacles and litigation that would have seemed excessive in an estate many times larger. However, the precarious state of Ringling's affairs at the time of his death offered the Norths a minor advantage. In effect, the mass of claims formed a sort of *triage* of natural priorities. In the first group were claims that had to be settled at once or the estate risked being dissolved. Next came claims that could be put aside for a later day, to be examined and if necessary paid in compromise. Last were the claims that on examination could be expected to prove wrongful.

Two claims posed an immediate threat: the court-ordered sale of

Ca' d'Zan and a tax sale certificate against the John Ringling Hotel. Liquid assets were slim indeed. Cash on deposit was found in two accounts: one for $15.51 and another for $208.82. One real estate corporation, the Ringling Isles, had funds on hand. Its cash balance was $4,717.[7] These were modest sums to be placed against the two critical claims. John North acted quickly, even before he was qualified by the court as an executor. To halt the sale of Ca' d'Zan, he engaged two Sarasota attorneys, and, taking Ringling Isles office manager and auditor James Haley with him, went at once to Tallahassee to enlist the support of Governor David Scholtz and Attorney General Cary Landis. To satisfy the judgment, two payments were made from admissions money at the museum, a step that state officials held was an improper use of funds. One of North's attorneys, Henry Williford, reminded the contentious attorney general that the money would have to be found—if not there, then somewhere else. The house, he said, was a vital part of Ringling's bequest, and it would be protected from efforts to remove it from the estate.[8]

Less than a week after the executors were qualified, speculators sought to purchase all outstanding tax sale certificates against most of Ringling's Sarasota real estate and the Ringling Isles Corporation. One of them threatened to force a sale of the John Ringling Hotel under a tax sale certificate for $7,000—on a hotel worth nearly a quarter of a million. Again, without waiting for the ponderous procedures of the court, the executors raised the $7,000 by selling an ancient dragline belonging to Ringling Isles and by quietly raising some money through one of the short line railroads owned by Ringling. Such steps were of questionable legality, but the Norths had to choose without delay either to take them or to risk the immediate loss of principal assets.

The threat posed by tax sale certificates meant that the estate needed court protection until any delinquent taxes could be verified and the arrears paid. Taxes unpaid to the city, county, and state amounted to about $200,000. By no means was that assessment all legitimate tax. Much of the amount had been levied earlier in the scheme to protect the museum from the threat of foreclosure by Ringling's creditors. To prevent any loss of property, the executors now filed two suits for the estate, halting all further sale of certificates.[9] Other unpaid taxes were pending in Montana and Wisconsin. Altogether, these obligations presented a bleak prospect for an estate with less than $5,000 in liquid assets.

The next top priority was finding a means to refinance the 1929 circus note. Allied Owners held that obligation in the principal amount of $800,000, due 6 November 1937.[10] Bound to that note was a further debt, already reduced to one-third of its original sum, owed to the Manufacturers Trust Company bank of New York and secured by three valuable paintings pledged as collateral. The three canvases were kept in a New York warehouse, guarded by a nontransferable receipt. Moreover, a substantial share of the Allied Owners note was obligated to the Manufacturers Trust, making the whole an extremely convoluted obligation. Allied Owners, Ringling's creditor, was itself in receivership. Unless this burden could be lifted, the circus and the art museum were almost certain to be lost in a distress sale. It was at once apparent to North and his attorneys that if satisfactory financing could not be obtained, the estate most likely would be declared insolvent.[11]

Not all the issues that arose at Ringling's death was confined to impersonal banks and corporate creditors. Bertha Verby, the housekeeper at Ca' d'Zan, was among the last of Ringling's live-in servants. In her first appeal to John North, Verby wrote: "my funds are all exhausted. I am absolutely without a cent. . . . I don't know of any place I can go to ask for help." A few days later: "I just don't know where to turn to purchase anything in the line of food for me and the dog."[12]

The housekeeper's distress reveals poignantly how the settlement of this estate affected real people who endured delays and postponements as the larger issues moved slowly to solution. Tradespeople and merchants were caught up in this process—unpaid-for work on the house, painting, repairing the roof, cleaning draperies damaged by a winter storm. James Haley missed ten months' pay in 1936 as auditor at Ringling Isles; Ringling's nurse, Ina Sanders, was unpaid for three years, claiming more than $10,000. John M. Kelley, the circus attorney who was best with troubles stemming from his share in the circus tax fraud, claimed payment for services performed for Ringling personally.[13] His abandonment of John Ringling to join the cabal of Edith, Aubrey, and Sam Gumpertz meant that he could expect little sympathy from the

Norths. His claim was allowed to drag on, delayed by whatever stratagems the executors could devise. Al Roan, formerly captain of the Ringling yacht, was moved from his guard post at the Ritz Carlton on Longboat Key to occupy the Venetian guest house on the estate so that he and his wife could become caretakers of the vacant property.

The executors named a team of attorneys to assist them. The leading attorney was Henry D. Frost of Cincinnati. The choice seemed curious. Frost was an experienced attorney of the first rank. He had never met John Ringling, but he was well known to Randolph Wadsworth (son-in-law of Ida North).[14] There was a certain advantage in his being free from local involvement among Sarasota factions, but the probate process also demanded a competent Sarasotan to establish smooth working relations with the court, with other counsel, and with cabinet officials in Tallahassee. John Burket was an ideal choice, respected locally and a longtime associate and friend of Ringling and of the Norths. Burket was thoroughly familiar with the apparatus of Florida courts. Ringling had found that Sarasota attorneys preferred to deal with their local colleagues, tending to be cool to outsiders.[15] Harold R. Brophy of New York was engaged to deal with issues centered there.

In the initial phase of settlement, the executors were on the defensive. Their authority was always diminished by the latest conflict between the terms of Ringling's will and the stated or implied changes contained in the codicil. For more than eighteen months, North withheld it from probate. He informed the court that he was "advised and believed that it was not a valid and legal codicil."[16]

Neither Brophy nor Frost could counter the massive weight of the circus note, the unpaid taxes, and the ambivalent attitudes encountered at Tallahassee. Added to these were suits brought by Edith and Aubrey for more than half a million dollars, Emily's constant barrage of claims to her dower, and the noisome heirs at law. What the executors needed were legal skill and pressure greater than those of their adversaries. Almost a year passed, with the estate always mired in procedural detail, unable to gain credibility.

The assistance they needed to turn things around came from an unexpected quarter: the partners of the large and prestigious New York law firm of Newman and Bisco. Almost at once, they devised an effective strategy. Leonard Bisco, a man of elegant mien and language, now took the lead. Sydney R. Newman was counsel to and an officer of the Manufacturers Trust Company, and Bisco had been principal negotiator in refinancing the circus note; the Norths had become acquainted with him then. For the next ten years, Bisco set the pattern, controlled events, and outmaneuvered the somewhat clumsy efforts of the Norths' adversaries. In Sarasota, where nearly every local attorney represented a claimant, a relative, or a Ringling adversary, the feeling grew stronger, as each action ensued, that the executors were gaining advantage through the clever tactics of their big city lawyers.[17]

What led these two rich and important lawyers to take up the cause of an estate that was barely solvent, beset with a host of problems, and sunk in litigation for which they might never collect their fee? While their firm seems never to have represented Ringling, there was a long-standing association between Ringling and the Manufacturers Trust. Perhaps recapturing the circus from his enemies was an inviting prospect. Much billable time was required, yet none was charged or paid during the ten years of litigation, except the expense of travel and accommodation. The firm was compensated only after all the bequests were settled. Bisco was far too astute to permit his substantial fees to show up on the periodic reports of the estate.

Before any progress was made, the true status of the estate had to be determined by a careful inventory of assets and a compilation of claims. Auditor James Haley conducted the inventory of assets in stages. Throughout the liquidation process Haley's report was kept confidential, a tactic favored by Bisco to prevent the information from reaching the claimants. Of the seventy-one claims, many were small; only a few exceeded $10,000, but those were substantial. Apart from federal taxes and the circus note, the largest were unpaid attorney fees in New York and Sarasota. Loans owned to Ida North and family accounted for other major debts.[18]

In his last years Ringling had been living on the edge of receivership, not because he had lost his wealth but because his assets were pledged as collateral. More then $600,000 in negotiable securities was included in the collateral posted for his debts.[19] It was perhaps his final piece of good fortune that the crisis of receivership never happened. Then, from the moment of his death, his estate was protected by the mechanisms of probate and the repeated delays granted to the executors by the indulgent Sarasota court.[20] Time was an ally in these matters, for the delays tended to make creditors amenable to compromise.

The affairs of thirty-five corporations were examined to learn what Ringling had left. Several, including his Cardinal Oil Company, were merely vacant shells; others, like the Rockland Oil Company, were functioning with more or less vitality. For each corporation, the executors had to establish the degree of Ringling's interest, to name directors where vacancies arose, and to uncover any power of attorney or proxy arrangements that he had been forced to sign. These holdings were affected by the laws of at least eight states.[21] In addition to the Florida land, there were large properties in Oklahoma and Montana, smaller ones in Nebraska, Indiana, and Wisconsin. His four short-line railroads were troublesome assets; they generated little income, and their affairs were hopelessly tangled with the Interstate Commerce Commission (ICC), the Bureau of Internal Revenue, and the Treasury. These lines could not be abandoned without permission from the ICC.[22] The work of the executors was made doubly difficult by lack of access to Ringling's personal records. His papers had been seized by the Bureau of Internal Revenue and removed to Miami, where they were held unavailable until 1941, when the income tax was paid.[23]

The executors were continually harassed by family members and often impeded by Florida officials. Their attorneys suggested wisely that every step be placed before the court for permission to act; afterward, the completed action was submitted for approval. The result was an unassailable record of every transaction and the authority given for it. At the same time, the state was protected by having full knowledge of what went on. If there was one characteristic that pervaded this ten-year process and its forty-five volumes of documents, it was mutual distrust among all parties to the case.

The circus note for more than $800,000 was due 6 November 1937. Unless paid or refinanced before then, a forced sale of all Ringling's collateral would be necessary.[24] Once the initial crisis debts were paid, all other claims had to await a settlement of the circus note. If that effort failed, all other claimants would receive little if any payment. Moreover, the transactions of 1932 placed New York Investors and their representatives in control of the circus, which was supposed to be a major revenue-producing asset of the estate. The New York Investors group was itself in receivership; at least twelve of the officials were under federal indictment for irregularities in corporate affairs. It was imperative for the estate to be removed from this unsound grasp. It was equally important for the circus to be returned to the control of the Ringling family and restored to a profitable condition. The executors searched for refinancing across the country, then back to New York.[25] Finally negotiations led to a proposal from the Manufacturers Trust Company, already holders of a personal note from John Ringling.

In the terms laid down by the Manufacturers Trust Company, the circus was to be returned to "the harmonious control of the Ringling family."[26] In the operation of the circus, all parties were united by a desire to see the show prosper, pay its debts, and produce its former generous dividends. But outside that central concern, there was no harmony. Each faction sought to gain control, while the state of Florida had to be assured that its one-third interest (under the terms of Ringling's will) would regain an investment value however its shares were ultimately disposed. The bank, as lender, was satisfied with an arrangement that offered operating harmony until the note was repaid. After that, the Ringlings were free to indulge in whatever disharmony they chose. *Fortune* magazine called the squabbling "Ringling wrangling,"[27] and it became increasingly rancorous in the succeeding years.

Two factions—the estate, headed by John North, and the Edith-Robert-Aubrey group—comprised the board of directors of the circus, with a chairman, William P. Dunn (a vice-president at Manufacturers Trust), named by the bank. The chairman had the controlling vote since the estate had three seats and the Edith Ringling faction also held three. The bank agreed to refinance the circus note and grant an extension of time on their own note owed by the estate, provided the legal details could be worked out. New York Investors and Allied Owners regained nearly a million in cash, but they also demanded that in payment for their voting trust, arrangements must be made to purchase their 10 percent of the circus shares and a similar amount of the second corporation, owner of the five circuses that Ringling purchased in 1929.

The negotiations led to at least twenty contracts, agreements, and releases. Further complications arose in attempts to free $450,000 in impounded Santa Fe Railroad bonds owned by John Ringling personally from the U.S. Treasury. The bonds were ultimately released, but only after one federal suit and another action against John Ringling were withdrawn. The new loan was finally closed only two days before the 6 November deadline. The cost of this maneuver was $67,000—an obligation the circus was required to pay to the estate.[28] The Santa Fe bonds, now freed, were sold above par for a half million, an amount used at once to reduce the new note by nearly half.

With the circus note safely refinanced, the estate—and the circus—were reasonably safe from a distress sale. For the first time there was reason to contemplate the bequest of the art collection and museum as more than a shadowy promise. On many occasions Ringling had stated that he intended to give his museum to the public. The terms of his bequest to Florida were drawn with the greatest care and with the advice of attorneys skilled in phrasing conditions that would bind the state to his wishes. Ringling had been prepared for the possible reluctance of the state to accept the gift; hence, he named the city of Sarasota as an alternative. But his greatest fear had been not that the state would reject his bequest, but that it would be accepted and then disperse his collection through gifts or loans to various courthouses and public buildings throughout the state.[29] He had wished to make certain of the complete integrity of the museum beyond his lifetime, that it should pass intact to the state and remain so. He had also made provisions for additions to the collection to give it a dynamic, growing quality in the future.

The location of the collection was another problem. Various objects, paintings, rugs, and even furnishings were not housed in the museum or the residence. Some were pledged as collateral in New York, some were mortgaged to Emily, others were in a storehouse on the estate, and still more were at the John Ringling Hotel. To be sure that all his possessions were included, his will explicitly specified all the classes of the bequest: paintings, antiques, tapestries, antiquities, sculptures, and art books—whatever properly belonged in the museum or the residence. Whatever was held in the name of the Rembrandt Corporation—or any other corporation where he held the power of disposition—was embraced in his bequest to the state of Florida. However, his intentions were not clear regarding such objects as china, silver, jewelry, furnishings, and personal property that were neither antiques nor objects of art. Moreover, until the mortgages on the contents of Ca' d'Zan were discharged, the entire contents were subject to Ida North's claim against the estate for loans to her brother.

To further protect the museum as a memorial to Mable and himself, Ringling attached certain conditions: "said museum shall always be known as 'The John and Mable Ringling Museum of Art' without power in anyone to change said name." And again to maintain integrity: "no change by sale, trade, or other means shall be made in any of the paintings or objects of art. . . ."[30] While this was a restrictive provision, it was by no means unusual for a donor to insist that none of a bequest should be disposed of by later administrators.

Keeping in mind Ringling's concern that the collection remain intact, the executors consulted with the governor, the attorney general, and leaders of the legislature. Together they framed a restriction in the proposed legislation: "All property received under the will and codicil shall not be removed from the city of Sarasota, Florida."[31]

James Haley, office manager of the Ringling Isles Corporation, had given his word to Ringling that he would never cease to do what he could to prevent any raid on the collection.[32] Haley kept his promise, though he could not have known, when he conversed with Ringling about ways to prevent dispersal, what forceful attempts would be made to frustrate the intent of Ringling's bequest. After all was settled, the first director of the state-owned museum gave testimony to Haley's promise: "the one who more than any other living man saved this great collection of masterpieces for the people of Florida . . . James Haley, representing the Ringling interests, fought against schemes, intrigues, and plans to sell the pictures, to dispose of them out of the state, or to get them away from the state of Florida. Few persons not intimately connected with the Ringling entourage know and appreciate the vital importance of the fight that Mr. Haley made to preserve the pictures for the state and its people."[33] Some thirty years later, as a congressman, Haley wrote to Robert Gray, Florida secretary of state, "I don't believe that in my lifetime I will ever be able to get away from the John Ringling estate."[34]

Legislation was required for acceptance of the bequest by the state. Lobbying in support of such a measure began early in 1937, in advance of the April legislative session.[35] Publicity appeared throughout the state urging prompt approval. Newspaper editorials supporting the bequest were in agreement that the splendid museum should be kept as a cultural asset. Most stressed its value as an educational institution for Florida and the entire South.[36]

While other parts of the state voiced public enthusiasm for state ownership, official feeling in Sarasota was divided and uncertain. With the support of Mayor E. A. Smith, one faction accepted the idea of making the museum and residence a Sarasota possession. Smith claimed that the city could afford to assume ownership with the aid of a small appropriation from Tallahassee. The mayor was probably sincere, yet unknowingly he was aiding the schemes of those who wanted Ringling's will to be overturned. Ineffective city ownership would measurably help their cause.

Both factions were lining up support. The key figures in the legislative decision were a state senator, Wallace Tarvin of Bradenton, and a state representative, John Early of Sarasota.[37] Early proposed that legislators should be invited to visit and inspect the museum and that a fund to entertain the visitors should be collected. There was no response to his suggestion. Knowing that the museum building showed signs of decay, the executors may have suspected Early's motives, since he had announced that he would urge his fellow legislators to reject the bequest. Early conferred with the president of the Senate, who stated publicly that he expected the legislature to be guided by whatever proposal he and Early put forward at the session in April.[38]

Intervention for which the supporters of state ownership were unprepared appeared in the form of an unsigned, polemical feature in the *Literary Digest*, a national weekly of some repute. The *Digest* described the museum as a "legal orphan" that had fallen into a sad state of disrepair. Some of the paintings were "an affront to art"; mildew was threatening to destroy parts of the collection, fast losing its value for want of care. Outdoor statues "lie in broken heaps . . . beyond any hope of restoration." The museum storage area was described as a mass of sagging shelves and smashed "Venetian" [*sic*] glass. The writer asserted, without citing authority, that few of the paintings were authenticated—that there was no verification of their genuineness.[39] This article, clearly derived from a malicious source, was especially damaging because it was released just before the Florida legislature would be discussing the worth of the bequest and the probable cost for the state to maintain it.

Verman Kimbrough, head of the Ringling School of Art and Design and a highly respected figure in the community, took up the public defense. He acknowledged that mildew had invaded some of the Rubens works; the secretary of the American Association of Museums had stated that unless repairs were carried out within four or five years, the damaged canvases could not be restored. On the question of challenged authentication, Kimbrough declared that of the works hanging in the museum nearly all attributions were established. His most significant comment was a surprise. He said that Ringling had shown him about 200 paintings in storage, removed from the galleries because connoisseurs had told him that there was a doubt of their authenticity.[40]

Jonce McGurk, a well-known authority, was engaged by the estate to appraise the art collection. He labeled the *Digest* article as the work of someone unfriendly to John Ringling—as propaganda aimed at prejudicing the legislature against accepting the bequest. McGurk rejected the implication that Ringling had no knowledge of art: "Ringling's genuine knowledge was well known to every prominent dealer in Europe and America. No one could read that *Digest* article without feeling that a great wrong and a great injustice had been done to the memory of a great man and a great patron of the arts."[41] McGurk was perhaps somewhat generous with his "greats," but he knew that he was a professional in the field and his adversaries were amateurs.

The *Sarasota Herald*, after supporting the case for state ownership and after printing the editorials of other papers urging state acceptance, changed its position. The *Herald* now asked for support of Representative Early's bill for Sarasota ownership. Further reports of a deteriorating museum building similar to those in the *Literary Digest* were circulated locally and in Tallahassee. John North responded by engaging the museum's builder, Lyman Chase, to examine the roof to determine the accuracy of rumors that damage was severe and the building was in imminent danger of further damage. Chase declared that the building had been sufficiently repaired to protect it from further damage. Then North spoke out: "There seems to be a determined effort in some quarters to low-rate both the museum and the gift, for what object it would be hard to say. . . . the Ringling museum is outstanding among art collections of the world. It is receiving the best care possible until the estate is settled. . . ." North rightly questioned the motives of many who opposed state ownership. Probably, city officials wished to secure the best settlement for Sarasota; yet they appear to have been manipulated by the claimants against the estate. At the urging of those who opposed state ownership, the still inactive codicil was introduced into the dispute by Mayor Smith.

Wittingly or not, Mayor Smith fueled a controversy that lasted until 1947. The dispute over ownership by state or city was a disguise for a more fundamental issue. If the principal bequest of Ringling's will could be turned aside from his expressed wish, then the opponents of the executors could exploit the opportunity to have the Norths dismissed and other relatives named as heirs. Their objective was to gain possession of the Rembrandt Corporation and all the paintings in Ringling's collection.

John North, with astute counsel to guide him, kept his public and lobbying efforts focused on two practical issues: the condition of the museum and the increasingly sound condition of the estate. He insisted that repairs to the structure were adequate to preserve the fabric of the museum and its contents.[42] Although North had the builder's reassurance to support his claim, the museum was undeniably showing signs of decay. Phillips had met Ringling's wishes by designing an exceedingly handsome building, but some of the necessary economies in construction had compromised the durability of the structure.[43]

On the matter of viability of the estate and its potential to emerge from its burden of debt, the executors were on stronger ground. Their lobbyists at Tallahassee, J. Velma Keen (formerly a Sarasota attorney) and James Haley, were the principal defenders. Each assured the legislators that other assets of the estate could readily pay off the obligations, leaving the residence and museum free from all claims and ready for state ownership.[44] Mayor Smith and Representative Early, with equal vigor, urged the state to reject the gift. They argued that state ownership meant only that the museum would become a political tool, a target for those who would distribute the collection.[45] Ringling's will and codicil were published by the *Sarasota Herald* to convince the people of Sarasota that the museum and its collection must remain forever in Sarasota.[46]

Pressed by both sides, the legislators wavered; first the house voted in committee for state ownership, and then on a second vote, rejected it. Mayor Smith and local landowner and real estate broker A. B. Edwards again appeared before the legislators, urging that debts were about to overtake the Ringling estate and that the museum-residence complex was in jeopardy.[47] Both senate and house committees presented bills to accomplish state ownership. Safeguards against breaking up the collection were included and cabinet control established for the transition from the estate. Early of Sarasota introduced a rival bill giving the museum to Sarasota, endorsed by Mayor Smith.[48]

The senate responded to the local legislators' customary privilege and voted to reject the bequest. Senator Holland of Bartow charged that the move was in reality "a wrangle between three of Ringling's heirs (the North family) and a larger group of heirs."[49] That was the nearest anyone came to exposing the conflict as one between factions of the Ringling family. There followed a move to reconsider. On a second vote, state ownership was approved by both senate and house. This grudging acceptance of the bequest was scarcely a mandate, but it gave the executors and the state, acting through the governor's cabinet, authority to proceed. The executors could now work to regain control of Ringling's assets and make them serve his intent by freeing the museum and residence from debt. On that score, the enabling legislation was specific.[50]

On 10 June 1937 the governor approved an act accepting the bequest. The executors and legislative committee members framed the act to embody John Ringling's wishes. The substance of his bequest was spelled out in a list of property—the museum, the home, the library of art books, and all paintings, pictures, works of art, tapestries, antiques, and sculptures. All this was to be received by the Board of Commissioners of State Institutions, free and clear of debts, claims, and obligations. A prohibition bound the state not to sell, trade, or otherwise remove any item from the collection. Last, a critical issue was settled: "all property shall be and remain in Sarasota, Florida . . . and shall not be removed from the city of Sarasota, Florida."[51] Florida's attorney general Landis estimated that two years would be needed to liquidate the estate—eight years off the mark.

Immediately after Ringling's death the estate had initiated a full inventory of Ringling's personal property, both to establish the worth of the bequest and for federal tax assessment purposes. Public estimates of the art collection, without basis in fact, had for some years ranged from $14 million to $40 million. When questioned, Ringling always refused to name a figure. But testifying in his divorce case, he claimed that he spent about $11 million, a figure that far exceeds the true amount. Henry North has estimated it to be about $3 million.[52]

At about the time an appraisal was to begin, the executors saw some encouraging indicators of the prestige the Ringling collection enjoyed beyond Sarasota. In January 1938, the editors of *Life* selected a number of Ringling works to represent Flemish painting in their series on the art of the world. In the following month, Dr. Herman Baruch visited Sarasota and offered high praise for Ringling's purchase. Baruch was a prominent financier, art collector and connoisseur, brother of Bernard Baruch, and a longtime friend of John Ringling. The two had often discussed their mutual interests, but this was Baruch's first opportunity to see the collection. He gave his opinion to the *Sarasota Herald:* "John Ringling had an instinctive knowledge of art . . . and while he gained it almost entirely through self-instruction there is no record of his ever having been fooled by a false painting. His ability to separate the wheat from the chaff in the thousands of pictures submitted for his approval was positively uncanny. Although I knew Ringling well and knew many of his art purchases, I was astounded and awed by my first glimpse of his museum."[53] Readers of the *Herald* were also impressed by the fact that Dr. Baruch was the son of Simon Baruch, a major on the staff of General Robert E. Lee.

The inventory was completed five months after Ringling's death. In the following year, expert appraisers established a value for every item listed. Haley (now superintendent of the museum) and his associates engaged four specialists to help them with paintings and tapestries, furniture, sculptures, and antiquities.[54] The two architects, Dwight Baum and John Phillips, submitted their recollections of the expenditures for the home and the museum.[55] Phillips agreed to come to Sarasota to take part in the appraisal, for he knew that almost no cost data were ever recorded.

The principal appraiser was Jonce McGurk, who had thirty years' experience as a collector, connoisseur, and appraiser; he was to value the paintings and tapestries. Among his credentials were similar tasks performed for Andrew Mellon, Percy Rockefeller, Henry Frick, and others whose collections had entered major museums.[56] Cypriote art—archaic and antiquities—was entrusted to Karl Freund. Freund had been at the Anderson Galleries in 1928, when the Metropolitan Museum auctioned their surplus antiquities. He had prepared the catalog for the sale where Ringling bought more than half the objects offered. Freund placed a greatly increased valuation on the objects, based on the rigid export controls in force on Cyprus and in Italy, enacted since the objects were sent to America in the 1870s.[57]

The team of appraisers omitted nothing in their meticulous pursuit of every tangible object on the home estate, on the islands, and in the John Ringling Hotel. Later, whatever remained in New York warehouses was added to the sum. The several hundred pages of the inventory tell much of John's and Mable's personalities and the particular time in which they lived. The household contained an immense variety of rococo court furniture, decorative objects, and bric-a-brac reflecting the eclectic tastes of the owners. The most highly valued objects were three tapestries from a series depicting Alexander the Great. Two exceedingly fine Aubusson rugs were of almost equal value. Yet the splendid Steinway grand piano in its European rosewood case was valued at only $500, probably because of its short keyboard.

Many of the possessions crowded into storerooms on the Ca' d'Zan grounds were of great interest. The house had no library or even a bookcase except in John's own suite, although there was a stored collection of a thousand or more books of standard nineteenth-century literature and current fiction. Many art objects that came from auctions and sales remained undisturbed in their cartons and crates, never opened until the estate appraisers examined them.[58]

Among pictures that had never been moved to the museum were eight ceiling panels, which could have been intended for the Ritz Carlton. Two were signed "Spiridin," a twentieth-century French painter best known for his murals and later his portraits. A more important panel was the work of Cesare-Auguste Detti. A late-nineteenth-century artist, Detti was highly regarded in modern Italy. A number of excellent frames were stored with the ceiling panels. Three complete paneled rooms, never uncrated, were found among the stored objects. Two were French from the eighteenth century; the other was an Italian room from the sixteenth century. No records were found to identify their provenance or when and how they were bought.[59] All these crated and stored objects of art raised the valuation of Ca' d'Zan to $2 million.

The old homeplace bought from the Thompsons in 1911 still retained its furnishings, which would soon exceed the value of the house as the old structure continued to fall into a state of decay. The furnishings of John Ringling's New York apartment were sold. Objects of real value had long since been removed from the apartment, including the Frans Hals portrait impounded as loan collateral. What remained was a collection of souvenirs and one or two fine pieces. There was a splendid pair of rock crystal chandeliers, each with more than 100 pendants in the shape of various fruits. Ringling's gold rococo bed was admired by more than a thousand curious visitors who inspected the items on the day before the sale.[60]

It is difficult to assess the work of appraisers examining a home fifty years ago. An ever-changing market determines value and price. There were some works of art at Ca' d'Zan that greatly increased the overall appraisal—the tapestries, the large rugs, the organ, some eighteenth-century mirrors—but most of the furniture was from the 1880–90 era of reproductions from the styles of the French court, popular with the owners of New York's great mansions.

The inventory of Ringling's total assets, next produced by the court-appointed appraisers, was revealing and in some respects controversial. The search identified seventy-nine separate assets with a total appraised value of $23,476,818.30. The report revealed the depredations brought about by unpaid taxes. Whole blocks of Oklahoma real estate were entered as worthless, their value more than consumed by outstanding tax bills. Nearly $50,000 worth of paintings were hanging or stored at the John Ringling Hotel; at one New York warehouse there were forty-one paintings. Two more New York warehouses held five paintings mortgaged to Emily Ringling and three to the Manufacturers Trust Company. Some valuable items were not listed.

The inventories and appraisal raised many questions, never fully answered. The Florida attorney general objected vigorously to the personal property appraisals and the fees that were charged to the estate. He saw them as highly inflated, useful only for increasing an estate tax.[61] In several respects he was more nearly correct than the experts. Values ascribed to statues and columns at the museum were unrealistic. Cast-stone statues mounted on the roofline over the loggia of the museum were appraised as pre-seventeenth-century sculptures; such misconceptions call into question the competence of the appraisers. James Haley, one of them, was never certain that all Ringling's paintings were accounted for in the inventory. He believed that some were missing, though he could not cite any examples.[62]

In the meantime, the Ringling family had once more secured possession of the circus, but harmonious control among its warring factions seemed impossible. The show was freed from the moneylenders and Sam Gumpertz, but there were other issues, some political and some financial. The estate had a claim of $750,000 against the circus for funds Ringling had paid personally toward the purchase of the American Circus Corporation. Edith and Aubrey not only refused to acknowledge that the circus owed any money to Ringling's estate; they brought suit for approximately $600,000, claiming that Ringling had used circus funds for his own personal business without their knowledge or consent.[63] The estate won a major victory when the Edith-Aubrey suit was dismissed and they were required to recognize the large debt owed to the estate by the circus. With the support of the bank member who was chairman of the board of directors, North became general manager and senior vice-president of the circus. The widows' trust (Edith and Aubrey) voted to give North the managing authority; they recognized that he held the vote of the estate share, which would visibly protect the circus asset. North had at last gained his principal objective, although his authority was tenuous, for he shared ownership with relatives who were declared adversaries. He found the organization in poor shape, riddled with discontent and burdened with unrealistic contracts and labor disputes. By the following season, under North's command, the circus was again making a profit.[64]

Florida state officials watched with amazement the squabbles of the circus family, aware that the state was to become owner of a third share in an extremely unconventional enterprise. Attorney General G. C. Gibbs grew more and more disquieted as he contemplated several major battles over the Ringling estate and the disposition of its assets. Gibbs regarded the executors as usurpers, but his campaign to remove them came too late. Two pervasive issues were already settled—the circus note was refinanced, with its attendant transfer of control to the Ringlings, and the museum-residence bequest had been accepted by the state legislature. Gibbs went ahead with his attempt to expel the executors, knowing that his actions could result in chaos, years of litigation, and dissipation of Ringling's assets in the struggle. Gibbs was thus allied with the self-styled "heirs" who also demanded that the Norths should be dismissed. Their combined pressure was not enough to influence the Sarasota court. The court consistently upheld the Norths but had to give way on the issue of posting bond, a step demanded by Gibbs because he regarded the Norths' strategies as mismanagement of the estate.[65]

Unperceived by at least some of these participants, the focus of the probate process was subtly changed. The purely financial questions of the first two years were becoming less critical as the flow of cash into the estate steadily improved its viability. Real estate sales were expanding, the Ringling Hotel was fully operational and profitable, and recognition of the circus debt to John Ringling's estate had added a substantial asset. Money matters involving debts and claims could safely be entrusted to accountants and attorneys. And so the emphasis moved to the courtroom. As fiscal viability increased, the legal battles became more intense—Emily and her divorce and dower, the construction of the will, interpretation of the codicil, claims of the relatives for possession of the art collection.

From this point in the process, John North was often away from Sarasota, busy with the circus as its general manager. He was unavailable except for signing documents, and even that could often be left to his co-executor, Ida North.

The "harmonious control" of the circus by the Ringling family barely survived the final payment to the Manufacturers Trust Company. Since Edith and Aubrey controlled two-thirds of the circus stock, they were in a position to oust John North at any time. In 1943 Edith used that power to place her inexperienced son Robert in charge. North's managerial style had been reminiscent of John Ringling's—exceedingly autocratic, but generally effective and successful. The nation's worst-ever circus disaster, a fire on the overcrowded grounds in Hartford, Connecticut, occurred on 6 July 1944. The fire consumed the big top in twenty minutes, killing 169 people and injuring more than 500—many of them children killed by falling poles and flaming canvas or crushed by the fleeing crowd.[66]

Connecticut courts found the circus management guilty of neglect and dereliction of duty; involuntary manslaughter charges sent six circus executives to jail or prison, including James Haley, Aubrey's new husband and executive vice-president of the circus, who saw Robert's feeble courtroom testimony as a tactic calculated to lay primary blame upon him. Indemnities of about $4 million were agreed upon, paid over the next fifteen years. Although convicted, Haley received a very short sentence.

Within the Ringling family, recriminations sharpened old conflicts, which grew more intense as the North and Edith-Aubrey factions battled for control of the organization, thought by many to be doomed after the catastrophic fire.

Another two years of acrimonious family battles followed, for each faction threatened to dissolve the organization rather than yield control to the other. By his marriage to Aubrey, Haley had become a key figure. Although he disliked John North, Haley was ready to join him, for he felt a bitter enmity toward Robert for failing to defend him in court. Haley voted (as proxy for Aubrey) to move her one-third interest to

John North's side of the directors' table. By 1948, deprived of Aubrey's shares, Edith abandoned the fight and let the circus return to North's control. Robert, now in poor health, wanted no more Ringling wrangling.[67]

To John North the circus was the central feature of the estate. However, other matters of less interest to him could not be separated from the survival of the estate. One of them was the question of what impact Emily Ringling's claims could have if she were to win a reversal of the divorce decree. The executors were now the defendants, represented in the Sarasota court, the state circuit court, and New York Supreme Court. Brief upon brief—one of 800 pages—was filed in Emily's efforts to claim her dower. North, impatient and frustrated, was ready to settle for a substantial sum. For once, the attorney general insisted that the case should be heard. It proved to be a wise decision, for Emily lost and one-third of the estate was safe from a dower settlement.

While Emily's dower hopes were unrealized, her personal claim on the estate was a valid one. Her prenuptial loan had increased by interest accumulation since 1930 to $72,000. To collect from the executors, Emily foreclosed on the five paintings that were made over to her by the 1933 bill of sale. The five were among the collection's more valuable and well-known works.[68] It has been speculated that Ringling deliberately made the paintings subject to Emily's claim to protect them from the possible future claims of creditors. To halt the foreclosure, the Sarasota court acted without the executors and named a special master in chancery to sell two paintings to pay off Emily's loan: Rembrandt's *St. John* and Frans Hals's *Olycan*. Hoping to prevent the loss of either painting, North attempted to borrow from the Manufacturers Trust. The bank refused because North could not produce unobligated collateral. What free collateral remained in the estate was under federal tax lien and could not be pledged. The bank's Vice-president William Dunn, the bank representative on the circus board, explained that the Ringling collateral generally did not meet standards of good banking practice; the circus note, he said, had never been considered a prudent loan.[69]

The *St. John* could not be saved. It was sold to the Boston Museum of Fine Arts through a private sale. The sale fell a few thousand short of

Emily's claims, but she agreed to take the remainder in installments. A court decree then enabled the executors to obtain a release on the mortgage on the remaining four, one in their possession (the Frans Hals) and three safely locked in a New York warehouse.[70] Florida's attorney general was so outraged by the sale that he again demanded the removal of the executors, arguing that they were destroying the collection and thereby violating Ringling's intent.

The estate was not finished with Emily. She had removed two cassoni (Italian dower chests) and two tall carved chests from the New York apartment. Ringling had once stated the value of the carved chests as $25,000, part of the famous Gavet collection of the sixteenth-century French ecclesiastical furniture that he acquired from Mrs. O. H. P. Belmont.[71] Bisco was adamant about recovering the four chests. He argued that if they were left in Emily's possession and later were found in the commercial market, the integrity of the Ringling collection would be permanently damaged. Again and again, agreements were prepared for Emily to sign, and she would change her mind. Eventually she gave up the chests; the estate paid her $7,500.

The sale of Rembrandt's *St. John* and the recovery of the antique chests were more symbolic than important. The Rembrandt was a minor work, but bore the great name. J. Tom Watson, now attorney general, blamed the Norths for losing it and redoubled his efforts to discredit them. This time he focused his complaints on lack of detail in the annual reports of the estate. In Watson's view, if the federal tax claims went to trial, the estate could not effectively resist federal demand. The Bureau of Internal Revenue had researched Ringling's affairs in depth. Their claim for nearly $13 million included taxes as far back as 1921, nearly twenty years' interest, and an estate tax based on the appraisal. All these claims were set forth in a letter from the Bureau; its forty-seven pages named 149 separate items of income that were disputed.[72]

Negotiations dragged on with little progress until 1941, when possible compromise sums were mentioned by the Bureau. The estate tax was eliminated because the entire estate, except Ida's annuity, had been left to a public entity. By early December a tax of $850,000 was agreed upon, almost the same amount that had been offered in a compromise just before Ringling's death.[73] Bureau officials were at pains to make clear why they accepted this compromise—not on the merits of any counterclaims, but because of the difficulty of wringing money from the estate through long and costly court appearances, plus the time of a team of federal accountants. The tax was paid with another loan from the Manufacturers Trust.[74] In return the Bureau gave a closure, ensuring that the case could not be reopened unless fraud or misrepresentation were found. The Miami office of the Bureau withdrew its suit demanding receivership; the estate had survived its last serious threat.

At the beginning of December 1941, the nation was poised to begin converting its entire infrastructure and industrial base into a war economy. Despite the upheaval created by the war, the expanding economy worked to the advantage of the estate, enabling the executors to convert assets into cash. Oil revenues continued to accumulate; Ringling Isles and the John Ringling Hotel moved cash into the general funds of the estate each month. By mid-1943 the Manufacturers Trust Company note was reduced to one-fourth its original sum.[75] The estate was becoming increasingly solvent.

When a new note was negotiated to pay off the income tax, the Florida National Bank at Jacksonville asked to become the lender. Attorney General Watson tried but failed to press the Sarasota court into denying permission for the executors to make the new loan with the New York bank. Then Governor Spessard Holland intervened. It became prudent for the estate to bring its business into Florida. John North and his lawyer Leonard Bisco did not object; they no longer needed the reassuring support of a major New York bank, and the estate and its affairs were better served by a more visible presence in Florida. A new loan was arranged with the Florida National Bank to pay off the New York loan and to provide credit for the needs of the estate.

Once again the collateral was excessive: several million dollars' worth for a loan of $300,000.[76] On such terms, the Florida bank could scarcely be considered reckless in choosing to deal with this often-controversial estate. However, this was the last migration of the Ringling collateral before the settlement, when Florida would receive the bequest. Now, all tangible assets were located in Florida and thus, for the first time, were placed under the jurisdiction of the Florida courts.

Excessive collateral characterized all the Ringling loans from the time of John Ringling's surrender to New York Investors. The prevailing belief among bankers was that the Ringling estate was always vulnerable, that it could suddenly dissolve into empty promises and worthless paper. Lenders became less nervous as months and then years passed and the estate continued to gain stability. Still, its essential weakness lay in its circus holdings. A circus is a highly volatile enterprise that can abruptly lose almost its entire dollar value. Once a circus is bankrupt, it has no real plant or invested capital to show for its former worth. After 1929, when the Ringling circus became a monopoly, there was even less trust in the credit-worthiness of any circus.

The Florida bank loan was well insulated from any precipitous loss. The entire art collection and all the oil company shares, far more valuable collateral than the circus shares, assured the loan officers that their funds were safe. The estate was now a client of one of the state's leading banks; several influential Floridians were among the advocates of the Ringling estate. On a more practical level, the new loan included funds to pay Ida North's claims, thus relieving the Ringling Isles property and the contents of Ca' d'Zan from her mortgages.[77]

This loan, like its predecessors, needed to be repaid from the sale of unencumbered assets. There were several large properties awaiting clearance, plus the railroads. The small lines, with one exception, were losers even in the heavy wartime traffic over the nation's lines. The trunk lines refused to buy them because the traffic was too sporadic and the labor costs were high. Essentially they were valued now as scrap, provided that salvage was not prevented by any protest to the Interstate Commerce Commission. One sale was halted by resident clamor. The rest were sold for nearly $200,000, inflated by the wartime price for steel. Only the White Sulphur Springs–Yellowstone line remained intact. Ringling had taken genuine pleasure in owning 49 percent of the shares and in holding the position of president. The majority shareholder was Chicago, Milwaukee, St. Paul and (Northern) Pacific Railroad.[78]

The war economy also stimulated buying of marginal farm and ranch properties as the demand for food products increased dramatically. Buyers soon made offers for the two largest Ringling properties—the

33,000-acre sugar bowl tract in southeastern Sarasota County, an area largely passed by in the land boom and in the Depression, and the 80,000-acre Montana range lands, which the executors had fenced and improved.

The Sarasota tract was leased to two ranchers. One of them made an offer which the Ringling Isles Corporation, holder of the title, accepted; the other promptly exercised his option to buy the whole at any price offered by another prospective buyer. Then the cabinet at Tallahassee demanded open bids, giving a chance to a prominent cattleman in Tampa. Another complication was introduced when the Humble Oil Corporation claimed the state bounty for an oil discovery on sugar bowl lands in Collier County, raising once more the question of oil on the Ringling lands.[79] After a year of disputes, the first lessee secured his title at a price just about 300 percent greater than Ringling had paid twenty years earlier.

An eager buyer offered to take all 66,000 acres of the Montana ranch lands although they were titled in a checkerboard fashion. The state, the school districts, and the Northern Pacific Railroad held alternate blocks next to the Ringling properties. Title and abstract were delivered to the purchaser only to have him protest that he was being given the most defective title in all Montana.[80] Ringling had haphazardly acquired many small parcels, then later manipulated the deeds for several of his arcane transactions. (He had never paid much attention to the niceties of recorded titles.) Moreover, he once "sold" much of the property, then repossessed it—a transaction that he failed to record. The Bureau of Internal Revenue traced it and called the repossession "income."[81]

To redeem this floundering sale, the executors first attempted a "quiet proof" of title, only to be confronted with the Soldiers and Sailors Relief Act, which protected the interests of servicemen and servicewomen in their absence. The list of potential defendants filled seven pages. Two or three years were needed to untangle the records of ownership. Fortunately the buyer was still eager. He offered a new plan whereby he would gain possession and assume the risk, and in return would receive a more favorable payment plan. The estate accepted and was free from all future claims to prior ownership.[82]

By 1944 the estate had sold off enough unencumbered assets to make it evident that the Florida National Bank loan would soon be repaid. Financial problems receded, largely because of the flow of cash into the estate—sometimes as much as $50,000 a month.[83] Whereas at the outset, emergency measures had been required to settle claims that threatened solvency, in these later years questions of Ringling's intent assumed critical importance.[84] There remained executors' and attorney's fees still unmet, including Ringling's Sarasota divorce costs of nearly $200,000. Several legal questions were also unresolved, pushed earlier into the background largely on Bisco's advice. Sooner or later all these issues would demand settlement.

Though the years of probate activity, in only a few instances had the Florida attorney general been able to have his way against the executors and Leonard Bisco. The cabinet decided to engage a new special counsel. They chose Doyle Carlton, a former governor of Florida, who was adept in the court and administrative system of Florida. Carlton and Bisco found they could work together without necessarily trusting each other, for the interests of their clients were not always identical. The skills of both were needed to cut through the remaining burdens on the estate.

Instead of allowing all parties to become engaged in a ruinous dispute, Bisco had guided the executors into a course of action that led to an early transfer of the museum, the collection, and the residence to state possession. He must have realized that once the bequest became state property, there was little prospect of its surrender without all the authority of the state being brought to defend that ownership. This placed the state of Florida in an anomalous position; successive attorney generals distrusted the executors and wished to oust them, but the cost might well have been an upheaval so violent that the entire bequest could have been lost and then dissipated among the greedy heirs.[85]

The plan to bring about the early transfer of property succeeded because there were sufficient assets remaining in the estate to cover outstanding claims. The executors and their attorneys agreed to waive their personal claims against the property devised to the state. To induce other claimants to sign similar waivers, they subordinated their own claims to all others that were still unpaid. In late January 1946, the

Norths announced that they were ready to turn over the museum and the residence and that all conditions laid down in the 1937 legislation had now been met.[86] In the intervening years since 1936, the executors had cleared judgments and settlements totaling more than $15 million.

The Norths met with Governor Millard Caldwell in the museum courtyard to formally present the Ringling gift. In their letter to the governor (phrased in Bisco's careful language) the conditions expressed in Ringling's will were repeated, conditions to which the state had to assent by its acceptance of the bequest.[87] Those conditions established the museum within a lasting framework that confirmed the wishes of John and Mable. The stamp of Ringling's personality as expressed in the collection was permanently fixed.

The process of liquidation was by no means finished. There were large legal fees still unsettled and major assets not yet converted to cash for the trust fund that was to be administered for the benefit of the art collection. Foremost in the minds of state officials was the question of how much of the yet-undivided value should be used to pay the executors' fees and those of their attorneys, Newman and Bisco. The fees had been accumulating since 1937, yet no mention of them had ever been made in the periodic reports of estate accounts. If North and Bisco had an agenda of their own, the time for action was growing short, for Florida officials were bound to lose interest in the whole affair after the principal bequest was transferred to the state.

The autumn of 1946 seemed to promise a lengthy and unproductive period of inaction. Bisco's strategy of holding back the three most valuable assets now left the state with the challenging prospect of possessing and administering one-third of the circus, the Ringling Isles property in Sarasota, and the Oklahoma oil interests. Then, in a dramatic move to resolve all remaining issues, Robert Gray (chairman of the cabinet committee overseeing state interests in the Ringling estate) suggested an acceptable formula to close out the whole estate. Let North and Bisco take all remaining assets, said Gray, in lieu of their fees. They could settle remaining claims against the estate and pay the difference in value to the state for its trust fund. In return, North would gain total control of the circus and Bisco could develop the island property and place it on the market. This arrangement required a year of negotiation. The state rejected North's initial offer but ultimately agreed to accept $1.25 million, to be paid into a Ringling trust fund.[88] A new corporation named Ringling Enterprises was formed—wholly owned by North and Bisco—and a state-held mortgage allowed them to take title to all remaining assets.

From the viewpoint of the state, the city of Sarasota, and the family of the executors, the outcome gave mutual advantage. The future of the museum was assured, once the public apparatus of state administration began to function. The presence of the Ringling art collection remained an ever-growing cultural asset to the city. To the Norths the advantages were more mundane but nonetheless gratifying. John North owned a major share of the circus, the principal object of his ten years of effort. The increase in national wealth of the postwar years and the growth of Sarasota as a resort steadily enhanced the value of Ringling's island property, bringing closer the realization of another Ringling vision.

Ida and John North had fought for ten years to redeem the estate from its discredited condition and to protect the gift that John and Mable had conceived and built for the people of Sarasota and Florida. The Norths may not have been wholly altruistic, but they were determined that the estate should not be dismantled by their adversaries. In time, the executors and their attorneys succeeded. Ultimately they benefited personally; but the greatest benefit accrued, as Ringling had intended, to the generations of museum visitors who experienced the Ringling bequest.

Leonard Bisco's skill, while not the only factor, was the primary force that led the Norths to achieve John Ringling's great memorial. The estate had been faced with formidable obstacles of debt, taxes, and a throng of claimants and litigants. In the end the museum, the art collection, and the residence were safe from depredation by humankind. There remained the equally formidable tasks of preserving those same, now public, possessions from the depredations of time and nature.

John Ringling Redux

OCIETY DEMANDS little from those who have ceased to be rich. It asks only that such people become invisible, thus assuring that their former associates are spared the embarrassment of chance encounters. In New York it was easy for Ringling to melt into the anonymity of a large city. In Sarasota his illness and his divorce effectively limited participation in the more public events of social life. Still, in his own unruffled way, he kept up a measure of visibility in Sarasota, conspicuous in his ancient Rolls Royce, chauffeured by his nephew Henry North. In his home city he became an anachronism in his own lifetime, a symbol of the 1920s in the grim Depression years of the early 1930s. In consequence, a new set of legends about his financial distress surrounded him, including rumors of assets hidden from the Bureau of Internal Revenue and from his creditors—all containing little more truth than the earlier accounts of his boundless wealth.

But there were millions enough to begin Sarasota's transformation into a fashionable metro-resort. Twenty-five years before his bequest was conveyed to the state of Florida, he used much of his accumulated capital to acquire most of the Sarasota keys and become the foremost developer in Sarasota history. With his diverse building projects in the mid-1920s and with the arrival of the circus quarters in 1927, he stood out among the principal economic assets of the community, the largest employer of Sarasota's small working class. By 1932 his own forced retrenchment and the devastation of the Great Depression hastened his fall from grace. In the small arena of Sarasota's daily life, Ringling's declining status may have seemed unique. In fact, much more than his personal eclipse was taking place. Across the nation a new Depression-induced populism rejected the superficial, free-spending culture that thrived in the affluence of the 1920s.

Then, starting in 1936 with the slow liquidation of estate, the Ringling name began a lengthy process of recovery. Each parcel of his holdings, when turned into cash, helped to rebuild his image, culminating in the gift of his home and museum to the state of Florida. In the interval, World War II had altered the balance of classes within the nation's social order. An expanded middle class in a newly mobile society—many more of whom were going to college—increased the potential audience for John and Mable Ringling's gift. The museum and its collection epitomized a particularly rich and colorful stage in the splendid visual heritage of West European culture that had been transported to America. And Ca' d'Zan was a museum in itself—an intriguing example of a vanished era in America.

Attendance fell off sharply in the war years; in 1942 visitors averaged nine or ten people per day, representing a drop of about 20,000 in the first four months of the year. After the war, attendance figures quickly climbed again.

During the long years of probate the museum, the house, and the grounds had suffered from a lack of funds. The fallen statues and columns, overgrown weeds, uncared-for trees and plants made them seem unattractive and unloved, though minimal care had prevented them from falling into ruin. Money and professional direction were needed for repairing the museum structure, for reclaiming pictures harmed by climate and dust, for bringing Ca' d'Zan back to its former glamor, and for making the grounds into an ordered setting for the whole.

Ralph Caples, the adjoining neighbor, had little faith that public ownership would restore the place to its former appearance. The procession of animals by night and rattlesnakes by day that invaded his property from the museum grounds spurred him to action. He addressed a sarcastic appeal to the Park Board of Sarasota: "I am constrained to say, however, that I do not believe that the Park Board, the Mayor and the City Council of Sarasota can be interested to any great extent in the $20-million museum property, when they are unable to agree on the construction of a comfort station."[1]

Caples's protest was more than a neighbor's frustration. It was a sign of regret for the estrangement of the last years that had separated him from John Ringling. His concern also revealed a lasting regard for his former neighbors and friends. He grieved to see their "once glorious monument" fallen into neglect and decay.

Karl Bickel was similarly dismayed at what he saw.[2] Bickel was a retired head of the Associated Press wire service. He had come late to the circle of local companions who shared occasional social evenings with Ringling in his later years when he lived alone at Ca' d'Zan. Once the state gained control, Bickel became a strong and vocal advocate of the museum's effort to regain its glorious image.

The appearance was more depressing than the actual condition of the buildings. In 1945 $78,000 was spent on the museum and residence to halt the worst assaults of rain and humidity.[3]

The Florida climate is particularly hostile to structures and grounds that are not constantly maintained. The museum was especially vulnerable because of its structural defects caused by inadequate funding when it was being built. It also suffered from the lack of professional curatorial supervision. John North was often absent from Sarasota for lengthy periods with the circus; in Sarasota or away, his attention was fixed on the vital financial affairs of the estate and his own campaign to claim control of the circus. Henry North, who was a trustee of the estate but not an executor, was more closely concerned with the museum and its collection and was fully aware of the urgent need to restore several damaged pictures. He surveyed the technical qualities of the entire collection along with Dr. William Suida, whom the Norths engaged in 1940 to prepare the museum's first catalog. Suida seemed anxious not to offend his employers. He reported that overall the state of preservation was satisfactory but added that expert help was needed for some urgent conservation. Stephen Pichetto was chosen to start the work.

Pichetto was then senior restorer for the National Gallery in Washington and for the Metropolitan Museum in New York. Ten pictures were sent to his New York studio, including a tondo by Bartolomeo, mystical scenes by Francken and Rubens, Sir Joshua Reynolds' *Marquis of Granby,* and one Guardi.[4]

The condition of the museum structure had begun to deteriorate rapidly even before Ringling's death, mainly because of the climate. An overview prepared for the estate in 1942 gives a dismal picture:[5]

> Tapestries are being eaten by moths and rotting and tearing around the edges. A hundred or more of the valuable paintings are greatly in need of expert attention. Mold and dirt have accumulated in many cases to where the original is almost obliterated.
>
> The roof is in deplorable condition, leaking badly all over and water is not only doing serious damage to the woodwork, floors and wainscotting, but it is seriously damaging many of the pictures and tapestries and other pieces of art.
>
> It is noted that termites are doing considerable damage to the floors. The window frames all need new putty . . . the water comes in and runs down on the window sills and on down the wall, in some instances on the floor.
>
> The concrete surface of the passageway behind the statue of David leaks so badly that the plastering is bulging out and doing serious damage to the walls and woodwork in the passage below. [The curved gallery beneath the 'bridge' was intended to be used to display the cypriote, antique collection.][6]

By the time the executors were prepared to transfer the museum and the residence to the state, many of the worst problems had been arrested if not removed. Roof repairs, termite control, and window repairs halted the dangerous decay and unsightly appearance of the interior. However, unused building supplies, fallen and broken statuary, and surplus columns continued to make the grounds hazardous, hidden among the waist-high weeds. The balustrade of the seawall, broken and fallen from storm damage, lay where it had fallen a number of years before.[7]

The first step toward complete recovery was the selection of a professional to head the institution. The Florida Board of Control, after assuming responsibility for the museum, wanted the new director to restore and convert it into an effective public facility. Its Italian Renaissance palace structure was suited to displaying the collection of a rich owner with eclectic tastes, but it lacked such essentials as space for offices, workrooms for conservation, and public conveniences. It had been designed in the tradition of a royal picture gallery. Böhler called it a jewel; the *American Magazine of Art* compared it to the palaces of southern Europe, an art exhibit itself.[8]

Edward Forbes, director of the Fogg Museum at Harvard, had known John Ringling and he understood the problems and strengths of this unusual bequest. He recommended A. Everett Austin, Jr., as the best man for the immense task ahead.[9] Austin was then director of the Atheneum at Hartford, Connecticut, a museum enriched by gifts from J. P. Morgan, and coincidentally the site of an authoritative collection of Italian Baroque paintings. He brought more than his knowledge of painting and art history. He was young and energetic, and he possessed a modest fortune, which freed him from dependence on the salary that the state was prepared to offer. That was indeed fortunate, for there were no funds to pay him for some months after he came to Sarasota.

Since repairs had temporarily protected the building from further weather damage, the collection was Austin's first consideration upon arrival. Like Böhler and Verman Kimbrough before him, he found that Ringling had begun to divide his collection into two classes—those that met his standards for permanent ownership and the remainder that were suited for trade, sale, or other disposition. Ringling's successors were denied that option, for his will forbade any sale, trade, or other change. Some paintings were in good condition and would remain so indefinitely with routine conservation. Others were beyond redemption, or if subjected to restoration would cease to exist as the original work of the artist. The third and largest class comprised those in need of restoration or conservation to retain their worth and to prevent further deterioration.

In the autumn of 1946, Austin began the long, costly program of restoration. While the executors managed to stem the progress of decay for the museum building, more repairs on the interior were needed.

Austin found the gallery walls uniformly dark and forbidding, stained by water from the leaking roof and windows. He began immediately to sheathe the gallery walls with plywood, then added another covering surface to halt any further invasion of dampness into the canvases or into the even older paintings on wood panels.[10] Starting with the south wing, he had the windows converted to opaque louvers to protect the pictures from direct sunlight. Austin mistakenly believed that in his wish to recreate a traditional palace art gallery, Ringling wanted to have the galleries sidelighted from windows rather than overhead lighting in the manner of the newer museums built expressly to hold pictures. Ringling had requested overhead lighting or skylights but was overruled by the architect.[11]

Despite their extremely hard marble-dust composition, some of the roof-line statues were starting to fracture. Austin let them wait for several years before he asked for funds to replace them. He found at the Cesana Gallery of Art in Venice an adequate supply identical to the first seventy-six statues bought by Ringling twenty-five years earlier, made at the same shop. These six-foot statues, delivered, were less expensive than the cost of repairs to the broken and weakened figures on the roof.[12]

Many of the pictures were peeling, and some canvases darkened by old varnish were actually curling out of their frames. Restoration not only saved them, but laid to rest the lingering doubts about the worth or attribution of many of them. "They were, for the most part," Austin later reported, "thought to be replicas, copies, or forgeries by serious students everywhere. Instead, after restoration, many were proved to be better pictures by better painters than had originally been thought."[13] In his first year about twenty smaller works were sent to New York for restoration with some of the new techniques that had been developed since Ringling's day. Within eighteen months more than 100 pictures had been treated.

Methods for the conservation and restoration of paintings were no less controversial in 1946 than at any other time since the inception of programs for that purpose. The museum under state ownership was feeling its way in a field where experts often failed to agree. Among the specialists who worked to restore some of the most vulnerable pictures was Cesar Diorio, engaged each summer from 1946 to 1953. Most of his work was done at Sarasota rather than at the New York studio. Diorio was among the first to use radiographic films to study layers of paint to reveal what might lie underneath.[14]

For two seasons the work of cleaning and restoration was done wherever a picture could be propped up—in a gallery, in the entrance vestibule, even outside on the loggia, where pictures were tied against columns to resist sudden gusts of wind. The next summer, work was adjourned to the terrace over the front door, in the space between the two attic stories. Hot summer sunlight rendered new varnish sticky, tempera curdled, and flying insects became embedded in the sticky surfaces.[15]

A studio was finally improvised by converting a garage storeroom adjoining the circus galleries—providing another attraction to curious visitors who crowded around the work in progress. The chief novelty was an improvised pressure table weighted with discarded slabs of marble and broken statues found at the rear of the building. A number of large canvases were relined with the makeshift equipment: Gainsborough's *General Philip Honywood*, Snyders's *Still Life*, and two by Rubens, *Departure of Lot* and *Pausias and Glycera*.[16]

The oldest works in the collection were painted on wood, some dating as far back as the 1300s. Panels in need of repair were entrusted to the museum's carpenter. He had to improvise a device to press a reinforcement panel or cradle to the back of a damaged panel. He was able to use the low ceiling of the basement carpenter shop, wedging lengths of board vertically between the ceiling and the protected panel on his worktable. Despite this cleverly contrived apparatus, carpenter shop repairs were failures on two valuable pictures—*Portrait of a Woman*, then attributed to Rembrandt, now to Reynier van Gherwen, and Pagni's *Medici Madonna*. Some of the damage was beyond repair.[17]

By 1950, some 200 of the 460 works listed in the Suida catalog were cleaned, relined, and restored. Austin's restoration program was unmistakably successful, praised by Julius Böhler and by Edward Forbes of the Fogg Museum.[18] The larger paintings had to await additional funding. Canvas of the size needed for the great Rubens cartoons had to be specially woven. Such large seamless sheets could only be purchased in Belgium or Ireland. Those canvases would take a year to produce and the cost was estimated at $5,000.

Through the Suida catalog and a series of journal articles stimulated by new professional interest in the Ringling pictures, the museum was gaining scholarly recognition in America and abroad. Most gratifying was the publicity from a loan of Rubens' *Departure of Lot* to the Philadelphia Academy, where it was among the most popular paintings in the Diamond Jubilee Exhibition.[19]

Austin found that administratively the museum was also in bad condition. The net assets were a few hundred dollars in cash, kept in a tin box. John Garland, state auditor for the estate, had been working with the executors' business agent, O. P. McLeod. McLeod had taken the place of James Haley when he left the museum following his marriage to Aubrey Ringling. The rest of the staff consisted of the doorman, William Robertson, who had been in Ringling's employ from the time the museum opened to the public in 1932; Al Roan, the superintendent of buildings and grounds for the estate and formerly captain of the *Zalophus;* George Lord, a guide; and a small number of grounds-keepers. "The institution," Austin later recalled, "had something of the air of the circus with its various concessions. There was no money available for expenditures."[20]

❧ Ca' d'Zan, closed during the ten years of probate, had suffered some damage and neglect, but much less than the museum. Owen Burns had built it to offer greater resistance to the hazards of Florida weather and climate. There was some water damage and plaster had broken away from the walls. Much of the upholstered furniture had become ragged, with lumps of stuffing pushing through the torn fabric.

Under the terms of Ringling's will, many of the furnishings, because they were not antiques or objects of art, were not specified to become state property. The executors and the state reached an agreement by which Ringling's personal effects, one-half the silver and china, and the contents of the closet in the third-floor vault were retained by the North family. All else, valued at $865,000, remained in the home.[21]

Ringling had stipulated in his will that the house was to become a museum of Venetian art. With a small fund provided by the governor and the cabinet, Austin acquired several pieces of antique Venetian furniture, including settees made by Michelangelo Pergolisi. He bought yellow damask to cover the walls and curtain the windows of the reception room and the ballroom. To hold down the cost, Austin himself performed much of the labor.[22]

In his redecorating Austin attempted to maintain what he called the Ringlings' "statement of magnificence" and at the same time to correct what he considered to be certain faults in their decorating tastes. "We should make every effort, it seems to me, to invalidate the criticism so constantly leveled at the interior: that it is tasteless and ponderous and to some people of taste even hideous and laughable."[23] He was never able to understand why the Ringlings chose to buy at auctions their gilded reproductions of rococo court furniture rather than investing in fine originals of the eighteenth century. In this regard he sometimes overlooked the fact that the distinguishing feature of Ca' d'Zan and the reason for its preservation was its unique character, however unconventional, as a product of its time and its owners' personalities.

Austin was beset by conflicting aims. He wished to disarm the critics who were looking at the 1920s with their tastes of the 1940s. At the same time he wished to preserve the Ringling approach in the decoration of their residence. After partly redecorating the first-floor rooms, he abandoned his plan to create a series of small, second-floor galleries of Venetian art and left most of the rooms very much as they were.[24]

The several other buildings on the estate were in worse shape. The old family home, an 1895 frame house with a shingle roof and no heating system, was past repairing. The furnishings were still inside, where they stood in 1924 when the house was moved to make way for Ca' d'Zan. For a time it was covered with a canvas umbrella to keep out the weather, then finally demolished. A caretaker's house, the pink Venetian Gothic cottage designed by John Phillips, was in fair condition, now providing a home for caretaker Al Roan and his wife. An old dairy barn—long unused—and a dormitory built for construction workers, plus a small servant's house, were all worthless. Roofs had caved in, one was partly blown down by the severe winter storm of 1945. Only a stone-block storehouse and the garage, constructed of hollow tile like

Ca' d'Zan, were in good shape. Each of these held more than $10,000 worth of frames, pictures, and other objects awaiting a suitable home.[25]

As part of the general refurbishing, the old frame structures were demolished. The red Georgia clay tennis courts reverted to grass. Mable's rose garden, its pillared, wrought-iron gazebo only slightly askew, was newly manicured.

Ca' d'Zan was ready to show in December 1946. On opening day a throng of 15,000 visitors came to see how the Ringlings had lived. The few who remembered the large afternoon parties and musicales, the small dinners for important visitors, did not come, for they knew they would find that much had changed. For all others, the great house had always been a mystery, a fantasy behind a forest of palms and Australian pines.

Mark Girouard, in his history of great British houses, states that those of long family occupancy present a "slice of life." An observer can perceive the changing image of generations in their various alterations of the structure, their personal possessions, even their apparel and servants' uniforms.[26] Ca' d'Zan presents a slice of life of only one generation, for the opposite reason. It was occupied only briefly. No one but John and Mable Ringling decided how it should look. Unaltered by other owners, it is a picture of the life of one couple, a couple who wanted a palace.

❦ From the time when the museum was opened to the public in 1932 until its first director was named in 1946, it remained wholly outside the mainstream of American art museums. In the early years, publicity appeared chiefly within the popular press. The Ringling collection, because it did not pass to a major museum like the gifts of Havermeyer, Morgan, and Mellon, never attracted the attention of scholars or art critics. With the appointment of the first director, it began to be taken more seriously in the literature of the museum and art community. *Art News Annual* in 1950 reported it to be the "greatest collection of Baroque paintings in America today."[27] That issue was circulated widely in the United States and in Europe, profusely illustrated. Two years earlier, in 1948, A. H. Mayor, curator of prints at New York's Metropolitan, had written: "Probably no collection outside Europe gives so rich an idea of taste from 1600 to 1800 by assembling so many large paintings by artists who have had great reputations."[28] The museum was beginning to emerge as something more than a rich man's personal memorial.

Late in 1947, Karl Bickel arranged for Julius Böhler to come from Lucerne to consult with the museum staff and the Florida Board of Control regarding the future of the museum. Böhler hoped to impress upon the director and the trustees that a definite line should be stated and that all purchases would be required to follow that line. He feared that without such a plan the collection would become diffuse and un-coordinated and would lose the focus that John Ringling had developed.[29] Böhler, of course, represented "old Munich"—a city where art was concentrated in the eighteenth century and earlier ones.

Along with the appointment of a professional director, the passage of time also changed the way the museum was perceived. In the perception of Ringling himself there had always been a conflict between the image of the circus man and the art collector—between the popular culture of the circus and the elitist culture of the art world. The fiction of the immensity of his fortune helped to bridge the strained credibility of the two diverse images. One interviewer predicted that John Ringling's own generation and one more would recall him as both a circus king and a patron of fine arts. Beyond that, the source of Ringling's money would be obscured and the donor would be remembered as the builder of the splendid museum.[30] For almost any other name, that judgment holds. But the Ringling name was destined to remain a household word, a synonym for "circus," despite his other achievements. Time has shown that in spite of his efforts to assume a posture of the millionaire-entrepreneur, Ringling's image has remained that of the circus man who also collected art and built a museum.

The events that began in 1932 displaced John Ringling as the local circus king. He was dethroned by his adversaries; the fiction that he retired because of ill health soon gave way to the common knowledge that he was forced out. By 1946 the circus came to mean John Ringling North, the man who restored the vigor and viability of that floundering giant.

Ringling's estate exemplified the tropical-paradise fantasy that enveloped Florida and inspired the land boom of the mid-1920s. If it had not become state property, it would have remained as it began, a rich man's eccentric pleasure. State support aided by professional expertise converted an elegant but impermanent structure into a stable, environmentally safe museum, housing a collection that increased steadily in prestige as its quality and rarity became known.

Throughout Ringling's Florida career and the surfeit of publicity that followed his celebrity image, his character was never clarified. The Sarasota power structure perceived him as a convenient mix of self-serving and civic loyalties, yet even his detractors could not deny that he possessed qualities that enabled him to draw the community in his train, using his larger fortune to assume larger risks. In an era when developers had not yet learned to risk only borrowed money, he financed development that placed Sarasota in a favorable position for its later growth. Much later, the post–World War II boom finally created the metro-resort that Ringling envisioned.

The cultural impact of Ringling's bequest can now be seen as twofold: on the one hand, art and art education have become a permanent characteristic of Sarasota life; at the same time, the Ringling estate, the art museum, and Ca' d'Zan present an enduring reminder of the Florida dream. Here the three great joys were once found in abundance: the joy of life, the joy of profit, and the joy of art.

❦ NOTES ❧

Abbreviations Used in the Notes

MCHA   Manatee County Historical Archives
SCHA   Sarasota County Historical Archives, Sarasota County Department
            of Historical Resources
RESF/FSA   Ringling Estate Subject Files/Florida State Archives
RMA   John and Mable Ringling Museum of Art
FSCA   Florida Southern College Archives
PROBATE   Sarasota County Court records, liquidation of John Ringling's estate
  FILE

Chapter 1

1. Fred Bradna, *The Big Top* (New York: Simon and Schuster, 1952), 66.

2. Melvin D. Hildreth, "Memorial," *New York Times*, 3 December 1836; Circus World Archives, Baraboo, Wisconsin.

3. Alf T. Ringling, *The Life Story of the Ringling Brothers* (Chicago: R. R. Donnelley and Sons, 1900), 70–75.

4. Charles Ringling notes, private collection.

5. Report of the Danish Consul General, New York, 14 July 1937, cited in the affidavit of Harold Brophy, counsel to the executors of Ringling's estate, RESF/FSA.

6. Robert H. Gollmar, *My Father Owned a Circus* (Caldwell, Oh.: Caxton Printers, 1965), 15–16.

7. Marian Campbell Rischmueller, "The Ringlings of McGregor," *The Palimpsest* (June 1944).

8. J. M. Kelley, Ringling Bros. reminiscences, *New York Times*, 6 May 1923, Section 6; Alf T. Ringling, *Life Story*, 29–30.

9. Charles Ringling notes, private collection.

10. "Ringling Bros. Circus Year by Year," *White Tops*, Ringling Bros. Golden Jubilee Issue (July–August 1933), 16ff.; Charles Ringling notes, private collection.

11. *Billboard*, 9 January 1936, RMA Archives.

12. *Sarasota Times*, 19 April 1922, 1; *New York Times*, 15 November 1919, 9.

13. Route records of 1892 show clearly that a circus was outside the established social order. "At Bolivar, Mo., on September 26, a very fierce battle was fought between the show people and the people of the town and vicinity. Many of the local bad men were badly injured. The show got out after a very exciting experience without suffering any injury." *Billboard*, 29 April 1933, 28–29.

14. *New York Times*, 3 December 1936, 27.

15. Charles Ringling notes, private collection.

16. *New York Times*, 23 June 1906, 1.

17. *New York Times*, 6 May 1926, Section 6, 6.

18. "The Big Top," *Builders*, 20 July 1957, 8.

19. J. M. Kelley to J. B. Brandenburg, Circus World Archives, Baraboo, Wisconsin. Diary of Fanny Cone, McGregor, Iowa, 31 July 1890. Cited by Marian Campbell Rischmueller, "The Ringlings of McGregor," *The Palimpsest*, State Historical Society of Iowa, June 1944, 191; J. M. Kelley, Brief, *Wisconsin State Journal*, 20 May 1923.

20. John Ringling, "We Divided the Job but Stuck Together," *National Magazine*, September 1919. Charles was initially the Ringlings' "opposition man" according to *Billboard*, 11 December 1926, 86.

21. Conversation with John Lentz, Circus Galleries, June 1985.

22. *Sarasota Herald*, 4 December 1930, 3.

23. *Fortune*, April 1930, 3.

24. *The Literary Digest*, 5 October 1929, 37–40.

25. Martha Dreiblatt, interview with Ringling, *Brooklyn Daily Eagle*, 14 July 1929, 5.

26. Ibid.

27. Members of the DeKos family to Ringling, June 1933, RMA Archives.

28. Kurt Eisfeldt to Ringling, 25 December 1934, 27, RMA Archives.

29. George Ade, article in *This Week in Sarasota*, 14 October 1924, 27.

30. Fred Bradna, *The Big Top*, 66–67.

31. May Wirth, unpublished diary, courtesy of Margaret Fisher, Circus Galleries, RMA Archives.

32. Seattle, Washington, *Post Intelligencer*, 28 August 1927, RMA Archives. Mable's family insisted that she had never been with the circus. A telegram to John L. Sullivan, Circus Museum, 11 May 1963, St. Augustine, Florida, read

"Mable Ringling born near Moon's Post Office, Fayette County, Ohio, March 16, 1874. She at no time performed in Circus. Regards. Amanda Wortman [*sic*]," RMA Archives. Mable's birth certificate states that her birth date was 4 March 1875.

Chapter 2

1. Janet S. Matthews, *Edge of Wilderness—A Settlement History of Manatee River and Sarasota Bay, 1528–1885* (Tulsa, Oklahoma: Cuprine Press, 1983), 132.

2. Dudley S. Johnson, "The Railroads of Florida," Ph.D. diss., Florida State University, 1965, 267.

3. *New York Times*, 8 February 1891, 17.

4. Dudley S. Johnson, "Railroads," 8.

5. Conversation with Lillian Burns, September 1990; Dudley S. Johnson, "Railroads," 12.

6. Ibid., 272.

7. Alfred P. Tischendorf, "Florida and the British Investor," *Florida Historical Quarterly* 33, no. 2 (October 1954), 123.

8. Lillian G. Burns, "John Hamilton Gillespie." In *Sarasota Origins*, Historical Society of Sarasota County, Summer 1988, 19–45.

9. Karl Bickel, *The Mangrove Coast* (New York: Coward-McCann, 1942), 10, 276; Alex Browning, "A Pioneer Railroad and Its Conductor," SCHA.

10. *New York Times*, 3 January 1885, 3.

11. Walter P. Fuller, "Manatee County 1860 Census," Manatee County Historical Society, 1968; Julia F. Smith, *Slavery and Plantation Growth in Antebellum Florida, 1821–1860* (Gainesville: Univ. of Florida Press, 1973), 26.

12. *Sarasota Times*, 16 April 1914, 4; 22 April 1915, 1.

13. Helen C. Gruters, unpublished analysis of Sarasota's 1916 population, n.d., SCHA.

14. *Sarasota Herald-Tribune*, 17 March 1963, 24; *The Weekender*, Sarasota, 28 February 1986, 10.

15. *New York Times*, 10 November 1890, 10.

16. *New York Times*, 4 February 1892, 20.

17. Ibid.

18. Elmer G. Sulzer, *Ghost Railroads of Sarasota County. An Account of Abandoned Lines of the County and City.* Sarasota County Historical Society (Sarasota, 1971), 7.

19. *Sarasota Herald-Tribune*, 7 February 1949.

20. Sulzer, *Ghost Railroads*, 31. In May 1903, the name of the line was changed to Florida & West Shore Railroad. In 1909, the property and franchises were sold to the Seaboard Airline Railroad. Browning, "Pioneer Railroad."

21. *Sarasota Times*, 30 March 1905, 2.

22. *Sarasota Times*, 13 April 1911, 9; 31 December 1914, 2; "Sarasota Ten Years Ago," *Sarasota Times*, 3 June 1915, 9.

23. Andrew Meserve, *General Directory of Manatee County, Florida, 1897*, 85. The directory lists 200 adults.

24. *Sarasota Times*, 9 May 1912, 1.

25. *New York Times*, 11 November 1910, 2.

26. "Looking to Florida," *Sarasota Times*, 9 October 1911, 1.

27. Shell Beach was mapped by Emil Broberg of Manatee, Florida, filed 26 September 1895, and registered in Manatee County Plat Book 1, 121, MCHA.

28. *Chicago Sunday Tribune*, 23 January 1910; SCHA; A. B. Edwards recollected that Mrs. Palmer responded to an advertisement that he had placed in the *Chicago Tribune*. Transcribed interview, 23 July 1958, 19, SCHA.

29. *Sarasota Times*, 21 February 1910, 1; 3 March 1920, 3 (an advertisement); 23 February 1911, 1; 19 March 1910, 3.

30. *Sarasota Times*, 9 March 1911, 2; 16 March 1911, 2; 28 August 1927 (obituary).

31. Burns to Gillespie, 23 May 1910, Burns Papers.

32. Quit Claim Deed, Owen and Vernona Burns to John Ringling, 22 March 1922, RESF/FSA.

33. Minutes of the Sarasota Board of Trade, 1 January 1910.

34. *Sarasota Times*, 10 October 1912, 1; *Sarasota Herald-Tribune*, 7 February 1949 (obituary).

35. Sarasota Board of Trade, *Sarasota, Florida and the Sarasota Bay District of Manatee County. 1914–1915* (Sarasota: ca. 1913), SCHA.

36. Ibid.

Chapter 3

1. Taped interview with Captain Arthur Rowe, captain of Ringling yachts. Burns Papers.

2. *Lloyds Register of American Yachts*, 1912.

3. Manatee County Deed Book, S, W.D. 270, 16 August 1895; Plat Book No. 1, 212; Manatee County Deed Book, U, W.D. 84, 17 December 1898, MCHA; *Tampa Tribune*, 22 October 1911, 11.

4. *Sarasota Times*, 19 January 1911, 3; 26 January 1911, 3. The newer Thompson home was later removed to make way for the home built by Charles Ringling for his daughter Hester.

5. *Sarasota Times*, 14 March 1912, 4.

6. The 1925 Caples home was designed by John H. Phillips of New York.

7. "Indian Beach," brochure (ca. 1913), SCHA.

8. Manatee County Deed Book 33, W.D. 9, 16 April 1912, MCHA.

9. Charles Ringling added to his property with a further purchase from the Thompson estate. Manatee County Deed Book 35, W.D. 17. 6 January 1913; *Sarasota Times*, 2 January 1913, 4.

10. Manatee County Deed Book 30, Quit Claim Deed 473, 11 April 1919; Book 55, W.D. 171, 11 April 1919; Book 57, W.D. 253, 12 April 1919, MCHA.

11. Conversation with Henry R. North, November 1986.

12. The Fifth Avenue apartment became the Ringlings' domicile. They regarded it as their home until Ca' d'Zan was built in Sarasota in 1926.

13. *Sarasota Times*, 12 October 1911, 5. The frame guest cottage was allowed to fall into disrepair. It was replaced with a masonry building designed by John H. Phillips in 1925.

14. *Sarasota Times*, 26 October 1911, 5; 2 January 1913, 4.

15. Dwight James Baum (architect for Ca' d'Zan) to Jonce McGurk, 5 January 1938, SCHA.

16. The Shell Beach side of Sarasota Bay was too shallow for a yacht of that size (83 feet). The wood dock at the Ringling home was shared with Caples. Agreement recorded with the warranty deed, Manatee County Deed Book 29, 543 and 562, 24 February 1912.

17. *Sarasota Times*, 19 February 1920, 1; *New York Times*, 19 February 1920; transcribed interview with Mrs. Al Roan, Eaton Florida Room, Manatee County Central Library; *Sarasota Times*, 16 February 1922, 1; *New York Times*, 17 February 1922, 3. Ringling engaged a private pullman to convey his guests to New York after they had recovered from the accident.

18. *Brooklyn Eagle*, 14 July 1919, SCHA.

19. Alice Coerper, "The Ringlings of Baraboo," in Charles P. Fox, *A Ticket to the Circus* (New York: Bramhall House, 1959), 19.

20. *Sarasota Times*, 4 July 1912, 2.

21. *Sarasota Times*, 6 August 1914, 1.

22. *Sarasota Times*, 31 December 1914, 2.

23. *Sarasota Times*, 12 February 1914, 1.

24. *Sarasota Times*, 30 August 1917, 1. According to the 1931 *Lloyds Register of American Yachts, Zumbrota* was later sold to E. C. Finkbine and registered at Los Angeles. In 1986, it was renamed *Vellron.* Owners included Mae West and Douglas Fairbanks, Sr. Now restored to reflect tastes of previous owners, *Vellron* is available for charter out of San Diego, California. *San Diego Log,* 10 January 1986, 9-A.

25. Bickel, *Mangrove Coast*, 210, 276. Following Berthe Palmer's first visit, her son Honoré chartered the houseboat *Ruffhouse* for tarpon and kingfish sport; Harry Payne Whitney, a millionaire sportsman, next chartered it. *Sarasota Times*, 1 April 1910, 3.

26. *Sarasota Times*, 21 September 1916, 1.

27. *Sarasota Times*, 18 March 1915, 1. Richard Ringling participated in the town's traditional St. Patrick's Day auto and boat races.

28. *Sarasota Times*, 19 November 1927, 1.

29. *Daily Ardmoreite*, 19 November 1927 (Ardmore, Oklahoma); Circus World Archives, Baraboo, Wisconsin.

30. Testimony of Eugene L. Garey, hearing held at the New York Bar Association, 26 August 1938, RESF/FSA.

31. Affidavit of Harold Brophy; *Daily Ardmoreite* (Ardmore, Oklahoma), 2 December 1936.

32. Ibid.

33. James A. Haley to Robert Gray (Florida secretary of state), 8 September 1969, Haley Papers, Florida Southern College.

34. Taylor Gordon, *Born To Be* (New York: Covici-Friede Publishers, 1929).

35. R. M. Calkins to Ringling, 28 July 1916, RMA Archives.

36. Affidavit of Harold Brophy.

37. The Bureau of Internal Revenue cited each claim on Ringling's tax returns and disallowed each one of their ninety-day notice of federal claim to unpaid taxes. Affidavit of Harold Brophy.

38. Correspondence assembled by Ringling relating to mining issues in tribal lands and lease dated 25 June 1921, RMA Archives.

39. Frank G. Curtis to Edward Horske, 28 October 1921, RMA Archives.

40. John M. Kelley, memorandum of 21 October 1921. Tribal land correspondence, RMA Archives.

41. Conversation with William Perry, April 1987. The famous 1914 Rolls Royce was sold for about $2,500 at the request of Henry Ringling North. Ownership was transferred from the John Ringling estate to enable North, as registered owner, to obtain gasoline ration coupons during World War II.

42. H. R. North, *The Circus Kings*, 171–77; *New York Times*, 14 March 1919, 18.

43. Willis Hayles, "And the Circus Went on Just the Same," *White Tops*, (December 1938–January 1939), 8. This article compares the problems and hazards of the 1918 season with those of the 1938 tour.

44. J. M. Kelley, *Brief*, 12. Kelley's *Brief* is the subject of an examination of circus economy in "To Make a Circus Pay," *Fortune*, (April 1933), 38–44. The valuation of Alf T. Ringling's one-third share of the circus at $83,943 indicates that the war years had depressed the value of the circus. Its future worth was then far from certain. *New York Times*, 8 April 1923, 6.

45. *Sarasota Times*, 25 September 1919, 1. The Alf T. Ringling estate "Ringling Park" at Oak Ridge, New Jersey, passed to Richard. It had been a combination summer home for Alf T. and family and a retreat for circus animals from the "R. T. Richards" circus (Richard Ringling's show, so named to avoid the use of "Ringling" in any other show than Ringling Bros.).

46. *Sarasota Times*, 22 January 1920, 1.

47. Ringling kept Mooser's check for $200 and the note of thanks for the loan, RMA Archives; *Sarasota Times*, 17 March 1921, 1.

48. Ringling to Burns, 27 July 1923; 9 August 1923; Burns Papers.

49. *Sarasota Times*, 23 March 1922, 1; 24 May 1923, 1. The *Times* published a long editorial and a detailed description with an array of figures to emphasize the

great size and complexity of the Ringling organization. The detail suggests an effort to establish the Ringlings as men of substantial wealth.

50. Charter of John Ringling Estates, Inc., Burns Papers; *Sarasota Times*, 16 October 1924, 1.

51. Conversation with Lillian Burns, June 1985.

52. Ringling's income tax return for 1916 was an example. RMA Archives.

53. *Sarasota Times*, 26 January 1922, 4; 9 February 1922, 5.

54. Ibid.

55. *Sarasota Times*, 26 January 1923, 2.

56. *Sarasota Times*, 7 December 1922, 1; 4 January 1923, 11; 11 January 1923, 1; 1 January 1923, 1.

57. *Sarasota Times*, 18 January 1923, 4.

58. *Sarasota Times*, 12 April 1923, 1; 3 May 1923, 1, 8.

59. Jennings Perry, "John Ringling of Sarasota," *Suniland* (February 1925), 33–35, 98.

Chapter 4

1. Kenneth Roberts, *Florida* (New York: Harper and Brothers, 1926), 9, 266.

2. *New York Times*, 13 September 1925, Section 8, 10.

3. *New York Times*, 6 February 1925, 19; 3 July 1925, 13; 29 September 1925, 40.

4. Ringling to Burns, 27 June 1925, Burns Papers. "It seems to me that the proposed island for power plants and terminal would eventually be an industrial site with fishhouse, warehouses right in front of our development which we are spending a whole lot of money on to get exclusive elegance."

5. Burns's first two companies were the Burns Dock and Commercial Company, 1911, and Burns Realty Company, 1912.

6. *Sarasota County Times*, 16 March 1921, 1.

7. *Sarasota County Times*, 16 March 1922, 1; Ringling to Burns, 20 March 1923, Burns to Ringling, 29 March 1923, Burns Papers; *Sarasota County Times*, 3 May 1923, 1.

8. *Sarasota Herald-Tribune*, 10 July 1963, 3. The house was demolished in 1963.

9. *Sarasota Herald-Tribune*, 22 June 1952; *Sarasota Times*, 16 October 1924, 3.

10. *New York Times*, 27 August 1925, 1.

11. Conversation with John McCarthy (asst. archivist, Sarasota County). Information provided by Helen Caravelli, 29 March 1988.

12. Conversation with Dorothy Kahle McDaniel, December 1987; *Sarasota Herald-Tribune*, 28 June 1952. Gumpertz's gift to the Boy Scouts on Siesta Key was known as Camp Gumpertz. *Sarasota Herald*, 2 December 1934, Section 2, 2. Conversation with Merle Evans (circus band leader), February 1987.

13. *Sarasota Herald-Tribune*, 22 June 1952.

14. *Sarasota Herald,* 11 May 1927, 1. James A. Haley also claimed credit for the move. Conversation with Alice Myers (administrative asst. to Congressman Haley), June 1985.

15. *This Week in Sarasota,* 27 November 1924, 3.

16. *Sarasota Times,* 4 January 1923, 1.

17. Burns to Ringling, 19 April 1922 and 24 October 1922, Burns Papers.

18. Burns to Ringling, 22 April 1924, Burns Papers.

19. Ringling to Burns, 19 April 1922 and 24 October 1922, Burns Papers.

20. Sarasota County Agricultural Fair Association and Sarasota County Historical Commission, Sponsors, *A History of Sarasota County, Florida,* ca. 1976, 8, 11. Wild cattle that could not be rounded up and dipped were usually shot to halt the spread of tick fever.

21. Ringling to Burns, 28 November 1922, Burns Papers.

22. *Sarasota Times,* 18 January 1923, 4.

23. *Sarasota Times,* 15 February 1923, 1.

24. *Sarasota Times,* 31 July 1924, 1; Ringling to Burns, 7 July 1923; Burns to Ringling, 6 August 1923, Burns Papers.

25. Burns to Ringling, 27 March 1923; Ringling to Burns, 3 April 1923, Burns Papers.

26. Burns to Ringling, 23 March 1923; Ringling to Burns, 30 March 1923, Burns Papers; *Sarasota County Times,* 5 April 1923, 1.

27. Memorandum of Agreement, Owen Burns, John Ringling and R. O. Holton, n.d., Burns Papers.

28. *Sarasota Times,* 12 April 1923, 1; 3 May 1923, 1; 24 May 1923, 1; Ringling to Burns, 30 March 1923, Burns Papers.

29. Memorandum of 8 March 1926. Burns was to have five lots on St. Armands or Lido instead of ten lots on St. Armands. Ringling was to select fifty lots on St. Armands and two or three Gulf lots on Lido. In a contract of 30 June 1925, Ringling reserved ten acres on Sarasota/Wolf Key and two hundred acres on Longboat Key. Burns Papers.

30. Ringling to Burns, 27 July 1923 and 12 August 1923, Burns Papers.

31. U.S. Department of the Treasury, Bureau of Internal Revenue, to Officers and Shareholders of the John Ringling Estates, Inc., 18 September 1929. RMA Archives.

32. Haskins and Sells (auditors) to St. Armands Realty Corp., 8 November 1944. Estimated costs for Longboat and Lido for 1925, 1926, and 1927 were $389,000. Office records were insufficient for the auditors to establish costs. John M. Garland (special auditor for the Ringling estate) to Julius Parker (special counsel). List of real estate owned by the Ringling estate in Sarasota and Manatee counties, November 1945. Purchase and development costs were estimated at $1.65 million. RMA Archives.

33. Ringling to Burns, 11 September 1923, Burns Papers; *Sarasota Times*, 3 January 1924, 1.

34. *Sarasota Times*, 15 February 1923: "that this league is strongly in favor of a city planning commission which will have as its special work the removal of the railroad tracks running to the very front at Strawberry Avenue."

35. *New York Times*, 19 April 1924, 10; 27 April 1924, Section 9, 5; 16 August 1924, 5.

36. *New York Times*, 28 June 1923, 1; 29 June 1923, 9; February 1923, 12; 19 July 1925, Section 10, 1; *Sarasota Times*, 3 July 1924, 1. Others associated with Ringling in the new Garden were J. S. Hammond, Frank Erle, Kermit Roosevelt, John Duys, and Ringling's secretary, Richard Fuchs.

37. *Sarasota Times*, 28 June 1924, 1; Burns to Ringling, August 1924, Burns Papers.

38. Burns to Ringling, 22 August 1924, Burns Papers.

39. *Sarasota Times*, 22 May 1924, 1. Ringling's gesture was also reported in the *Palm Beach Post*, 24 May 1924.

40. *Manatee Evening Journal*, 31 December 1924.

41. *Sarasota Times*, 24 October 1924, 1.

42. Ralph C. Caples, Letter dated 27 December 1924, Burns Papers.

43. Donald W. Curl, *Mizner's Florida, American Resort Architecture* (Cambridge, Mass.: MIT Press, 1985), 140–41.

44. *This Week in Sarasota*, 1 January 1925, 4.

45. *This Week in Sarasota*, 23 April 1925, 1; *Sarasota Herald*, 3 May 1926, 1.

46. Ringling to Burns, 16 October 1923, Burns Papers. Conversation with Lillian Burns, June 1986.

47. *Sarasota Herald*, 10 January 1926, 1; 23 March 1926, Magazine Section, 2.

48. Contract, John Ringling Estates, Inc., and Hageman and Harris Corporation, 7 February 1926, RMA Archives. By an addendum, the contract was assigned to Ringling's Ritz Hotel Corporation of Sarasota.

49. *Sarasota Herald*, 3 March 1926, 1.

50. *Sarasota Herald*, 13 April 1926, 1.

51. *Sarasota Herald*, 6 June 1926, Section 1, 8.

52. *Sarasota Herald*, 29 October 1926, 4. Reprinted from the *Tampa Tribune*.

53. *Sarasota Herald*, 3 November 1926, 2; 27 November 1926, 1.

54. *Sarasota Herald*, 12 September 1926, Section 2, 4; 14 September 1926, 4.

55. *Sarasota Herald*, 3 November 1926, 2; 27 October 1926, 1; 28 October 1926, 1.

56. *Sarasota Herald*, 5 November 1926, 1.

57. *Sarasota Herald*, 3 September 1926, 1; 10 December 1926, 1.

58. *Sarasota Herald*, 20 September 1926, 1; 21 September 1926, 1.

59. *New York Times*, 5 December 1925, 1; 13 December 1925, 25.

60. *Sarasota Times,* 21 September 1916, 1; *Sarasota Herald,* 9 September 1926, 1.

61. Ibid.

62. *Sarasota Herald,* 9 November 1926, 1.

63. *Sarasota Herald,* 26 April 1928, 1; 27 April 1928, 1.

64. *New York Times,* 3 March 1936, 16; 10 March 1936, 7; 27 April 1936, 3.

65. Conversation with Henry Ringling North, November 1936. Conversation with Merle Evans, February 1987.

Chapter 5

1. Sergeant George H. Tighe (New Jersey State Police) to Ringling, 8 February 1934. Tighe wrote: "The former, deceased Mr. Ringling would come over to our quarters and set in the rose garden and talk with me and the rest of the troopers."

2. 21 January 1932. Assertion made in testimony supporting Ringling at a hearing to determine his legal residence. When the Fifth Avenue apartment house was torn down to make way for Rockefeller Center, the Ringlings moved to 270 Park Avenue.

3. Fourth Annual Report of Executors (for 1940) filed 31 March 1941, Probate File, Sarasota Circuit Court. Report lists proceeds of sale of personal property stored in New York ($3,562) less storage fees and sales expenses ($2,822), net $740.

4. See auction catalogs from Silo Auction House, 26 November–1 December 1923 and 1–12 April 1924, RMA Archives.

5. "John Ringling to Spend Millions on Development," *This Week in Sarasota,* 11 December 1924, 20; "John Ringling Starts Three Million Dollar Development," 1 January 1925, 6.

6. Mark Girouard, *Life in the English Country House* (New York: Penguin Books, 1978), 1–5.

7. *Sarasota Herald,* 19 June 1928, 1. Reprinted from *Christian Science Monitor,* 14 June 1928.

8. Editorial, *Sarasota Herald,* 26 October 1925, 2.

9. Roger F. Sears, "A Venetian Palace in Florida," *Country Life,* October 1927, 35.

10. John Garland (state auditor) to J. T. Diamond (secretary to the Board of Control), 27 May 1946, RMA Archives.

11. Photographs of the Shell Beach property from 1895 to 1910 show a seawall and balustrade. Manatee Historical Association collection, Eaton, Florida history room, Manatee County Main Library.

12. *The House that John and Mable Ringling Built* (Sarasota: John and Mable Ringling Museum of Art, n.d.), 4–5.

13. Ringling to Burns, 9 August 1923, Burns Papers. See also James T. Maher, *Twilight of Splendor* (Boston: Little Brown, 1975), 110.

14. Ringling to Burns, 9 August 1923, Burns Papers; Richard Thomas, *John Ringling, Circus Magnate and Art Patron* (New York: Pageant Press, 1960), 128.

15. Ringling to Burns, 9 August 1923, Burns Papers.

16. Burns to Ringling, 12 August 1923, Burns Papers.

17. Ibid.

18. Ringling to Burns, 13 October 1923, Burns Papers.

19. Robert H. Raynor, "Dwight James Baum, Architect, 1886–1939," M.A. thesis, Univ. of Florida, 1976, 1; "The Architecture of Houses, Discussed by Dwight James Baum," *Country Life* (October 1927), 52.

20. Charles C. Baldwin, *Stanford White* (New York: Dodd Mead, 1931), 316–26.

21. Matlack Price, *The Work of Dwight James Baum* (New York: William Helburn, 1927), 6.

22. Marcus Whiffen and Frederick Koeper, *American Architecture 1607–1976*, (Cambridge, Mass.: MIT Press, 1981), 215.

23. "Developing a Regional Type, with Particular Reference to the Work in Florida of Dwight James Baum," *American Architect* (20 August 1926), 144–48; Raynor, "Dwight James Baum," 87–95.

24. Sears, "Venetian Palace," 35.

25. Raynor, "Dwight James Baum," 1; Baum to Jonce McGurk (appraiser of the Ringling estate), 5 January 1938. Letter enclosed with the appraisal, SCHA.

26. *Sarasota Herald*, 6 February 1931, 7. In 1931, Baum returned to Sarasota with a photographer (Gottscho) to document his work. More than ninety photographs of Ca' d'Zan appeared in that series. Cynthia Duval, then curator of decorative objects for the RMA, obtained copies from Columbia University, which held the rights to the photographs.

27. Misconceptions about the appearances of Ca' d'Zan have been common. In 1937, the *Saturday Review* published a photograph of the museum court, mistakenly captioned "The Ringling house—meant to resemble a Doge's palace."

28. Raynor, "Dwight James Baum," 60–81.

29. Baum to Jonce McGurk, 5 January 1938, SCHA.

30. Plans for the residence of Mrs. John Ringling, January 1924. Drawings show many changes during planning and construction. Earl Purdy made the drawings at Baum's studio in Riverdale, New York.

31. "Ca' d'Zan, the John Ringling Residence" (Sarasota: The John and Mable Ringling Museum of Art, n.d.). Includes a floorplan and brief description.

32. Burns to Ringling, 19 August 1924, Burns Papers. Lyman Dixon was Baum's Sarasota office manager. Antique Spanish tiles, doors used in the building are described in *This Week in Sarasota*, 26 February 1925, 19.

33. Burns to Ringling, 19, 23, and 30 April 1924; Ringling to Burns, 8 May and 9 August 1934, Burns Papers. Details of construction appear in a flurry of messages: Burns to Ringling 19 and 30 April 1924, 29 May 1924, 4, 5, and 25 June 1924; Ringling to Burns 4, 24, and 25 June 1924. A series of photographs labeled "Spanish tiles for Mr. Owen Burns," Foto Wunderlich, Granada, Spain, from C. F. Wicker to Burns record the journey of the antique roof tiles from Granada to a ship bound for the United States, Burns Papers.

34. Samuel G. Wiener, *Venetian Houses and Details* (New York: Architectural Book Publishing, 1929). Illustrations in this text show details of the exterior of Ca' d'Oro and the Palazzo Pisani S. Polo, which are similar to those seen on the exterior of Ca' d'Zan, pp. 10, 24, 89, 93, 95, 104.

35. Ibid.

36. For stories of Mable's wishes regarding Ca' d'Zan, see Robert Wernick, "The Greatest Show on Earth Didn't Compare to Home," *Smithsonian* 12 (23 September 1981), 62–71; Maher, *Twilight of Splendor,* 103, 108–9.

37. Conversation with John McCarthy (asst. archivist, Sarasota County), June 1988.

38. *New York Times,* 29 April 1924, 21; 30 April 1924, 32. On the first day Mable spent $4,500 on furnishings, including a carved walnut and tapestry screen, a gilt screen of the same style, a Louis XV marquetry table, and two gilt armchairs. The next day she added (among others) six carved and gilded armchairs for $1,680.

39. Conversation with Henry Ringling North, November 1987.

40. S. G. Rains, Auction Catalog, Emerson McMillin and George Crocker million dollar sale, November 1924, RMA Archives.

41. *Sarasota Herald,* 7 May 1926. Pogany was one of the most popular illustrators for the war posters during World War I. He created sets for the Metropolitan Opera's *Coq d'Or,* and his ceiling and wall decorations were sought for homes in New York City and on Long Island. At Ca' d'Zan he also decorated the third-floor playroom, covering the walls and ceiling to represent the *Fete Micareme* in Venice. Among the figures were John and Mable, her pet cockatoo Laura, Ringling's parrot Jacob, Tel the Alsatian, and Mable's four miniature Dobermans.

42. Inventory of furnishings in the John Ringling home, room #3, Probate File, Sarasota County Court.

43. Baum to McGurk, 5 January 1938, SCHA (copy for James A. Haley inserted in the appraisal of Ringling's personal property). When Baum estimated the value of Ca' d'Zan's furnishings in 1938, he generally was not figuring their cost at time of purchase. "This does not include the value of the paintings because I do not know which ones are still in the house. It includes the tapestries, the pipe organ which cost approximately $50,000, the decorative paintings on the ceiling mostly done by Willy Pogany, etc. It is rumored that Mr. Ringling's bedroom furniture was the original set used by Napoleon III at Fontainbleau, for which he paid $35,000."

44. *Sarasota Herald,* 22 March 1926, 1.

45. *Sarasota Herald*, 26 October 1925, 4.

46. Editorial, *Sarasota Herald*, 26 October 1925, 4.

47. Hugh F. McKean (president of Rollins College) minority report of the museum survey panel, 1953, RMA Archives. Owen Burns may never have received full payment for his work on Ca' d'Zan. In April 1925, when the main structure of the house was in place, Burns signed a general release. In it, he discharges John Ringling from "all manner of actions, etc., suits, claims, or for services rendered in purchase of land, property, improvements, development, causeway, construction of home." 15 April 1925, Burns Papers.

Chapter 6

1. *Sarasota Herald*, 27 November 1926, 1.

2. Conversation with Henry Ringling North, November 1987; *Sarasota Herald*, 14 January 1927, 1; 18 January 1927, 1.

3. The messages were routinely alike. The roster of addresses shows that most were railway executives, government officials, and friends in the world of entertainment. RMA Archives.

4. Fuchs to Ringling, exhibit attached to divorce proceedings in the Supreme Court of New York, John Ringling defendant, 8 May 1935, RESF/FSA.

5. *Sarasota Herald*, 13 January 1927, 1; 14 January 1927, 1; 23 February 1927, 1; 24 February 1927, 5.

6. *Sarasota Herald*, 27 February 1927, 1.

7. *Sarasota Herald*, 23 February 1927, 1; *Sarasota Times*, 16 October 1924, 3. "Samuel Gumpertz—largely interested in one of New York's largest financial institutions."

8. "Oil! Oil! Oil!" editorial in the *Sarasota Herald*, 22 December 1926, 4. The editorial praised the drilling project for its avoidance of a frenzied stock promotion and the wild speculation that so often accompanied oil discoveries.

9. *Sarasota Herald*, 26 November 1926, 1. The banner headline announced that carloads of drilling equipment had arrived in Sarasota from El Dorado, Arkansas.

10. *Sarasota Herald*, 1 February 1927, 1, 2.

11. *Sarasota Herald*, 27 February 1927, 1.

12. *Sarasota Herald*, 5 March 1927, 1.

13. The Humble Oil Company later claimed the bounty and offered to donate this sum to the University of Florida and the Florida State College for Women, Letter from Humble Oil to the Commissioners of State Institutions, 22 November 1943, Probate File.

14. *Sarasota Herald*, 13 March 1927, 1.

15. *Sarasota Herald*, 1 December 1927, 4.

16. *Sarasota Herald*, 9 December 1926, 1.

17. *Sarasota Herald*, 6 February 1927, 4.

18. *Sarasota Herald,* 13 February 1927, Section 1, 3 (full-page advertisement).

19. Ibid.

20. *Sarasota Herald,* 15 February 1927, 4; 17 February 1927, 4 (editorial).

21. *Sarasota Herald,* 17 February 1927, 1.

22. Burns's letter addressed to the corporation was clearly a statement for the record, dictated by an agreement with Ringling, 28 December 1925, Burns Papers.

23. Garland (state auditor for the Ringling estate) to Caldwell, 12 July 1943. The doors were found to be 90 percent damaged. "They were believed to have come from the old Waldorf Astoria, purchased 13 years ago by John Ringling," RESF/FSA.

24. Circus publicity probably written by Alf T. Ringling.

25. *New York Times,* 31 March 1925, 20. Mable Stark's fourteen Bengal tigers were transferred to the menagerie and the great star herself reverted to an equestrienne role.

26. *Sarasota Herald,* 23 March 1927, 1; 9 April 1930, 1.

27. Congressman James A. Haley to Joan Tramantano: "I was one of the men who persuaded John Ringling to bring the Circus quarters to Sarasota many years ago," Haley Papers, Florida Southern College; Conversation with Alice Myers, June 1985, at SCHA.

28. *Sarasota Herald,* 23 March 1927, 1.

29. *Sarasota Herald-Tribune,* 4 October 1975, 19.

30. *This Week in Sarasota,* 31 March 1927, 1.

31. *Sarasota Herald,* 8 June 1927, 1.

32. *Sarasota Herald,* 12 May 1927, 1.

33. *Sarasota Herald,* 10 May 1927, 5; 2 October 1927, 11. Summarizes Ringling's investments in Sarasota.

34. *Sarasota Herald,* 10 June 1927, 1.

35. Receipts for Mable's Paris wardrobe, RMA Archives.

36. A. E. Cummer, interview, SCHA.

37. Conversation with Henry Ringling North, November 1986; Estate of Charles Ringling, Probate File, Sarasota County Court; Conversation with Merle Evans, February 1987.

38. *Sarasota Herald,* 18 January 1927, 4. The source is not identified, nor did the *Herald* point out the errors.

39. Souvenir Menu Card, John Ringling Testimonial Dinner, 27 January 1928, at the El Vernona Hotel, SCHA.

40. *Sarasota Herald,* 7 February 1928, 10; 12 February 1928, 6.

41. Ibid.

42. *Sarasota Herald,* 29 February 1928, 7.

43. Interview (transcribed) with Gordon Higel, former mayor of Sarasota, 25 October 1973, SCHA.

44. Visitors included Pierre du Pont, chief executive of the family-controlled

firm, and Mr. and Mrs. Barclay Warburton. He was the former mayor of Palm Beach; she was a daughter of the late John Wanamaker, whose yacht the Ringlings had chartered.

45. *Sarasota Herald*, 26 January 1921, 1; 29 January 1929, 1.

46. *Sarasota Herald*, 24 February 1929, 1.

47. *Sarasota Herald*, 15 March 1929, 8.

48. Conversation with Henry Ringling North, November 1987.

Chapter 7

1. Henry Ringling North, "John and Mable Ringling Museum Has Much of World's Greatest Art," *Sarasota Herald*, 5 December 1937, Section 2, 1. Julius Böhler confirmed Ringling's earlier purchases in a meeting with Kenneth Donahue (museum director), *Sarasota News*, 26 October 1962, 1.

2. Ringling was then a major shareholder in the old "Garden."

3. Henry Ringling North, "John and Mable Ringling Museum."

4. Linda H. Roth, *J. Pierpont Morgan, Collector—European Decorative Arts from the Wadsworth Atheneum* (Hartford: Wadsworth Atheneum, 1987), 37; Baldwin, *Stanford White*, 280.

5. *ARTnews* 26 (18 February 1928), 14.

6. S. G. Rains, Auction Catalog, McMillin and Crocker Sale, Mahwah, New Jersey, 27 October–1 November 1924, RMA Archives.

7. Galerie Georges Petit, *Trois Importantes Tapisseries du xvii siecle, Paris, Le Mardi, 22 Mai 1928*, 64, RMA Archives.

8. American Art Association, *Paintings, Furnishings and Architectural Fittings of the Astor Residence, 840 Fifth Avenue, New York*, auction catalog, April 1926, RMA Archives.

9. Kristi Nelson, "Jordaens and Three Alexander Tapestries at the Ringling Museum," *Ringling Museum of Art Journal* 1, no. 1 (1983), 204. Paper presented at the International Rubens Symposium, 14–16 April 1982.

10. In 1955, Parke-Bernet inventoried and appraised a mass of objects stored in the museum basement. Few had artistic merit, many were damaged; e.g., a bird cage listed as "Delft or Rouen Blue and White Faiance, imperfect: $25." In 1924 Ringling bought it at the Fifth Avenue Auction Rooms: "Rare antique Delft bird cage, late 17th century, finely decorated: $125."

11. Executors' report, 14 December 1936: "Ringling prior to his death, agreed to allow the use at said (John Ringling) Hotel of any desirable furnishings that might be in his residence at Shell Beach," Probate File. Pictures at the hotel were valued at $50,000; those at the garage storeroom at $100 each.

12. *ARTnews* 26 (5 May 1928), 1.

13. Ibid.

14. *International Studio* 92 (March 1929), 8.

15. Robert Benson and Evelyn Benson, *Catalog of Italian Pictures*, privately printed (London: Chiswick, 1914), vii.

16. *ARTnews* 20 (1 October 1928), 1.

17. *Art Digest* 5 (October 1930), 22; *New York Times*, 15 October 1930, 11. The figures were believed to be the artist and his first wife, Isabella Brant. The Belgian government wanted the painting, but the low value of the franc in 1924 made the purchase impossible. Arthur Newton held ten of the Westminster pictures. Ringling bought six. *ARTnews* 24 (31 October 1925), 2.

18. *ARTnews* 26 (5 May 1928), 2. Ringling named Böhler curator; directors were Henry Walters, Langdon Douglas, August L. Mayer, Max J. Friedlander, Albert Keller, Sir Joseph Duveen, and Baron Von Hadeln. With those distinguished experts, *ARTnews* noted that "it should be impossible to question the authenticity of any of the paintings or works of art," 10.

19. For the Berenson-Duveen association, see Thomas Hoving, "The Berenson Scandals, an interview with Colin Simpson," *Connoisseur* (October 1986), 132.

20. Communication from Julius Böhler III to the author; inventory of the contents of Ca' d'Zan, 1937, books in John Ringling's bedroom, SCHA.

21. "Ringling," *Fort Lauderdale Daily News*, 15 May 1957, RMA Archives.

22. *Christian Science Monitor*, 14 June 1928. Reprinted in the *Sarasota Herald*, 19 June 1928.

23. Ibid.

24. Julius Böhler, "Ringling—Collector and Builder." In Murray, *The Ringling Museum.*

25. Ibid.

26. Peter Tomory, "John Ringling, the Collector," in *Catalogue of the Italian Paintings before 1800*, ix—xiii.

27. Hans Makart's *Diana's Hunting Party* sold for $8,500, highest price at the Metropolitan Museum sale. The canvas measures 15' × 32'3". *New York Times*, 8 February 1929, 14. The Makart was hung in the auditorium gallery when the museum opened. It has since remained in storage.

28. *Time*, 12 October 1931. Reprinted in the *Sarasota Herald*, 4 November 1931, 1.

29. Bernadino Luini's *Madonna and the Child with Sts. Sebastian and Roche* was exhibited at the Reinhardt Galleries in late 1925.

30. Telegram, Ringling to Mable Ringling, 23 April 1926, RMA Archives.

31. Peter Tomory to Nora de Poorter, Kunsthistorisches Museum, Antwerp, 18 July 1972. RMA Curatorial File.

32. The three withdrawn from Christie's auction were *Gathering (Descent) of the Manna, Abraham and Melchizedek,* and *The Four Evangelists.* The fourth cartoon (not offered at auction) was *The Defenders of the Eucharist.* Communication from the Westminster Archives.

33. *New York Times*, 22 April 1926, 10. Ringling's purchases at the Astor sale are recorded in his copy of the auction catalog. See also *New York Times*, 6 May 1925; "Astor dining room," *New York Times*, 6 December 1925, Section 9, 3.

34. *New York Times*, 22 April 1926, 10.

35. Paul R. Baker, *Richard Morris Hunt* (Cambridge: MIT Press, 1980), 346; Andrew Tully, *Era of Elegance* (New York: Funk and Wagnalls, 1947), 13. See also Michael Condorti, "The French Interior: Style and Symbol in Nineteenth-Century America," paper presented at The John and Mable Ringling Museum Symposium, November 29–30, 1984, RMA.

36. *History of The John and Mable Ringling Museum*, prepared by Frances Hoersting, 1982, B-8. The room was there reported as having been removed from a palace in Savoy (then Italy) and moved to New York. In "The French Interior," Condorti credits Allard with original construction in the Astor home. For details of the southeast salon, see the American Art Association catalog, *Paintings, Furnishings & Architectural Fittings*.

37. Mark Girouard, *Houses of Historic Britain* (London: Peerage Books, 1984), 122.

38. American Art Association catalog, *Paintings, Furnishings & Architectural Fittings*.

39. *New York Times*, 22 April 1926, 10.

40. Georgio Vasari, *The Lives of the Painters, Sculptors and Architects*, 4 vols. (London: Dent, 1963), vol. 3, 54.

41. Julius Böhler, *Art Museum*, 19.

42. *New York Times*, 4 February 1927, 1. Prices reported for the Van Loo $3,500; Bellini $6,000; *ARTnews* 25, 22 January 1927, 12; February 1927, 1.

43. Böhler to Ringling, June 1927, Curatorial File, RMA.

44. *The Times* (London) 15 July 1927, 14; 16 July 1927, 14.

45. *The Times*, 16 July 1927, 14. Now titled *A Sultana of Venice*, the painting was originally called *Catarina Cornaro* and then *Sultana Rossa*. The second Holford portrait bought by Sir Joseph Duveen was presented to the government of Cyprus.

46. *The Times*, 18 July 1928, 11; 19 May 1928, 11, 17; *ARTnews* 26, 17 March 1928.

47. Tomory, "John Ringling," 50.

48. Ibid., 4.

49. *New York Times*, 17 November 1927, 1.

50. Tomory, "John Ringling," 6, 7. Julius Böhler, 21.

51. Karl Freund added a foreword to the appraisal of John Ringling's collection of classical antiquities, 60, 61, in the McGurk appraisal of the Ringling estate. Cesnola sold some of his collection to European museums, but most of it came to the Metropolitan, where he served as a trustee, secretary, and president until 1904. John L. Myers, *Handbook of the Cesnola Collections of Antiquities from Cyprus* (New York: Metropolitan Museum of Art, 1914), 14–19; John Taylor Johnston, "The

Cesnola Collection of Cypriote Antiquities in the Metropolitan Museum of Art, New York," 455: appendix to Cesnola, *Cyprus, Its Ancient Cities, Tombs and Temples* (New York: Harper and Brothers), 1887, 451–56.

52. Tomory, "John Ringling," 12.

53. The Bourdons were damaged by water in the 1960s and were treated by Edward Korany; their condition at the time of Ringling's purchase in 1929 cannot be determined.

54. *An Allegorical Representation of the Crucifixion.* The allegories are the virtues: Caritas, Humilitas, Obedienta, and Patienta. No certain attribution; possibly an early work of Guariento di Arpo, active in Padua and Venice (1338–68). William E. Suida, *A Catalog of Paintings in The John and Mable Ringling Museum of Art* (Sarasota: published by the Museum, 1949), 7. For a later opinion, see Tomory, *Italian Paintings*, 116. Ringling's Flemish works totaled 42; there were about 50 Dutch (25 labeled anonymous, follower, or imitator).

55. *ARTnews* 27 (23 March 1929), 21. From A. C. R. Carter's comments on the sale of 1 March 1929. Carter had been present at the 1888 sale when the Bonheur was sold to W. H. Smith. The article in *ARTnews* contained material from Carter's report in the *London Daily Telegraph*.

56. Ibid.

57. Ringling's record of checks drawn on his account at the Chatham and Phoenix National Bank, New York. Also, Christie's sale records for 31 July 1931, RMA Archives.

58. Böhler, 17.

59. One, *Saint Eloi* (1515), was sold to the Boston Museum of Fine Arts in 1930. See E. Moliniere, Catalogue Raisonné; 186. The Yarbrough "Rembrandt" was never authenticated. It was at one time in the collection of H. O. Havemeyer in New York.

60. J. H. Guttman (consultant), Memorandum, 13 August 1964, on his study of frames at the Museum, RMA Archives.

61. Executors' report, 14 December 1936, Probate File.

62. Emily Ringling denied having asked Ringling to sell the paintings: "How could I ask him to sell pictures when I knew they were all pledged to New York investors?" Supreme Court, New York, N.Y. County, Emily Ringling plaintiff, 325, SCHA.

63. The cottage was built by Hageman and Harris. *The John and Mable Ringling Museum of Art* (Sarasota: RMA), ca. 1949, 3.

64. *Brooklyn* (N.Y.) *Daily Eagle*, 6 December 1936; interview with J. H. Phillips, RMA Archives.

65. Böhler, 17.

66. *Brooklyn Daily Eagle*, 6 December 1936, RMA Archives.

67. Deed of Gift, 7 September 1927 and 21 January 1930, RMA Archives.

68. *The John and Mable Ringling Museum of Art*, 4.

69. *Sarasota Herald,* 3 August 1927, 1. The initial building permit was for an estimated cost of $235,000, about one-fourth of actual cost. A second expansion lengthened the south wing 145 feet. *Sarasota Herald,* 16 August 1927, 4.

70. J. H. Phillips, claim against the Ringling estate for plans of a proposed art school at an estimated cost of $75,000, 8 March 1937, Probate File. The large quadrangle and extension of the north wing appear in the Phillips drawings. Julius Böhler to Karl Bickel, 29 December 1947.

71. Grace and John H. Phillips to Marian Murray (museum staff), 3 October 1949, RMA Archives.

72. Claim against the Ringling estate by J. H. Phillips of Haff and Farrington, Jamaica, N.Y., for $5,741.12, filed 8 March 1937, Probate File. Phillips to Jonce McGurk, 4 January 1938, SCHA.

73. North, "John and Mable Ringling Museum."

74. Phillips to Jonce McGurk, 4 January 1937, SCHA.

75. Grace and John H. Phillips to Marian Murray, 3 October 1949, RMA Archives.

76. Ibid. A drawing from Phillips's studio is dated 24 January 1936, RMA Archives. Phillips's claim for work on the catacomb and vault, $2,152, 8 March 1937, Probate File.

77. Conversation with Henry Ringling North, November 1986.

78. Letter from J. H. Phillips, *New York Times,* 5 December 1937, Section 12, 13.

79. J. H. Phillips, notes on architectural drawings for the museum, 2 September 1926 and 5 October 1926, RMA Archives.

80. The *New York Times* and the *Sarasota Herald* published photographs of the "Palmieri" door frames and wainscot panels. The same photographs were provided by Ringling for the initial catalog of the Ringling School of Art and Design, published by the school in October 1931, RMA Archives.

81. Emile Moliniere, *Collection Emile Gavet* (Paris: Imprimerie de D. Jouaust, 1889), i.

82. *Sarasota Herald,* 27 December 1929, 9. Inventory of paintings, attached to the Minute Book of the Rembrandt Corporation, 25 July 1932, FSA.

83. *Sarasota Herald,* 4 October 1931, Section 3, 3; Section 1, 9. A partial inventory was published in Section 2, 1.

84. *Art Digest* 6 (1 October 1931), 32; *Sarasota Herald,* 8 October 1931, 1.

85. *New York World,* 16 March 1930 (extract), SCHA.

86. *Sarasota Herald,* 19 June 1928, 1. Reprinted from the *Christian Science Monitor,* 14 June 1928.

87. Conversation with Henry Ringling North, November 1987.

88. Ludd Spivey to Ringling, 15 February 1930, FSCA.

89. Ringling to Spivey, 16 April 1930, FSCA.

90. Ringling to Spivey, 27 May 1930, FSCA.

91. Spivey to Ringling, 29 May 1930; Ringling to Spivey, 11 June 1930; Spivey to Ringling, 17 June 1930, FSCA.

92. Spivey to Ringling, 17 June 1930, FSCA.

93. Addresses of Spivey and Ringling at the dedication of the museum and opening of the school of art/junior college, *Sarasota Herald*, 4 October 1931, Section 1, 5.

94. Spivey to Ringling, 5 March 1931. The trustees accepted the arrangement, which was at best an improvised scheme, lacking any protection from liability in the event of failure. Southern College, *The Southern*, 3 April 1931.

95. *Bulletin No. 1*, Sarasota, Ringling School of Art and Design, 1931, RMA Archives.

96. Spivey to Ringling, 2 September 1931, FSCA.

97. *Sarasota Herald*, 2 October 1931, 1; 3 October 1931, 18.

98. *Art Digest* 5 (1 May 1931), 27; (15 May 1931), 27; 6 (1 October 1931), 28.

99. Spivey to Richard Fuchs (Ringling's secretary): "Unless Ringling pays this account, I must pay it personally. Please see if you cannot do something," 12 July 1932, FSCA.

100. Spivey to Bern Pullard (faculty member), reply to faculty round-robin letters of 1 and 12 December 1932, FSCA.

101. Spivey to Ringling, 23 December 1932; Spivey to Mayor E. A. Smith, 29 April 1933, FSCA.

102. Ringling Trust and Savings Bank statement, 29 April 1933, FSCA.

103. Ringling to Spivey, 18 August 1933, FSCA.

104. Spivey to Atty. E. C. Rice, 16 May 1933; Spivey to H. W. Chandler, Univ. of Florida, 11 March 1933. Spivey's files for 1933, 1934, and 1935 contain nearly one hundred letters seeking payment for art school debts.

105. Ringling to Verman Kimbrough, n.d.; J. H. Phillips to Kimbrough, 14 May 1935; Robert E. Perkins, *The First Fifty Years—Ringling School of Art and Design* (Sarasota: The Ringling School, 1981), RMA Archives.

106. *Sarasota Herald*, 17 January 1932, 4.

107. *Sarasota Herald*, 18 February 1932, 1; 29 February 1932, 1.

108. North, "John and Mable Ringling Museum."

Chapter 8

1. *Sarasota Herald*, 11 July 1930, 1.

2. Ringling to the Advisory Committee of the Out-of-Door School, Sarasota, 18 March 1929, RMA Archives.

3. *Sarasota Herald*, 30 December 1935, 4, editorial.

4. *Sarasota Herald*, 21 January 1930, 4.

5. George D. Lindsay to Ringling, 19 May 1934, RMA Archives.

6. Trial Balance, Eastland, Wichita Falls & Gulf Railroad, 31 August 1930, RMA Archives.

7. U.S. Department of Treasury to John Ringling Estates, Inc., 18 September 1929, RMA Archives.

8. *New York Times*, 4 September 1929.

9. Ibid.

10. William Carey (Madison Square Garden Corporation) to Ringling's attorneys, 15 February 1930. Draft contract dated February 1930, RMA Archives. Circus rent was to be $5,000 per day, excepting $4,000 on Sundays. Letter prepared by William Saxe, endorsed: "We agree to put this contract into effect." Signed by John Ringling and W. F. Carey, RMA Archives.

11. "Prince Dexter, Master of Ballyhoo," *American Magazine* (March 1930). Reprinted in *Sarasota Herald*, 2 March 1930, Section 2, 1.

12. Charles F. Noyes Company (real estate) to Ringling, 5 September 1929, RMA Archives.

13. *The Bandwagon*, published by the Circus Historical Society, n.d., RMA Archives.

14. North, *The Circus Kings*, 219.

15. *Sarasota Herald*, 12 April 1931, 1.

16. Conversation with Merle Evans (circus band leader), February 1987.

17. *Sarasota Herald*, 4 February 1930, 1.

18. *Sarasota Herald*, 4 February 1930, 1; *New York Times*, 5 February 1930.

19. *Sarasota Herald*, 6 February 1930, 1, 2; 7 March 1930, 1.

20. *Sarasota Herald*, 14 February 1930, 1; 29 August 1930, 1.

21. *Sarasota Herald*, 16 April 1930, 1.

22. TAMS Inc. (Yacht Brokers and Naval Architects) to Ringling, 31 May 1934; Ringling to TAMS, 9 April 1934, RMA Archives.

23. *Sarasota Herald*, 14 March 1930, 1.

24. *Sarasota Herald*, 26 January 1930, 1; 13 March 1930, 1.

25. *Sarasota Herald*, 19 March 1930, 1 (banner headline).

26. *Sarasota Herald*, 14 February 1930, 1.

27. U.S. Department of Treasury, Bureau of Internal Revenue to officers of the John Ringling Estates, Inc., 18 September 1929, RMA Archives.

28. Richard Fuchs testimony, appeal by Emily Ringling to the Supreme Court of Florida, 229, 230; letter from Fuchs to Ringling, 23 January 1934, attached as an exhibit to the proceedings.

29. Sarasota County Court Chancery Orders, #2135, book 20, 131. Ringling had secured an injunction to prevent the removal of the disputed bonds from the safety deposit box.

30. *New York Times*, 20 November 1930, 38; *Sarasota Herald*, 24 November 1930. The report of Mable's personal property at $750,000 is most likely an error.

Her personal property was mostly in the form of jewelry. Without an appraisal, no value can be placed upon it, but $75,000 seems reasonable. Mable left no will, an inaction that would be out of keeping for an estate of nearly $1 million.

31. Affidavit of Harold R. Brophy, 12 July 1946, Probate File.

32. Conversation with Lillian Burns, August 1986; *Sarasota Herald*, 14 September 1931, 1. No transfer was recorded to verify the sale.

33. *Sarasota Herald*, 27 April 1931, 9.

34. There are actually twenty-two galleries. The Round Gallery under the bridge between the north and south wings was used to store the Cesnola and Julien Grau collections. It was not open to the public. *Sarasota Herald*, 9 January 1930, 9; 21 March 1930, 1; 25 March 1930, 1; 31 March 1930, 1.

35. *Sarasota Herald*, 16 November 1930, 1; 21 November 1930, 1; 1 December 1930, 1.

36. Testimony of Emily Ringling, Supreme Court of New York, New York County. Emily Ringling, plaintiff, 8 May 1935, 63. Appeal to the Supreme Court of Florida, 2 November 1937, 268, SCHA.

37. Testimony of John Ringling, New York Supreme Court, 8 May 1935, 579. Testimony of Emily Ringling, 66, SCHA.

38. Testimony of Frank Hennessy, ibid., 272; Emily Ringling, 77; John Ringling, 586, SCHA.

39. Conversation with Harriet Burket Taussig, June 1986; *Sarasota Herald*, 26 December 1930, 4.

40. *Sarasota Herald*, 28 December 1930, 7.

41. *Sarasota Herald*, 13 January 1931, 3; 14 January 1931, 3; 1 March 1931, 6.

42. *Sarasota Herald*, 23 January 1931, 7; 28 January 1931, 3.

43. *Sarasota Herald*, 18 March 1931, 1.

44. *Sarasota Herald*, 31 July 1931, 1.

45. Testimony of Emily Ringling, appeal to the Supreme Court of Florida from the Circuit Court of Sarasota County, 7.

46. *Sarasota Herald*, 20 February 1931, 7.

47. *Sarasota Herald*, 5 April 1931, 1; Conversation with Merle Evans, February 1987.

48. *Sarasota Herald*, 31 August 1931, 1.

49. *Sarasota Herald*, 22 April 1922, 5.

50. *Sarasota Herald*, 17 September 1932, 1; 20 September 1932, 1.

51. *Sarasota Herald*, 1 April 1932, 1.

52. *New York Times*, 25 May 1932, 23; *Sarasota Herald*, 24 May 1932, 1. Ludd Spivey urged Ringling to state a formal opening with the museum trustees present, but Ringling preferred to open the museum without ceremony. Spivey to Ringling, 17 November 1931, FSCA.

53. *Sarasota Herald*, 4 March 1932, 3 (editorial).

54. *Sarasota Herald,* 12 July 1932, 2; Testimony of Richard Fuchs, Appeal to the Supreme Court of Florida, 232.

55. *Sarasota Herald,* 12 July 1932, 2. Reprints from the *New York World Telegram,* 17 July 1932; *Chicago Tribune,* 12 July 1932, SCHA.

56. Testimony of Richard Fuchs, Appeal to the Supreme Court of Florida, 232.

57. Conversation with Henry Ringling North, November 1986.

58. Testimony of John Ringling, Appeal to the Supreme Court of Florida, op. cit. 95. Testimony of Emily Ringling, 308–9.

59. Details of the New York Investors note and negotiations are contained in the affidavit of Henry D. Frost, attorney for the John Ringling estate, 1 May 1944, FSA.

60. Francis T. Pender, for Allied Owners, 25 June 1937, Probate File.

61. Affidavit of Henry D. Frost.

62. Minutes of the meeting, Board of Directors, Rembrandt Corporation, 26 July 1932, FSA.

63. Letter from John Ringling to the Rembrandt Corporation, 26 July 1932, FSA.

64. Stock transfer sheets, Rembrandt Corporation, FSA.

65. John Ringling, letter giving proxies, etc., August 1932, RMA Archives.

66. *Sarasota Herald,* 13 September 1932, 1.

67. *Sarasota Herald,* 3 October 1932, 1.

68. *Sarasota Herald,* 12 December 1932, 1.

69. *Sarasota Herald,* 9 August 1932, 1; 11 August 1932, 1.

70. *Billboard,* November 1932; *Sarasota Herald,* 17 November 1932, 1; *White Tops,* Golden Jubilee Issue, July–August 1933; *Sarasota Herald,* 25 November 1932, 5; 2 April 1933, 1.

71. Conversation with Henry Ringling North, November 1986.

72. Testimony of Richard Fuchs, Appeal to the Supreme Court of Florida, 235, SCHA.

73. Testimony of Ina B. Sanders (nurse to John Ringling), ibid., 164.

74. Testimony of Richard Fuchs, Appeal to the Supreme Court of Florida, 242.

75. Testimony of Ida North, ibid, 434; Ch. Mortgages Book 7, 331, 4 August 1933, Sarasota County Court.

76. Ringling to Ida North, 24 August 1933. Courtesy of Henry Ringling North, private papers of Ida Ringling North.

77. Chancery Orders, book 7, 345, 1 September 1933, Sarasota County Court. Ringling retained the right to hang the paintings in his home and at the museum.

78. Chancery Orders, book 29, 483, 1 September 1933, no. 1983 (motion and order dismissing petition of John Ringling); *Sarasota Herald,* 27 July 1933, 1.

79. *Sarasota Herald,* 26 November 1933, 1; 15 December 1933, 1.

80. *Sarasota Herald,* 4 January 1934, 1; 7 June 1934, 1.

81. Testimony of Dr. Joseph Halton, Appeal to the Supreme Court of Florida, 169.

82. Arrears on the Madison Avenue office rent were paid in June 1934 with funds from the Rockland Oil Company sent by Tide Cox to John North. Grocers, Rolls Royce rentals, and other New York suppliers were increasingly persistent in their demands for payment. Memorandum of taxes for 1931, 1932, 1933, and 1934, RMA Archives; C. G. Strohmeyer to Ringling, 19 August 1935, RMA Archives.

83. Richard Fuchs to Ringling, 27 February 1934.

84. Ibid.

85. Response of the executors of the John Ringling estate to the petition filed by the State of Florida demanding that they post bond, 75, FSA.

86. Eugene L. Garey, petition for payment of legal fees, April 1937, Probate File.

87. *Sarasota Herald,* 4 March 1934, 1; 5 March 1935, 5.

88. Tax receipt, Clerk of the Sarasota Circuit Court, 7 October 1935, RMA Archives; Leo Ritter (Pacific Finance Corporation) to attorneys for John Ringling, 19 July 1935, RMA Archives; Sarasota County Court, Assignment of Mortgages, book 14, 371, 504; Darden Haley (general and salvage contractor) to Ringling, 2 August 1934, RMA Archives.

89. Petition by Albert E. Fitzpatrick for legal fees assigned by Choate, La-Rocque, and Mitchell, 29 April 1939, FSA.

90. *Sarasota Herald,* 15 July 1934, 1.

91. "Mr. Ringling's Own Three Ring Domestic Circus," *American Weekly* (16 February 1936), SCA.

92. Ringling to George Lindsay, editor of the *Sarasota Herald,* 5 November 1934, RMA Archives. Draft letter for publication prepared by Ringling, n.d., RMA Archives.

93. Conversation with Henry Ringling North, November 1986; Transcribed interview with Mrs. Al Roan, 27 October 1981, Eton Florida Room, Manatee County Central Library.

94. Eugene L. Garey, Deposition, 25 June 1946, Probate File.

95. Testimony of Eugene L. Garey, Ina B. Sanders, and Frank Hennessy at the New York Bar Association, 27 August 1937, FSA; Report of investigation in New York, Doyle E. Carlton, FSA.

96. Doyle E. Carlton, report. Hennessy said that Ringling told him he had destroyed the codicil.

97. Private correspondence, Ringling and Ida North, North Family Papers.

98. Ringling's draft letter to the press, n.d., RMA Archives.

99. Conversation with Merle Evans, February 1987.

100. *Sarasota Herald,* 21 May 1936, 12.

101. *Business Week,* 27 April 1935, 22, 23.

102. *Time,* 27 July 1935.

103. *Sarasota Herald,* 11 November 1936, 1.

Chapter 9

1. *New York Times,* 5 December 1936, 19; *Sarasota Herald,* 6 December 1936, 1; *Billboard,* 12 December 1936, 1. Lengthy biographies appeared in the *New York Times,* 2 December 1936, 27; 3 December 1936, 25.

2. *New York Times,* 3 December 1936, 25.

3. Affidavit of Henry D. Frost (attorney for the executors), 1 May 1944, RESF/FSA.

4. Codicil to John Ringling's will, dated 2 November 1935; submitted to the Sarasota County Court, 12 December 1936; entered for probate, 12 September 1938, RESF/FSA.

5. Heirs of John Ringling recognized by the court at the beginning of the probate process: Ida Ringling North, 62, sister; Robert Ringling, 39, nephew; Hester (Mrs. Charles) Sanford, 43, niece; Henry Ringling, 30, nephew; Alice (Mrs. Rollo) Coerper, 47, niece; Mattie Burnett, 49, niece; Lorene Cowgil, 52, niece; Paul Ringling, 16, grandnephew; Jane Ringling, 15, grandniece; Mable Ringling, 12, grandniece.

6. Emily Ringling entered her claim to dower rights on 23 December 1936, Probate File. Petition granted, 23 December 1936, reopening the divorce suit of Emily vs. John Ringling, substituting the executors and heirs as defendants. *Sarasota Herald,* 11 February 1937, 1; 21 February 1937, 1; 27 February 1937, 1; Conversation with Henry Ringling North, November 1986.

7. First report of executors, 31 December 1937. Cash at the time of Ringling's death was $296.33, Probate File. The cash balance of the Ringling Isles Corporation was $4,717.74.

8. The sum of $9,000 was paid from museum admissions on 6 January 1937 and again on 28 February 1937. State objections were based on lack of proof that the residence was part of the museum. Transcript of hearing on 25 May 1939, testimony of John North, respondent. Testimony of John Burket, application for attorney fees, 1 March 1943, 34, 96.

9. *Sarasota Herald,* 1 January 1937, 1.

10. Affidavit of Harold R. Brophy, 12 July 1945, RESF/FSA.

11. Ringling's loan from the Manufacturers Trust Company had required impounding three paintings in a warehouse with a nontransferable receipt. They were Titian's *Nobleman with a Page,* Veronese's *Portrait of a Lady,* and Moroni's *Portrait of a Man* (1936 attributions). Memorandum in James Haley's copy of the estate appraisal (undated memorandum), SCHA; H. R. Brophy affidavit, RESF/FSA.

12. Bertha Verby to John North, 12 December 1936; 15 December 1937, RMA Archives.

13. Claims against the estate of John Ringling. Claimants were allowed eight months for filing. Petition of executors, 3 May 1945, Probate File. A lien for $146.96 was filed by Martin Roehr against Ca' d'Zan for repairs; Sarasota County lien book 5, 197.

14. Conversation with Henry North, November 1986.

15. Ringling cited that local prejudice in advice to Emily, urging her to engage Sarasota counsel only in contesting his divorce suit.

16. Petition of John and Ida North upon placing the will of John Ringling in probate, 12 December 1936. The codicil was only deposited, Probate File.

17. Conversation with Lillian Burns (daughter of Owen Burns), January 1986.

18. Claims included: Henry L. Williford, approximately $200,000 for the Ringling divorce; Choate, LaRocque and Mitchell, $200,000; Eugene L. Garey, $43,000; John H. Phillips, museum architect, $5,700. Family loans included: Ida North, $79,899 (1933–34); Salomé Wadsworth (daughter of Ida North), $2,000; Randolph Wadsworth (husband of Salomé), $15,000. Emily Ringling claimed $78,085.33 (her $50,000 loan plus interest since 1933).

19. Collateral pledged by Ringling included Santa Fe Railroad bonds with a face value of $450,000 and $100,000 in Sarasota County bonds. Inventory of Assets, Probate File.

20. "John Ringling Properties to Go on Market," *Sarasota Herald*, 7 March 1937, 1; 11 March 1937, 1; 21 March 1937, 1.

21. Ringling's estate was subject to laws of Delaware, New Jersey, Florida, Oklahoma, Nebraska, Wisconsin, Indiana, and Montana.

22. H. R. Brophy affidavit, 12 July 1946, RESF/FSA. Executors petition, 1 October 1937, Probate File.

23. Ibid.

24. At the time of Ringling's death, there was an unpaid balance of $1,117,320.67 on the so-called circus note held by Allied Owners (subsidiary of New York Investors) personally endorsed by Ringling. Note due with 6 percent interest on 6 November 1937. Balance on note to Manufacturers Trust Company was $124,402.99. Collateral consisted of nearly all his assets. H. R. Brophy affidavit.

25. Approaches were made to D. E. Ryan, vice-president of Investor Syndicate of Minneapolis; John F. Fitzpatrick and Clarence Bumberger of Salt Lake City; Carl Beal of Los Angeles. H. R. Brophy affidavit.

26. Ibid.

27. *Fortune* 6 (1 July 1947), 114, 161–67.

28. Court approval of the loan agreement between the executors and the Manufacturers Trust Company of New York, 11 October 1937.

29. James A. Haley to Governor Collins, 3 May 1954, SCHA; Conversation with Alice Myers (administrative assistant to Congressman Haley), June 1985.

30. John Ringling will, 19 May 1934; entered for probate, 12 December 1936.

31. Chapter 18131, Laws of Florida, 1937.

32. James A. Haley to Governor Leroy Collins, 3 May 1957, Haley Papers, Florida Southern College.

33. A. Everett Austin, Jr. (director of the museum). Budget request for 1952, RMA Archives.

34. James A. Haley to Robert A. Gray (Florida secretary of state), 8 September 1969, Haley Papers, Florida Southern College.

35. The lobbying effort led by the executors to secure state acceptance included John Burket and James Haley of Sarasota, and Velma Keen of Tallahassee. Later, the state objected, claiming that the executors had wrongfully charged the costs to the estate.

36. Editorials cited in the *Sarasota Herald* included: *Miami Daily News, Tampa Tribune,* Jacksonville *Times Union,* and Arcadia *Arcadian.*

37. *Sarasota Herald,* 12 March 1937, 1; 9 April 1937, 1, 8; 18 April 1937, 1.

38. *Sarasota Herald,* 22 April 1937, 1; 23 April 1937, 1.

39. "Ringling Art Museum Decaying, Circus Millions in Treasure Suffer Lack of Care," *Sarasota Herald,* 8 April 1937, 1. Reprinted from the *Literary Digest,* 10 April 1937.

40. *Sarasota Herald,* 8 April 1937, 1.

41. *Sarasota Herald,* 24 April 1937, 3. Ida North declared that "The executors are at a loss to know what possible news angle could have prompted the story."

42. "Gift Football," *Literary Digest* 123 (29 May 1937), 24. Contains a partial retraction of the earlier article of 24 April 1937 about the decayed condition of the building and the collection. The second article attempts, with an array of statements, to maintain the same position. *Sarasota Herald,* 29 April 1937, 4 and editorial; 14 May 1937, 1.

43. Phillips Exhibition, Ringling Museum of Art, prepared by Marian Murray, released 17 August 1949, 6.

44. *Sarasota Herald,* 29 April 1937, 1.

45. *Sarasota Herald,* 14 May 1937, 1.

46. *Sarasota Herald,* 6 May 1937, 1.

47. *Sarasota Herald,* 2 April 1937, 1; 23 April 1937, 1; 24 April 1937, 1.

48. *Sarasota Herald,* 18 April 1937, 1.

49. *Sarasota Herald,* 9 April 1937, 1; 28 May 1937, 1.

50. Chapter 18131, Laws of Florida, 1937.

51. Last Will and Testament of John Ringling, 19 May 1934, Section 2, Part C; Chapter 18131, Laws of Florida. The conditions that were embodied in the legislation were agreed upon by the governor, the attorney general, the leaders of the Florida legislature, John Burket of Sarasota, Henry D. Frost (attorney for the

estate), William Davis of Ardmore, Oklahoma, Velma Keen of Tallahassee, Harold R. Brophy of New York, James A. Haley, estate attorney, and the executors.

52. Conversation with Henry North, November 1987.

53. *Sarasota Herald,* 13 January 1938, 1; 10 February 1938, 1.

54. Sarasota County Court, executors' appointment request, 30 November 1937; Court order, 31 December 1937, Probate File. Inventory of the Ringling estate, 51-2, SCHA. James Haley to George Higgins (chairman, museum board of trustees), 10 February 1960, Haley Papers, Florida Southern College.

55. Dwight James Baum to Jonce McGurk, 5 January 1938; John H. Phillips to Jonce McGurk, 4 January 1938, SCHA; *Sarasota Herald,* 4 February 1938, 1.

56. Jonce McGurk, résumé of his qualifications and experience, n.d. Copy attached to James Haley's copy of the estate appraisal, SCHA.

57. Karl Freund, Foreword to the section on Cypriote and classical antiquities in the estate appraisal. Freund's appraisal of some objects tends to support the attorney general's opinion that the estate was assigned greatly inflated values. Roof statues at the museum valued at $2,000 were later replaced from the original source at $130. New columns valued as "pre-seventeenth century" were listed at $2,000 each. Those errors alone inflated the estate by some $200,000.

58. Inventory of objects located in the storage rooms at Ca' d'Zan.

59. Ibid. The three crated rooms (French and Italian) are no longer at the museum.

60. Fourth annual report of the executors, 31 March 1941, Probate File.

61. Objection by the Florida attorney general, filed with the Sarasota County Court, 30 April 1939, Probate File.

62. Conversation with Alice Myers, June 1985. Appraisers' fees were disputed. Petition for the appraisers' fee filed 8 October 1938. Executors petition to the court, 7 January 1942; court order, 20 January 1942. McGurk was paid $3,000 upon completion of the appraisal. He waited three years for the next payment. He later demanded $30,000 and settled for $15,000. Haley and Van Dame charged the estate $23,000.

63. With the circus note refinanced the money lenders' clique was evicted from control. The New York Investor–Allied Owners team resigned from the circus directors: Sam Gumpertz, Francis Pender, William Greve, and T. Grant Caldwell. Carl Hathaway, a longtime and trusted member of the circus staff, was named general manager. *New York Times,* 10 December 1937, 28. For the Edith and Aubrey Ringling claims and counterclaims, see Report by the executors, 12 August 1937. Claim filed by Edith and Aubrey Ringling, 4 August 1937; Objection filed 13 June 1938. Executors' response, 30 June 1939; Executors' petition for settlement, 7 August 1940; Circus debt recognized by Edith and Aubrey Ringling, 19 October 1940; Agreement ordered by the Sarasota County Court, 5 November 1940, Probate File. The sequence is indicative of the slow pace of estate affairs, generally working to the advantage of the executors.

64. "Ringling Wrangling."

65. Bill of complaint, Florida attorney general, 6 November 1939. Appeal by state of Florida to reverse court order regarding posting bond by executors, 11 October 1940, Probate File.

66. Petition by the executors regarding the Hartford fire, 27 June 1945. Petition of Robert and Hester Ringling, 26 March 1946, Probate File.

67. Agreement of 26 January 1940. Newman and Bisco and Allied Owners Corporation, Goldwater and Flynn, attorneys to Newman and Bisco, 26 January 1940. Bisco to Carl Loos (attorney), 19 April 1940, Probate File. By this maneuver, Bisco captured the one hundred circus shares that Ringling had allowed to fall into the hands of Allied Owners. In a complex series of steps, fifteen shares were delivered to Edith and fifteen to Aubrey. Seventy shares went to John North, who later acquired three hundred shares from the estate, plus three hundred from Aubrey Ringling. *New York Times*, 16 November 1947, 65.

68. One day after his first divorce suit was withdrawn in August 1933, Ringling gave Emily chattel mortgage on the five paintings. In return, Emily renewed his note for $50,000 for four years at 6 percent. In the agreement, Ringling forfeited title but retained the right to hang the following paintings in his home and in the museum: Moroni's *Benvenutti*, Rembrandt's *St. John* and *Portrait of a Lady*, Hals's *Olycan*, and Titian's *Queen of Cyprus*. Sarasota County Court, Mortgages, Book 7, 345, 1 September 1933. Following Ringling's death, Emily filed for foreclosure in Circuit Court. Chancery Orders, Book 50, 262, 28 March 1937. Special Master Barringer was given court authority to sell two paintings, but only *St. John* was sold to satisfy the debt.

69. William F. Dunn to John North, 24 May 1939, RESF/FSA.

70. Sarasota County Court, Satisfactions and Judgments, book 6, 445; third annual report of the executors, 30 March 1946, RMA Archives.

71. Bisco to Doyle Carlton, 11 January 1946. Settlement with Emily Ringling, Probate File.

72. Executors petition for court approval of tax compromise, 18 February 1942; court approval, 24 March 1942, Probate File.

73. James A. Haley to Robert A. Gray, 8 September 1969, Haley Papers. Newman and Bisco retained the firm of White and Case to assist them through the final settlement. Claim for fee submitted by executors, 16 March 1945, Probate File.

74. Executors petition to the court. The executors and their attorneys' fees had been subordinated to the bank's note. The new note was to run for only one year, but the executors were informally assured that the bank would not damage the integrity of the estate by forcing the disposal of assets to pay off the note, 18 February 1942, Probate File. Court response to petition required that the circus must pay off its note to the estate before any dividends were paid to shareholders. State opposition, 13 March 1942, 24 March 1942, Probate File.

75. Sixth annual return, 31 December 1942. In 1942, the estate realized more than $700,000 income, 28 May 1943, Probate File.

76. The Florida National Bank stipulated in its loan proposal that it would insist on a mortgage on the paintings in the museum as part of the collateral, 23 March 1942, Probate File.

77. Petition by the executors. Collateral was to include Ida North's shares (998) in the Ringling Isles Corporation, the St. Armands Realty shares, circus shares (300), the shares of the Sarasota Oil Company, the Rockland Oil Company, and the Rembrandt Corporation, Probate File.

78. Petition of the executors, 17 September 1943. H. R. Brophy affidavit, 12 July 1946; court order, 10 April 1944, Probate File.

79. Director of the state geological survey, Hiram Gunter, added fuel to the controversy. He testified at a hearing that "sugarland" in Collier County had been found to have oil deposits. Belief persisted that the Sarasota area would produce oil someday. Hearing, 15 January 1944; Humble Oil Company letters to the trustees of the Internal Improvement Fund, 22 November 1943.

80. Petition by the executors and court order approving the sale, 31 March 1944, 24 May 1944, Probate File; Bisco to Carlton, 22 August 1945, RESF/FSA.

81. Disallowed loss claimed on Ringling's 1931 income tax return. H. R. Brophy affidavit, RESF/FSA.

82. Court order and summary of Montana land transactions, 30 July 1945, Probate File.

83. Court approval for transfers of funds: Ringling Isles and John Ringling Hotel, 26 August 1947, Probate File.

84. Report on investigation in New York, prepared by Carlton, n.d.; Bisco to Carlton, 30 October 1945, RESF/FSA.

85. Heirs at law vs. John North and Ida North, taken to the Florida Supreme Court, 13 June 1947. Appeal to the Sarasota Circuit Court, 8 September 1947; Bisco to Carlton, 6 December 1946. Sarasota County Court, final decrees, 3 January 1947. Claim of the surviving relatives of John Ringling dismissed, 23 January 1947.

86. Executors to Governor Millard Caldwell, 26 January 1946, RESF/FSA; *Sarasota Herald*, 27 January 1946, 1. Executors return for 1946, 15 May 1947. Values established for the bequest: Ca' d'Zan contents, $865,000; Rembrandt Corporation, $11,095,305. Five additional paintings at New York warehouse, $41,000.

87. Executors to Governor Caldwell, 7 February 1946, RESF/FSA.

88. Bisco to Carlton, 16 August 1946. In April 1946, conversations began on the idea of a syndicate to take over all remaining assets of the estate, RESF/FSA. Robert A. Gray, "Brief History of the Ringling Estate," unpublished memorandum, n.d., Robert Gray Papers, Florida State Archives, Tallahassee.

1. Caples to Dr. J. B. Scully, Sarasota Park Board, 6 January 1945, RESF/FSA.

2. Recollection of Karl Bickel, 1946, *St. Petersburg Times*, 16 December 1956, RESF/FSA.

3. Bisco to Carlton, 4 February 1946, RESF/FSA.

4. Memorandum by William Suida, 9 April 1941, RESF/FSA; Conversation with Henry Ringling North, November 1986.

5. Suida memorandum.

6. Unsigned memorandum, probably by W. E. Suida, n.d., RMA Archives.

7. Caples to Dr. J. B. Scully, 6 January 1945, RESF/FSA.

8. "Field Notes," *American Magazine of Art* (23 October 1931), 337.

9. Report of the Survey of the Ringling Museum of Art; Director's report to the committee, 12 January 1953, 6ff.

10. Report to the director, 7 November 1946; Report of February 1949.

11. Ringling Museum' of Art Release for the Phillips exhibition of sketches, 7 August 1945, 5, RMA Archives.

12. Director's budget request for 1951–53, RMA Archives.

13. Report of the director,16 November 1950, RMA Archives.

14. Diorio's films were thought to be a fire hazard. In consequence, they were destroyed by the museum staff.

15. Caesare Diorio, "Report of my Employment as a Restorer," New York, 22 June 1953, 6, RMA Archives.

16. Ibid., 9. Using the discarded pieces of marble as weights for pressure, Diorio double-relined other large canvases, such as Jan Fyt's *The Calydonia Hunt*, J. de Ribera's *The Flaying of Marsyas*, and Frans Snyders's *Still Life.*

17. Ibid., 13, 17, 23, 26. The carpenter's work was not wholly responsible for the damaged condition. The Madonna was also damaged in transit on its return journey from Naples, where it had been on exhibition. Interventions on the Rembrandt—the panel was shaved (reduced) on the reverse, the joints were filled to excess with gesso—cannot be undone.

18. Director's report, April 1948, May 1949, RMA Archives.

19. Director's report, December 1949, RMA Archives.

20. Report of the Survey of the Ringling Museum of Art, 12 January 1953, 6; Director's report to the committee. Panel members were Francis Henry Taylor, director of the Metropolitan Museum of Art; Daniel Cotton Rich, director of the Chicago Art Institute; Charles H. Sawyer, dean of the Yale School of Fine Arts; and Hugh F. McKean, president of Rollins College.

21. Executors return for 1946; Executors to Governor Caldwell, 8 February 1946; Memorandum of Robert A. Gray, 27–29 November 1948; Gray to the Board of Commissioners, 3 December 1948; Gray to the Board of Control, 12 August 1954, RESF/FSA.

22. Director's report 1949, RMA Archives.

23. Ibid.

24. Director's report to the Board, 7 November 1946; Report of the director, 9 December 1949; Annual report of the director for 1949, RMA Archives.

25. John Garland (state auditor) to J. T. Diamond (Board of Commissioners), 27 May 1946, RMA Archives.

26. Girouard, *Houses of Historic Britain*, 8.

27. *ARTnews Annual*, 1950, 3.

28. A. H. Mayor, "The Greatest Show Down South," *ARTnews* (June 1948), 47.

29. Julius Böhler to Karl Bickel, 29 December 1947, RMA Archives.

30. *Atlanta Journal* (Georgia), interview with John Ringling. Reprinted in the *Sarasota Herald*, 26 October 1931, 1.

❧ BIBLIOGRAPHY ❧

The principal documentary sources for an account of John Ringling's Florida career are found in papers relating to the liquidation of his estate. The Ringling Estate Subject Files at the Florida State Archives are papers assembled by state officials plus correspondence with the executors of Ringling's estate. A probate file at the Sarasota County Courthouse contains material produced by the executors, claimants against the estate, and correspondence with the court (forty-five volumes). Archives of Florida Southern College at Lakeland, Florida, include correspondence between Ringling and the college president and former head of the first Ringling School of Art, Ludd M. Spivey.

Sarasota newspapers contain voluminous material; I drew heavily on the *Sarasota Times* (1911–25), *This Week in Sarasota* (1925–26), and the *Sarasota Herald,* 1926–47. The *Manatee River Journal* (and its successors) and the *Bradenton Herald* contain little of Sarasota news. Sarasota County court records for 1921–47 and Manatee County records for 1911–21 contain complete records of Ringling's real estate transactions. His personal papers were seized by the Bureau of Internal Revenue. Files taken to Miami were for investigation into his Sarasota activities; files taken to New York were part of the investigation into the circus tax fraud that extended from 1918 to 1936.

"A. Everett Austin Appointed Director." *Museum News* 24, no. 3 (15 June 1946): 3.
Albee, Luella A. *Doctor and I.* Detroit: S. J. Block Publishing, 1951.
Albrecht, Ernest, J. *A Ringling by Any Other Name.* Metuchen, N.J.: Scarecrow Press, 1989.

Andrews, Wayne. *Architecture, Ambition, and Americans.* New York: Free Press, 1978.

Arsenault, Raymond. *St. Petersburg and the Florida Dream 1888–1959.* Norfolk, Va.: Donning, 1988.

Arslan, Edoard. *Gothic Architecture in Venice.* Translated by Anne Engel. London: Phaidon Press, 1972.

"Astor Residence." *American Architect and Building News* 48, no. 1017 (22 June 1895): plates.

Austin, A. Everett, Jr. "The Baroque." *ARTnews* 19 (1950 annual): 12–32.

Baldwin, Charles C. *Stanford White.* New York: Dodd Mead, 1931.

Baum, Dwight J. "The Architecture of Houses." *Country Life* 52 (October 1927): 52–53.

———. "Mediterranean Beauty in America." *American Home* (4 April 1930): 38–39.

———. "Small Italian Villa Comes To Dwell among Us." *Ladies Home Journal* 42 (April 1925): 24.

Beatty, J. "Dexter Fellows, the Master of Ballyhoo." *American Magazine* 109 (March 1930): 62–67.

Benson, Robert E., ed. *The Holford Collection—Dorchester House.* 2 vols. Oxford: Oxford University Press, 1927.

———. *The Holford Collection, Westonbirt.* Privately printed for R. E. Benson et al., 1924.

———. and Evelyn Benson, *Catalog of Italian Pictures Collected by Robert and Evelyn Benson.* London: Chiswick Press, 1914.

Bickel, Karl A. *The Mangrove Coast.* New York: Coward-McCann, 1942.

Böhler, Julius. *The Art Museum John Ringling Built.* Sarasota: John and Mable Ringling Museum of Art, 1949.

———. "Ringling—Collector and Builder." In Marian Murray, ed., *The Ringling Museum, a Magnificent Gift to the State of Florida.* Sarasota: The John and Mable Ringling Museum of Art, RMA Archives, ca. 1949.

Bradna, Fred A. (as told to Hartnell Spence). *The Big Top—My Forty Years with the Greatest Show on Earth.* New York: Simon and Schuster, 1952.

Browning, Alex. "A Pioneer Railroad and its Conductor." Unpublished memoir. Sarasota County Department of Historical Resources, 1931.

Burns, Lillian G. "John Hamilton Gillespie." In *Sarasota Origins.* Sarasota: The Historical Society of Sarasota County, 1988.

Burns Papers. Letters, telegrams, and photographs, ca. 1910–39. Most are from Owen Burns's Sarasota business affairs, including his dealings with John Ringling. Privately owned by Lillian G. Burns.

"Catalog of Paintings in the John and Mable Ringling Museum of Art by W. E. Suida." Review. *Art Quarterly* 12, no. 4 (1949): 386.

Cesnola, Luigi Palma di. *Cyprus, Its Ancient Cities, Tombs and Temples.* New York: Harper and Brothers, 1887.

"Circus Taxes, Income Tax Frauds." *Time* 28 (27 July 1935): 54, 65.

Coerper, Alice. "The Ringlings of Baraboo." In Charles P. Fox, *A Ticket to the Circus.* New York: Bramhall House, 1959.

Cordner, Frank. "The Original Building of the John and Mable Ringling Museum of Art." *Florida Architect* (September–October 1970): 16–19.

Dearing, Albin P. *The Elegant Inn. The Waldorf Astoria Hotel 1893–1929.* Secaucus, N.J.: Lyle Stuart, 1986.

"Developing a Regional Type with Particular Reference to the Work in Florida of Dwight James Baum." *American Architect* 130, no. 2503 (20 August 1926): 144–48.

"Died, John Ringling." *Newsweek* 8 (12 December 1936): 48.

Eco, Umberto. Translated by William Weaver. *Travels in Hyperreality.* New York: Harcourt Brace Jovanovich, 1986.

Fenlon, Paul E. "The Struggle for the Control of the Florida Railroads (1867–1882). A Case Study of Business Enterprise in Post-Civil War Florida." Ph.D. diss. Gainesville, University of Florida, 1955.

Fitch, James. *American Building: The Forces That Shape It.* Boston: Houghton Mifflin, 1948.

Folsom, Merrill. *Great Mansions and Their Stories.* New York: Hastings House, 1963.

Frankfurter, Alfred M. "John Ringling's Greatest Show." *ARTnews* 19 (1950 annual): 3–11.

Fuller, Walter P. "Manatee County 1860 Census." Manatee County Historical Society, 1968. Unpublished manuscript.

Galerie Georges Petit. *Trois Importantes Tapisseries du XVII Siècle.* Paris, 22 May 1928, 64.

"Gift Football: Florida Politicians Wrangle over Ringling Museum." *Literary Digest* 123 (29 May 1937): 24.

"Gift of the Ringling Museum to the State of Florida." *School and Society* 46, no. 1182 (21 August 1937): 248–49.

Gollmar, Robert H. *My Father Owned a Circus.* Caldwell, Ohio: Caxton Printers, 1965.

Gordon, Taylor. *Born to Be.* New York: Covici-Friede, 1929.

Grace, John P. "Ringing Bros. Circus Year by Year." *White Tops* 7, no. 3–4 (July–August 1933): 16–19.

Gray, Robert A. "A Brief History of the Ringling Estate." Unpublished personal memoir. Robert Gray Papers, Florida State Archives, n.d.

Grismer, Karl H. *The Story of Sarasota.* Tampa: Florida Grower Press, 1977.

Hale, John Rigby, ed. *Renaissance Venice.* Totowa, N.J.: Rowman and Littlefield, 1973.

Harner, Charles J. *Florida's Promoters—The Men Who Made It Big.* Tampa: Trend House, 1973.

Harrower, Ina M. "Famous Paintings in the John and Mable Ringling Museum." *Apollo* 61 (May 1955): 133–35.

"Historical, Architectural, and Archeological Survey of Sarasota, Florida." Bureau of Historic Sites and Properties, Division of Archives, History, and Records Management. Florida Dept. of State. Miscellaneous project report series #51. August 1982.

"How Dear to My Heart Are the Memories of Sarasota." *White Tops* 34, no. 2 (March–April 1961): 3.

"How Ringling Made the Greatest Show Greater." *Literary Digest* 103 (5 October 1929): 36–40.

Jennings, Perry. "John Ringling of Sarasota—The Man to Whom the Wonder City Owes Her Sudden Leap into Prominence." *Suniland,* Tampa (February 1925): 33.

The John and Mable Ringling Museum of Art. Sarasota: John and Mable Ringling Museum of Art, ca. 1949.

Johnson, Dudley S. "The Railroads of Florida," Ph.D. diss. Tallahassee, Florida State University, 1965.

Johnston, John T. "The Cesnola Collection of Cypriote Antiquities in the Metropolitan Museum of Art, New York." Appendix to Cesnola, *Cyprus, Its Ancient Cities, Tombs and Temples.*

Kelley, John M. *Brief in re Estate of Henry Ringling, Alf T. Ringling before the Board of Appeals and Review, Inheritance Tax Division, Treasury Department.* New York: Evening Post Job Printing Office, 1923.

Knecht, Karl K. "Another Story of the Brothers Ringling." *White Tops* 7, no. 3–4 (July–August 1933): 20–23.

Lauritzen, Peter. *Venice: A Thousand Years of Culture and Civilization.* New York: Atheneum, 1978.

McElroy, Annie M. *But Your World and My World.* Sarasota: Black South Press, 1986.

"Madison Square Garden." *American Architect* 128, no. 2487 (20 December 1925): 513–23.

Maher, James T. *The Twilight of Splendor: Chronicles of the Age of American Palaces.* Boston: Little, Brown, 1975.

———. "A View of the Water. American Palaces by the Sea." *Holiday* (July 1966): 48–57.

Marth, Del. *Yesterday's Sarasota, Including Sarasota County.* Miami: A. E. Seeman Publishing, 1973.

Matthews, Janet S. *Edge of Wilderness: A Settlement History of Manatee River and Sarasota Bay, 1528–1885.* Tulsa, Okla.: Cuprine Press, 1983.

———. *Journey to Centennial.* Tulsa, Okla.: Centennial Heritage Press, 1985.

Matthews, Kenneth, and Robert McDevitt. *The Unlikely Legacy: John Ringling, the Circus and Sarasota*. Sarasota: Aaron Publishers, 1979.

May, Earl Chapin. *The Circus from Rome to Ringling*. New York: Dover Publishing, 1963.

Mayor, A. Hyatt. "The Greatest Show Down South." *ARTnews* 47, no. 4 (June 1948): 46, 61.

"Medieval Architecture in a Modern Museum: Views and Plan." *American Architect* 140 (September 1931): 70.

Meserve, Andrew. *General Directory of Manatee County, Florida*. Braidentown, Florida, 1897.

Moliniere, Emile. *Collection Emile Gavet-Catalogue Raisonné*. Paris: Imprimerie de D. Jouaust, 1889.

Murray, Marian. "John Ringling's Home." *Palm Beach Life* (17 January 1956): 29.

———. "Phillips Exhibition." From John and Mable Ringling Museum of Art release, 7 August 1949. Watercolors, drawings and photographs, mostly from J. H. Phillips, RMA Archives.

———. "The Ringling Museum." *Palm Beach Life* (26 March 1957).

———, ed. *The Ringling Museum, a Magnificent Gift to the State of Florida*. Sarasota: The John and Mable Ringling Museum of Art, RMA Archives, ca. 1949.

"Museum Renovated." *Art Digest* 6 (15 December 1946): 13.

Myers, John L. *Handbook of the Cesnola Collections of Antiquities from Cyprus*. New York: Metropolitan Museum of Art, 1914.

Nelson, Kristi. "Jordaens and Three Alexander Tapestries at the Ringling Museum." *Ringling Museum of Art Journal* 1, no. 1 (1983). Paper presented at the International Rubens Symposium, 14–16 April 1982.

North, Henry R. "John and Mable Ringling Museum Has Much of World's Greatest Art." *Sarasota Herald* (5 December 1937): Section 2, 1.

——— and Alden Patch. *The Circus Kings—Our Family Story*. New York: Doubleday, 1960.

Paintings, Furnishings, and Architectural Fittings of the Astor Residence, 840 Fifth Avenue, New York. Auction catalog. New York: American Art Association, April 1926.

Parker, Jere. "Federal Naval Raid on Sarasota Bay, March 23–27, 1874." In *Sarasota Origins*, 1–9. The Historical Society of Sarasota County, 1988.

"Pausias and Glycera Added." *International Studio* 98 (January 1931): 44–45.

Perkins, Robert E. *The First Fifty Years—Ringling School of Art and Design 1931–1981*. Sarasota: Ringling School of Art and Design, 1981.

Perry, Jennings. "John Ringling of Sarasota." *Suniland* (Tampa) (February 1925): 33–35.

Plowden, Gene. *Merle Evans—Maestro of the Circus*. Miami: Seeman Publishing, 1971.

———. *Those Amazing Ringlings and Their Circus*. Caldwell, Ohio: Caxton Printers, 1967.

Pozzetta, George E. "Foreigners in Florida: A Study of Immigration Promotion 1865–1910." *Florida Historical Quarterly* 53, no. 2 (October 1947): 164–80.

Price, Matlack. *The Work of Dwight James Baum, Architect.* New York: William Helburn, 1927.

Raynor, Robert H. "Dwight James Baum, Architect, 1886–1939." M.A. thesis. University of Florida, 1976.

"Residence of John Jacob Astor, Esq. Northeast Corner Sixty-Fifth Street and Fifth Avenue, New York." *American Architect and Architecture* 57, no. 1128 (7 August 1897): plates.

Ringling, Alfred T. *The Life Story of the Ringling Brothers.* Chicago: R. R. Donnelley and Sons, 1900.

Ringling, John. "We Divided the Job but Stuck Together." *National Magazine* (September 1919): 56. Reprinted in Charles P. Fox, *A Ticket to the Circus.* New York: Bramhall House, 1959.

"Ringling Art Museum and School." *American Magazine of Art* 23 (October 1931): 336–39.

"Ringling Art Museum Decaying." *Literary Digest* 123 (10 April 1937): 24.

"Ringling Art Now in Home Which is Museum of Architecture." *Art Digest* 5, no. 18 (1 July 1931): 32.

"Ringling Museum of Art. J. H. Phillips Architect: Views and Floor Plan." *Architectural Forum* 56 (June 1932): 561–62.

"Ringling Museum Renovated." *Art Digest* 21 (15 December 1946): 13.

"Ringling 1933 Circus." *White Tops* 7, no. 3–4 (July–August 1933): 14–15.

"Ringling's Rubens." *Art Digest* 5 (1 November 1930): 8.

"Ringling's School at Sarasota, Florida." *Art Digest* 5, no. 15 (1 May 1931): 27.

"Ringling Wrangling." *Fortune* 36, no. 1 (July 1947): 114, 161–67.

Rischmueller, Marian Campbell. "The Ringlings of McGregor." *Palimpsest* 25, no. 6 (June 1944): 161–92.

Roberts, Kenneth L. *Florida.* New York: Harper and Brothers, 1926.

Roth, Linda H., ed. *J. Pierpont Morgan, Collector—European Decorative Arts from the Wadsworth Atheneum.* Hartford: Wadsworth Atheneum, 1987.

"Sarasota as Art Center." *Art Digest* (15 March 1935): 14.

Sarasota Board of Trade. *Sarasota, Florida and the Sarasota Bay District of Manatee County. 1914–1915.* Sarasota County Historical Archives, ca. 1913.

Sarasota County Commission. *The Truth about Florida.* Sarasota: County Commission, 1925.

"Sarasota Retrospect." *Florida Architect* (September–October 1976).

Schmidt, Pete. "John Ringling, His Impact on Sarasota." *Sarasota Life* 4 (December 1970): 13.

"School of Fine and Applied Art of the John and Mable Ringling Museum of Art." *Bulletin* 1, no. 1 (May 1931).

Sears, Roger F. "A Venetian Palace in Florida." *Country Life* (London) 52 (October 1927): 34–40.

Shaw, Andrew. "The Ringling Brothers and Barnum and Bailey Circus: A Century of the Greatest Show on Earth." M.A. thesis. Durham, N.C.: Duke University, 1971.

Smyth, G. Hutchinson. *Life of Henry B. Plant*. New York: G. P. Putnam's Sons, 1898.

Soby, James T. "The Ringling Art Museum." *Saturday Review* 40 (15 January 1957): 30–31.

Stockbridge, Frank P., and John H. Perry. *Florida in the Making*. New York and Jacksonville, Fla.: De Bower Publishing, 1926.

Sturtevant, C. G. "The Ringling Brothers." *White Tops* 4, no. 3 (July 1950): 7–9.

Sulzer, Elmer G. *Ghost Railroads of Sarasota County. An Account of Abandoned Lines of the County and City*. Sarasota: Sarasota County Historical Society, 1971.

"Survey of Dwight James Baum's Florida Work. Developing a Regional Type—with Special Reference to the Work in Florida of Dwight James Baum." *American Architect* 130, no. 2503 (20 August 1926): 144–48.

Sutton, Horace. "Booked for Travel—John's House." *Saturday Review* (2 March 1957): 31–35.

Taylor, Robert L. *W. C. Fields, His Follies and His Fortunes*. New York: Doubleday, 1949.

Thomas, Richard. *John Ringling, Circus Magnate and Art Patron*. New York: Pageant Press, 1960.

Tischendorf, Alfred P. "Florida and the British Investor." *Florida Historical Quarterly* 33, no. 2 (October 1954): 120–29.

"To Make a Circus Pay." *Fortune* 3 (April 1938): 39.

Tomory, Peter. "John Ringling, the Collector." In *Catalogue of the Italian Paintings before 1800*. Sarasota: The John and Mable Ringling Museum of Art, 1976.

U.S. Department of Commerce, Bureau of the Census. 16th Census 1940. *Population—First Series Number of Inhabitants, Florida*. Washington, D.C.: U.S. Government Printing Office.

Wernick, Robert. "The Greatest Show on Earth Didn't Compare to Home." *Smithsonian* 12 (23 September 1981): 62–71.

Whiffen, Marcus, and Frederick Koeper. *American Architecture 1607–1976*. Cambridge, Mass.: MIT Press, 1981.

Wiener, Samuel G. *Venetian Houses and Details*. New York: Architectural Book Publishing, 1929.

Williamson, Edward C. *Florida Politics in the Gilded Age, 1877–1893*. Gainesville: University Presses of Florida, 1976.

Wittcower, Rudolph. *Architectural Principles in the Age of Humanism*. New York: Random House, 1965.

❦ INDEX ❧

Ringling, Charles, 6, 7; initial role of, as circus orchestra leader and violinist, 11; lifelong role of, as manager of circus crew, 11; relationship of, with JR, 20, 109–10, 255; purchases Shell Beach property, 48; initially little known in Sarasota, 60; named director of Bank of Sarasota, 79; and Sarasota Home Building Co., 93; forms Ringling Trust and Savings Bank, 93; death of, 108–10; popularity of, 110; *Sarasota Herald* reprints inaccurate description of, 157. *See also* Ringling Bros. Circus

Ringling, Della (Mrs. Alf T.), 230

Ringling, Edith: as new partner in circus, 146; attitude of, toward JR, 156; resents JR's independence, 219; and circus control, 219; and sports arena, 222; entertains for Emily R., 228; alarmed by Depression's impact on circus, 230; forms circus voting trust, 230–31; joins JR's creditors, 236; becomes manager of circus, 238; abandons circus control to John North, 278

Ringling, Emily: alleged dislike of, for art collection, 196; appearance of, 226; JR courts, 226; loan from, to JR, 227, 244, 278–79; signs prenuptial agreement, 227–28, 244; marries JR, 227–28; urges JR to resist money lenders' pressure, 235; domestic conflicts of, with JR, 242; refuses to sign for Ca' d'Zan mortgage, 243; divorced by JR, 244, 245–46, 248; escapes court summons, 244; in JR's will, 258; seeks to reverse divorce decree, 259; dower suit of, dismissed, 278; collects prenuptial loan, 278–79; estate recovers Gavet chests from, 279

Ringling, Henry: comanages Adam Forepaugh-Sells Circus, 12; purchases winter home at Eustis, Fla., 50

Ringling, John: ancestry of, 5; birth of, in McGregor, Iowa, 6; start of circus career of, 9–10; marries Mable Burton, 23–24; establishes John and Mable Ringling Museum of Art, 198; marries Emily Buck, 227–28; divorces Emily, 248; final illness and death of, 254. *See also* Ringling, Emily; Ringling, Mable; Ringling Museum of Art

—business of: Sarasota real estate purchases, 41, 73–74, 91; New York office, 51; as Madison Square Garden Corp. director, 52; as Chatham and Phoenix National Bank director, 52; Oklahoma, New Mexico & Pacific RR, 61–62; Rockland Oil Co., 62; Sarasota Oil Co., 62; Northeast Missouri Land and Gravel Co., 62; St. Louis and Hannibal RR, 62; Cardinal Oil Co., 62; White Sulphur Springs & Yellowstone Park RR, 63; Dayton, Toledo & Chicago RR, 63; Eastland, Wichita Falls and Gulf RR, 63; Montana ranch land, 64–65; international livestock market, 64–65; accounting practices, 65; Crow Indian tribe oil leases, 66; with Owen Burns, 74–75; charters JR Estates, Inc., 75; named director of Bank of Sarasota, 79; named chairman of Bank of Sarasota, 153; Sarasota bond issue, 89; vision of Sarasota's future, 115; status of, derived from investments, 136; cuts price of island lots, 143–44; severs working relationship with Burns, 166; El Vernona Hotel, 226; debt of, to Madison National Bank, 229

—and circus: cofounds circus with brothers, 8–9; as clown in, 11; becomes manager of, 11; as only surviving Ringling Bros. partner, 136; as sole decision-maker of circus, 146; purchases American Circus Corp., 219;

of personality of, 168; intellectual aims
of, 169; as art collector, 173, 180; egocentrism of, 174; reputed prodigious
memory of, 179; attitude of, toward Old
Masters, 180; perception of self as a
rich man, 199; loses public approval,
215; judgment error of, in making
circus loan, 219; Owen Burns mistrusts,
225; intransigence of, 234; latent anti-
Semitism of, 250, 286; seen as distant
and arrogant, 255; estranged from R.
Caples, 241; contradictory behavior of,
279

Ringling, Mable: family and early home
of, 22, 23; marriage of, to JR, 23, 24;
avoids publicity, 24; injured in *Salomé*
fire, 54; role of, in Sarasota society, 76;
proposes railroad causeway, 92–93;
fondness of for Italian decor, 114, 119;
helps design interior of Ca' d'Zan, 121–
22; researches Venetian buildings, 123;
lavish entertaining of, at Ca' d'Zan, 156;
illness and recovery of, in Europe, 160;
death of, in New York, 167; commitment of, to founding art school, 206;
estate of, disputed, 224

Ringling, Marie Salomé, 5, 6, 7

Ringling, Marjorie, 253, 282

Ringling, Montana, 63

Ringling, Oklahoma, 62

Ringling, Otto, as treasurer of circus, 9;
character of, 9; impact of death of, on
Ringling brothers, 14, 48–49

Ringling, Richard: Montana ranch holdings of, 65; and Crow Indian oil leases,
66; inherits circus shares, 72; relationship of with JR, 89; attitude of toward
circus, 146; death of, 230

Ringling, Robert: starts opera career, 72;
testifies on Hartford, Conn., circus fire,
277; loses control of circus, 278

Ringling art school: faculty appointments

to, 209; JR and Spivey accept plan for,
209; students of, required to attend
church, 209; emphasis of curriculum on
marine and landscape painting, 211; financial failure of, 212; Ringling Museum school dissolved, 212; new school
formed, 212, 213

Ringling Bros. and Barnum & Bailey
Circus: merger of, 13, 71–72, 148; and
rail strikes of 1921–22, 77–78; publicity
for, 102; move of winter quarters to
Sarasota, 146–55; wild animal acts of,
148–50; effect of 1934 typhoid epi-
demic on, 247; under N.Y. Investors'
control, 247, 275; tax fraud of, 254;
Sam Gumpertz gains control of, 266;
Robert Ringling replaces John North as
manager of, 272; effect of Hartford fire
on, 277; family factions battle for control of, 277–78. *See also* Ringling,
John—and circus; Ringling Bros.
Circus

Ringling Bros. Circus: origins of, 7–9;
roles of brothers in, 8–11, 13, 14, 55,
56; social barrier separates crew and
audience of, 11, 300*n*13; purchases half
of Adam Forepaugh-Sells Circus, 12;
combines with Barnum & Bailey, 13,
71–72, 148; ethical character and standards of, 13; prospects for future management of, 72. *See also* Ringling,
John—and circus; Ringling Bros. and
Barnum & Bailey Circus

Ringling Isles, 89–92, 93, 95–96,
225

Ringling Museum of Art (John and Mable
Ringling Museum of Art
—building of: location of, 197; Italian design of, 197–99; architect of, 197–98;
Italian relics included in, 198; Hageman
and Harris start construction of, 198; financial straits halt building of, 198;

witnesses codicil to JR's will, 251; testimony on JR's last moments, 252

Sarasota: location and climate of, 26; history of, 26–29, 31; 1916 population of, 32; public schools of, 32–33; rail service to, 34, 35; conditions of, in 1911, 36–37; attracts winter visitors, 38; Shell Beach developed, 38; Bird Key, 38; bay channel authorized by Congress, 41; Board of Trade formed, 41; Ringlings initially not involved in local society of, 43–44; developers' dredge and fill operations add value to, 67; Manatee County limits growth of, 69; courts formed in, 69; potential of for development, 75; and hurricane of 1921, 77; JR credited with progress of, 79; as possible deepwater port, 83, 103–4; lack of industry in, 90; JR builds causeway from, to St. Armands Key, 92, 93, 96, 100, 153; League of Women Voters of, 93; publicity for in circus advertising, 96, 102; city limits of reduced, 104; bond issue purchased by JR, 105; JR's promotion of Lido Beach, 105; welcomes tin can tourists, 106–7; impact of land boom's collapse on, 131–32; social composition of in early 1920s, 133; Siesta Key, 134; tangible benefits from land boom in, 137; Chamber of Commerce of, 138; JR named president of Chamber of Commerce of, 138, 153; JR seeks development investment of, 139; oil exploration in, 139–42; Sara de Sota festival of, 159–60; Depression's impact on, 216, 238, 286–87; sports arena proposed for, 222; arena rodeo proposed for, 222; impact of unpaid taxes on, 229; school department funds of, depleted, 229

Sarto, Andrea del: *Vision of Saint Matthew,* 189

Schueler, Dulcie (sister of Mable R.), 76

Schueler, George, 225

Seaboard Airline RR, 92; Sarasota benefits from, 58; expands to Fort Myers, 82

Selby, Marie, 93, 95

Sells-Floto & Hagenbeck–Tom Mix combined show. *See* American Circus Corporation; Ringling, John—and circus

Sheridan, Gen. Philip H., 172

Sinclair, Harry F., 108

Smith, E. A., 268, 270

Smith, Gov. Alfred E., 108; at Sarasota, 161

Snyders, Frans: *Still Life,* 292, 329n16

Southern College (Lakeland, Fl.), 208, 231, 232

Spanish-American War, 35

Sparks, Clifton, 257

Spiridin, 274

Spivey, Alan, 232

Spivey, Ludd M. *See* Southern College

Stillman, C. C., 188

Suida, William, 288

Sutherland, fourth duke of, 30

Tait, Selwyn, 29

Tamiami trail, 50, 107–8

Tapestries: JR's purchases of, 171–72; *History of Alexander the Great,* 172; *Fides Catholica,* 172; *Triumph of Faith,* 172; critics' view of JR's, 173

Thompson, Charles N., 32, 46, 47

Tin can tourists, 107

Tintoretto, 174; *Young Lady with a Dog,* 180

Titian: *Palladin and Page,* 184; *Queen of Cyprus,* 180, 189–90

Titus, Hazen, 196

Tyler, W. T., 73

Valdo, Pat, 160

Vanderbilt, William K., 191